A LOOK IN THE MIRROR

THE DISINTEGRATION OF OUR MORALS, VALUES, ETHICS AND SOCIETY

CAN AMERICA BE SAVED?

DARRELL CASS

A LOOK IN THE MIRROR is available at special discount for bulk purchases. The
author is available for special events.

For more information, updates and comments please call 413-454-2815

Library of Congress Cataloging-in-Publication Data
Cass, Darrell
A Look in the Mirror / Darrell Cass
Revised edition
p. cm.
This book includes bibliographical references
ISBN - 978-0-692-84797-8 (hbk) ISBN - 978-0692474228 (pbk)
ISBN - 0692474226 (electronic)

Text set in 12 point Garamond
Cover Design by Martin Lee and Kiana Cass

To my little girl Kiana, who's not so little anymore.
Without you, I never would have lived.

Bill Moyers
A true hero to democracy and people's champion
who inspired millions of people, gave us hope,
and made sure we were never alone.
May his tenacity never wane and fire be spread but never extinguished.

Contents

Contents

Introduction

Like a lot of people in these parts, I remember the days of giant family gatherings on the farm listening to the baseball game on the radio and friends chatting away in my grandmother's small town family restaurant. Not all that far removed from the same lifestyle of our founding fathers, we were living the American dream - big families on big farms with lots of friends and family with whom we shared our good fortune. When some of the new farmers arrived in town after the great stock market crash of 1929 unable to get bank loans they needed to establish their own business, my grandfather came through like their knight in shining armor and personally gave them the loans. We had faith in our fellow Americans and helped each other back in the community barn raising days. We were free and our own bosses in control of our destiny for generations. Like our founding fathers, we believed in a free government without tyranny, democracy without oppression, civic responsibility that freedom demands, and true patriots rise against all those that stand against these beliefs.

My family has historically been a rather well-to-do, independent, business oriented group of Republicans who acquired their upper middle class status through shrewd land acquisitions, our own businesses, hard work, and stock market investments with an emphasis on oil related industries. We were often upscale country farmers with a get-a-way house on the lake and hunting cabin reminiscent of President Theodore Roosevelt's western years. My grandmother was the county Chairman during the Eisenhower administration, and the whole family was staunch supporters of both his and the Nixon administrations.

However, they were the last of the moderate progressive Republicans who followed the philosophies of American heroes Abraham Lincoln and Theodore (Teddy) Roosevelt, then his Democratic cousin Franklin Delano Roosevelt (FDR) and fellow farmer Harry S. Truman. So like millions of Republicans after the infamous Watergate scandal, and the radicalization of the lost party that started in the 1960's with paranoid extremists such as Lewis Uhler, Barry Goldwater, and Ronald Reagan, the family broke ranks and switched alliances to the Independent Party our founding fathers crafted their vision of the country after.

After getting just one bad apple that brought hard times to the family party and seeing our lofty position quickly disintegrate, I've now lived in both worlds of the upper middle class who could afford nearly anything they pleased and the new struggling lower middle class. My unusual path through life has left me a more learned, civic minded individual with deep ethical and moral convictions that I hope will resonate to you.

While many have taken the high road and written what you want to hear about society's great unraveling, (usually from their multimillion dollar homes in Washington or New York City about the Ebenezer Scrooge aristocrats they blame for our predicament) they have just covered the tip of the iceberg. Although they are a main cog, it goes far beyond them and the two cities that bear little resemblance to the other 99% of America - yet spread their evil throughout the land. I will, instead, share with you a trace of history cascading back to relevance as well as experiences from family, friends, neighbors, and people like yourselves that typify our newfound greed, selfishness, ideals, and social problems. Plus, inside secrets from my perch upon crony local governmental agencies that vehemently affect us all.

This embarrassing Noam Chomsky, Socrates-like analysis of modern day society illuminates the ingenious ways our self-serving elite have percolated their morals, values, and ethics down throughout society at **any** cost: One that was willingly hypnotized, brainwashed, duped, and molded into playing its role in this play for modern day privateers through a comprehensive list of cancerous infections we've all spread throughout every segment of society for **their** benefit. As did they, I throw down the gauntlet and proclaim this self-reflection shall set you free! While America has tens of millions of good, honest, hardworking, kindhearted people and does many wonderful and incredible things, I don't hesitate pointing out the evil ones and our own faults that now outweigh them and tilt the scale the wrong way.

I assure you this book is for the little people, the laymen. Not pompous, arrogant, crony capitalists who have no conscience, sold their souls, poisoned every well, and captured and imprisoned all counter-weights that balance our society... though they would be advised to read it and get a conscience. This is a hard "look in the mirror" to reeducate those 99% of Americans and the world that have been bullied, programmed, and beaten into delusional submission by master sorcerers.

My hope is to convince those of you who have succumbed to their sorcery to join us and take action.

We'll discuss our social degradation started by Wall Street, politicians, and Super Pac's in the 1980's with just a few selfish, corrupt, moral less narcissists on board. But by 2000, when the train pulled out of the station, it was packed full of ordinary Americans under their spell. You will quickly realize for the last 35 years we've been nothing more than a highway for political ambitions, an extremist punching bag they beat to a pulp, and puppet they played like a violin for their amusement.

When a guy's watching a football game on his big screen TV he often can't afford, he doesn't think about why he has that mega-tube when he used to be satisfied with a 25" one, and the electricity it uses will slowly drain his wallet, or the detrimental effects on the environment. People don't think about why they buy expensive computers, games, and $700 iPhones with contracts that put them in the poor house and their addictive and often deadly, destructive powers. Or the media's influence and why they're wearing $200 sport shoes, supersized pants, and idolizing destructive, violent rappers. They don't consider their schools, environment, and most things they ever do, use, or see as Wall Street and the affluent blatantly cashing in on them at any cost to society and the planet! Like the opium addicted Chinese the British government created in Hong Kong in the 1830's - complete with warships to insure their continued addiction - they don't see themselves as manipulated dupes in their diabolical master plan.

Time and again we charge that football like Charlie Brown and follow their plan as if they sincerely are not going to pull that darn ball away, then continue to follow that Scrooge of contemporary society - COMMERCIALISM - right off the cliff!

Who falls for the charlatans insufferable, boorish sales pitches? Who lines up outside of stores waiting for days to buy their newest gizmo or gadget, then stampede, trample, and kill each other to quench their insatiable thirst? Who buys their mammoth TV's, jewelry, fashions, and automobiles stuffed to the hilt with the latest expensive gadgets on borrowed money? Who really empowers the billionaires, politicians, and banking establishments that are more dangerous than standing armies and helped push the self-destruct button?

This book is about the inauspicious forces affecting society from a much broader, previously ignored, non-tunnel vision, look in the mirror perspective that points out it takes "two to tango." Who's really responsible for our misguided, irrational, self-absorbed, materialistic, often violent, and cruel society and how did it happen? Is it Wall Street and the behemoth banks, the titans of industry, or the federal government? How about the guys at the repair shop, factory workers, and the town inspector and his secretary? Perhaps it's the mayor, farmers, janitors, preachers, and school teachers. Maybe it's all of them… maybe it's you!

Most of the material I use comes from a lifetime of living a rural and suburban life with my eyes open and not accepting the public brainwashing that has descended over us like a plague. I've observed our world through Spock-like logic, reality, and facts. Callus and brutally honest in spots, with a grandfatherly heartfelt love and contempt in others, we'll cover a wide variety of intertwined, controversial subjects, addictions, and perverted things we go through to serve our masters. My short history lessons set the stage for the knockout punch, with the reoccurring themes – "Just because you can doesn't mean you should" and through "Greed, Selfishness, Ignorance, Arrogance, and Thirst for Power - the U.S. refuses to learn."

We'll talk about extremism in every way, shape, and form and its overwhelming role in our new morals, values, and ethics. As does the stock market corruption that's been around since inception, numerous things stoke the fire and you've experienced some of them yourself. This is the most comprehensive, current analysis and results of our newfound attitude, expectations, fascinations, addictions, lifestyle, state of society and recurring financial calamity.

There are multiple cancers feeding on us, so each subject is akin to a mini-book highlighting and explaining the role and effect of the privileged elite, fanaticism, and those five hideous attributes we refuse to learn from. It's not important that you know every facet of our demise to get the picture, or every detail about the menagerie of cancers the mad sorcerers spread throughout society for their own benefit at the expense of our social conscience. I just want you to open your eyes and realize we've been a whipping boy, bamboozled, and like a kid in a candy store, we took the bait hook, line, and sinker. But unlike Timex – we took a licking and did not keep ticking! We're broken, our problems are extensive, and they cannot be fixed by a band aid here and there. A radical attitude change and makeover is necessary – possibly, another revolution!

Hopefully, I've filled in the pieces to this sorted puzzle so you can comprehend the entire finished product and in the end you'll learn the lessons I did, perhaps even have an epiphany. I'll hit a sore spot in everyone sooner or later and bust your chops a bit, but it's not just about us individuals as it is the country as a whole, the sum of its parts. Most of the time I'll be piling heaping helpings of blame on the privileged, so don't blow a circuit down our slippery slope "looking in the mirror."

As the Rockefeller's realized from their burden of enormous wealth and my grandmother did after the collapse of our social standing; I too now believe that old saying "Money is the root of all evil!" So like Teddy Roosevelt, I'm taking a contrarian stance and proclaiming "too much is no good." In the 1960's and 70's, when we denounced our over materialistic, self-centered lifestyle that's dwarfed by our present day one, we realized something we have since forgotten: The voracious predators stalking us are only the means - we are their vehicle!

Since the 1980's, many of us contrarians have warned of the addictiveness of video games, the internet, social media, and texting that helped take society down a dark path. We warned of the corruption and shaky deals on Wall Street long before the 1987 stock market crash and Savings and Loan disaster that were falsely propped up by the unscrupulous using junk bonds, government insured savings, mortgages, and pension funds. Then they added hedge fund and derivative scams, and this new phenomenon called IRA's to manufacture insidious CEO bonuses, phantom profits, and market returns. We sounded the alarm it was imminent history was to repeat itself time and again with their newfound selfish, abusive mentality and little regulation.

But us unflappable realist were blackballed and ridiculed for decades as being alarmists, lunatics, and delusional in attempts to conform and silence us, resulting in the rest of the country being decades and one disaster after another behind. History most often vindicates us, so if you weren't with us before reading this, you better be after! Acquiescence has set in, civil disobedience strangled, and we've fallen for every trick and trap that allowed evil to usurp our power and oligarchs rule. We chased the glitz and glamour long enough; a storm is brewing as never seen since the great depression. Social Armageddon is upon us. We hang by a tenuous thread and desperately need your help righting the American ship, and henceforth the world's, before it's too late!

My hope is that each and every reader will share in the overall message we've all willingly done something that's led us down this dark path. From those abusing our democracy, freedom, capitalistic system, and the kindness of others, to those suckers who unwittingly participate and allow them to do so, to those who complain about their politicians, then turn around and vote for them time and time again, we've all played our part in this drama. And I myself for too long have selfishly worshiped many of the wrong ideals and ignored my civic duties and responsibility in this chokehold on our dwindling free democracy.

I sincerely hope that you too will look in the mirror and admit to playing your part, no matter how small. Have you tried your best to set a good example and guarantee a just and noble society for your kids and future generations by volunteering and participating in your community and country as our forefathers did? Do you help your fellow man as in the old barn raising days, or have you followed Hollywood, the media, marketing, and greedy narcissists, then passed these values along to your kids. If so, join the crowd sucker, you've played right into their hands.

With each wrong answer the oligarchy gets nearer and society slips father downstream. A long trail of abuses tangles the tidy narratives we tell ourselves that keep us from fulfilling our civic duties and make America the country that for generations was the shining beacon of democracy President Kennedy referred to in his inaugural address: So "Ask not what your country can do for you; ask what you can do for your country." If it hurts seeing what this country has become, then DO SOMETHING ABOUT IT! DON'T JUST COMPLAIN ABOUT IT!

You say you don't have the time because you're too busy with two jobs and raising the kids? I say you don't have time NOT to do something about it, because your lack of civic engagement has caused your low paying job and that's why you're working two jobs to raise your kids! We old farmers know getting up at 4:00 in the morning and working sometimes until 9:00 o'clock at night was what our founding fathers had to do to maintain social justice. They knew a true, equal democracy didn't come easy and worked day and night to make sure their vision became a reality - and we must too!

We need a healthy mind, body, and spirit devoid of profiteer's materialistic, systemic, commercial ideology. We must reinstall civics classes, the arts, and physical education in our schools and communities. Then do as Bill Gates and the late Steve Jobs preached. Get off of your butt, shut off your electronic gadgets and get out of the house as previous generations have! If the ultimate techno geeks saw the light and minimized their kid's electronic use, why should you and yours be abusing their creations?

We can no longer follow the plutocrat's deceitful, destructive, itinerary! Remember the old saying and a main theme of this book: "Just because you can, doesn't mean you should!" Let's be a little less self-centered, compromise, objectively educate ourselves, use some common sense, help one another, and return to the days of fiscal and environmental responsibility. Let's all pitch in and recycle, grow our own gardens – kids love it - and volunteer in our community, state and national parks and forests. We have the greatest national treasures in the world, so let's support our fellow Americans by traveling here before heading overseas. Then do as the signs say my little girl put on our bedroom doors to remind us of the most important thing every day – "I will help someone today!" That's a feeling no amount of self-indulgence or electronics can give you!

It's the old fashion little things that will give us the foundation we'll need to rally and pull together as we did in WWII to defeat the modern enemy within our ranks. While the aristocrats and politicians across the board push their inauspicious, lamentable, unsustainable lifestyles and sail the high seas in their nuclear powered subs and aircraft carriers, we're in our row boats awaiting their orders.

But there's hope people! America is finally waking up from the poison apple and millions are hopping on the bandwagon of reform! I've personally battled the titans and scaled their mountain so immense that I couldn't see the top! Yet I didn't back down and cower in the corner like every shaking fiber of my being wanted to. If a frightened little pion such as myself shaking in my boots can do it – YOU CAN TOO!

So let's discuss where we stand, how we got there, whose responsible, and what we have to do to restore our liberty and society, sink their moral-less mighty fleet, and pull the country back out of "Davy Jones's locker." Because there are other Theodore Roosevelts like Senator Bernie Sanders waiting to bite the hand that feeds them!

Prologue
A Look in the Mirror

What could transform the United States of America from the world power President Kennedy spoke of into just another crumbling ex-superpower?: The same country that preached its democratic form of government, social values, and capitalistic system to the world as a role model for all. Can we put our finger on any one particular reason that could explain the transformation of THE richest, most powerful, generous, moral country, empire, or dynasty the world has ever known into the oblivion of history in so many ways?

That answer might depend on your perspective. If you think a country's fate is predisposed by one major influence, such as their financial institutions or form of government, you could oversimplify this downfall. For instance, you could say the Roman Empire and the Third Reich with their superior technology and military might simply expanded until they stretched the seams too far and burst, while ignoring other unpredictable forces such as disease, weather, food supply, and natural resources. Or, the former United Soviet Socialist Republic (USSR) was doomed from the start under what we called "Communism" from a severe bout of paranoia, ignorance, and propaganda reasons.

I believe the United States of America failed for many reasons that have been festering since the industrial revolution, when like the Romans, Germans, and Russians, need was replaced by greed and we began to pillage and plunder until it reached critical mass in the late 20th and early 21st century: A form of boom-to-bust, caused by greed, selfishness, special interest, and a corrupt government rotten to the core you would normally expect from a third world dictatorship or communist country. Then a heavy dose of socially accepted changes with catastrophic consequences pushed by our sensationalistic, propaganda spewing, special interest media, and our refusal to learn from our mistakes finished us off.

We followed Federal Reserve Chairman Alan Greenspan's economic theory of self above all else until democracy, liberty, and freedom were kidnapped! Delusional from privateers, marketing, the stock market boom of the 90's, and stratospheric home appreciations, expectations changed dramatically and we no longer appreciate what we have.

Imprisoned by our own whims and desires, we feel we're entitled to the best, and things that were once considered a luxury or treat are now a daily expectation and demand. A feeding frenzy of excess has been embedded in our brains by those who profit most, leaving our priorities and ethics a disgrace and our values disappearing like a ship on a flat earth. We've become enraptured by people such as original proprietary trader Jay Gould - who was despised and outcast by his peers in the 1850's as Wall Street's most despicable trader - yet would be glorified and worshiped today. Humble and contrite, we obediently serve our masters, and the vast majority of people now worship Greenspan's self-centered opulent lifestyle, Wall Street gluttony, and the almighty dollar!

Dozens of websites for kids, including powerful billionaire Warren Buffett's animated "Secret Millionaires Club," with the theme "the more you learn the more you'll earn," and books such as "Time for Kids" get kids thinking like a market tycoon early in life. A national stock market competition for kids as young as ten, combined with financial literacy classes taught at schools nationwide with stock market investments as the main theme, have our kids flooding into Wall Street's church by graduation. Everyone both young and old continue to buy into Greenspan's preaching's, with 81% of college freshman now saying they want to get rich above all else, often dooming themselves to jobs they hate and moral dilemmas, while denying themselves fulfilling, successful careers. Meanwhile, we are selfishly ignoring our elderly, neighbors fellow townspeople, countrymen, and planet, but most importantly, our civic duties that freedom demands.

As if in a trance, we've followed the wishes of the Federal Reserve Board (Fed) and Wall Street bankers into becoming a nation of debtors, with the federal government (feds) leading the way by owing $22 trillion, of which 6 is owed to other countries and 4 to "individual brokers and mutual funds." It got so deplorable they turned the Debt Clock back on in 2002 just two years after laying it to rest. And the people have borrowed nearly $12 trillion that many are supposed to pay back on federal minimum wages always decades behind inflation - leaving 77 million adults with debt at collection agencies for more than six months.

Aristocrats continue to abuse, expand, and guard their position with an iron fist Stalin would be proud of to suppress the lower and middle classes they depend on for their pot of gold. Now 90% of Americans are poorer than they were in the 1980's! Sound familiar? Isn't that the underlying reason all the other major dynasties crumbled? Without a doubt, in my opinion, the five most important factors of our social demise are: Greed, Selfishness, Ignorance, Arrogance, and a good old fashion *Thirst for Power;* often interchangeable and one feeding off the other like a cancer, slowly and agonizingly torturing its unsuspecting victims into submission.

Extremism and gluttony replaced moderation at all levels of society, and fanaticism is as rampant as the fraud on Wall Street that infiltrated our soul until it tore the country apart at the seams. From gargantuan insurance company's falsifying damage reports after natural disasters to avoid paying claims to $720 Nike shoes to mom and pop home repair services - few can be trusted in this new "age of greed."

Despite our decline from record prosperity, we're still spoiled rotten. We forget and ignore how good we have it, even complaining about unemployment above 5%, though it hit 35% during the last great depression of the 1930's and nearly every year the rest of the world is 2 to 10 times higher. The average supermarket carries "40,000 thousand items," store shelves are piled high with the latest fashions, and record size homes with electricity and running water are filled with gizmos and gadgets galore. We've paid just a fraction of the price for power, gas, and fuel as Europe and most of the world by plundering the world and environment for more than 100 years running - using between 20% and 25% of the total energy to power our colossal economic machine, over consumption, and Yuppie lifestyle – while ignoring those we stole from and future generations. Following our destructive example, China claims "the U.S. did it the last century, now it's our turn." Don't you just hate it when they're right?

We've followed our leader's example until respect for our fellow man hit the skids. As legislators do their fellow lawmakers, we despise our neighbors, and inner cities are now killing zones thousands of times larger than the famous Hatfield and McCoy murderous feud of the 1800's. Ignoring millions of socially conscientious gun owners, hunters, shop owners, 315 million non NRA citizens, and history; time and again every Republican in Congress has turned their back on their brethren shot in the head, claiming to protect the antiquated second amendment used by gun lobbyist and drug cartels to spread their paranoia, kidnap freedom, and money. Now, despite the Militia and gun Control Acts restricting their use, assault weapons and ammo bans in many cities, seven states, and guns being banned in public places such as Tombstone throughout the country for centuries; over 300 million guns, some capable of killing thousands in minutes, are allowed in our supermarkets, coffee shops, and public places just waiting for carnage in some states.

Certainly a number of other social and political factors have led the U.S. into being perhaps the most corrupt, fraudulent, selfish, spoiled, greedy, materialistic, wasteful, and environmentally destructive nation the world has ever seen in the name of... CAPITALISM! Add a splash of religious fanaticism here and a psychoanalysis explosion there with a total breakdown of morals, values, and ethics, then combine with an unbridled disregard for history, and voila, a recipe for another world class society about to disappear into the vast confines of history.

Let us look at some of these and other factors that are leading to the ultimate, possibly irreversible social and economic collapse of perhaps the richest and mightiest nation in history. While some reasons may be of greater significance than others, all like any great recipe combine to produce the final product, with each one as crucial and intertwined as the next in this perfect *"Sorcerer's Brew."*

But where should we start? There are so many things. We idolize our richest and poorest, most corrupt, evil, conscienceless, and greediest. We've become a country in total contradiction between plutocrats and everyone else that resembles an oligarchy. We worship Hollywood stars and celebrities that are often the worst parents in the world, and drugged out singers such as Ozzy Osbourne, supermodels, and ghetto rappers who make hundreds of millions of dollars, while the real heroes of society toil in animosity near the bottom of the pay scale and many get nothing at all!

These mistaken ideals have convinced us we are entitled to the largest, fanciest, and grandest of everything, from our houses, autos, TV's, and other electronics to our bellies... even though most of us can't afford it. Many people have vacation homes and traveling homes that cost as much or more than their primary homes. We have the fattest 218 million pets on earth that resemble ourselves from lack of exercise and gorging on both ultra-high calorie luxury pet food and human food! Sixty percent of our pets are so obese, pet weight loss centers sprang up like their human counterparts to take advantage of the monstrous creatures with every amenity, including tread mills and swimming pools.

The majority of people has either forgotten or doesn't want to cook real, healthy, homemade meals. Instead, they go out to restaurants and get fattened up akin to hogs being readied for slaughter on their supersized meals that often come with a price to match. Many that do eat at home are like a lady on TV that is so lazy, she says cooking rice is too much trouble and instead buys everything premade and ready-to-eat. Others who don't want to cook at all or can't afford the better restaurants, go to their local fast food chain to indulge in massive amounts of calories before retiring in front of their TV's, computers, and other electronic gadgets all night - making us not only the most sedentary industrialized nation on earth, but the "fattest and sickest." Crash test dummies even had to be enlarged from the previous 167 pounds to 270 to reflect our true girths.

Materialism became the "national religion," prompting pop star Madonna to idolize us with her breakthrough hit "Material Girl" 35 years ago, and we haven't looked back since. Frugality disappeared until it was too late. Now, tens of millions of people spend more money than they earn, usually on frivolous or convenient luxuries they don't really need on borrowed money. Many buy so many things they never use they store it in their garages collecting dust - leaving their automobiles outside exposed to the elements. Even basic items they need and use daily, such as winter coats, gloves, and boots go unnoticed when their kids lose them at school. Now, schools have tables overflowing with unclaimed clothing they wind up donating to charities year after year. And every year our little state claims about 1 in 10 people have unclaimed property waiting for them in state coffers. Last year it only returned $112 million out of $2.4 billion nobody noticed missing!

We have members of our society that are just plain evil with no conscience. A number of psychos, such as Jeffrey Dahmer, go ballistic and stalk their human prey, kill them, dismember them, then eat them. And hunting students of all ages at schools, along with everyone else, everywhere else is the newest fad. We have white supremacist thugs such as Klu Klux Clan leader and former Louisiana Congressman David Duke who follow Hitler's white superiority theories - stalking, taunting, torturing, and killing anyone who isn't white like them. Others prey on the elderly with scam after scam to steal their money, often large sums or all of it, leaving them crushed and crying in despair. One guy even held four elderly men prisoner in his garage with little furniture or food to steal their social security income and veteran's benefit checks for more than a year. Some are just lunatics, like the guy who locked his sister in her room, boarded up her window, and left her covered in her own bodily fluids with nothing but a portable toilet for seven years before she was found. Another kidnapped three girls for 20 years for sexual favors before one of them got to a phone and called police.

Some kids bully people from their own schools both physically and by way of social media into committing suicide and then bully their surviving loved ones, as well as those on the growing list of public exterminations. While others fraudulently said they were at the Boston Marathon bombings and tried to collect charity money for their injuries and suffering. And some people sink so low, they steal Christmas presents off of people's front doorways after the deliveryman drop them off. One guy even had his 2-year old daughter steal one and bring it to her stroller before fleeing!

Some steal our identities by hacking into our personnel computers, or strolling through social media websites looking for our personal information so they can get into our bank accounts and steal everything we have. The biggest and best hack into sophisticated corporate and government computers to get their information, then sell it to black markets around the world, while others just do it for the adrenaline rush. Many do it for fun, and others the challenge, or to expose government operations. Some disgruntled lunatics just do it to make life miserable for everyone who does business with any of them. And the feds... well, they hack into anything they please!

Everywhere you turn, trusted organizations such as the Boy Scouts, Catholic Church, and the government ignores or covers up thousands of crimes from members, leaders, and hierarchy. For decades, the Scouts and Catholics, from priest to the Pope, collaborated to cover up one sexual abuse conspiracy after another. And the Vatican Bank was so crooked many countries refused to do business with it! Not to be outdone, government agencies from police departments to the president cover up everything you can imagine in a "shield of secrecy."

We have an economy of incentive based fraud falsely propped up by our preposterously corrupt, sociopath politicians and Wall Street with insanity at the controls. Fund managers across the board put people's money into high commission expensive mutual funds while simultaneously stuffing their own money into low cost index funds.

Many days the Dow Jones Industrial Average (30 large handpicked price based corporations) forces the market in the complete opposite direction of many other important stock market indicators, resulting in up to 100 individual stocks setting record highs while the majority of stocks decline from disturbing news. Wild swings in minutes, even seconds, strike for no logical reason with computers at the controls. Most Internet companies make no money (and never have), yet sell billions in stock. Then companies such as Facebook gamble billions buying them hoping to strike gold, as they did with WhatsApp, paying $19 billion, despite it having no paying customers over $1 a year and a stratospheric price to earnings (P/E) ratio. Then they bought Instagram for over $300 a share (300 times their P/E) when 14-17 is the norm.

The Dow became mostly irrelevant in representing the real world of finance after CEO bonuses, company buybacks, crooked ratings companies, the Fed, a few behemoths, and supercomputers took over, which now run it based on thousands of news and social media websites looking for good news to keep it perpetually moving upward. Days when economic news is ghastly, computers programmed by Wall Street's greediest zealots push it into record territory time and time again, ignoring the shaky economy, staggering fraud, and "our version" of high unemployment. In the first quarter of 2014, as the economy was contracting and bank profits were shrinking from higher interest rates and a reduction in mortgages (normally a scenario that would set off panic and a selling spree), the Dow instead set record highs! Then, as the Russell 2000 index - a much better barometer made up of smaller companies - was dropping 15%, the Dow set more record highs! Don't you just love computers at the controls? Apparently, the Dow's were feuding with the Russell 2000 ones that year.

After legislators, banks, and financial institutions partnered to destroy the economy in 2008, the Federal Reserve artificially lowered interest rates they charged them so they could loan it back to the federal government, homeowners, and small businesses to lower their own debt and prop up the economy. But the banks borrowed the cheap money and bought back record amounts of their own stock at huge discounts, then sold it right back to Wall Street at stunning profits! They then used the dubious free profits to create fraudulent hedge fund and derivative schemes that continually push the market higher and higher, year after year, so they can swim in ever larger pools of fictional money until it

7

crashes. Then do it again and again! Adding insult to injury, those of us who followed their recommendation to save money watched our CD's and savings accounts lose money to inflation from the record low rates, forcing some to invest in risky junk bonds and other shady deals looking for higher yields. The results are never pretty.

In this continuing revolving door between the government, banks, and investment firms, the government sold treasury bonds to the same financial institutions that own and run the Fed. The Treasury then printed trillions of dollars and bought them back, plus interest, along with eighty percent of the countries home mortgages to artificially stimulate their bottom lines, Wall Street, and the economy. Despite record corporate profits year after year, it continued infusing the economy with $85 billion a month while the market cheered the free cash. It was no surprise, though, with nearly every recent Treasury Secretary, Securities and Exchange Commissioner, and Federal Reserve Chairman working for Wall Street and the government... and dare I say *'both at the same time.'*

Insanity and gluttony has been the order of rule for years. Those in suit coats and ties have become the enemy of the people, with white collar crime penetrating every orifice of society, especially the stock market, financial institutions, and governments across the nation. With every headline I warn my daughter never to trust any of them. Stock market and insurance fraud runs rampant and capitalism's been hijacked and abused! As a result, we've become a country that President Carter claims is an "oligarchy," with patrimonial families like the Walton's, Koch brothers, and Warren Buffett at the helm.

We literally created the Taliban, Al Qaeda, ISIS and chaos around the world resembling Armageddon when we stuck our big, fat, greedy, ignorant, arrogant noses into everyone else's country to pillage and plunder for our own self-interest, weapons manufacturers, corporate profits, and executive bonuses; leaving every country in the Middle East in shambles and civil war, with starving, thirsty, homeless citizens burying their dead in droves and us despised by millions across the globe. We're so arrogant we cling to the Standard measurement system even though everyone else on the planet converted to metric eons ago.

We're a backwards democracy where the smallest of minorities rule every facet of society, and our national slogans seem to be... If it's broken don't fix it, and if it's not fix it. If it's needed don't do it, and if it's not do it. In Massachusetts, the School Building Authority went bankrupt adding onto and building new schools with so few kids they had to close 40 of them! Then turned around and did it again just five years later, only this time, bankrupting local taxpayers rather than themselves by building schools and additions in towns and cities with plummeting enrollments while ignoring those bulging at the seams.

Because of our outdated constitution and capitalistic greed, we ignored both history and Mother Nature while losing our identity with a Wild-West like immigration policy with no control of our borders that slowly fractured our society. People of every religion, color, and creed infiltrated our soul in a mixed hodge-podge of distrust, with Islamic terrorist embedded throughout the land. They tied the hands of the Border Patrol then opened the Mexican border, prompting Mexicans to proclaim they were going to take everything back they lost in the Mexican-American War - and they did! Now, 100 million illegal aliens (including their kids) comprise more than 50% of the school population from Texas to California. They were allowed to flood the country in such mass, the largest corporations and politicians started courting them for their buying power, influence, and possible votes at election time while simultaneously using and abusing them as slaves and complaining about our lack of border control for political posturing.

The minor holiday, Cinco de Mayo, was forced upon us in the 1980's by the media and advertisers that run it to pad their wallets. Now, five boys in California were sent to the principal's office and asked to turn their patriotic tee-shirts inside-out for being "insensitive and disrespect-ful" to their Mexican classmates on Cinco de Mayo day. Meanwhile, Spanish nationalists are allowed to wear and display their former countries flags in schools, courtrooms, cars, and every other public place across the land, including our own Independence Day celebrations.

We've become inundated with Spanish heritage events and parades since the "occupation," even giving them their own month! And things such as planned parent workshops are now in Spanish with English translations so they don't have to assimilate. Many places look more akin to Latin American countries with places like Miami requiring teachers to teach in both English and Spanish - giving kids half a day to learn. Some Charter schools in our area arc mandated to teach kids a second language starting in first grade, and it's spreading to all public school systems nationwide. Guess which one is at the top of the list?

All sports and every show is broadcast in Spanish on Spanish TV. And now the world wide symbol of America – football - was broadcast in Spanish on CBS and part of the Sunday night game from Dallas on NBC, leaving the rest of us clueless and turning it off.

Latin Americans get away with protesting our lack of an immigration policy that allows them to illegally sneak into our country and stay here, and then want the same rights as U.S. born citizens. They also got President Obama to sit in on one of their protests, causing decent from the more sane Americans... especially the tens of millions of LEGAL immigrants, including my wife, her sister, and even Mexican old timers who waited decades to get here by FOLLOWING THE LAW! We court immigrants to such an extent; we've been giving them ultra-low interest loans for decades to start their own business while denying Americans the same privilege!

A media feeding frenzy promoting radical leftist groups gave rise to the equally radical Tea Party in order to balance the scales, and the majority centrist have been caught in the crossfire ever since. The fanatically left feminist groups led by the lesbian, gay, and transgender communities have relentlessly badgered us through every media outlet available for decades. Despite celebrities like the famous Greek writer Arianna Huffington writing a book "The Female Woman" in 1974 proclaiming most women didn't agree with their stance and they were bullies, and the Canadian band The Guess Who with their 1970 hit song "American Woman" - "stay away from me."

To this day we're pummeled to such an extent, millions of woman are embarrassed to be straight, traditional, heterosexual woman who just want to lead traditional lives – not take over the world like they want to. And my daughter and I will be sent to a rubber room if they don't stop their incessant prejudicial rhetoric she too despises.

These overbearing groups dominating society led to Donald Trump's presidency, and were as much a factor the over liberal Democrats took a shellacking in the 2010 through 2016 elections as the over conservative Tea Party was for the Republicans in 2008, despite a total economic recovery, low unemployment, and record high stock markets and corporate earnings. To both escape, and join these groups, we turn to technology that isolates us from the outside world and choose to associate electronically with only those who think like us, rather than socializing with our families, neighbors, and fellow townspeople.

We've become a nation of cliques that separate us from early childhood through adulthood. For instance, developmental soccer leagues start in kindergarten and separate our kids into cliques before they even get to know their classmates. By the age of twelve there's a premier league for the most dedicated kids, who play on both teams, giving us cliques within cliques. My daughter's team had three: the premier league players, developmental league players, and bench players; all practicing, warming up, and playing in their own separate groups. Arrogance is not only tolerated at this young age, but encouraged, leaving us with another generation of arrogant, rude, spoiled adults America is known for and the term "spoiled rich kid syndrome."

Perhaps our downfall started with that world renowned arrogance, or perhaps our equally renowned financial system and its partner in crime – Capitalism. I remember in the 1980's, Donald Trump was the epitome of all three. He borrowed hundreds of millions of dollars until he was the poorest person on the face of earth, yet the banks continued to give him more. In fact, they gave him so much for his titanic failures, he arrogantly told them and his junk bond holders to lower his interest rates or he would make them take his Trump Plaza Hotel and Casino and run it themselves. Twenty five years after giving in, with six bankruptcies, many subcontractors and employee lives in ruin, billions in debt from his casino owning years, and federal charges for money laundering and being a threat to the financial system and terrorist attacks, his last casino was finally closed when the Taj Mahal closed Oct 2016. As a reward, he is president and we have the first "foreign born" First Lady.

Former CEO and Vice President Dick Chaney's own Halliburton has been accused of everything from overcharging in Iraq to bribery in Nigeria. General Electric's so arrogant since Ronald Reagan was their spokesman; they are repeatedly fined by the Securities and Exchange Commission (SEC) for everything from accounting and securities fraud to a kickback scheme with Iraq. Even with nearly 700 settlements a year, the SEC just can't keep up with all the Wall Street crime.

How about our so-called "democracy" or our world-renowned media? How about Hollywood? Does the media and Hollywood control the way we think? I'm not talking about the subliminal messages they insert into their broadcast from time to time. I'm talking about their overly powerful influence on a strategically dumbed-down, uneducated, easily brainwashed, bored society - one that elected a president who only ran as a publicity stunt! And the three teenagers that shot to death a college student jogging by said they were bored and looking for someone to shoot all day! Society has completely lost its identity, perspective, and soul. Family life has deteriorated and disappeared almost into extinction from drugs, gangs, electronics, and too many hours worked by all in an attempt to live the rapidly unreachable, unrealistic, twenty-first century American dream. With so few parents married and raising their own kids (more than half born to unmarried mothers under 30) and with computers, Hollywood, and day care facilities doing it for them, our kids grow up more like clueless drones.

They no longer socialize in person or are taught social skills like eye contact when talking to someone or calling their friends on the phone to hear their voice. Respectful things, such as hello ma'am and sir, disappeared with thank you and your welcome, and table manners have been replaced by electronics at the dinner table... if there is a dinner table!

With both parents working and single parents often working two jobs to put their kids through college in this new "perceived" age of higher education or be left behind, they and their kids have piled up enormous mountains of debt only Wall Street bankers can be proud of. Leaving us with the highest percentage of adults under 35 unable to buy a house since Ronald Reagan became president in 1980. With President Bush's No Child Left Behind Act, they've come off the assembly line programmed for the four main purposes of the act: science, technology, engineering, and math. They've forgotten how to do critical thinking, including problem solving, which other countries realize is more important than memorizing data and test taking techniques. Instead relying on computers and other electronic gizmos to do their thinking for them, forgetting the most important trade skills America perfected other countries have not.

Sustainability has taken a back seat to the greedy oil, gas, coal, and mining industries. They created a phantom energy shortage, then filled the top positions at the Environmental Protection Agency (EPA). Including George W. Bush's own EPA Administrator, Jeff Holmstead, a leader in the coal industry who wrote the environmental bills then had their people in Congress pass them. They got the government to issue them permits to mine our national parks and forest, yet kicked the native Shoshoni Indians wild horses off of them. With congress bought and paid for, we were one of just a handful of countries that refused to sign the Kyoto Protocol and other world regulating pollution and nuclear arms control agreements so they could continue to rape and bully our people, country, and world. We even fought three wars for the oil barons in the White House.

Big oil actually had contrarian geographer Pierre Desrochers telling the world oil made cities "cleaner" and regenerated America's forest by allowing the roads and railroads to bring in people wanting to save them.

Fanatical Super Pac's (political action committees) have sprouted up in every orifice of society and taken over the government at all levels with absolutely no conscience. Extreme wealth, influence, and their own personal agendas are all that matter to them. Maniacal organizations, such as the American Legislative Exchange Council (ALEC), have kidnapped democracy and relentlessly try to abolish the same public school system that has been America's backbone ever since the Revolutionary War by handing it over to big business for hideous profits. And the most powerful industries partner with ALEC to make sure their top corporate and political leaders continue raking in billions of dollars every year at society's expense.

Is it just me, or do you see something wrong with this whole picture? Everybody's been warning us that our dubious lifestyle can't continue, yet we don't listen and continue to ignore history time and time again - putting democracy, the environment, and every segment of society on trial. Insanity, fanaticism, and gluttony are at the controls! As a result, despite being the wealthiest nation on earth, we've fallen behind with our usual short term, short sighted, money grubbing way of thinking brought about by our dysfunctional, crooked, self-serving, gorging, hypocritical government. One that was once set up for the prosperity and fairness of all and run by some of the more honest, insightful, and visionary men of the time, has become an outdated liability easily abused by the unscrupulous and wealthiest.

Society has changed so much and so rapidly since 1980, you can see why it's impossible to pinpoint one single reason for our demise, or who's responsible. But I think if you stick to those five original denizens of destruction in the name of a capitalist, consumerism culture and an over the top unsustainable way of life, we can start with the main ingredient to this perfect *"Sorcerers Brew."*

1

The Stock Market and Financial Institutions

PIRATES!!! - Hoist the sails! Load the cannons! Batten down the hatches!

Wall Street! New York, New York! Home to the most powerful forces of evil the world has ever known - the New York Stock Exchange, New York Mercantile Exchange, and a host of the ultimate "Too Big to Fail" financial institutions. Modern day pirates, fraud, and corruption have ruled for decades, lurking around every corner. Nowhere on earth has anyone seen such a Pandora's Box of greed, power, selfishness, and arrogance assembled in one place and hosted by a city equally willing to burn in hell. By the 1990's, it was a place where innocent young college kids were lured and forced into the deepest darkest bowels of hell by their evil superiors, burning throughout eternity with those who forced them there. Others eagerly went looking for riches never before so easily attainable from a city where 1 in every 22 people is a millionaire. Pirates could never have dreamed of such widespread wealth.

Few escaped this scenario, but those who did, turned against their own evil corporations and joined millions of us fighting them in a massive showdown between the people, Wall Street, K Street, and the government in a movement called "Occupy Wall Street." In the end, though, integrity was banned, and the luckiest and most honest that told their horror stories were easily drowned out by the roar of corruption. Even the Street's most prized symbols - the rampaging Bull and Bear - represent the strength and oppression of the powerful beast. Like a Greek God, the enormous bull sits perched outside the market to remind every worker of his duty to the "Gods of Wall Street," but these are cruel and destructive Gods.

Capitalism was stampeded by gluttony, with Wall Street and K Street Super Pac's partnering with the feds to control all aspects of life in the United States. Even our 'free unbiased media' is controlled there. Nearly all money in the U.S. flows through there; and in a country obsessed with wealth, power, and an overly greedy and self-centered lifestyle - it became a ticking time bomb. There was no need for our enemies to put any effort into destroying us; we were perfectly capable of pushing the self-destruct button on our own. Just as all other failed dynasties, the power is focused in one place amongst a very few people. In this country, they are called "the top one percent."

How did this all come about? Bankers and Wall Street have been partners in crime since 1859, when hated Wall Street railway baron Jay Gould began his speculative trading schemes based on short sales. Then Joseph P. Kennedy, father of John, Bobby, and Edward (Teddy) Kennedy brought that corruption back to the front burner.

Proclaiming himself the youngest bank president in the country at 25 in the early 20th century, Kennedy jumped on unregulated banking of the roaring twenties like a fly to flypaper. Perhaps, no politician was more crooked and ruthless than Joe Kennedy. Known for his ties to the mafia, and with his banking background, he was the premier forerunner of today's modern day hedge fund and derivatives' most prolific abusers, pillaging and plundering at will. Manipulating the market, he artificially inflated the market and then sold at the peak for stunning profits. Kennedy proudly told his friends he had to make all the easy money he could before someone passed a law against it, and ultimately hustled investors and the public out of millions before the Glass Stiegel Act (banking regulations put into place after the 1929 stock market crash) outlawed his abuse. Then he reportedly turned to bootlegging during the prohibition era of the 1930's and made Hollywood movies to become the wealthiest Irish American in the country.

Still, that wasn't enough for the greedy Kennedy who wanted to get into President Franklin D. Roosevelt's (FDR's) Cabinet. So he raised the unheard sum of $200,000 for his 1932 campaign, despite Roosevelt despising him. For one reason or another, with both using each other for certain gains, Roosevelt appointed Kennedy - the man he said he would never trust - to be the first chairman of the new Securities and Exchange Commission, therefore becoming the first Wall Street fox to guard the hen house. As the youngest bank president and market manipulator, Kennedy knew where the money came from and how to use it in his unscrupulous climb to the top.

Like most countries, the money starts at the Federal Reserve Bank. Although it is distributed to 12 regional Fed bank offices across the country, eventually, most of it winds up in New York at what is now known as the "too big to fail" financial institutions and corporations.

It gets there through a vicious circle of insiders the sitting presidents appoint at key departments, including the Federal Reserve, Treasury, and Comptroller of Currency, as well as financial government watchdog agencies like the SEC. They work for the government and then switch alliances to the mega Wall Street banks and investment firms as executives or consultants, where they teach them how to get around federal laws while learning the inside scams of the industry. Then are appointed to run those same agencies that are supposed to regulate their former employers and lead us into one financial crisis and market crash after another.

Former Treasury Secretary Robert Rubin is the poster child for insiders who worked both sides of the table. He led Goldman Sachs through the early years of President Reagan and Clinton's deregulation era before Clinton chose him to lead the Treasury. After the Savings and Loan collapse he helped orchestrate, Clinton must have figured he knew exactly how to get around the system so he hired him to run the Treasury, where he could help control America's entire money supply - printing money, collecting taxes, and managing government debt instruments.

It's similar to internet security companies who hire ex-hackers to show them how to make unhackable systems. Akin to hackers who should be rotting in prison, Rubin, like all the others, was rewarded for his corruption. This became the normal way of doing business between Wall Street and Washington. The Street did whatever it wanted and the politicians supported them at any cost. Eventually, his former company Goldman Sachs and last one Citigroup, (two of America's most well-known oversized financial institutions) helped lead the country into the ultimate financial collapse of 2008-09 from a flurry of scams he helped bring to fruition.

Thanks to the financial industries' buyout of Capital Hill with hundreds of millions of dollars in campaign contributions that culminated with the Financial Services Modernization Act of 1999, and their power over federal entities entrusted to control them, they convinced Congress to abolish the Glass-Stiegel Act of 1932 that separated banks from investment firms. This left them virtually as unregulated as the roaring 20's that led up to the 1929 market collapse. So they freely merged the largest commercial banks with the largest financial investment institutions at will.

They were now free to do as they pleased. And that was to wreak havoc on every country in the world while wallowing in the resulting mountains of wealth. They were so free in 1995; future House Speaker John Boehner went around the House floor handing out tobacco lobbyist checks from the industry to fellow Republicans. Then in 2011, only one and half years after the banks destroyed the world's economy, as Speaker, he had the audacity to tell them to fight Wall Street bank reforms the people were demanding - and it worked.

Banking didn't used to be this way. It used to be a pleasure for most folks up to the latter part of the 20th century. They were your nice friendly community banks that you trusted with your money, and why wouldn't you? You had a personal relationship with them. Sometimes they were your neighbors and often your friends or school mates. They looked out for you, putting your money into a nice safe savings account that paid around 5% interest when you were just a kid. As you got older you put your money into a checking account, or perhaps a Christmas club account. If you had a fair amount of savings, you would move it up to a certificate of deposit (CD) and collect a pretty reasonable amount of around 7% interest a year. You could also go to your neighborhood bank for your home mortgage, business, or even a farm loan.

Those few people considered well off with extra money to burn went to their friendly neighborhood financial planner or investment broker, who was often their accountant and friend as well. They did their taxes and tried their best to protect any stock market investment they might attempt - since people knew little about this mysterious entity in New York - except it crashed badly in 1929 and spearheaded the great depression. Ever since that, people were cautious about investing large amounts of money. The first thing their representative would do for them was warn them: "You should not invest any money unless you can afford to lose it!" Don't count on it going up in value because about three out of four people throughout the history of the market have lost money, many staggering amounts - some everything!77

On the other hand, the main purpose of large Wall Street financial institutions, such as insurance corporations and jumbo commercial banks, was almost exclusively for sizable infrastructure projects. Things like roads, bridges, airports, and shopping malls. This new breed of colossal investment banks and insurance firms were not the good old friendly ones we had all grown up with. These monstrosities created by

Presidents Carter, Reagan, and Clinton's deregulation of the industry came to represent the changing face of America - one of pure greed, arrogance, and selfishness by those with no conscience. These bankers and money managers came straight from down under, and the nuclear chain reaction that debilitated society had begun.

They were now so arrogant they would lie right to your face and tell you there was no need to be afraid of investing your free cash, pension money, Individual Retirement Account (IRA), or retirement money into the stock market. They told you back then and to this day, "throughout history, the market has been the greatest investment in the world, outperforming every other investment, including real estate." Of course, they never told you 90% of millionaires got their wealth through real estate before deregulation, including Donald Trump's father.

Remember that 90's commercial with Peter Lynch, head of Fidelity's behemoth Magellan Fund and face of Fidelity Investment Services? He said we "shouldn't be intimidated, and everyone can do well in the stock market. You have the skills and intelligence and it doesn't require any education. You only need patience and a little research and you're good to go." He convinced me, I signed up! They all seemed to have a million good things to say about the market and made it seem impossible to lose. Nearly everyone seemed to agree a sure fire way to financial security was to diversify your portfolio by spreading your money around between stocks and bonds - all with lucrative fees attached!

Let me tell you, they all lied through their teeth! Investing is a guessing game even to the best minds on the Street. Nobody told you there was almost no data available to the general public in some areas like the incredibly confusing and secretive 401, 401(k), and Roth IRA's. And obscene amounts of confusing data available in other investments that the most experienced market analyst admittedly could not decipher in their lifetime.

There were other pieces of crucial information that was omitted from their "buy stocks pitch" - including 75% of investors historically lost money and many all of it. And the three times the market did have substantial run-ups in the roaring 1920's, 1987, and the internet bubble of the 1990's, all ended in meltdowns caused by maniacal manipulation from deregulation and unwarranted trust brought on by the mass hysteria of the booming market. Combined with the internet bubble and cash infusion from IRA's, pension funds, tax cuts for the wealthy, and government backed securities, the Dow shot up ten-fold from 1000 in the mid 1980's to 10,000 in about 15 short years, before crashing nearly 40% the next two.

The reality of it is, the market has been nearly a guaranteed loser most of its existence, including long stretches of many years. Multiple crashes and inflation was driving the 'great market returns.' Take a loaf of bread for example. It used to cost a nickel when my mom was a kid, but inflation has made it $2.00 now. That is almost a 4000% increase in inflation alone - not including any smoke and mirrors. Did your stocks go up more than that? If not, you lost money.

After 1990, it was mutual funds, IRAs, manipulation, and scoundrel executives whose bonuses were tied to stock performance in the form of stock options that drove the market up, not higher profits. One of the best tricks in the book is for companies to buy back their own stock, forcing the price up, then chief executive officers cash in their voluminous options, dragging it back down. The massive sales that would normally start a price decline and the impression a CEO might be leery of their future, are hidden by the company buybacks that force the price right back up, then the cycle starts anew.

Warren Buffett doesn't even attempt to hide his buybacks. In just 3 years from 2011 to 2014, he forced his Berkshire Hathaway's A-shares up from $100,000 a share to a record $227,900 by using its colossal cash holdings acquired over the decades. The truth is, most of the market returns simply don't exist, yet CEO's, like any great sorcerer, create the illusion they do. To make money on the market, like real estate, you simply have to be there at the right time - and that is always after the farcical antics of deregulation.

One interesting contest has people, including experts, trying to pick stocks that will do the best over a 6-month period using $100,000 in virtual money. The sponsor of the competition picks stocks by throwing darts at those listed on the New York stock exchange. In nearly every competition the darts beat the people that are trying their best, despite using all the most recent and sophisticated technology to pick a winning portfolio. Those who win are usually retired stockbrokers who use the real world scam of buying mammoth amounts of a stock to force the price up a bit. Then turn around and sell it, taking the small gain while simultaneously forcing it down, and then repeating the process over and over again: Sound familiar CEO's?

With the public unaware of the above, and widespread financial gains from the internet boom and housing market, an attitude based on unrealistic, unsustainable, materialistic expectations emerged - especially among the younger college age kids. An, I want the biggest and best money can buy society emerged that corrupted many into a "keep up with the Joneses" mentality like never seen before; one with brutal disregard that didn't give a damn about anyone but themselves. For the first time in history, many going to college would choose careers based on money rather then what they wanted to do for a living, which is exactly what the pirates on Wall Street were pushing. With encouragement from the government and investment banks, people would for the first time start spending more money than they earned through unlimited borrowing tied to their rising home equity and investment gains.

How They Set You Up and Reeled You In

Tax Shelters - Through the years, K Street and the feds had conspired finding ways for the wealthy and corporations to legally hide their money and infuse the Street with capital through tax shelters. Most of Apple's $257 billion in excess profits (more than all the gold in Fort Knox) and a total of $32,000,000,000,000 is estimated to be hidden in offshore bank accounts to evade paying taxes on. With trillions at stake, Switzerland openly courts and encourages the wealthiest to cheat the IRS by shipping it to their banks, where attorneys and accountants set up shell companies, "scrub dirty money," and launder it.

But it's not just happening offshore: 1209 North Orange Street, Wilmington, Delaware, is home to 285,000 firms and politicians setting up shells and dodging taxes, 16 times more than the Ugland House in the Cayman Islands. Amongst them are Walmart, Apple, and Coke of the Fortune 500 companies, with Bill and Hillary Clinton and Donald Trump - who always preach cracking down on outrageous tax havens - leading the politicians. Trump alone has 378 of his 515 companies (most not his, they just bought his name for marketing) using the Delaware loophole that allows firms to legally shift earnings from taxable states.

Since the 1929 fiasco, the market had done very little until these tax shelters for the demigods accidentally spilled over to the public. They had a plan to aggressively publicize one tax shelter in particular, the IRA, and trap tens of millions of ordinary people to boost both savings and the economy while artificially pumping up Wall Street and the ruling class to achieve their "trickle-down" philosophy.

Economists have a theory I call "the economic circle of life" and what they and President Reagan called "trickle-down economics," more formally known as "Supply-Side Economics." His theory was, the rich would get richer from his tax reductions and deregulation, and then reinvest it in their corporations, which were then supposed to invest in more equipment and hire more people. This gives people more money to spend on the economy and reinvest in their employers. This strategy, in turn, keeps the market, our economy, and everybody's pockets filled with money, theoretically forever, keeping the ball rolling right along for eternity. Companies have a constant flow of capital from all that money we put into the market, and we spend our newfound wealth from these investments on their goods and services: A real win-win for all, right?

Yeah right! Did you get any part of that $32 trillion hidden offshore or the tens of billions of cash profits back in dividends? So much for the theory of trickle-down economics!

IRAs

For years the government said we didn't save enough money for such a wealthy nation. By the 1980's, pension plans became too expensive and difficult to run and investment strategies and tax laws became more complicated. When companies discovered a tax loophole used by millionaires they knew it would save them money and they could pawn the responsibility of investing it off to their employees. However, Wall Street banks and investment firms had their own plans for the upper class loophole.

They jumped on this opportunity like a lion on a wildebeest. Their scheme to make themselves and their corporate partners loaded beyond their wildest dreams was kept secret. They pushed the corporate tax break on the general public as IRAs and then proclaimed they were better than pension plans. We could save our money "tax free" they bellowed from the highest mountains to the lowest sea, and then went about helping firms set up these retirement accounts faster than a bobsled down the Matterhorn. Needless to say, the public was sold the tax free part, not the you had to invest it in the incredibly fraudulent and dangerous Wall Street "Death Star."

The most popular and one of the easiest ways to save money for ordinary folks were the 401 plans. The 401s expanded into the hybrid 401(k), which was, and still is a very popular tax deferred account for market gains. Soon they came up with Roth IRAs, where you prepaid taxes before putting the money in. Many corporate and public employees were offered both pension funds and IRAs, many with matching contributions to their IRAs. The problem with these saving schemes was you had to put your money into the Death Star. This money that you would normally put into a federally insured savings account, CD, or perhaps government bonds was now at the mercy of the uninsured, mostly unregulated market.

As the years went by and corporate profits reached god-like status, the more expensive pension funds dwindled from being offered at nearly half of the companies to around 4% so the IRA took over as king of the hill, going from 6% of Americans invested to 43%. By 2013, the APs Josh Boak wrote: "Americans hold $4.2 trillion in 401(k) plans" and "an additional $6.5 trillion in IRA's." Now you see why Wall Street just had to have your retirement money.

This seemingly easy way to save money is more complicated than the average person can fully understand. They're laced with tax penalties if you don't follow the IRS rules exactly. Even the highest executives in banking claim they're too complicated for the average person. So much so, private equity firms with people like presidential candidate Mitt Romney use them to get around IRS laws for their wealthy clients and themselves. He himself has up to $100 million stashed away somewhere in one. Retirement money be-came the most sought after money in history. Still, many people came to long for the good old days of investing their savings in safe, simple, government insured savings accounts, CD's, and savings bonds

That's because after you open your account, you usually have to choose a mutual fund with dozens of companies and have no idea which to pick, or calculate how long you'll work and what amount of your pay check should go into them. You won't consider dividends over the years and the shady market, or how to leave money to a loved one or charity. But most importantly - can you trust the funds they offer? Like most people, my brothers and mom couldn't make heads or tails of all the gibberish in theirs in the 1990's. They didn't know anything about the stocks in their two choices and had no idea which to pick.

Confusing things further, companies offer their own stock, often at a discount. So the biggest mistake many people make is picking too much of their own company's stock or not investing in their 401 at all. When that happens, employers take money out of their pay check and invest it for them without ever notifying them, then they progressively deduct a higher percentage every year and invest it in whatever *they* want. The market found out if people sign up on their own only 56% sign up to put their money in the ultimate criminal enterprise, yet 90% do if it's automatically done for them.

Why would they do this? Greed of course! There are literally thousands of funds to choose from and thousands of individual stocks making up those funds, so the industry makes it easier for corporations by making deals with them. I know what you're thinking, but I'm sure it's all legitimate... and pigs have wings. For a certain percentage, or fee, they set up the IRAs for them but only allow their own funds to be offered to the employees. With trillions of dollars available - the choice is easy.

Most people would think this is illegal, yet they claim these are not illegal kickbacks and they're only helping the employers with educational services and advice. After thousands of complaints, the Department of Labor, which regulates employment retirement plans, and President Obama disagreed. They told them the fund salesmen are acting as financial advisors, and by law, as salesmen, they have a fiduciary duty to tell their customers they are pushing their funds for their own profit, not theirs. But the massive fund industry temporarily stopped the department's effort to regulate them. They claimed they were brokers and only had to prove the funds they were selling were suitable for their customers. President Obama didn't buy it and made them list themselves as fiduciaries obligated to put their client's interest ahead of their own, but Trump - in his infinite wisdom - reversed it.

Brokers are the worst. They're paid by commission on the value of securities and mutual fund shares sold and a markup on bonds, making them predatory sharks that put your money into whatever brings in the most profit no matter what the returns are. They constantly buy and sell securities within a retirement account (called churning) to fleece you out of more fees, and then talk you out of low cost employer plans for their higher fee IRA's. They call it "revenue sharing," we call it "kickbacks!"

Anyone who ever had an IRA and tried following it closely will tell you, the funds their firm's offer are not suitable for the average person. It's just a game for the greedy financial services industry that secretly hides what companies or industries you put your retirement money into. Their prospectus lists dozens of firms you never heard of, making dozens of products you probably never heard of, and a bunch of other mumbo-jumbo. Worst of all, your 401 retirement money "can and is" used for political campaigns by some CEO's and board of directors regardless of who you support! Did they put that in their prospectus? Or the banks and investment firms use it to pay off their highly leveraged earth rattling investment schemes through third parties? That's why the Fed had to bail them out after the 2008 financial collapse. It wasn't only plutocrat's money they bet - but theirs too!

For all your efforts to understand this quagmire, you personally get charged all kinds of fees instead of your employer. The biggest annual fees are usually the management fees, but they also stick you with retirement and early withdrawal fees of around 10% that often hit people when they're most desperate for money... think after every stock market crash. Switching from one type of IRA to another is also very popular for managers, and for a very good reason. They receive a commission every time they move your money around. It got so outrageous, the government instituted rules that only allowed it under special circumstances. They have you coming and going. If you stay on the job they get you and if you retire they get you. A person with an annual fee of 2% over a 40 year career can pay as much as two-thirds of their gains to the plans administrators.

Shiss... Don't tell anyone there's a cheaper way they never tell you about. Warren Buffett knows it. He had a ten year running bet using the Vanguard S&P 500 Admiral index fund with five highly paid expert fund managers and he kicked their butt's silly. Their funds went up a "whopping" 2.2% a year... his 7%. Actively managed funds (churned funds) are much more costly than index funds that only charge a one-time fee around .2% and are tied to the less risky indexes like the S&P 500. That means all your dividends and gains go to you instead of them after the upfront fee. They also have very little chance of beating the long term index funds. Especially with all those extra churning, I mean, "transaction fees," which is why fund managers normally put their money into index funds and yours in actively managed ones no matter what the ramifications. In fact, the Wall Street Journal reported, in a study of over 700 top performing domestic equity funds, 77% of those in the top quartile had dropped out within a year - most for poor performance - and none lasted four years.

In the 1990's, most people never questioned the fees or risk because they were making enormous amounts of money and ignoring the fact the entire S&P 500 was trading at 40 times the price to earnings ratio, nearly triple the historic average. Some over exuberant people such as money manager, lecturer, and author Harry Dent Jr., were actually predicting the Dow would hit 40,000 and the NASDAQ as much as 20,000 by 2008 before the bubble burst. Of course, we didn't know he was getting paid $50,000 a pop to fire up mutual fund employees and brokers at the same time, or he started his own company serving as sub-adviser to a mutual fund. Would you trust that character?

With internet nobodies becoming overnight millionaires and billionaires, the stars seemed aligned and the ingredients perfectly mixed. So many people, including myself, were convinced the party had just begun. Salesmen (not yours of course) never let on that you were gambling in the stock market and the fees were eating you alive, or over the long run you can receive as little as one third of your money back. When, and if, you found out you had to put it in the market, they gave you that old song and dance about the market has always been the best place for your money and always will be. Do we have signs on our butts that say - Kick Me Hear?

This is good for Street hogs feeding at the trough and hiding behind the flag of capitalism, but dreadful for Americans. It's not just working folks who got caught up in this scam. Many people, including my mom, and a vast majority of older folks were talked into cashing in their life long belief of putting their extra money into safe, government insured accounts (usually CD's) for these newfangled 401s. Many had no idea their money was going into the market under this hideous investment bank and government conspiracy to boost the market and their own personal wealth. This was an awful fright to those who found out, especially at their age. They all grew up living through the unbridled corruption of the 1920's and the ensuing depression, now they were in the mouth of the monster up to their necks. Yet, they, along with millions of others, took solace in the fact the market was indeed doing what they were told it would.

Isn't it ironic that most of the state and national congressmen are older people themselves who constantly talk about protecting their own and count on the elderly votes to get elected, then turn on them and feed them to the lions if they and their cronies can make a buck off of them?

The warnings of over 200 years from accountants, money managers, brokers, and investment companies to never put your money into the market unless you could afford to lose it had vanished. No more warnings, it was now a game for the filthy-stinking-rich and ordinary folks should have stayed away. They didn't fully understand the way 401's, pension plans, and the market really worked. No longer were investment brokers like any other professional you went to for their expertise and fiduciary commitment that protected your best interest. These new money managers were in it for the mind-blowing amounts of money, and the previous warnings were never heard from again once the power of the 401s, pension money, and deregulation reared their ugly heads.

Their ill-conceived plan to infuse Wall Street with trillions of dollars was now complete. They had no idea the internet would be invented and cause the market to boom to heights never imagined - that was a bonus never before seen in history. Young and old alike had to hope for the best with their home equity and retirement savings locked into the market. And after experiencing the 1929 catastrophe, retired folks were forced to sit on pins and needles the rest of their lives praying history would not repeat itself.

The stage was set and all the stars were aligned after congress abdicated their responsibility. People were spellbound and the stock market was the talk of the day, every day. It seemed like the perfect plan. Imagine an inexhaustible perpetual flow of money with nowhere else to go. More money than all of the oil and gas ever discovered. An amount so vast, it seemed like a temptation sent straight from the devil himself; preying on a repeated weakness man has demonstrated time and time again. We've never been able to control ourselves with the thought of vast riches so easily attainable. Even the most powerful country the world had ever known would surely stray and self-destruct just as all the others before it. Everyone's heard the old saying – "Those who ignore history are doomed to repeat it." Like it or not, the people of United States of America were about to test history again.

Day Trading Springs to Life in a Market Out of Control

We were mesmerized and under the sorcerer's spell. Nothing could stop this out of control beast that was about to be unleashed and would change the world, and even our perception of who we were. Nobody seemed to be satisfied with what was perceived as a normal life anymore. The bar was being raised in the eyes of many, and the personal computer in conjunction with rising wealth and a new breed of super computers led the way. A new industry called "Day Trading" sprung out of nowhere, and suddenly ordinary people were quitting their jobs and chasing the ticker-tape on Wall Street at day trading facilities that popped up everywhere. The blistering market was so hot, brokerages started after hours trading for day workers who couldn't do it during normal hours, and the Dow would actually open the next day based in part on the previous night's trading.

As I mentioned earlier, the market volume had ballooned immensely by the 90's, with perhaps five times the previous trade volumes. When the stock market imploded in 1987, people like me had to wait up to a week before getting confirmation of their trades going through. The 400 million shares traded that day were more than the computers of the day could handle. After experiencing Hell for the six months it took me to get back to even, I finally sold and vowed never to touch the market again. However, computers were now capable of handling billions of shares a day and the unscrupulous Street took full advantage of the new supercomputers trading powers, tempting me to get off the fence once again.

Day traders could follow the market at home by watching a channel called MSNBC. They posted the live ticker-tape you would normally see in an investment office. Then, overnight, it seemed to be everywhere! The market was on fire! Everybody in the media wanted up-to-date reports for their viewers, and the viewers now included almost everyone in the country, from housewives and grandparents to steel mill workers. People spent their lunches scurrying to television sets in restaurants, bars, or anywhere they could find one to get updates and often traded during their lunch break. A down day was usually followed by notorious bounce backs the next few days until the next profit-taking day came along. Indeed, the record would show the market rising vastly more often than not in a sea of green on the ticker-tape.

Everyone was unsuspectingly sucked into the jaws of the monster. Pure human greed, or the devil, was having their way and everyone was in for the ride. You had to keep your hands and feet inside the ride at all times; for this was to be an unprecedented dangerous one. Veterans of the street were aghast! Mouths open in astonishment one minute; lips pressed tight the next from what they were seeing. Time and again, day after day, insanity pressed on, driven by this inexhaustible money supply, privy CEO's, and internet related stocks! Nobody on Wall Street seemed to be able to put two and two together.

I'll never forget the stunned head shaking every time a so-called "expert" on the market was asked to explain the insane run ups, followed by equally outrageous selloffs explained as "profit taking." I'm not talking about one or two big gainers going up a few dollars a day as in the past. I'm talking across the board rallies of unprecedented leaps and bounds! Individual internet stocks doubling or tripling in price in one day and vast quantities of other stocks like Amazon and Yahoo jumping 30 or 40 dollars in hours and well over a hundred a week!

People who were normally very conservative with their money, now started feeling left out as their friends and co-office mates began telling their joyful stories of success. It seemed the ticker-tape was always green and everyone was getting rich except them. That's just what an episode of mass hysteria needed to finish them off. And after vowing never to get back in the market, I myself couldn't stand on the sidelines any longer.

Only two other times since the Philadelphia Stock Exchange originated in 1746 had the market seen run ups this impressive, the madness of the 1920's and just before Black Monday 1987. Both imploded in meltdowns, with people committing suicide after the 1929 one. One of my rather well-off grandfathers was amongst the victims of that insanity. All because Congress ignored the Sept. 1920 bombing of J.P. Morgan's Wall Street bank that rocked the Stock Exchange after decades of protest bombings that had industrialist John Rockefeller, Andrew Carnegie, and William Vanderbilt on the "hit list" as well.

The 1929 travesty changed the course of history in banking and investment industries here and around the world. The less greedy of the day realized what had happened shattered the country and implemented a plan that stood for generations to come. Congress installed the Glass Stiegel Act, restored the integrity of the banks, and left the stock market to those who could afford it. It actually took a couple of decades and federal guarantee of deposits before the people truly trusted them again. Even the well-off stayed away for decades, putting their money back into their businesses or hiding it somewhere.

Slowly the memory of the 1920's faded as Franklin D. Roosevelt helped save millions of people and the country from further damage with his famous "New Deal." Regrettably, memories fade and history always repeats itself. The stock market run-up and crash of 1987 was just a tune-up for the madness the 90's would bring.

The U.S. Office of Government Ethics and states around the country brought back some old fashion values to the industry and won back some of the people's trust, but it was an unwarranted trust. Suckered in again by a false sense of security, history was repeating itself... as was I. Internet stocks that emerged out of nowhere would soar in this internet bubble, only to vanish from the face of the earth overnight and take down millions of investors with them. Even the largest corporations with solid backing and a hail of media coverage would vanish before long, and the bubble everyone was waiting for to burst - finally did.

Borrowing on Margin

Unfortunately, the euphoria of the 90's was short lived for some who put all their eggs in one basket by borrowing on margin (a very risky bet with borrowed money that the market or whatever you invest in will continue to go up). They bet the powers to be would be with them for just a few more days, because like everyone suckered into this horrific, unscrupulous game for the affluent, they wanted on that bandwagon of treasure too. Like the run-up before the 1929 crash that was sowed by widespread borrowing on margin, it seemed as though the market only went up in historic leaps and bounds on a daily basis, making borrowing on margin a less risky affair. Only those who lived through it can imagine the enormous temptation day after day to gamble everything you owned knowing you could double or triple your money in a week. The trickle-down effect had everyone thinking of getting rich quick, not just the fat cats on Wall Street.

For some desperate people (mainly the handicapped and disabled), they couldn't resist the temptation of improving their plight, sometimes betting everything after seeing what they perceived as one last chance for security. It wasn't about getting rich for them, but about the dignity, self-respect, and security some felt robbed of others were born with. Desperate people will do desperate things that are light-years outside their normal way of thinking under such extraordinary circumstances. Even the most conservative tight-wads will follow a dangerous path to destruction if they're desperate enough. Others were just caught up in the insanity one can't possibly explain if you didn't live through it.

Betting the price of the stocks would continue to go up, more often than not, was a fatal mistake. Often they were bought from one of the many new discount brokers like I had during the 87 crash. They sold stocks with much lower fees than a full service broker because you received fewer services and got rookies handling your investments. Discount brokerage houses sprung up out of nowhere and hired the young kids just out of college with little to no experience, then trained them. This made dealing with them that much more dangerous than a full service broker, although in the "age of greed" and a runaway market, borrowing on margin happened with them as well. In a just and honest world, no broker would allow someone to borrow on margin and it would be illegal, however, this was the late 1990's and morality was on sabbatical.

Discount brokers, like others, started you off by opening an account. But then you were given nearly free reign over it. Computers willingly took your orders in a "shoot first and ask questions later" kind of mentality. With all the public information about all the companies listed on the exchanges available by computer, it was considered enough for you to research them yourself and make proper investment decisions on your own in a kind of "buyer beware" type of deal.

This new information age turned out to be the firm's best defense when people lost substantial amounts of money, sometimes everything, then sued them. Many even lost their homes!

Some people ordered extra shares by computer as part of their get-rich-quick plan, but sometimes unknowingly, therefore, in essence, borrowing on margin without ever knowing it. When done intentionally, only you and the computer knew it until you got a notice that you over borrowed, or the price had gone down. Then, if you were lucky, you got a call from a real person at the brokerage house to add more money to your account and cover the shortage. If you didn't have it, and most people didn't, they started selling your stocks to cover your losses.

This is where using a discount broker or computer trading devastated most people. They were never told of the corporate insider's trick that virtually guarantees you will never lose called a "limit down." Putting a limit down on orders tells the computer to automatically sell whatever you buy if the price goes back down to your agreed upon price. Usually this is your buying price so you won't lose your shirt in a big selloff. Since its inception decades ago, Wall Street traders have been using this tactic to virtually guarantee a profit on every share they ever traded. Sometimes you can double your money in days instead of the usual years buying on margin. But tragically, like most good market parties, this one left in the hands of rookies and no limit downs, more often than not, left people as broke as 1929.

This was a new world order powered by friendly computers and unscrupulous brokers that would let you do anything foolish - even if you lost everything. These were not the same slowpoke computers that would periodically start selling stocks in an ill-conceived computerized frenzy of selling like the 1987 crash. These computers were 100 times faster at creating carnage of a rigged market set up by numerous conspiracy's and occasionally reminded us of their infinite power of destruction.

By the 21st century, capitalism was kidnapped and held hostage, with half the companies in the U.S. offering different 401 plans and 19% ($10,000,000,000,000) of American's money invested in them, and thus the stock market. It was going up at a fast and furious pace again, which as you know, always precedes disaster. With our short memories and history repeating itself yet again, just as in all the other run ups, nobody seemed to care they had staggering amounts of money in the nearly unregulated, illogical, irrational, volatile, artificially inflated, highly corrupt and leveraged market because of the vast amounts of money they were making.

Once again nobody was questioning why. Then, reality set in and half of that $10 trillion was wiped out in the blink of an eye during the financial meltdown of 2008 and the ensuing housing crises of 2009. Leaving 60 million people once again stunned, jaws dropped, and worrying if they were going to lose everything like the 29 collapse and ensuing depression. Indeed, 2000-2010 was the worst decade ever.

Americans paid dearly for their trust in the most powerful and corrupt system the world has ever known. Millions were left with a house worth less than half of what they paid for it, unemployment was skyrocketing, and their retirement money took a shellacking. It didn't look good. A lot of these people had gotten used to living a lavish life and couldn't comprehend their new situation. Still, they did whatever they had to. They often drained their retirement funds down to nothing in an attempt to stave off total financial collapse. About 25% of people with IRAs used it all and others borrowed heavily against it.

Do you think the fund managers or sales people cared about what they did to 60 million people in their self-made world financial collapse? After skimming off their share of the seemingly inexhaustible money supply, they had enough money hidden offshore to last 1000 lifetimes. Adding insult to injury, an additional $18 billion in bonuses was dished out during the dismantling in 2008.

Learning from the internet bubble burst in late 2000, the vultures on Wall Street implemented new cons that fed off their friends and neighbors to cause the latest meltdown. Like Darth Vader, who became more powerful with every person he brought to the dark side, they started feeling like gods with infinite power and very few rules, then pushed the envelope to the max. Everyone, everything, and anything were now fair game. Their greed, selfishness, arrogance, and lust for power brought many to their knees, and others untold riches. But it also brought about the darkest, most sinister chapter in American history - and ultimately the fall of the United States of America as we knew it.

Government's insufferable manipulation of interest rates slowly forced the rates on peoples federally insured CD's to unthinkable historic lows, forcing anyone with a little extra money to put it in the market or real estate. Even Nobel Prize winning economist Robert Shiller, whose famous price-to-earnings ratio formula was accurate on all previous meltdowns and predicted this one, had to admit, for both young and old "there simply was nowhere else to go for a halfway decent return on their savings."

Guess what the Shiller P/E ratio says should happen again right about now?

The two largest schemes of the day that took advantage of this inexhaustible money supply and still the all-time champion of stock market profiteers are hedge funds and derivatives. They are the most spectacular, creative, secretive proprietary trading scams of all time. Let's look at how they rose from the dead in the years prior to the 2008-09 collapse to devour your money and are setting you up for the next one.

One woman, Brooksley Born, chairman of the powerful Commodity Futures Trading Commission and hero to justice and fair play, tried valiantly to stop them, but ultimately was crushed like a fly in the tidal wave of corruption.

2

Proprietary Trading on an Epic Scale
Hedge Funds and Derivatives

Newsflash: "Prosecutors accuse hedge fund company SAC Capital of being a criminal enterprise, where executives, including founder Steven Cohen, encouraged insider trading on a scale without precedent."

The hedge fund and derivative scams hiding in the closet for decades had escaped and were now terrorizing the world. Originally thought up around the time of the Korean War, hedge funds exploded onto the scene in the 1990's, and along with derivatives, they manipulated the stock market until it reached critical mass and imploded like a black hole, sucking everything down within its reach. Tools of Wall Street barons and investment bankers, hedge funds are secretive, risky bets on anything even remotely tied to the market, and usually bet on the market or whatever they invest in going either up or down.

They're supposed to follow the rules under the never publicized Investment Company Act of 1940 and other SEC regulations that set rules on investment companies and their fiduciary responsibilities. Not surprisingly, the act has a few gaping loopholes that allow the very wealthy to gamble as much as they wish, and that old saying – "Just because you can doesn't mean you should," has no meaning to these egotistical, greedy narcissists. One loophole allows funds which accept positions from one hundred or fewer people with more than one million dollars in net worth to be "exempt" from most of the regulations, and they take full advantage of their impunity. Unbeknown to public employees, they too are sucked into their cons through pension plans that gamble with their retirement money, all the while guaranteeing billions for the double-crossing thieves to play with. It's just $2.4 trillion of Monopoly money to them.

Another problem is computers and their algorithmic programs that run the market based on massive volumes of data, news, and monitoring social media websites, can and are set off on trading frenzies within milliseconds of any news they interpret as being bad. Without slowpoke humans to intervene, wild systemic sell offs and equally wild buying binges wreak havoc with markets worldwide. And never was that more apparent than when someone hacked into the AP computers and posted a news bulletin saying there were explosions at the White House and President Obama was injured. Within milliseconds the Dow free fell until the AP posted a newsflash that it was a hoax, then the market spiked right back up to which it came as though nothing ever happened.

You can see how volatile the market is nowadays with computers at the controls, and as time went by, these games for the affluent spilled over into the market and sucked down everyone and everything with it... Can you say 1929? With virtually no regulation, guaranteed taxpayer bailout, and fees of 2% upfront and 20% of the profit, how can hedge fund managers lose? It's like taking candy from a baby – a very rich baby.

They know if the market implodes again, as it has three times since 1987, they'll make many times what they may lose by buying everything back at bargain basement prices. That's the idea! Most hedge funds and derivatives count on this and bet the market will go down at some point. Since the broker is the one who actually buys the stock, commodity, or whatever they're gambling on and never transfers ownership - only the profits to the investor's accounts - the investors themselves rarely lose anything other than the upfront commission and dividends they pay. Naturally, if the market keeps going up, they have to pay the difference in the price between what the broker bought it for and the new price. But you know the old saying – "What goes up must come down," and when it does, its Bingo time baby and the "trickle-down" effect kicks in for the big shots again! Of course it kicks in for us too... just in more of a death spiral type of way.

Large investors and brokers have been colluding in manipulating the market like this since degenerate Jay Guild. It's nice for everyone if their investments make money in the short term. But pure hell for us and ecstasy for them if enough large speculations systematically go bad and dismantle the market from multiple short sales, as they did in 2008 with Lehman Brothers, Bear Sterns, Fannie Mae and Freddy Mac. They collect multimillions on their bets, and then buy back their investments and many others with their new fortunes at fire sale prices. The more it crashes the more they make, repeating their strategy over and over. When it reaches rock bottom it can only go one way and they're guaranteed stratospheric profits going back the other way... not that they're greedy.

What a racket! They know the government (taxpayers) will bail them out if things get really ugly and they'll get their money that much faster. This has proven to be the case ever since the Savings and Loan bank scandal took down the market in the 1980's, which has allowed the top 1% to reap the rewards of corruption with nearly 50% of the gains ever since and 99% after the 2008-09 fiasco.

I'll never forget the great S&L collapse of the 80's because I had my live savings in two of them. The panic started when crooked officials and the loaded went on the war path the minute the S&L's got word Congress abolished the rules dealing with deposits and loans in the Glass Stiegel Act. It was nerve racking. The S&L's (also known as thrift banks) could now use depositor's money to fund any type of risky loan, and they were dropping like flies in an insecticide factory just like 1929. Both that and the 2008-09 collapse saw gambling on real estate, from home loans to commercial office buildings as the 10 ton straw that broke the camel's back. The oil barren in the White House, Vice President George H.W. Bush's own state of Texas was at the center of corruption, as it was during George W Bush's infamous 2008-09 collapse. Commercial property nosedived, with office buildings taking the biggest hit, followed by vacant land that was supposed to be developed, oil, and residential property.

People were scared to death after the 1929 collapse but few were still around to tell us what happened. I asked one of my elderly customers, who was a teenager back then, what was going to happen to all of us who had our life savings in the banks. He assured me after things settled down everything would return to normal, so I put my faith in his 70 plus years of living and went about with life. However, it got so shaky in 1989, Congress decided to set a precedent by bailing them out after the Federal Deposit Insurance Company (FDIC) fund fell well short of covering people's losses. Some poor suckers sweated years before getting their money back.

By the late 1980's and early 90's, over 1000 banks had failed, with assets around half a billion dollars in 1980's money. Charles Keating's Lincoln Saving and Loan emerged as the leader of the pack. Five senators known as the Keating Five; four Democrats – Alan Cranston, Dennis DeConcini, John Glen, and Donald Riegle, along with GOP ring leader John McCain, were investigated for helping their buddy Keating - who conned both investors and the public out of their life savings.

All had been heavily financed by Keating, and they jumped right in head first to protect him when the hammer came down.

This time around it was extremely wealthy aristocrats like Dan Loeb, who became a billionaire with his hedge fund "Third Point" that was a perfect example of swindlers taking advantage of the system. He bought 60 million shares as a board member of Yahoo for Third Point worth $1.16 billion, forcing the price up, then turned around and sold 40 million of them for a profit of $665 million for himself and his hedge fund. He even got giant Dow Chemical to spin off its chlorine-alkaline division because of his mammoth investment. However, his was one of the few major hedge funds still thriving, with thousands of others doing rather poorly, despite their record investments of $2.4 trillion five years after they helped dismantle the world's financial systems.

You would think "Tweedledee and Tweedledum" (the House and Senate) would rein in hedge funds, derivatives, and junk bonds after they decimated the world's economies, but nope, they didn't go away after the meltdown, they actually got bigger! Junk bonds alone more than doubled after the 2008 collapse to a record $366 billion by 2013!

That's no surprise for the little regulated rogue industry that is more of a government set up pyramid scheme glued together by subsequent investors and unethical politicians than a legitimate investment. I've been telling people that for 30 years, but not until the recent crash have others come aboard. It's akin to gambling in Las Vegas. They bring in the suckers that lay down their money one after another, but there are very few winners, and eventually people realize the odds are heavily stacked against them. With guaranteed bailouts, loans near 0%, interest written off, and the carried interest loophole that allows them to pay 15% tax instead of 40%, those with grotesque amounts of money keep investing in the latest gimmicks while gambling the country and world away for their own benefit. It's just a sick twisted game to them and we get sucked in.

The large hedge funds that helped obliterate the market in 2008 had partially crashed the market in 1998, when hedge fund company Long Term Capital Management (LTCM) became the first post deregulation titan to collapse under its insanely leveraged high risk bets. Its lightning fast fall from grace temporarily took the market with it in Sept. 1998, and should have set off some bells and whistles in Fed Chairman Alan Greenspan's head. Yet the stubborn old coot wouldn't budge on his over capitalistic views and went about in 'Greenspan World' setting us up for more calamities. Even after Amaranth Advisors lost more than $6 billion playing the futures market collapsed in 2006, Greenspan and the SEC continued bailing out failed institutions and rigging the market for failure.

Both companies actually did very well at first with different schemes. LTCM used bonds of different maturities and very complex accounting methods, as opposed to Amaranths natural gas futures strategy. It wasn't until they started betting on more risky ventures and leveraging themselves to the hilt that they put the noose around their own necks. When nearly all of LTCM investments in Latin American, Asian, and Russian bonds went belly up in rapid succession, the hangman pulled the rope! Fearing total systemic collapse, Greenspan bailed them out by convincing some of their largest creditors to tally up hundreds of millions each and kick the full implosion down the road until another day.

How They Get Away With It

Hedge funds use highly complicated mathematical calculations and scenarios to try and predict the future market activities of big market movers - such as 401's and pension funds. If one can predict when a giant pension fund is going to buy or sell with relative certainty, they can make tens of millions of dollars for their company and millions for themselves by buying ahead of them. Therefore, they're hedging their bets.

Can you imagine the incentive for two power players to illegally collude in controlling the markets? You would be talking about billions of dollars buying each other's stocks, commodities, funds, or whatever they traded. They could collaborate to buy any agreed upon targets before the official trade – think insider trading with sophisticated computer programs that can trade milliseconds ahead of the official trades. Believe it or not, I have them on tape doing exactly that. Only on this day they didn't rely on lightning fast computers, just good old fashion *fraud.*

There have been claims of stock market rigging time and again, but the powerful Wall Street firms always called it circumstantial evidence. Although never officially caught collaborating with one another to control the market during the 1990's internet bubble, I can give you an example of one day in January of 1999… I believe it was, when I think they were caught red handed.

As I recall, it was another one of those days not uncommon for the stock market of the 90's. After a substantial run-up the week before, the market was due for a selloff. This profit taking phenomenon always followed the market run-ups. It was only a matter of time before large corporations would start selling from some minor excuse to ensure their gains.

The excuse on this day was the finance minister of Brazil had resigned the night before, giving the conspirators on Wall Street time to concoct a very lucrative scheme. It put the market in a pre-open lockdown. I had never seen this before! The market was in a panic before it even opened! When it finally opened, nearly every stock opened at mind-boggling lows and it was in a free fall! But this was not a computer generated free fall. This, I believe, was a precisely orchestrated effort amongst some of the largest firms on the Street to rig the system.

After plummeting for half an hour, the market dramatically reversed course and shot back up within an hour to the previous night's closing level. Stocks that had dropped as much as $40 or $50 a share bounced back for no apparent reason! For those familiar with the lunacy of the 1990's stock market on a day to day basis, this appeared to be just another strange, unexplainable day on the Street that left everyone shaking their head.

But was it? Or was there some sort of collaboration going on? This pre-opening lockdown for something I considered relatively irrelevant to the United States seemed strange to me. So I decided to tape MSNBC for a while to see if they had an explanation. They were as puzzled as everyone else! So Joe Cronin went down to the trading floor of the New York Stock Exchange and showed us a pile of buy orders immediately under the pile of sell orders that had caused the collapse at the opening bell.

Was this just a coincidence? I think not! Why would a number of major players on Wall Street sell such enormous amounts of stock and start a sell-off? Because this was a coordinated profit taking sell-off, one with a predetermined bottom followed by a predetermined frenzy of buybacks. On this day they had their cake and ate it too. I believe, to this very day, this unequivocally proves that massive corporations collaborated in rigging the market and pulled off perhaps the largest one day trading scam ever.

With their profits guaranteed from their limit downs in place, they undoubtedly made billions between themselves selling and buying back their own stocks, each other's, and all the others on the market at huge discounts they themselves had just created.

Limit downs are great for hogs feeding at the trough, but the market winds up having outrageous swings because a sizable trade of millions of shares will cause a chain reaction of computer buying or selling. For example, if a hedge fund, large company, or mutual fund buys a colossal amount of whatever they target, it forces the price up... let's say one dollar per share. The limit down price is put on with the trade order at the new higher price and those shares just sit there waiting to be sold if the price ever comes back down, guaranteeing them a one dollar profit per share. One million shares: a million profit. This has been done ever since the item was sold that first day it went on the market - the Initial Public Offering (IPO). And the henchmen have bought such staggering amounts and forced the price up every step of the way, they collect their ill-gotten gains at every step as it comes back down in reverse order.

When high rollers cash in their lot of shares around the market, it drops prices to the limit downs and they make their obscene sinister profits. That volume drops the price enough across the board to trigger multiple limit downs and other computer sales kick in, earning them their profit and triggering more and more sales. Now it's just a good old party for the computers, selling at will. The chain reaction then carries over to other stocks, commodities, and investments and everyone is along for the ride on the computer induced sell off. At this point and time, you just have to keep your hands and feet inside the ride at all times.

You can see the substantial incentive to collaborate on crashing the market. The big players on that day were counting on this chain reaction so they could gouge the system and buy everything back at tag sale prices. Because everything they buy has built in profits due to their large purchases and limit downs - they never lose! As I mentioned earlier, this is not real money like cash, it's just "paper money." Computer generated money derived from years of doing this since the first day every stock went on the market. None of their own money has to be given to the companies they're investing in after that first day. They can constantly reinvest their computer profits they make on every deal and it looks as though they make tremendous cash profits. In the real world, no company could ever pay all of their stockholders if they cashed in at the same time with only computer profits. This is another reason why many of us claim the stock market is not a genuine indication of anything, especially what a company truly earns at any given time - or its true value!

On this particular day we know the big shots involved made out like bandits. What we don't know is who and how many conspirators were involved in one of the greatest heist in the history of the market up to then. If the companies free falling at the opening bell were not part of the synchronized dance, they were left on the sidelines like the rest of us thinking this was going to be the devastating internet bubble burst we were all waiting for. Thanks to the well-played conspiracy it didn't come that day, but the market was still primed for an internet burst and everyone knew it.

Shortly after that crazy day, I ran into a former stock broker at a campground in Florida who confirmed my suspicions by revealing a trade secret at that time. He told me the largest traders on Wall Street acquired a computer program that only they could afford. Like a crystal ball, it could give any of their brokers the future price of any stock or fund a few seconds (now milliseconds) before the new official trade price. This allows huge brokerage firms to virtually guarantee themselves outlandish gains that eventually reach into the trillions all-toll. With limit downs programmed into the computers on every trade, it's all but impossible for them to lose. Unfortunately, as noted, this is phantom money that never actually comes from real deposits or purchased goods and only boosts a firm's bottom line and share price, therefore, creating an artificial market not based in any way, shape, or form on real sales or earnings. Facebook, Twitter and many other internet companies are proof of that.

Many of them were supposedly worth hundreds of millions, even billions of dollars one day without showing any profits and most nothing but losses – then, Bam!, nothing overnight. There were few customers exchanging real money for their goods or services, and very few of the upstarts made any real profits from their products. So investment bankers cashed in their shares and took their approximate $2.5 trillion of profits with them. Consequently, most of the internet bubble companies quickly vanished into that endless void of stock market oblivion, and predictably, the bubble burst.

Now that you know how rigged the market is, you can see why the more hedge funds made on companies the more they seemed worth to other investors. And a vicious cycle of hedge fund and derivative trading emerged as a way of making enormous amounts of money without need of receiving one dollar beyond the initial investments. The rest was all leveraged done by computers just chatting with each other. This paper money would eventually face reality and help obliterate the market in 2008 when margin calls popped up on these extremely complex, overly optimistic instruments. It was inevitable, and people on Wall Street, as well as the public knew it. But they were too busy enjoying the ride and waving their hands and feet outside the ride to care. What the Street didn't know, or care about, was the backlash and total collapse of the entire U.S. and world economy was coming nearer because of their greed and selflessness.

Derivatives $700 Trillion Involvement in the 2008 Crash

According to Merriam-Webster's dictionary; derivatives are "something made up from parts of something else or a substance made up from another substance." Sometimes it's something copied with a new twist. In the stock market, they're some sort of theoretical contract assembled, perhaps using parts of other contracts that say if this, that, and the other thing happens as we predict it well, this contract will be worth so and so much gross (after liabilities), which currently averages 2%. They hedge other investments and are basically gambling on almost any asset. Be it stocks, bonds, indexes, commodities or market, currency, land, and interest rate swaps - and are always set up to confuse their intended victim. They are the king of speculative trading and undoubtedly the most costly to the world's economy.

Popularized after the 90's internet bubble faded, they somehow kept avoiding regulation and wreaked havoc on global markets and econo-mies. Once again, we're talking about a highly speculative and leveraged form of trading, which is essentially borrowing on margin without any rules, except one - you get the economy imploding margin calls like LTCM, Enron, WorldCom, and Amaranth did when they couldn't pay their investors. I think it's safe to say that many of the country's largest investment banks made a staggering amount of their 'perceived' wealth by using a kaleidoscope of derivative schemes.

These contracts are very costly, secretive ones that are made up of fake market strategies that don't exist until created by a master sorcerer. Banks create them any way they want them to look, but always extremely complicated so they can fool the thousands of municipalities, like yours, who rely on outside expert advice to handle their investments. The more confusing the better, yet not so confusing they chase away the pigeons. If mutiny erupts and whistleblowers leak news about these secretive contracts, the mad sorcerers throw the mutineers in the brig, toss the key away, and their stories never see the light of day again. This in itself tells us everyone, including our hypocritical politicians and heads of media, are being silenced by the $700 trillion industry.

With ever bigger rip-offs dreamed up by their brightest scoundrels, Wall Street heavily pushed the tremendous amounts of money young people could make. As you know, stock market competitions are sponsored by bureaucrats in middle and high schools throughout the country, and shows like Buffett's have them hooked at a very early age. This insidious career was then pushed at college campuses for the hordes of high-tech employees they needed to carry out their plots. They knew the younger generation could be easily wooed and seduced into almost anything. Especially this new breed of high tech, materialistic kids hell-bent on getting rich and chasing the glitzy, glamorous lifestyle. In no time at all college kids were lured, trained, and selling derivatives and proprietary bets with no idea how they worked. That's the beauty of derivative scams – NOBODY knows how they work or what they're truly worth at any given time.

By 2008, derivatives made up about 'two-thirds' of the total trade volume. The ravenous lion was out of its cage and feasting on munici-palities across the globe. At first it fed mostly on Europe because it had few, if any, laws to protect their prey. These were the days after the Soviet Union and its Eastern Bloc countries broke up and they were all trying to get into the European Union so they wanted to look their best. Desperate for good reports of financial stability, they would do almost anything to achieve it… and anything they did.

One of the most popular derivative shams started out with a broker contacting their target and telling them they would buy millions of shares of their stock, forcing the price up. Sound familiar? This in turn resulted in an artificially pumped up price with profits to match, but came with a substantial fee to the pigeons. They were never told the money they were using to buy the stock was highly leveraged and a downturn in the markets would be catastrophic. The mad sorcerers were betting on the markets infinite rise, and they didn't care because they were making hundreds of billions of dollars. Like attorneys, it was impossible for them to lose. With their limit downs they always got paid. With friends and business associates like that, who needs enemies?: Talk about your Dr. Jackal and Mr. Hyde.

All the largest banks in America went into Europe with hundreds of investment bankers-brokers-traders-salesmen-hustlers (pick a name) to London, which had a market nearly as immense as ours with even less regulation. They were like a kid in a candy store, selling products all over Europe their clients didn't understand. In London, brokers from both sides of the pond (Atlantic Ocean) were getting exponentially richer and celebrated with lavish parties and enormous spending sprees. Finally, that trickle-down effect actually worked! At least temporarily, as these VIPS infused millions into the economy. But similar to derivative scams, it only worked a few years in making the markets do what they bet it would.

It was as if the old, lawless, roaring 1920's was back; everyone was just a pawn in their get rich schemes. Like the salesmen themselves, few stooges ever knew exactly how this all worked until it imploded. The more legal ways an employee could find around the SEC regulations here in the U.S. and lawless Europe, the more their company made and the bigger their bonuses were. It was, and still is, pure capitalism at its worst.

Interest rate swaps was their grandest of all illusions. The bank's best hustlers would go to towns and cities or anybody with a large loan, bond, or other sizable debt and promise magical results from interest rate reductions, lower debt, and better credit. Instead, they were mortified by skyrocketing adjustable rate loans, subprime loans, higher debt, wrecked credit, and their town, city, or country in financial ruin. Those who had an adjustable rate loan in the 1980's know they are tied to an index that can rise very quickly and cause their loan to explode. I had a customer who lost everything when all his investment property loans ballooned to 20% interest and had to start over from scratch.

The problem with these loans is nobody knows when they'll go up. And in this new 21st century scheme, small towns to entire countries wound up owing billions more than they had been promised, causing them to default - and ultimately go bankrupt.

Greece is perhaps the most famous tragedy. Like everyone in Europe after the collapse of the Soviet Union, they were trying to become a member of the European Union and had taken on a lot of debt. This was a perfect opportunity for Goldman Sacks. They stormed in with a deal to reduce their debt by 2%. It was an initial subprime loan of what is believed to be around a staggering 15% that would never get on the books and essentially make it look as if Greece's debt was much lower. This would make it look more competitive with other European countries and allow them to borrow more money at a much lower rate. They could pay off that phantom loan and afford to invest in other things if they accepted the proposal. Thinking they would save billions, they accepted at a cost of millions of dollars and went on a spending spree that to this day has desecrated their country.

With their economy in ruins, massive deadly protests spread around the country and eventually lead to the downfall of the government. Many other countries that followed their path wound up with the same fate, and eventually the U.S. economy followed as well. In the end, over a thousand lawsuits were filed by municipalities across Europe.

Usually, only those with very poor credit and a high probability of default will pay these kinds of rates known as sub-prime rates. Subprime loans were outlawed here in the U.S. because the pariahs preyed mostly on low income and desperate people. As pressure mounted to stop these extremely lucrative loans in the U.S., European countries became subprime loans, currency swaps, and "reduced interest rate" scams most lucrative market.

Municipalities and governments from around Europe were devoured by these maniacs. Goldman Sacks, JPMorgan, and the other humongous U.S. and European banks made a killing off their victims. They were no longer satisfied with annihilating just the U.S. economy; they decided to demolish the entire worlds.

The greatest "known" heist Wall Street ever pulled in the United States was in Jefferson County Alabama. They had to expand their sewer system and didn't want to raise sewer rates or taxes, so they put out a $3 billion bond to finance the huge project. They screwed up royally, and just as the proposed Gravina Island Bridge to nowhere in Alaska, they were left with lines to nowhere! This nearly tripled everyone's water and sewer bills, leading authorities to issue another $3 billion bond.

JPMorgan discovered this colossal project and sent their top hustler to the rescue. He offered them an interest rate swap that would be swapped around from a variable rate to a fixed rate, then back and forth several times. They were told it didn't really matter what the market did because they had a plan to protect them either way. Jefferson County officials must have fallen asleep during the news hour the previous ten years. Like most of the other interest rate swaps, the deal went belly-up and they filed the largest bankruptcy in U.S. history.

Not surprisingly, with such astronomical amounts of money being made, an investigation by the feds found a bribe of three million dollars was given to former mayor, Larry Langford, who was in charge of the project, and he was given a fifteen year prison sentence. Former county Commissioners Gary White was given 10 years and Chris McNair 5 on charges of bribery and fraud, while the JPMorgan broker got off the hook by receiving just three months in prison. But JP was ordered to pay a penalty of $25 million and forgive the county $697,000,000!

The crooks on Wall Street would eventually sell these interest rate and currency swap contracts to schools, hospitals, and a host of municipalities across the country, costing us taxpayers and victims as much as a trillion dollars. Many-a-time people insisted these types of speculative trading funds be declared illegal, but each time bought out politicians working for the markets were able to sweep public decent under the carpet.

With such vast amounts of money flying through their computers at light speed, employees started questioning where it was all coming from and where it was going. Everything seemed to be based on just getting as rich as you can, as fast as you can, then ignore how you did it. For some, their consciences started getting to them and the spellbound finally woke up, asking, am I just a cog in this enormously unscrupulous machine swindling everyone's money, and is this worth selling my soul to the devil?

They knew they were taking the U.S. and world down the path of no return financially, morally, and ethically. It was no longer a job of helping good people invest their hard earned money. Led by former Wall Street employees and people from every facet of life, the new protest movement "Occupy Wall Street" sprang up around the country. For months, starting in summer and continuing through cold fall nights, scores of protesters from around the country occupied the Street day and night. Then protesters everywhere joined in, occupying parks and other public places across the land with crowds not seen since the Vietnam and Gulf Wars.

In New York City, every day became more and more violent between police and citizens, with neither wanting to give in. Something had to give… and it did. The police were granted court orders to disband the people on grounds of unsanitary conditions, disrupting the peace, and a host of other charges. When the people ignored the court order to disband, they were hogtied, beaten, and pulled from the parks by hundreds of police who had showed patience for weeks. But they hung themselves when they decided to line up protesters screaming in fear and doused them with pepper spray!

Energized by their actions, a small group of former traders that had gotten loaded from the shady deals they helped pull off were so sick about what they and their companies had done to the innocent people of the world, they decided to fight their former bosses. They were now the enemy and tried to write new legislation their previous bosses could not possibly find a way around and then presented it to the fired-up legislators.

Politicians acted like they were as furious as everyone else and put on a jolly good show for the people. They held meetings with everybody involved in the meltdown. It seemed nobody would escape their wrath. They looked outraged and pulled in the bankers, the Federal Deposit Insurance Corporation, Ginny Mae, Fanny Mae, and Freddy Mac to get answers.

You would think exposing this information to the world would have set off some bells and whistles at the Justice Department, SEC, and the FBI. Still, no investigation of top management ever followed! Why? Many people believed the SEC (which is supposed to make the laws for Wall Street), the Justice Department, and the FBI (who are supposed to enforce them) have turned into powerful government agencies that are instead run by the major cooperation's they are supposed to be policing - often called "regulatory capture." Powerful Wall Street had the big three enforcers in their hip pocket and was free to run hog wild without fear of prosecution. It was just too easy!

A financial reform committee was set up, with Barney Frank and Christopher Dodd putting together a bill to reform the S.E.C. rules and reign in corruption on the Street known as the Dodd-Frank Financial Reform Act. It was apparent to them Wall Street was controlling the SEC rather than the other way around, so why didn't they do something before the meltdown? Perhaps because Frank was the chairman of House Financial Services Committee from 2007-2011, and the committee took in $21 million in donations between 2008 and 2010 from Street lobbyist and bureaucrats. Overall the banks and financial institutions spent $150 million in 2009 alone lobbying legislators.

Peter Wallison of the Atlantic claims he also led the push in the 1990's to give low income people mortgages they couldn't afford through the Affordable Housing Act, which forced banks and other mortgage originators to give between 30 and 55% of the total mortgages to people making less than the medium income. I remember it well. That's when President Herbert Hoover's promise of "a chicken in every pot and car in every garage" had been up-scaled to a "house for every renter."

Dodd's excuse was, he had been one of the Street's closest allies and represented a state where many of them lived. In fact, Dodd had always been heavily financed by four of the biggest players in the financial collapse – Citigroup, AIG, Bear Sterns, and Merrill Lynch. In 1991, he actually helped set up the financial collapse by successfully attaching the amendment to FDIC legislation dealing with the Savings and Loan bailout of the late 1980's, which allowed the oversized financial institutions and insurance companies to be bailed out by the Federal Reserve - although we were still paying for the S&L one.

Everyone who knew anything about hedge funds and derivatives knew this was coming. After getting hammered in 2011, Warren Buffett said the highly leveraged, complicated, and secretive credit default swaps and other complex derivatives were "weapons of mass destruction." As Bill Moyers put it, "They made the arsonist the fire chief."

Slowly but surely the committees reforms were whittled down to nothing by their Street buddies and fat cat corporations, leaving all the major players of the financial collapse singing all the way to the bank – their bank. They quickly began ringing up record profits again, and the four largest too big to fail financial institutions that were supposed to be downsized, actually grew another 40% and are still controlling 90% of the hedge funds and getting $83 billion a year in taxpayer subsidies! That's justice American style folks!

The FDIC once again reminded the world who was running things. When at a meeting to discuss reforms with bankers and the Office Of Complex Financial Institutions, whose job it is to stop any more systemic financial failures, the FDIC told everyone at the hearing: "We will not tell the banks what to do, they will tell us what to do!"

Gee, I bet you didn't see that coming!

The Dodd Frank bill was supposed to set up a $50 billion fund the charlatans would have to fund themselves instead of the FDIC for any future bailouts, but was heavily opposed by Republicans, who said it would create more bailouts. Three dozen experts, including hedge fund investor and owner of Kynikos Associates, President Jim Chanos, warned Congress they were unanimous in the fact the reforms did not go far enough to prevent future collapses. "Wall Street is right back to piling on leverage and leveraged buyouts," he said. It soon proved it with another hedge fund scheme that let people bet on Hollywood movie box office receipts.

As during his Reagan years, former Fed chairman Paul Volker (who was always leery of deregulation) proposed going back to the Glass Steagall Act. The Volker rule was proposed, but after lobbyist got done with regulators it had 300 pages of exemptions, all but defeating the former Wall Street workers attempt at reform. The agency to protect the people by insuring this would never happen again had sold out just two years after the swindlers destroyed the world economy.

Confirming who was pulling the puppets strings, multibillionaire Buffett proclaimed: "If there was a power struggle between the one percent and 99 percent... my side won." The bankers then put the final stake through our hearts by getting the feds to increase the amount of money a regulated bank trading swaps up to $100 million annually to $8 billion. This left virtually everything the same as before the crash and confirms what I told you in the beginning - we are perhaps the most corrupt, arrogant, ignorant, selfish, greedy capitalist country in history and we refuse to learn!

Did I hear someone ask how much the meltdown cost the US economy? Although it's impossible to put an exact figure on the destruction, the U.S. Government Accountability Office (GAO) set it at $22,000,000,000,000!

Seven Years Later

Here we are in 2017 and no investment bank president or top executive has ever been prosecuted. It would seem the ethics commission and federal prosecutors from the SEC and Justice Department just vanished. This regulatory capture allowing the bloodthirsty sociopaths to continue a dossier of total impunity was the primary factor in the eventual downfall of the United States, both financially and morally. Had the country learned nothing from history?

The Supreme Court in their Citizens United vs the Federal Elections Commission case gave Wall Street and the beltway bandits substantially more power to abuse the world. Their absurd ruling allowing the rich and powerful to donate unlimited amounts of money to any politician's campaign through Super Pac's would be the death blow to both Wall Street and campaign finance reform, all in one of the Supreme Courts worst decisions in history. They now seemed to have all three branches of the United States government in complete control. But were they really in control?

May 6, 2010, computers gave the world a taste of who was really controlling our destiny, when they once again unleashed their powers of destruction to both rich and poor alike. They unexplainably decided to go on a selling rampage as never before seen in history. In minutes the Dow was down 1000 points for no apparent reason. By now humans were too slow for computers trading in milliseconds and had no way of stopping them. They were now programmed to get the data they based their trades on from thousands of news sources around the world. No one could say why they started selling or what spooked them. What we did know in our real world of finance was one of the world's largest and most widely held stocks, Procter and Gamble, was down almost 25%, and some companies such as Accenture were completely annihilated - dropping from $40 a share to 1 penny. Then, as usual, and equally unexplainable, they bounced right back up. It's days like those that spurred one of the stock markets all-time greatest quotes when newsman Brian Williams quipped: "The dirty little secret is the world has no money and the emperor now has no clothes."

By 2012, three of the Street's superpowers had merged; JPMorgan bought Bear Sterns and merged with Chase, all huge players in the 2008 implosion. JP was the expert rip-off artist before and apparently had no desire to stop being the number one thug. Shortly after the implementation of the heavily watered down Dodd Frank Financial Reform Act and Volker Rules, they were once again in front of government officials trying to explain their way out of a total loss of more than $17 billion nine months into the year. As was expected from the rest of us, they had already circumnavigated around the few laws regulating them.

Their London man executing these contracts known as the London Whale, Bruno Iksil, told people he couldn't keep the scam going any longer and he didn't know when they wanted him to stop. He thought it was insane! And those involved claimed the orders came from the top, in other words, chief investment officer Ina Drew. All-toll, JPMorgan lost $2.6 billion in the scandal.

Drew, who had resigned after news broke of their shenanigans in the derivatives market, claimed she was deceived by the London office. She claimed they misrepresented the potential risk to their latest con job and projected losses, so she never knew about the risky contracts. Haven't we heard that one about a thousand times?

When government investigators found they had reported losses of $1.2 billion in their internal report, yet $580 million to the Office of Comptroller and Currency, they wanted answers! The panel told them they had not followed their own internal rules, and eventually the feds made a deal that made them pay a pittance for the world's largest investment firm - $100 million for a firm that took in hundreds of billions hustling.

The FBI is once again investigating them and other players for the umpteenth time. But as you know, no top corporate official has ever been successfully prosecuted from the 2008-09 meltdown - despite many employees coming forward with stories of banks' lending 5 or 6 times more money to federal agencies and other large customers than they were capable of paying back. Then they bet on them to fail, where they had billions of dollars waiting in profits. Even after the great crash, with the Fed charging them interest rates near zero, the denizens of destruction continued peddling nothing but debt and highly leveraged borrowing.

For years Washington Mutual was giving millions of individual home owners and businesses subprime loans they knew couldn't be paid back and then sold them to the feds - which insured them. Lehman Brothers was committing outright fraud in the hedge fund and derivatives markets, and when whistleblowers (who are purportedly protected by law) came forward, including Matthew Lee, vice president of Lehman - they were fired on the spot! Mr. Lee wrote a letter to four different departments that should have been policing the company, including the chief risk officer, general council, and head of internal audits, only to be terminated immediately.

The head hunters weren't the only players in on the racket. It takes "two to tango" you know. Accounting firms auditing their books helped them pull off the heist. In this case it was the auditing firm Ernst Young, who was supposed to catch the cheaters in on the fraud, yet gave the companies a clean review. Future Federal Reserve chairman Timothy Geithner said their hands were tied because the banks that regulate them (instead of the other way around) didn't give them any authority to do anything about it - like a fire truck with no water. Many whistleblowers came forward and told exactly how the morons were committing blasphemy, and they all got fired! Meanwhile, the deranged criminals were rewarded with billions!

To make it look good, the FBI and the Justice Department went after the mid and low level management who could be more easily prosecuted and imprisoned then the moguls. And the SEC fined major corporations but never jailed any top executives.

By 2013, the clueless central bank was supporting the market with record amounts of liquidity (cash) that would be used by the criminally immoral financial sector to borrow record amounts on margin for their bets. This caused valuations to be stretched, near record phantom profit margins almost double historic averages, and price to earnings ratios nearly 50% above historic norms.

After supposedly regulating derivatives starting in 2014, the U.S. House immediately and overwhelmingly voted to exempt them from regulation if firms do it through an overseas subsidiary. So after using up all the North American and European countries, banks led by industry leader JPMorgan are now running their rackets in China (the world's most populous country and second largest economy) as well as other Asian countries, including Japan. Combined with Supercomputers capable of selling at warp-speeds of nearly half a million trades per second and humans unable to control them, it could only result in one thing - history repeating itself yet again. And it did just that in China!

Hopefully, if nothing else is done to drive Wall Street out of the highly leveraged derivatives market and stop the artificial numbers they cause on our economy, the government fines well at least recoup the money it takes to run these agencies that are supposed to regulate them and oversee their operations. That way, at least someone will break even from these scams because you know it won't be us! Unfortunately, they're a tax write off and we only net about two-thirds of the measly fines.

Now let's look at a couple of the greediest psychopaths in history.

Jon Corzine

In 2011, Jon Corzine, chairman, CEO, and 40% stockholder of MFG Global (MFG) caused the worst single bet collapse in Wall Street history. Jon seemed like a really nice guy to everybody that ever met him, but greedy arrogance lay under that kindly exterior. He polished his deception at Goldman Sachs, where he was a respected and well liked chairman, CEO, and senior partner. After disagreeing with major partner Henry "Hank" Paulson about his dangerous investment style, he used over $100 million of his Wall Street fortune to become a New Jersey senator and then Governor in 2006.

By 2008, as did many other Street insiders, he became an advisor for President Obama. But after losing reelection he went back to do what he did best - steal everyone's money via derivatives at MFG; a cash and derivatives brokerage firm that provided trading and hedging solutions (his specialty) in commodities, futures, and other investments. MFG was in dire straits and thought they had found a savior in Corzine, but shortly after arriving, he pushed the limit and no risky investment was too risky for him. He loved interest rate gambles and lost badly when he bought into the European scam with a huge proprietary bet, eventually totaling $6 billion on European bonds going up.

Like many scheisters, he was able to con people with the help of accountants. By Wall Street accounting law, as soon as you make a trade with expected future profits you can use them to "cook your books" and make a company in trouble look pretty impressive. He did this by hustling other commodities companies into buying products that, even professionals like themselves, "claimed" they did not know exactly what they were investing their client's money into. The product was sovereign bonds, and Corzine, as most government run departments do, simply shifted money from one of the firms other departments to his bond scheme. We do it all the time here in town, as does the school district. The only difference is we do it legally... I hope.

Corzine, who was literally a god to the Commodities Futures Trading Commission, set up his ruses by telling them it would be a huge mistake regulating them - so they didn't. Being a former presidential advisor, senator, governor, and Goldman Sachs big shot, he got what he wanted and kept betting until he annihilated his company just 2 years after the collapse and Fed bailout. It was as if it never happened.

Who knows how many other commodity brokers put their client's money into MFG. Not only did he screw all of his trusting associates, but auditors found over $1.5 billion missing from costumer accounts, which are supposed to be kept separated from MFG's. It would appear the money was stolen from costumers to pay off a substantial margin call from JPMorgan, whom Corzine borrowed it from. Because he personally stole so much from so many, this was considered the worst single bet in history up until then.

Originally, Corzine nor anyone else at MFG was prosecuted, despite having no explanation for misplacing the $1.5 billion. In July of 2013, the CFTC finally charged the former CEO and executive Edith O'Brian with the unlawful misuse of about $1 billion in customer funds related to the firm's October 2011 collapse. And believe it or not, the CFTC finally did something right and banned internal borrowing!

In a city and place where everyone's money is fair game, Jon Corzine would soon be outdone by a bigger and better "mad sorcerer." One who had been working on the most impressive scam in history for decades and had the best of them under his spell.

Bernie Madoff

Hero to some on Wall Street for his ultimate greed and ruthless, deceitful, in your face Ponzi scheme, but criminal con artist and mad sorcerer extraordinaire to everyone else: Bernie Madoff pulled off the greatest individual con the world has ever seen. A scam so amazing it will go down in the annals of history. He took his family, associates, "friends," and some of the world's largest banks for a total of $65 billion in paper money and $17 billion in cash over 20 years to achieve his ultimate goal of fame and fortune. He is such slime; he even stole from charities and was the ultimate psychopath in a capitalistic system gone wrong.

Ponzi's have been around for centuries and are almost identical to pyramid schemes, only on a multimillion dollar level. They can focus on almost anything but are most popular in the stock market and real estate arenas. Like Pyramids, they take in money from their victims on promises of extraordinary gains in a short period of time. Then use each subsequent investor's money to pay off the unusually high interest rates, dividends, or whatever is promised before they move up the list and get their money.

This is actually how the whole stock market works and just about all forms of investments. Stocks, mutual funds, insurance, and even Social Security are a few of the things that couldn't pay off current investors without subsequent investors to keep them going. Your home mortgage is literally a Ponzi or pyramid as well, because the banks borrow from the Federal Reserve and peoples deposits in exchange for your future payments. In that way our entire financial system is a Pyramid and Ponzi! That's why market crashes keep happening after every deregulation. When Wall Street gimmicks are conceived, phantom money is created through bookkeeping scams such as that of Madoff's accountants. Then they create phony books and records to hide their double-crossing ruse from everyone else. If I said it once I said it a thousand times: A great accountant is about the most important person in any business... especially crooked ones!

Like most government officials who turned to the dark side, Madoff was the former chairman and co-creator of the NASDAQ and advisor to the SEC on electronic trading. He then used his lofty position and contacts to finance his fraudulent securities company. With the conviction of a dictator and charm of a prince, he intimidated his loaded pigeons into investing sometimes tens of millions of dollars each and mutual and hedge fund managers hundreds of millions. To win their confidence, he wined and dined them at his lush parties while establishing himself as a god-like figure in the eyes of everyone on the Street. For years nobody questioned the success of the great and powerful Oz. Those that did were bullied into submission by his personality and personal handling of every investor, successfully keeping his investments a secret.

His charade worked better and longer than most because he didn't brag about his enormous returns and ran another reputable company as middleman between buyers and sellers. He went on his track record of consistent returns over many years, including the meltdown of 2008. That's what got him in trouble! People couldn't figure out how did it legitimately because no one does that good in an implosion. The SEC had been warned by multiple experts for years, yet Madoffs friend SEC chairman, Arthur Levitt, ignored his own SEC's reports of Madoff's questionable investments.

For his efforts, Madoff got 150 years in prison, has to pay restitution of $20 billion of the $65 billion he stole, and one of his sons that turned him in committed suicide. On the strength of his assistant Annette Bongiorno's testimony, five of his closest employees also stood trial for conspiracy and fraud, including her. They were convicted of aiding and hiding the spectacle, and had to forfeit everything they gained, including their multiple lavish multimillion dollar homes, vacation properties, and real estate investments.

The nation's largest bank, most fined in history, and my top fraudster award winner JPMorgan Chase, had to pay a slap on the wrist $2.5 billion in penalties for Bank Secrecy Act violations in a deal that kept CEO Jamie Dimon out of jail, but infuriating the 4000 duped investors. JP had a 22 year relation with Madoff, and according to the NY Daily News, during a jail interview, Madoff claimed they and other banks were aware of his scam and it was very obvious to them what was going on. He said, "they turned a blind eye with me." Federal prosecutor Preet Bharara claimed Madoff funneled $150 billion through just a single account without ever buying any stock or raising an eyebrow. Prosecutors fingered JP as the main accomplice Madoff used for his money laundering scheme, and they not only ignored the alerts the computers were posting in 2007 and 2008, but shut them down!

Bernie wasn't the only one running Ponzi's. There were hundreds of others using every source one can imagine. Real estate Ponzi's were everywhere, including vacation getaways. Cay Club Resorts and Marinas defrauded nearly 1400 investors out of $300 million by telling them they were building five star destination resorts and they would get a guar-anteed 15% return on their investment, plus $30,000 in upgrades to their units. As with all Ponzi's, investors lost everything, and the president and CEO, Fred Clark Jr., and his former manager and sales agent Cristal Coleman (now his wife) got millions along with the usual perks - planes, yachts, etc., then fled to the Cayman Islands to live in luxury.

Then it was Donald Trump's turn. After his airline, casinos, and other real estate investments went belly up, he too got into strikingly similar shady vacation resort deals that could well be considered Ponzi's.

Can we ever successfully stop these scams with deregulated financial institutions? I think the answer lies in the proposed international Basel III rules. It protects the public's money and collapses by limiting how much they can gamble on speculative trading. It would regulate them to some extent by strengthening their quality, consistency, and liquidity ratios by requiring the mostly behemoth U.S. and European Banks and financial institutions to hold more than double the current common equity. It would also require a higher leverage ratio of a minimum 3% and 6% for eight SIFI banks and 5% for their holding companies.

The U.S. Federal Reserve proposes implementing all the Basil III rules for institutions with assets of more than $50 billion and annual test with early remediation. If they do, maybe we won't repeat the devastation of 2008-09. As the Wall Street Journal put it - "Credit default swaps imploded, complex derivatives blew up, and banking stocks plunged or got wiped out." The scoundrels may be able to pay off most politicians, but so far they haven't successfully been able to pay off all the regulators. They are trying their best and have successfully pushed back the inauguration date to 2019, but good congressmen like Alan Grayson, John Conyers, Bernie Sanders, and Elizabeth Warren were demanding higher capita, particularly cash reserves, and tying executive bonuses to performance - not stock.

If Tweedledee, Tweedledum and Donald Trump fail to reign in these weapons of mass destruction that brought the world to its knees and caused the Dow to gain 18,000 points the last 8 years, after taking 87 to hit 1000, it doesn't take a crystal ball to predict what's coming again!

3

Political Action Committees
Are We Still a Democracy?

NO! It's just that simple! With insanity at the controls, Wall Street's influence over the state and federal governments led the country into a state of which, short of a miracle, only a civil war declared by the 99%ers could destroy. From this unlimited Capitalistic power, came the special interest organizations "Political Action Committees" that grew into that criminal enterprise "Super Pac's." Originally small fundraising organizations similar to Parent Teacher Organizations (PTO's), they morphed into a massive abomination that hijacked democracy when they unofficially replaced government in running the country. Like K Street's ideology, their sole purpose is to amass as much wealth and power as they can while pushing the agendas of the insidious aristocrats and the Street's largest powerbrokers. As a result, once again, Reagan's trickle-down effect would come into play for all Americans, unfortunately, not in the beneficial way he envisioned.

Two Princeton and Northwestern University professors have unequivocally verified the over 300 million Americans and mass based interest groups, such as environmental and political reform organizations, have "virtually no impact on our national policy!" The plutocrats and corporate interest groups get what they want nearly 100% of the time from Congress… and you can bet the farm, from many state politicians as well.

How did they get so powerful, and how did that help them play their part in demolishing the United States of America? After all, the media had been exposing these groups for decades. Always a friend to the little people, Republican President Theodore Roosevelt got the train rolling by exposing the tyrants of industries corrupt, ruthless abuse way back in the early 1900's. After being "bought" by them for his 1904 re-election, he turned around and bit the hand that fed him when he jumped all over the robber barons privy, abusive butts and defeated them and their union murdering hitmen. Recognizing their importance, yet need to control them as "creatures of the state," he started by banning corporate and national bank donations for federal election campaigns through the little known Tillman Act of 1907. Then got Congress to break up their monopolies, rule against the oligarchs on key issues, (including instituting worker's rights) and installed what is now the understaffed Food and Drug Administration.

Despite fiery protest from the affluent Republicans he betrayed, Roosevelt championed the environmental movement and started the National Park system to protect public lands from them. For the next 60 years, progressive Republicans and Democrats alike continued to level the playing field and bring prosperity to Americans. They expanded the Tillman Act twice with the Federal Corrupt Practices Act of 1910 that put limits on campaign spending for national elections and full disclosure of monies contributed, then again in 1925, when they replaced both laws and set the modern day spending limits. However, leaving enforcement up to Congress made it rather useless, and eventually things shifted back to the privileged through Super Pac's. Now, monopolies are back and worker's rights have taken a shellacking. As one of the Republican Party leaders in my own town boldly exclaimed: "We have the money and we're going to keep it that way!"

For more than 100 years, Democrats had been a small government, anti-big business, agrarian, slavery party with few wealthy people. That changed after the three consecutive anti-government, anti-regulation GOP presidents of the 1920's Warren Harding, Calvin Coolidge, and Herbert Hoover led us into the doom of the great stock market crash of 1929. Led by the nation's top swindler, Joe Kennedy, Democrats increased their wealth to help balance the scales. With Theodore's cousin Franklin Roosevelt implementing his "New Deal," the democrats took hold of the White House for all but two terms from 1932 to 1968. Their reforms during that time created the great middle class that pushed the country to greatness, only to disappear from the selfish greed of the newest deregulation era.

When a show called 60 Minutes first aired in the 1970's exposing crooked people, politicians, and organizations, many thought the country was saved from shenanigans like corporate abuse and President Richard "tricky Dick" Nixon's Watergate break in. After all, most people were raised honestly back then with a small-town-like upbringing and they'd be way too embarrassed to be caught doing the unthinkable things they were exposing. What most of us didn't realize, though, was psychopaths have no morals or ethics. Instead of things getting better, they thrived by the thrill of the game and possibly being caught, so both corporate and political crime took off.

The captains of industry and Washington went berserk. Fortunately, mass protest by the people spurred prosecution of both Nixon and corporate buffoons. We even defeated the big bad tobacco industry as recently as the late 1990's, forcing them to temporarily poison and kill the rest of the world rather than us. Unfortunately, the country stopped the massive social protest of the 1960's and 70's, and by the 1990's corruption learned that media coverage alone was not enough of a deterrent to stop their dominance of the country's politicians. There was no modern day Roosevelts so Pac's simply no longer cared if they were exposed.

These contemporary pirates are the greediest people outside of Wall Street and are literally a spinoff of corporate greed. Based mostly on K Street in Washington D.C., they slowly built up power from around the time of the Reagan administration and his failed small government, financial deregulation, supply-side economics. When President Clinton completed the deregulation policies, it led to a complete mora
l and ethical collapse at the highest levels of society. Pac's became greedier, with the mightiest players on the Street funneling billions of dollars annually to control Wall Street's and the state and federal government's every move.

Any big time politician that runs for office is now a puppet with strings attached. They even set up their own private organizations with both politicians and themselves as joint members writing the laws, thus making them their official proxy. With the Supreme courts passing of the Citizens United case giving maximum influence to the wealthiest tycoons and Super Pac's through unlimited corporate donations, they essentially bought the state and federal governments. Now they control every facet of the country in every way, from the food we eat to the most powerful and feared governmental agency - the Internal Revenue Service (IRS). Not one entity of either the private or public sector has escaped their command.

As political campaigns became more and more expensive, legislators became prisoners of their own doing. They created the beast they now depend on for their campaign financing. No one can get elected without enormous amounts of money anymore, so the most powerful Pac's and well-to-do are both their best friend and worst enemy. Disappoint either one of them and they make sure you're not elected, keep them happy and you almost assuredly win.

How do they do it? Politicians learned a lesson years ago when John Kennedy and Richard Nixon had the first televised presidential debate in 1960. Nixon hurt his leg, was in pain and had the flu, so the young tanned Kennedy made Nixon look old and tired with not only his looks, but confidence and overall appearance. Ever since that day, they put more and more emphasis on appearance instead of their message.

So now they collect large sums of backdoor money from the wealthy, where it is used for the most crucial campaigns. Armed with nearly unlimited funds, they buy politicians thousands of T.V and radio ads that make you look good and your opponent look like an idiot, criminal, or both with vicious attacks whether they're true or not. Then they hire swarms of professional services to get you elected and beholden to them for life. They even pay for their travel and teach them things like body language and wardrobe to address the "Nixon affect."

Politician's lives became simply a revolving door of fundraisers with no time left for running the government, especially the House of Representatives with their two year terms. They only have a few months to actually write a bill, submit it to the sub committees, and advance it to a vote before their fundraising has to begin anew. This short term approach makes it all but impossible to present any controversial legislation, such as gun control, for fear of not being reelected in GOP states. It's always an election year to them and nobody dares try and pass that kind of legislation in an election year.

To show you how much money is now being raised on elections, President Obama and Mitt Romney went about raising nearly half a billion dollars of the $7 billion total in the 2012 presidential elections and 2016 rang up the same tally. Economist agree, if Super Pac's, large corporations, and Wall Street thieves put all the money they hid in offshore bank accounts and paid anywhere near the former tax rate of 70% the past 30 years, there never would have been a federal deficit. When Reagan took office in January of 1981 and the country in a recession, the deficit was just $79 billion. When he went for reelection four years later and the economy booming, it had gone up a staggering 135% to $185 billion and it never looked back. It was clearly the tax decreases and bank deregulation pushed through under pressure from Pac's that caused the deficit they claim - and for once they are right!

The American Legislation Exchange Counsel

The American Legislation Exchange Counsel (ALEC) is another extreme, mostly conservative, Republican organization hell bent on destroying the U.S. They push relentlessly at the state level, where most legislation takes place, to privatize and control everything from schools to state operations, then work their way up to federal programs like Medicare. They put the titans of industry in control so they can rule with an iron fist more representative of the old Soviet Union hammer-and-sickle way of life. If they get their way, we'll regress back to when all unions were abolished and collective bargaining outlawed as in the present day ALEC controlled state of Wisconsin. The deadly old guard GOP ways of slave labor by Ford, Rockefeller, Vanderbilt, and Carnegie of over 100 years ago will return. All labor, voting, living wage, environmental, and medical compensation laws will be severely restricted or eliminated. And everything from schools, prisons, and Medicare to the IRS will be run by their for-profit companies.

President Carter says "they'll stop at nothing to make money for their corporate members and gain as much power and influence as they possibly can to reach their objective – a complete subversion of government." They bulldoze public education by lying and cheating on tests and writing one horrendous report after another in an attempt to divert public money to their private corporate partners. The parasites even tried making all schools virtual schools with their Virtual Public Schools Act bill, isolating and denying our kids of ever making real friends. Instead, condemning them to students who never feel the joy of social interaction, sports, or working together as a team on projects and social issues. After pushing it with an army of lobbyist, they only got one state foolish enough, or corrupt enough, to pass it - Tennessee. They don't give a hoot about our kids' lives or education, only corporate takeover and profits for slime like junk bond king and prisoner turned virtual school owner Michael Milken... whom we'll discuss later.

Originally started by a religious fanatic in the late 1970's to Christianize America, ALEC was bolstered and praised by many religious leaders, along with conservative Presidents Reagan and George H.W. Bush, who said he valued their partnership and looked forward to continue working together in the future - in praising their partnership with state and corporate leaders.

ALEC is now the most powerful secret lobbyist for corporate privatization of America in history. They claim the same traits as those of hard core Republicans, such as small government, free unobstructed capitalism, and individual liberties. And contend with the NRA as the most influential of all Super Pac's, despite their claims of being a non-profit educator. Unlike the NRA, they get their greedy little claws into everything you can imagine rather than focusing on a single objective. This allows them to control a wider range of governance - from a phony Wall Street bond company posing as a tax exempt nonprofit 501©(3) online school for the disabled, to getting eight governors elected in the 2012 elections.

ALEC could easily be the GOP's poster child for greed, power, arrogance, and corruption. It's led by business tycoons Charles and David Koch, whose Koch industries is the second largest privately held company in the country. They're also among the world's largest commodities dealers with their many environmentally destructive endeavors that include chemicals, fertilizers, polymers, oil refineries, and pipelines. Made up of dozens of right wing fanatical groups such as the Koch's Super Pac "Americans for prosperity" and others that include The Tax Foundation, The Heartland Institute, and the NRA; ALEC pushes through beneficiary legislation for themselves and their allies while securing state contracts behind closed doors, and often skirting their way around competitive bidding laws. The Koch brothers alone and their foundations reportedly pledged somewhere around $400 million throughout the country to get what they wanted in the 2012 elections. And that figure was closer to $1 billion for 2016. They even got the Public Broadcast System (PBS) to drop a documentary on them or the David Koch Foundation would pull their millions in funding – forever!

Others, such as Steven Moore of the Wall Street Journal (and ALEC Board of Scholar member) control the media and push cutting taxes further for the loaded in that old trickle-down economics myth and greed. And the Freedom Foundation pushes their small government, corporate agenda, while private sector members like Leonard Kilroy and his Reason Foundation merrily proclaim victory in many cities in which they control almost all public and private sectors.

ALEC is supposed to be a nonpartisan, nonprofit, public-private partnership organization made up of legislators and businesses. But they are far from it, with about 2000 legislators and 300 jumbo corporations that are often represented by hordes of lobbyists embedded in them. Nearly 100% of their income comes from them and their trade and foundation groups, along with grants from the largest ones in America. Each corporate member, including Koch Industries, Pfizer, AT&T, State Farm Insurance, UPS, all the major oil and gas companies, and hundreds of others pay up to $25,000 per year membership fees and $10,000 more to participate in any of the eight task forces. A seat at their policy workshops will cost you another 25 to 40 grand a pop. Meanwhile, the politicians only pay $50 a year in order for both them and their masters to discretely follow most states $50 gift to legislator's laws.

Because of the incredible difference in membership fees, most people would call the discount a gift subject to ethic laws, but not this heavily stacked predator. Thousands of ALEC "model bills" have been given to legislators to supposedly "review for the public good" that turn up as laws around the country, infiltrating every government agency, town, and state. Every year they send 1000 "model bills" to them in every state, with an average of 200 being passed each year! More would be passed except they don't allow compromise, so bills are rarely amended to what congressmen think they should be. It's their way or the highway. Does this sound like a nonpartisan, nonprofit, private-public partnership group to you?

How do they do it? Having President Reagan and the Bushes in the White House promoting their agenda for 20 out of 28 years didn't hurt. And George H.W. Bush's other son Jeb as governor of the second most populous state of Florida for 8 years at the same time his brother George W was president didn't hurt either. ALEC has set up 8 task forces comprised of hundreds of people with different objectives for each one. One of them focuses on education, another on legislation, and one specializes on the most dangerous products to the health and wellbeing of every American - the Civil Task Force. This demented task force's mission is to attack all government protections of the most dangerous and often deadly corporations and their products, including fracking chemicals, strip mining runoff, fertilizers, explosives, poisons, drugs, tobacco products, and assault weapons.

One by one, ALEC members control state legislators with two dozen lobbying firms employing hundreds of lobbyist who wine and dine them at the most luxurious places. Then sit in on their legislative meetings behind closed doors to personally hand them the laws they want passed in the form of model laws. Needless to say, the model laws are only from the point of view of the plutocrats plugging them. On top of that, they shake down legislators to tack on amendments for crucial infrastructure project legislation. For example, here they attached repairing the 100 year old gas pipelines with building more gas fired power plants in Massachusetts. ALEC is more than willing to let scores of people blow up from the 100 year old leaky pipes and cost more than $40 million in leaked gas annually if they don't submit.

In return, the double-crossing politicians get all expenses paid trips and an opportunity to get some of the wealthiest people and largest players to donate billions of dollars to their campaigns.

They're able to do this because they're registered as 501©(3) non-profit corporations, which allows them to be tax exempt organizations and still receive millions from corporate and private members and their foundations. Meanwhile, they get paralyzing tax write offs and anything they desire. Ethical and legal problems, from IRS statutes to state laws about lobbyist and reimbursing legislators, would make a normal person think this is all illegal and unethical. And indeed in our state everything ALEC does is! We're very clear about ethics violations. Matter of fact, in addition to all public employees, anyone who volunteers, participates, or works in or on a public board or committee must take the state mandated ethics test and abide by the laws or be fined or imprisoned if caught breaking them.

ALEC's secrete existence and claims it doesn't have to follow any state's disclosure or Freedom of Information Act laws may be coming to an end, as well as their reign of terror on the American people. They've been exposed by whistleblowers and ever larger protests greet them at meetings around the country. Thousands are protesting their bills, such as their Electricity Freedom Act for Fossil Fuels they're schlepping for the industry that would repeal renewable energy laws across the country.

As of now, it is fighting a complaint by one of America's true protectionist, Common Cause, who has filed their complaint to the IRS rightfully claiming they are a corporate lobbying group masquerading as a public charity. And Arizona's Steve Farley reintroduced his ALEC Accountability Act in an attempt to get them off the Tax Exempt list and on the lobbyist list - where they'll have to disclose who their members are and where they get their funding.

With the actions of legislator turned anti-ALEC spy, Mark Pocan, (D) Wisconsin and his speeches against them proclaiming things like "ALEC is a corporate dating service for lonely legislators and corporate special interest," the U.S. may stand a chance against the most powerful Super Pac in history. But I wouldn't hold my breath until then. Because currently, every legislator who exposed their illegal business practices and proposed bills to officially list them as high powered lobbyist has been voted out of office at reelection time! Don't forget, 90% of incumbents win reelection, so this is pretty convincing evidence who is really running our country. It's like the song "Hotel California." Once there, they can never leave!

Sadly, ALEC is just the tip of the iceberg. There are hundreds of powerful groups like Koch Industries and their Americans for Prosperity foundation, Donors Trust Fund, and Donors Capital Fund. Not to be outdone, the woman of America got into the choreographed world of business with Tracie Sharp's State Policy Network. She has 64 state operations known as "think tanks," and combined with the Heartland Institute and other right wing organizations; raise more than $80 million a year in donations to influence lawmakers. The best part of it for these groups is they use these so-called "donations" as tax write offs that often lowers their taxes down to nothing ...and even get refunds. Think tanks also get into the private takeover of our schools by operating as for-profit schools. Can you believe it?

This brings us to ALEC's most prized victory and blasphemous decisions ever handed down by the GOP handpicked United States Supreme Court: The infamous Citizens United vs. the Federal Election Commission case, which simply became known as "Citizens United."

Citizens across the country were sick and tired of gigantic corporations controlling our politicians. So many public watchdog groups got together and sued the F.C.C. in an attempt to stop their campaign money flowing into election coffers. They claimed the election process was meant for private individuals to contribute campaign money and not big business with its own self-serving agenda. But the Supreme Court ruled they were people too! Reasoning publicly traded companies were obviously owned by millions of individuals and private ones were owned by private individuals.

Naturally, we claimed millions of individual owners aren't the only owners of a publicity traded company. A variety of groups and organizations invest in them, including government agencies and their pension plans. Clearly our founding fathers could not foresee such things as Super Pac's when they stressed individual rights in writing the Constitution, Bill of Rights, and subsequent legislation.

Through the years, goliath corporations and the wealthiest became more and more influential over the election process and now have unlimited power. Before the ruling they were allowed to donate to any campaign they pleased, but amounts were strictly limited in each state and they had to identify themselves. By law, the political campaign committee had to keep a record for the state of how much was donated, by whom, and how it was spent. Generally speaking, amounts to individual campaigns was under $1000 and anything over, say $100, you had to disclose the donor's name, address, phone number, and employer. This "public discloser," or notice, is so nobody can hide their donations and anyone can inspect the politician's records.

The Court ruling allowed any amount of money to be secretly funneled through Pac's to push their personal agendas. They already had unlimited spending on ballot initiative laws that allowed them to place anything on any ballot throughout the country. This was just another feather in their cap!

As Franklin Delano Roosevelt put it: "We had to struggle with the old enemies of peace – business and financial monopoly, speculation, reckless banking, class antagonism, sectionalism, war profiteering. They had begun to consider the government of the United States as a mere appendage to their own affairs. We know now that government by organized money is just as dangerous as government by organized mob."

Where did this leave the average American? It left them feeling disenfranchised, powerless and like the little peons they are. Like Warren Buffett said: "If there was a power struggle between the 1% and 99% - my side won."

If that don't give hope – what will?

This useless, betrayed feeling destroyed our democracy. People are so despondent by the system that they simply drop out - and who can blame them? That's what the insidious puppet masters want. When the politician with the most donations always wins, why should we participate?

There are those who say it's our own fault because we elect the winners and many don't participate. The reality is, even with 100% participation it still won't matter. The low life Pac's will still get their people elected and write the legislation they want enacted, then have "their" legislators do it. We're just a highway for political ambition and disposable commodities to them.

Fortunately, some politicians such as presidential candidate Bernie Sanders and Senator Elizabeth Warren saw the truth and tried pushing through legislation asking for an amendment to the U.S. Constitution to repeal the Citizens United case. About 20 states joined in and Bernie actually raised hundreds of millions in small donations. A ray of hope emerged for our democracy, but, in the end, the mighty puppeteers triumphed... Checkmate!

It's my belief, until everyone is once again just an Independent voter and we abolish all other parties and their blood money like our founding fathers intended, there can be no legitimate elections in this country and nearly every election will go to those with the most "criminal" support.

With Pac's controlling the strings and government entities, it would be impossible to explore all facets of life affected by them. So let's look at the most influential and heinous one outside of ALEC: The one that cost the most lives, money, and suffering. With them around, you don't need enemies.

A Country Under Siege!
The National Rifle Association (NRA)

From 1979 to 1997, more Americans were killed by guns (651,697) than all our country's wars combined. So why did the NRA go from a rifle club with a single range for marksmanship to a paramilitary army Super Pac? Backed by the most religious and conservative members of the Republican Party and their partners in crime, weapons manufacturers, it is one of the largest and most powerful Pac's, and perhaps the most costly, destructive, polarizing one.

Their sole purpose seems to be to bring about the Apocalypse by terrorizing our media brainwashed nation with its irrational, immoral fearmongering and psychological warfare, then arm it with 300 million guns and military machine guns in the name of the antiquated 2nd amendment to destroy our governments, education systems, and peace.

They enlarged the very same government they wanted downsized, and cost every school department, emergency management center, police department, medical facility, and taxpayer across the land untold billions annually for extra equipment, personal, training, medical care, security equipment, property damage, and tens of thousands of funerals annually.

It's led by super paranoid and often anti-government vigilantes made up almost entirely of white rightwing Republicans who must believe the Apocalypse is here. For years they've followed the mythological creature and biblical tyrant "Moloch" in the human form of Wayne LaPierre and his four horsemen, led by the first horseman of war Charlton Heston. They methodically armed its members, gangs, drug dealers, terrorist in every country, and millions of psychotic nuts with the most ferocious arsenal of mass murdering high powered military style guns ever seen. Then, declared war against the government, 315 million non NRA members, police, and states who wanted to live in peaceful bliss.

LaPierre has slaughtered tens of thousands of sweet little innocent kids across the land as Moloch sacrifices, blasting them full of holes, with skulls, brains, and other body parts splattered across schools, colleges, shopping centers, movie theaters, streets, and homes across the land. And Heston fulfilled his part as the first horseman of war in the name of peace and religion... NRA style. Now famine is widespread, nations are warring, spilled blood and death is everywhere. Have the other horseman arrived in the form of Senate leader Mitch McConnell, ALEC, and the NRA, and have they started the Apocalypse?

Because of them, we have far more dead bodies scattered across the country year in and year out (nearly 40,000) than any other country on the planet. Police are under siege and robberies, murder and mayhem is so prevalent in neighborhoods across the land, many municipalities have bought triple their normal cruisers so officers can take them home and park them in their driveways in an attempt to thwart it.

Thanks to them and weapons manufacturers, you can get as many machine guns, rocket launchers, anti-tank artillery, and flame throwers as you want easier than a voter identification card - and some people do just that. Their fanaticism killed the very freedom they claimed they were protecting and we fought every war over by terrorizing and paralyzing society. Police are now armed with machine guns to protect themselves, and the people they're trying to protect are prisoners cowering in their own homes afraid of their heavily armed neighbors, spouses, gang members, and mafia style drive by shootings. Shades are drawn in cities and towns across the land, doors quadruple locked, and security camera companies unable to keep up with demand. Perhaps the saddest thing is, schools complete with metal detectors are locked down permanently, taking away the last bastion of spirit and freedom our kids used to enjoy.

Like a communist country, the politicians comprising the federal government responsible for this scenario has turned against its own people and is heavily guarded. Any disobedience from the parents of the kids whose body parts are scattered across America are dealt with swiftly and severely when they protest in the imprisoned Congress.

The NRA has pushed relentlessly to re-control the feds since they ticked them off by outlawing assault weapons under President Clinton, despite knowing countries like Australia hasn't had one murder in 20 years since banning them. Ironically, it was Republican icon Richard M. Nixon in the early 1970's that first tried banning any specific type of gun after the assassinations of Democratic President John Kennedy, his brother Bobby, Senator John Stennis, presidential candidate George Wallace, and Martin Luther King. He wanted to ban the hand guns known as "Saturday night specials" used by all but Lee Harvey Oswald.

Then GOP hero Ronald Reagan accidentally reignited the gun ban issue after the attempted assassination of Nixon's Vice President turned President, Gerald Ford, himself, and his good friend James Brady. That led to the NRA becoming the over powerful paranoid lobbyist we know to this day. Once again, going against history, the assassinations, and near assassinations of the past, the NRA relentlessly hammered their paranoia into everyone that could buy a gun and shackled the truth at every turn. They took over the gun regulating Alcohol, Tobacco, & Firearms (ATF) agency. Then got them to withhold their data on how many and which guns were used in millions of robberies and murders so reformers couldn't pinpoint which to ban like Nixon had.

With their estimated 300 million guns roaming the streets, the industry feared another multibillion dollar lawsuit the tobacco companies went through. So they got Congress to let the assault weapons ban expire, then banned literally all gun laws at the federal level, including making gun manufactures the 'only industry' exempt from prosecution. They partnered with legislators and K Street to turn small towns and cities from coast to coast with little to no crime into blood filled war zones, littered with bodies and illiterate drug gangs running escape proof cities just to fill their bloodstained, greedy little pockets in exchange for America's most prized possession – FREEDOM.

Somehow, the NRA kept twisting the second amendment around meant to defend our homes and country from invasion with ancient single shot guns, to include the most deadly arsenal of weapons on the planet. I'm talking about military assault weapons and sub machine guns converted to machine guns. Yes, those same weapons used in war to annihilate the enemy are now being used by anyone. Including little kids like the 11-year-old in Westfield, Mass., who killed himself when his insane Uzi-toting father took him to shooting practice and allowed him to try his Uzi! The gun, that is literally a powerful sawed off machine gun popular with drug cartels and mass murderers, went straight for his head when he pulled the trigger. Even Vice President Dick Chaney came close to killing a friend when he accidently shot one at point blank range during one of President George W.'s hunting trips on his sprawling Texas ranch. Everywhere guns go - death waits in the shadows.

Where would they get this philosophy that anyone can own and carry a rapid-fire gun with thousands of rounds of ammunition like a soldier, out of the more than 200 year old amendment based on many single shot guns that couldn't hit the broad side of a barn from more than a few feet away? We are talking about an era where you had to load a "Long Gun" by standing it upright, pull out the ram rod from its holder, pull a packet of gun powder out of their belt buckle pouch, tear off the tip with their teeth, and pack it and a lead ball down with a rod to seat it. Then replace the ram rod, pull back the trigger, prime it with a percussion cap, and then finally aim and fire it. All the time praying the gun wouldn't blow up in your face when fired (if it fired at all) and the enemy hadn't run up and killed you before you finished loading it.

The guns used at the time of the writing of the constitution were as much of a menace to the shooter as they were to the enemy. The only reliable thing on it was the bayonet, which was actually the principal killing tool in its day. Far more people were killed by it than the slug of lead that came out. Today's guns with magazines of 100 bullets could obliterate hundreds before a soldier got one shot off.

It's strange how the radically right keep stressing our founding fathers couldn't possibly have imagined all the government laws we have today, yet apparently think they foresaw high capacity guns and anti-tank and aircraft launchers in the hands of civilians. That was some crystal ball folks! Otherwise, how could the NRA and their crony politician's claim the second amendment - which clearly refers to the state militias in the 1792 Militia Act and amended 1903 one designating them and the National Guard the official legal ones - allows anything outside the single shot giant pea shooters used to pattern it after?

Plus, the 2nd amendment says nothing about regulating guns, tanks, missiles, etc. and courts ruled it legal time and again in the name of public safety. It makes no sense for civilians to own such high-capacity firearms, considering even the shaky guns used at the writing of the constitution have traditionally been banned in public places. Yet here we are watching ordinary citizens executing our beautiful little kids at will in schools, movie theaters, and stores across the nation, thanks in great part to the blood stained GOP controlled Congress. Even former party president H.W. Bush quit the NRA following the massacres below when nothing was done. His son, and avid hunter, George W. tried doing the right thing in nominating ATF Interim Director Michael Sullivan to be the full time director, but his own party blocked it, saying his gun control support was bad for the industry.

Let the Extermination Begin

The extermination of the masses that eventually included over 15 school shootings a year started with the 1989 and 92 massacres at a school in Stockton, Ca. and a café in Killeen, Texas, leaving 84 shot and 28 dead. But it was the 99 school massacre in Columbine, Colorado that stunned the world when two students gunned down their classmates in cold blood. They never shot a gun until the plan was hatched. But after killing the first few, they felt the thrill of the hunt rushing through their veins with these powerful killing machines and decided to annihilate as many kids and teachers as they could with their remaining ammunition.

One was a military brat who loved the thought of killing everyone, the other a rich kid. Combined, they successfully killed 13 classmates and wounded dozens of others in the first major public ambush.

The self-serving GOP and NRA didn't flinch. They tossed the executions aside like it was a freak thing of nature that had nothing to do with them, although both under aged kids got their guns and ammo illegally through the NRA's control of Capitol Hill at a gun show and retail store. The country was outraged, yet nothing was done.

Next up – Virginia Tech University: This time it was a university student who went off the deep end and obliterated a record 32 students and teachers, mowing down everyone in sight as he indiscriminately rampaged through the college. The public was outraged, scared, and too paranoid to send their kids to school. Once again the remorseless NRA got what they wanted. He was identified as being dangerous and they claimed the system failed to protect the students - their guns didn't kill anyone. It was just another sick kid they claimed after this one, and once again nothing was done about it.

Then it was - the Fort Hood military base in Texas, where two shootings came in five years. The first was a mass eradication of army soldiers that left bullet riddled bodies, blood, and body parts everywhere with more than a dozen dead and 30 wounded. Army psychiatrist Nidal Hansan, who was convicted and sentenced to death, walked inside a crowded building carrying two assault weapons loaded with high capacity magazines and shouted God is great in Arabic. At least this time the NRA and GOP could say it happened on a military base by a Muslim fanatic, and as they say in basketball - no harm no foul.

The second shooting left three dead and a dozen wounded when an unhappy soldier returned to the base after a heated argument and indiscriminately opened fire.

I won't let the military have all the fun – This time it was at a movie theater in Aurora, Colorado, where another rich kid, batman fanatic James Holmes, appeared at the Batman premier in body armor and gas mask, then opened fire inside, murdering twelve people and injuring 70 in one of the worst mass shootings in our history. This guy wasn't satisfied killing as many moviegoers as possible. He also stockpiled guns, 6000 rounds of ammo, 350 shotgun shells, grenades, and a batman mask. Then booby-trapped his apartment that was supposed to explode when police came looking for him.

This never should have happened, there were many warning signs about his mental stability. He suddenly was flunking out of school after years of brilliance as a neuroscience major, high school athlete, and camp counselor for kids. He was going to a psychiatrist but banned from the campus after failing an exam before quitting. He's so deranged the psychiatrist warned both the local and campus police after he had threatened him. He also sent a package that included a journal, notepad, and note with an infinity design and some burnt 20 dollar bills 8 days before his rampage. However, it wasn't found in the university mailroom until 2 days after.

This time the villainous NRA had no excuses. This is a highly educated, intelligent, honored student and community volunteer, with equally successful parents who quickly went from Doctor Jekyll to Mr. Hyde. He's the epitome of what can happen with 300 million easily accessible legal dismantling machines with high-capacity magazines just waiting for their chance at carnage. Humans simply cannot be trusted with these things. Any one of us can snap like a beautiful, loving, loyal, dog that one day turns around and bites the hand he loved just yesterday. We had one on the farm, and man's best friend did just that!

We didn't get a politician yet - The assassinations just kept coming. This time, it was at a new type of event reminiscent of the old days to let the public chat informally with their elected official called Congress on Your Corner. The first of its kind in recent times, it was set up in a grocery store parking lot in Tucson, Arizona, for anyone who wanted to talk to Congresswoman Gabrielle Giffords. It was just getting started when Jared Loughner rushed up to her and her staff and unloaded a barrage of 31 bullets.

This was a high profile ambush of important people with another high-capacity, semi-automatic weapon that if not for him dropping his second magazine, who knows how many would have been blown away? Not only was she a congresswoman, but a judge and some of her staff were also shot in this political execution. Surely the Republicans would finally break ranks with the NRA.

House Speaker John Boehner was horrified by the shooting and said, "An attack on one who serves is an attack on all who serve. Acts and threats of violence against political officials have no place in our society. Our prayers are with her and this is a sad day for our country."

He tried to rally his GOP allies for action. After all, these people on the Hill were highly educated and most of them lawyers who were old enough to remember the other assassinations. Now they, their kids, and their grandkids were the targets of these atrocities. Who would be next? If people want more open, friendly political access to their politicians, they can forget it now... thanks to you know who!

You would think after the other massacres, this high profile ambush on one of their own would make the Tea Party Congress finally banish these weapons again.

Nope – Apparently, this one didn't count either. Because like James Brady, who was shot in the head during President Reagan's assassination attempt, and Senator Stennis, she didn't die - plus she was a Democrat. The Tea Party - who pranced around in their 1770's wardrobes with guns from that era to assault weapons - couldn't have cared less. She was a Democrat and they didn't matter. It's kind of like the Hatfield and McCoy hillbilly feud the GOP and their Tea Party have with the Democrats. You can kill anybody fair and square in a feud, and in their eyes, everyone was off the hook again.

Doesn't that confirm how corrupt and fragmented the GOP was and still is to this day? They fought their own House Speaker after watching one of their own shot in the head and 6 others killed by a member of the newly formed arm of the party. This was a Tea Party ambush alright, but the NRA reminded us of who was in command of this ship, even if a few congressmen, their kids, and grandkids had to be gunned down in cold blood by these destructive weapons.

Let's get some more kids – Finally, the dismemberment of our kids in Newtown, Connecticut, on December 14, 2012 by another privileged kid. This ambush was the one that finally galvanized us 300 plus million NOT under the NRA's spell to demand background checks and ban assault weapons and high-capacity magazine.

Twenty more 6-year-olds and 6 teachers were mutilated, with dozens more wounded, as hundreds of other kids and teachers watched. The country was appalled after parents went in to retrieve their butchered, bullet ridden, bloody, blown apart little darlings. It looked like a war zone, with skull fragments and body parts strewn around the building. Police and other emergency responders were sickened and shocked. Surly this would be the massacre that broke the NRA's back.

The good people of the nation, including many respectable gun owners and weapons dealers, were determined to ban these genocidal weapons and screamed bloody murder at the GOP and NRA. Mass rallies were held in the freezing cold of winter all across this former great country that was now being crushed under the weight of Super Pac's and their lackeys.

The NRA strategically held back with only a minor response of sorrow and waited for the funerals to end before blasting everybody about our constitutional rights to own military assault weapons and high capacity magazines of 100 rounds each. We have a right to protect our homes and families they yelled from every corner of the country, with enough guns and ammunition to eradicate hundreds of millions. They even had the gall to call people on the federal do not call list, using a robo-call that told everyone to kill the proposed legislation banning any gun control of any kind. It was our second amendment and god given right to own these things and butcher anybody we please.

Again, nothing was done, despite the GOP's own presidential candidate Senator John McCain voting to reinstate the gun control and assault weapons ban.

We're not done yet – Then, out of nowhere came more killings. It seemed like an epidemic was spreading across the country - and indeed it was. The U.S. was covered in blood from bodies blown to smithereens in the multiple mass killings (100 in the year after Newtown, including 14 at schools). They now spread from coast to the coast when a former California police officer went on a shooting spree. This time he targeted his prior bosses little girl and her boyfriend. Loaded to the hilt with massive amounts of ammunition like the others, he shot a couple of his former brothers in uniform that got in his way, then sought a hiding place for his final shootout with authorities from all the agencies a mass cop killer attracts.

He wasn't out to get civilians this time, as he proved when he hijacked a man's pickup truck and told him he wasn't who he wanted to kill. Like all others before him with a death wish, he got what he wanted in his last stand. All they found left of this one was his charred remains in the burnt out cabin in the mountains of Big Bear, Ca. he chose for his gravesite.

I told my daughter, perhaps this string of high publicity atrocities was no coincidence. Like the Stoneman Douglas High shooter admitted, he wanted us to ban these things before someone like him uses them. Perhaps some were not the crazy, sick people the delirious gun proponents said they were. Like the highly intelligent murderous cult leader Charles Manson, who tried using gruesome murders back in the 1960's to start cultural wars between whites and blacks, maybe some figured only a string of horrendous events could break the NRA infused Congress, and they were willing to sacrifice their lives and others to get them to act. Some were telling us you shouldn't allow ordinary citizens to run around with machine guns and unlimited ammunition.

Still, everyone's efforts to do the right thing and save the country failed. If nonstop carnage that would be considered war crimes and a vast majority of the country couldn't get the axis of evil on board with the rest of us, was all hope lost? The tiny minority once again ruled.

These increasingly frequent mutilations infuriated most of us. Far and above the vast majority of people - including many hunters and gun manufactures' employees - thought assault weapons and high capacity magazines should have been banned again. President Obama, who refused to reinstate the ban earlier when he had an all Democrat government because two senators from Wyoming were up for reelection, again cried crocodile tears. Now, the GOP house made it once again impossible to institute reason over insanity and protect our kids and ordinary citizens: Those who just want to go see a movie, shopping, or just sit in the park without fear of being exterminated. In fact, a ban on assault weapons was never even put on the agenda in both houses of Congress - and the incomprehensible just kept happening.

Confirming this writer's claim, the United States Senate voted no to all gun control legislation. With parents of butchered Newtown children in the balconies, Congresswoman Giffords, and thousands of others at the Capital, the Senate had the audacity to shoot down all gun control legislation. Several of the parents that shouted "shame on you" were arrested and taken into custody for interrogation. Parents, police, first responders, and school administrators around the country were furious. And I for one was too livid and disgusted to write anymore on this subject for days. I always hoped they would prove me wrong, but I didn't think they would and predictably wrote all the above two months before the vote. I really wish they had made me re-edit this chapter!

A few days later - Another Boston Massacre! This 21st century tragedy at the annual Boston Marathon came just days after the Senate voted down all gun control legislation when terrorist detonated two kettle bombs near the finish line of the annual event. An unprecedented manhunt of the two suspected brothers, whose families were allowed into the U.S. under political asylum from the Chechnya region of Russia, ended in the oldest brother's death in a shootout with authorities. After being weakened by hundreds of rounds fired by police, the second brother was captured hiding in a boat behind a house near the first shootout.

The brothers were seen on security cameras along the route with backpacks like those used in the bombings and pictures were posted on every source of media worldwide. Instantly identified by hundreds of neighbors, friends, and fellow college students, they tried to flee around midnight armed with more kettle bombs, assault rifles, thousands of rounds of ammunition, and possibly grenades.

Renewed calls for gun control energized the victims of the failed Senate votes. But the old coot, Sen. Lindsey Graham, R-South Carolina, still insisted the gun control laws the rest of the world has proven protect innocent people from these atrocities "do not work."

I guess he never looked at statistics in those countries and states with some of the toughest laws. Massachusetts and New Jersey only have about 4 gun related deaths per 100,000 people, despite enormous amounts of relocated N.Y. city drug dealers, compared to states like Tea Party leader and NRA champion Sara Palin's extremely sparsely populated Alaska's 18. Other NRA infused states reflect similar dismembering statistics.

We forgot about the neighborhood watches - This high publicity murder was from a man who hunted down a teenager in the name of a neighborhood watch person and was done under a controversial law called "stand your ground," which some claim was a victory and an advertisement for the NRA. They claim the gunman, George Zimmerman, was an important piece of their master plan and a tool for them and the gun industry to sell more guns. The NRA claims we need to arm every neighborhood watch person throughout the country with concealed weapons because there's danger lurking around every corner. So high profile cases such as these allows them to prey on the public and push their paranoid agenda into the minds of every man, woman, and child. Then they advertise heavily to increase their sales.

Despite the NRA's best efforts, people are following ex-president Bush's example and the number of paranoid members and households with guns is dropping. Unfortunately, the most delirious have bought more so the number sold has increased to record levels, with just 3% owning 50% of all guns (averaging 17 each and some psychos over 100) with gun manufacturer Smith and Wesson reporting stunning growth in sales and profits. In fact, every high profile case and massacre sets off binge buying by those suckers who buy into the NRA's preaching's. Mr. Zimmerman - who is now a cult hero - was seen reluctantly signing autographs at a gun store as a pawn for the owner and NRA. He said he was paying them back for their support during his trial.

Keep them coming - Another man walked into an elementary school near Atlanta with an assault rifle to have a shootout with police. He said he wanted to see cops die. And don't forget about the 3 teenagers who killed a college jogger after being foiled in their attempt to shoot someone earlier in the day with one of the 300 million guns because they were bored. A couple weeks later, two more mass executions occurred in Washington DC and the new murder capital of the US – Chicago, leaving 9 and 12 more in coffins.

We don't want to be left out – Finally, some more action in my own back yard several years after the 11-year old kid blew his head to kingdom come. Baystate Medical Center was in lockdown after a man shot his wife then took her there for treatment. After an all-night standoff with police he eventually shot himself.

We need to get more of our kids in on the action - Kids are routinely getting accidentally shot by their brothers, sisters, and friends playing with their parent's guns. But some kids turn into cold blooded murderers by using their own guns. In 2009, another bright, athletic, eleven year-old shot and killed his future stepmother by shooting her in the head in a nice rural community. The boy was given the shotgun by his "out to lunch" dad for his birthday and now sits in an adult prison awaiting a life sentence and a wasted life... I guess Santa won't be stopping by his house anymore now that he's on the naughty list. Santa will have to start wearing full body armor from now on here in the gun and murder capital of the world. The NRA keeps telling us we need more guns with more ammo than the perpetrators to protect us from their guns – so I guess the father should have given his fiancé a machine gun!

Let's get some soccer kids this time - Figuring they didn't sacrifice enough kids for Molech, another unidentified person opened fire on a first grade soccer team in Missouri. Parents jumped on the kids to sacrifice their lives! But apparently the shooter was just messing with them, or it was a warning like the others of what's to come if something's not done. Whatever the reason, he didn't kill this day and only a pile of casings were found at the scene.

It happened again – Another disgruntled Muslim youngster in Roseburg, Oregon, went to Umpqua Community College with a flak jacket, six guns, and five clips of ammunition, then lined up the kids and asked them question pertaining to God and were they Muslim before blowing each ones head to smithereens one at a time - execution style. He got through eight kids and one teacher before turning the gun on himself.

Maybe it's not as bad as I think. After all, there are other ways to kill people. Back in the 1970's, there was a show set in New York City called All in the Family. When the daughter, Gloria, was sick about all the gun murders, she asked her dad Archie... "Do you know 65% of all murders in this country were committed by handguns?" And Archie, a staunch Republican gun lover, responded with the classic quote: "Would it make you feel any better little girl if they were pushed out of windows?"

According to the constitution, the premier role of the government is to protect the citizens of these United States of America from anyone trying to harm us, so why don't they do it? Here is a perfect example why they don't in the gambling capital of the world.

Las Vegas - When the good people of Las Vegas, Nevada, tried passing a law the corrupt congress wouldn't, the NRA got their buddies in ALEC to push a bill through the state legislature disallowing communities from implementing tougher gun laws than the states.

The city that depends on visitors from around the world for its survival, wanted to ban machine guns and submachine guns from the famed Las Vegas strip. When the NRA got word of it they jumped into action and summoned ALEC. They had their "Public Safety" and Elections Task Force write a bill for an unknown Nevada state politician that would ban the city from protecting their own citizens and the millions of tourists from around the world from machine guns, submachine guns, modern day black powder weapons, and muzzle-loading firearms. It followed ALEC's Consistency in Firearms Regulation Act and their model law prohibiting local governments from adopting different rules for gun control and ammunition than the states. It's designed to make sure nobody anywhere in the U.S. can pass laws tougher than the states.

So what do you think happened? A husband and wife yelled "this is a revolution" and killed two Vegas cops at a pizza place. Then left a swastika and flag that said "don't tread on me" on their bodies, before heading for a Wal-Mart where they managed to kill one more before killing themselves or being killed in a shootout with police. Video and police reports were inconclusive about the final seconds.

Then, a few months later, came two more victims as another insane parent let their 9-year-old daughter shoot another Uzi. Only this time, it went straight for the instructors head instead of hers when she pulled the trigger. Now, she has to live with her actions that her incredibly stupid parents and the Last Stop shooting range allowed. She is the real victim here, for the lifelong vision embedded in her brain is much crueler than his quick death.

October 1, 2017: Stephen Paddock opened fire on a crowd of concertgoers on the Las Vegas Strip from the Mandalay Bay hotels 32nd floor. Using over a dozen assault rifles and high capacity magazines he fired 1058 shots that killed 60 people and wounded 413, with the ensuing panic bringing the injury total to 869 to earn the title of top predator before killing himself.

Despite gun enthusiast organizations and shop owners that push for sane regulations, the bloodthirsty anarchists continue bashing all levels of government.

Iconic gun manufacturers themselves are imprisoned from their partnership with the NRA. Smith and Wesson suffered for years trying to do the right thing March 17, 2000, when they made an agreement with the feds for more regulations after they, gun control advocates, and dozens of city mayors sued them. After all, the government had more money than they did and could bankrupt them by filing thousands of cases around the nation if they pleased. Unfortunately, the NRA, other gun groups, and manufacturers told people to boycott their guns and buy them elsewhere. I bet you can guess where elsewhere was!

When I was growing up in the 1960's and 70's, I loved having friends over to the farm where we would shoot all kinds of things from tin cans to birds with pellet guns. We were considered just farm boys doing what farm boys do. But my Polish grandfather patrolled the farm as if he was still in World War I hunting down Germans with his shotgun. We had no trespassing signs up in numerous places that legally allowed us to shoot anyone on our property. It was like that old song from The Five Man Electrical Band that said "anyone caught trespassing would be shot on site!" So one day, good old grandpa shot one of my friends on site!

I was supposed to tell him in advance if one of my friends was coming over to fish, trap, or hunt. Oops, I forgot... and as usual he forgot who my friend was. My friend was on the other side of the pond with a heavy fall jacket and hat so he only received a few dimples in the back of his neck from the shotgun blast. Fortunately, this story had a happy ending thanks to the single shot gun he was using and a pond in between them. If he used today's weapons, my friend would have been riddled with bullet holes and laying in a pool of his own blood. All because I forgot to tell grandpa he was coming over to go fishing as he had many times before.

My grandfather knew and liked my friend but probably had what is now called Alzheimer's disease. He never recognized any of my friends no matter how many times he had seen them before. Even with a friendly welcome, he was half death and the kind of person to shoot first and ask questions later. This story, along with former Vice President Dick Chaney's should serve as a warning as to what can accidentally happen in even the friendliest mistakes.

I'm sorry to report, as of printing, the barbarians had not heeded these warnings and successfully killed all common sense federal legislation to ban these weapons of mass destruction or limit high-capacity magazines in these 'not so' United States of America.

Some sensible states like Connecticut and Colorado joined the lowest murder states that already banned them, but Congress was still sleeping with the henchmen instead of protecting us from them. So, 50 more were blown away in Orlando, 5 policemen in Dallas with an AK-47 and armor piercing ammo, and 17 at Marjory Stoneman Douglas High with dozens injured, traumatized and the rest of the civilized world shaking their heads AGAIN as to why we don't banish them nationally.

After all, in a Newsweek study of 6 million violent crimes involving gun owners, "99.2 percent were NOT able to use them to defend themselves" and "invaders got to them twice as often as the owner." Worse yet, states with the right to masquerade around town with guns have "more crime!" Furthermore, after the 1994 assault weapons ban expired in 2004, the number of gun massacres (6 or more) shot up "an astonishing 183 percent with a 239 percent increase in massacre deaths." Swat team deployment also went from 3000 to 45,000 a year and the rate of gun confiscations per 1 million air passengers has more than tripled, according to the latest numbers from the TSA.

So why don't the 315 million non-hallucinogenic citizens have the right to ban useless high-capacity guns, magazines, bump stocks, gun kits, and gun shows that sell them like candy? Where's our rights, as well as store owners and employees to live in peaceful bliss without fear of being mutilated at work, the movies, shopping centers, parks and our own homes and yards by neighbors or anyone armed with thousands of rounds of ammo? Where's our right NOT to bear arms?

At the tri-county fair in Northampton, Ma., I ran into 20 something Sam Johnson. I showed him my book about our brainwashed, selfish, me society. He admitted he had a 60" TV and an AK-47. So I asked, why do you need them? Not surprisingly, he said "I don't, I just want them," despite the AK-47 being outlawed here.

I wish I didn't have to put so much blame on the GOP for the destruction of our country - considering both parties equal corruption. As you know, my grandmother was the county chairman back in the 1950's and our entire family was staunch Republicans. But since then, the party has become as radically right as the Democratic Party has left, as Mitch McConnell proved when he followed Charlton Heston's stunt. At a convention of Republican big-shots for retiring Sen. Tom Colburn, he hoisted a riffle over his head and shook it in defiance of all the massacred kids, people, and their families. Is he the second horseman?

With about 40,000 people dying every year at the hands of guns, former N.Y. mayor Michael Bloomberg announced he was going to use $50 million of his own money to fight the NRA. That's more than double the NRA's normal annual figure. Is there actually hope for the future - or has the Apocalypse begun?

4

Our Dishonorable Government

As feared by our founding fathers, by the 21st century, the brilliant and visionary independent democratic form of government they instituted was besieged by corruption and multiple parties. The over 200 year old constitution that doesn't even recognize we've had an Air Force (originally called the Army Air division) since 1918, has become not only the oldest in the world but mostly obsolete. It's now an outdated liability without the reforms necessary to be effective in the modern world. With special interest gangsters abusing the system in mass, we became perhaps the most crooked democratic nation on earth. Because opposite to what our grandparents had taught us — honesty, morals, and ethics, selflessness and greed is the order of the day for governments across the land run by the "me generation" baby boomers.

There is a complete lack of both morals and ethics that escalated with the stock market boom of the 1990's. It seems white collar crimes at every level of the corporate and political ladder are on trial daily around the country for every conceivable violation of law you could imagine. In June 2014, the mayor of San Moreno, Ca., actually threw a bag of his dog's poop on a guy's doorstep who had complained about people letting their dogs poop on his small front yard! Why? Because he had signs on his front lawn that read "This is a no dog pooping zone," and the mayor said the small signs were ugly.

When politicians and big business can't get away with - pardon the phrase - pooping all over us, they do it through the tax code with wave after wave of tax reductions and deductions for themselves and the ruling class, then pay for them on the backs of the middle class and taking away our most valuable tax deductions. They then rig the electoral system to ensure their two party system remains just that.

After the most powerful and notorious lobbyist Jack Abramoff and 21 others went to prison for corrupting public officials, tax evasion, and fraud wrote a book detailing his life of crime bribing congressmen, how he did it, and listing people he did business with, you would think the new political ideology might be forced to change their ways. But as Will Rogers said: "We have the best politicians money can buy."

In a lecture at Georgetown University in Washington, Abramoff told us: "I spent $1.5 million a year on sports tickets alone in order to get policymakers to come with me so that I would have an opportunity to influence them and have them indebted to me in some way." He then went on about his lobbying years when he was king of the lobbyist and represented everyone from Native American casino owners to Russian energy companies, and buying that access is corrupt. He got to "100 congressmen," including his good friends' Republican House Majority Leader Tom DeLay and ally Bob Ney through their chief of staffs. Yet considered that a failure "because that leaves 335 offices that we didn't have a strong influence over. For lobbyist to make money they have to take it away from other lobbyist in an intense special interest competition." Bob Ney - who longed to become Speaker of the House - admitted they were in a "culture of corruption" and were in violation of the gift limit laws, along with many others.

Abramoff owned a bar that President George W. Bush's staffers packed daily and often conducted illegal business right out in the open. They tacked on special legislation to bills that were as confusing as derivatives and Ney claimed nobody read. It was all just a great big shell game. Of course with the king of shells in the White House – is anyone surprised?

Ney spent 17 months in jail for his part in Abramoff's dragnet that could have, and should have, included many other congressmen. DeLay was found guilty of money laundering from a fundraising scandal in November 2010 by 12 jurors who heard the testimony of over 40 witnesses and found the evidence sufficient for a guilty verdict. They also got him for funneling $190,000 in corporate money via the Republican National Committee to help elect GOP candidates to the Texas legislature in 2002. That allowed them to push through his redistricting plan and further entrench themselves.

Abramoff claims the whole system is bribery and almost everybody partakes in it! As former Ohio governor Ted Strickland told Charlie Rose: House Majority Leader "John Boehner told me, if he couldn't control them (the Republicans) he was going to let them loose and see what happens."

When Abramoff finally saw the light after 3 1/2 years in prison, (unlike the 12 congressmen and lobbyist who joined him and still call him a liar) he emerged like the other former Wall Street employees that turned on their own banks and sleazy Pac's. He admitted he was working for a system of "legalized bribery" on Capitol Hill. Then acknowledged his mistakes and said he used legal bribery to purchase political offices, and he hated term limits because he didn't want to spend the time and money to repurchase the same office. He's now joined the rest of us in going after his formidable industry and wants to close the revolving door between Washington DC, Super Pac's and the Street by banning legislators and their aids for life from ever becoming lobbyist. In addition, he wants to ban them from giving lawmaker's gifts or political contributions and instituting term limits for our tethered bureaucrats.

Once opposed to social and environmental groups who are fighting to free government from Wall Street and special interest's stranglehold, he suggested if we want to do something about how the lobbying industry is using legalized bribery and other things that corrupt our democracy, we should support their efforts. Like the Declaration of Independence says: "That whenever any form of government becomes destructive of these ends, it is the right of the people to alter or abolish it, and to institute new government."

As you know, the fed's continuous collusion with the Street and special interest made it nearly impossible to distinguish one from the other. Especially with career criminals like Henry Paulson (Chairman and CEO of Goldman Sachs) and Robert Rubin (former co-chairman of Sachs) appointed Treasury Secretary by George W. and Bill Clinton respectfully. Then it was New York Federal Reserve board member Jamie Dimon (CEO JPMorgan Chase) along with the SEC's Mary Jo White working both sides of the table.

With generations of 19th century families still entrenched in Congress and other governmental agencies, and Wall Street constantly recycling the same people back and forth through congressional positions, it became more entrench with insiders than ever. As Sen. Warren - who was appointed by President Obama to head the congressional panel overseeing the new Troubled Asset Relief Program (TARP) after the meltdown - wrote in her 2014 autobiography, former Treasury Secretary Lawrence Summers "urged her to be an insider." Like Rubin, Paulson, Dimon, Summers, and Mary Jo, thousands of prior federal employees work on the Street and vice-versa, switching alliances in key positions that regulate themselves – the fox guarding the hen house!

Another recent transfer was Timothy Geithner, the former president of the powerful New York Federal Reserve and U.S. Treasury Secretary under President Obama. He supervised the (TARP) after the implosion and took a job on the Street as president, partner, and managing director of the mega private equity firm Warburg Pincus LLC, where he's helping the firm with strategy, investment management, and investor relations. He joined former presidential candidate Mitt Romney and governor Duval Patrick in running firms that specialize in leveraged takeovers using borrowed money from the fed's historically low interest rates he himself helped set up. Like all private equity firms, he'll downsize their prey by firing lots of employees to make them more profitable and resell them for a major profit and 20% of the gains.

George W. had brought in Paulson in 2006 to run the Treasury Department at a time when everyone was waiting for the market to collapse from the unsustainable loose credit and bogus hedge fund and derivatives scams he was orchestrating. His firm's mortgage abuses later became the focal point of the housing meltdown and added more lawsuits, fines, and congressional hearings to its buyers Jamie Dimon's JPMorgan Chase's impressive list of indiscretions and abuse. Dimon's list of fraud was so long, it took "six pages" for the New York Times to list all the charges against him and his bank! So what does it take to get this guy in jail?

Those two were like the best computer hackers in the world hired by the best computer security companies to create the newest anti-hacking software. As the old saying goes – "It takes one to know one." Since Paulson knew all the Wall Street banking gimmicks, it only made sense to the unethical bureaucrats to hire one of the best to run the Treasury if you wanted to either prevent more of them, or run them at the federal level. Take your choice… if you dare!

One might question why someone would give up a nearly $11 million a year job with over $600 million in stock options to take a cabinet position. The capital gains tax alone would have been a staggering $90 million if it weren't for the collusion between banks and politicians. In 1989, they pushed a law through creating a tax loophole as an incentive to draw more corporate millionaires into government Executive Branch positions that exempted them from capital gains taxes. So Paulson and all the others got off TAX FREE. Do you think maybe that's why he took the job?

In Dimon's case, he was in banking his whole life and was CEO of JPMorgan when he was elected as a Class A director on the New York Federal Reserve by the regional banks that make it up. That powerful bank is the only one with a permanent voter of the twelve regional banks and votes on every issue... Checkmate Wall Street!

The Federal Reserve Board (Fed)

The Fed is supposed to be a shining example of a public-private enterprise, but could almost single handedly be blamed for our demise the last 35 years. For without their insistence we borrow money to get both into and out of debt - citizens, Wall Street, titans of industry, and the government itself could never have been so irresponsible and done everything they did to debilitate the country. The Treasury's nearly non-stop printing of money (specifically after the 2008–09 crash), combined with the Fed's cheap interest rates, has not only led nearly everyone into a black hole of debt and punished savers, but it set us up for the next meltdown and taxpayer bailout. When will it stop sleeping with the aristocrats and realize the country was most stable when we were NOT a country of debtors, but a country of fiscal middle class savers!

The powerful Fed is owned by the $700 trillion Rothschild family fortune through their Bank of London and Berlin, along with a few other powerful European and American banks and investment houses. It's made up of seven Governors who serve 14 year terms and are appointed by the Rothschild's – I mean president, and confirmed by Congress. Then there is the Federal Open Market Committee (FOMC), twelve regional Federal Reserve Banks located in major cities across the country and owned by the banks (depository institutions) that collect 6% dividends per year on their capital investments, as well as advisory councils and committees. The dividends are supposed to make up for the lack of interest paid on their required reserves held by the Fed, but in 2008 it started paying them interest as well. So you can see why there's a tremendous incentive for the scheisters to use the guaranteed dividends, plus interest, to bet on the market.

The Fed is supposed to be independent, except 'all national banks' must be part of it, and nearly 40% of all the others are members also. So how does that make them independent? Ones like Dimon's who play both the market and fund government borrowing by buying their bonds for everything that tax collections don't cover can't lose! Another problem is the so-called "independent board" that leads the commit- tees, studies current issues, and sets banking laws has no legal authority to control what the financial institutions do with the money once they lend it to them. Their abuse of this loophole led President Obama to angrily admonish them when the Fed lowered interest rates down to near nothing to stimulate the economy like in past recessions. Yet the morons didn't pass the low rates on to the people, instead, cashing in on them with their shady dealings.

The regional Feds main job is to hold the cash reserves of depository institutions, make loans to them, regulate the banks, and stabilize the financial industry. They sell government securities, process checks, handle the treasuries payments, and assist them with cash management and investments. The boards have one Class A director who represents their particular group of regional banks, and three Class B ones also elected by the banks to purportedly "represent the public" and the Federal Reserve Board. Bringing up the rear are the Class C directors for the public.

The problem with this system is in the voting. The Class A directors are elected according to the group of banks with "the most capital in their region" (i.e. the titans of the banking world) and the smaller ones vote for the Class B directors. Now you see why the Federal Reserve can be construed as just a shadow banking operation and 'nobody' has the authority to audit them or hold their butt to the fire!

While with the New York Fed, Dimon was directly involved with the $30 billion loan to bail out the failed Bear Sterns, as well as leading JPMorgan through all the proprietary scams around the world that caused the global crisis, including his buddy Bernie Madoff's historic Ponzi scheme. While on his watch, the nation's largest crook lost $17 billion of depositor's money, another $2 billion in 2012 on bogus hedge fund trades, and by the third quarter of 2013 had lost another $380 million of its own money - mostly from the ensuing lawsuits. Is this guy ever going to jail?

With his bank getting hammered from the unprecedented fraud, he continues to collect his $20 million paychecks year in and year out! Even after the FBI, Federal Reserve, and the SEC investigated his shenanigans that cost Morgan $20 billion in penalties! He is also a critic of the Basil III international financial regulations that have successfully stopped the countries that abide by it from the same cons and world financial destruction he orchestrates. When JPMorgan opened an online site about career advice, they had to shut it down they got so many furious people yelling and screaming at them!

It was no surprise President Obama carried on the tradition of appointing people tied to Wall Street. His economic advisers Robert Rubin, who lead Goldman Sachs into the ground, and former Treasury Secretary Lawrence Summers, along with Fed Chairman Alan Greenspan, were the architects of President Clinton's deregulation that centered on banishing the Glass-Steagall Act and self above all else. Together, Time magazine called them "the committee to save the world," but instead they put the fuse in the time bomb that became the 2008-09 world collapse.

Summers, the former professor of economics, Harvard president, chief economist for the World Bank, Bill Clinton's Undersecretary for Internal Affairs, and Treasury Secretary was nominated by Obama for the top spot at the Fed but was expediently shot down in committee. Still, Obama didn't give up! He finally got the prior managing partner at the hedge fund company D.E. Shaw & Co. appointed Director of the White House U.S. National Economic Council.

Another top appointee, Mary Jo White, spent most of her life switching alliances. She was U.S. Attorney, Wall Street defense attorney, and partner of Debevoise & Plimpton LLP, where she defended Dimon's mega-bank and investment firm from the SEC. Obama brought her back to the government side as his choice to run the SEC. That's right! The same bogus agency she fought against while defending Street insiders and Super Pac's that was supposed to regulate and defend the public from the same behemoth financial institutions she was defending! Can you believe it!?

I know what you're thinking, but no need to worry. I'm sure Mary Jo and her Wall Street super-lawyer husband - who also worked for the SEC - didn't have any conflict of interest. It was like the judge *and* jury sleeping with the defendant!

In a completely unrelated coincidence, (ha-ha) the SEC gave corporations hundreds of waivers since Mary Jo's appointment after replacing Mary Schapiro, who had worked honorably in government for many years. Schapiro had brought a record amount of enforcement actions and reformed the Street after the meltdown. She was also the only person to ever lead all three federal regulators of the Street: the SEC, Commodities Futures Trading Commission, and the Financial Industry Regulatory Authority.

After dismantling Schapiro's reforms, White decided to cross over and take a job on GE's board of directors for about a quarter million dollars a year, and a job as managing director of Wall Street consulting firm Promontory Financial Group LLC, where she joined President Clintons former SEC chairman Arthur Levitt. Many of her top employees at the SEC also joined her in the jump back, continuing that revolving door between government regulators and the Street.

Are you starting to feel like you're stuck in one of those giant revolving doors you push half way around to enter? Only this one reads Federal Positions on one side and Wall Street Executive Positions on the other? They may not have us fooled, but they sure have us where they want us - up a river without a paddle. For sanity sake, maybe we should pretend the system isn't rigged, the SEC doesn't hire hundreds of people that used to work for or do business with the Street, and they are now regulating them, introducing reforms, and enforcing them. Hey, stop laughing!

The grossly overpaid executives and previous federal officials that started the 2008 collapse at companies like Citigroup, JPMorgan, and the huge insurance company AIG - who all-toll cost the taxpayers a total $7.77 trillion in bailout money between 1985 through the big bang of 08 and 09 - were richly rewarded for this collaboration. They received $165 million in executive bonuses shortly after their bailout and millions more at private speaking forums and book deals. Former Fed chairman Ben Bernanke alone commands a quarter million dollars for each tainted speech!

Therefore, it should come as no surprise when I tell you until the people's revolt for Wall Street reform in 2012; it was perfectly legal for congressmen to participate in insider trading! Usually with industries they oversaw. The wealth of thousands of devious politicians across the country came in large part through the stock market, and you already know their pensions and IRA's are tied up in it.

What a joke! The beltway bandits yell and scream at each other in front of the cameras for their supporters, while laughing behind closed doors about which former Street executives and attorneys they're going to appoint next.

Are We Really That Stupid?

It's as if were back in Joe Kennedy's days: President George W. was a Wall Street inside oilman, as was his father and grandfather. Vice-President Dick Chaney was CEO of the world's second largest oil services company (Halliburton) and national security advisor and Secretary of State Condoleezza Rice was on the board of directors for Chevron - who named an oil tanker after her. Gee! I wonder why? By 2014, we taxpayers were giving the mega-rich fossil fuel industry nearly $600 million a year in corporate welfare for energy research!

Halliburton was given what became known as the Cheney Loophole. It exempted them and other fracker's from parts of the Clean Drinking and Water Acts so they could go hog-wild without any public safety regulations slowing them down. Even Commerce Secretary Donald Evans was the CEO of a natural gas company called Brown Inc. Meanwhile, the House was banning funding for protections under the Clean Water and Air Acts. And regardless of what the administrations claimed, they started two Gulf wars for cheap oil and big business profits in the bloody, oil stained White House; prompting protest from many Rutgers University students and faculty over Rice being picked to give the commencement speech in 2014. She knew she was a dead duck and gave in to the protesters, then forfeited her $35,000 speech fee.

Hundreds, if not thousands of large company's and greed misters were given corporate welfare, tax exemptions, deductions, reductions, off shore hiding places, and legislative laws meant to directly benefit them. Over the last 30 years these laws allowed the top 1% to gain nearly half of all income growth.

The huge biotech and chemical manufacturer Monsanto has literally annexed the U.S. Department of Agriculture (USDA), and was given so much power, they were allowed to force the major farmers of the food belt into buying their genetically engineered corn seed and other products or be forced out of business. They also wanted to sell farmers their super-toxic defoliate "Agent Orange" used in the Vietnam War and suspected of causing numerous cancers as an herbicide on their genetically modified corn and soybeans. Then they were accused of monopolizing our food supply, when on March 1, 2013, the Monsanto Protection Act disguised as the Farmer Assurance Provision was passed to protect you know who. It came as no surprise Monsanto board members worked for the EPA, President Obama's Advisory Committee for Trade Policy and Negotiations, and were advisors to the USDA.

Former Monsanto employee Margaret Miller was accused of overseeing a report on dairy cow growth hormone safety, then took a job at the FDA where she approved it. Their ex-lobbyists Michael Taylor was a USDA administrator and FDA deputy commissioner, and Islam Siddiqui helped write the USDA's food standards that allowed irradiated and genetically modified foods to be labeled "organic."

The Chaney and Monsanto loopholes, along with the Koch brothers and Karl Rove, were just the tip of the iceberg receiving special exemptions and regulations while raking in billions in government subsidies for their businesses: As Al Lewis put it - in referring to former presidential candidate Sen. John McCain's relationship with investment banks – "John McCain, the Republican senator from Merrill Lynch, Citigroup, JPMorgan Chase, Goldman Sachs, Morgan Stanley, UBS, and Credit Suisse." Warren Buffett never would have gone into the clean wind energy business if it wasn't for the Wind Energy Production Tax Credit. The government went bankrupt financing nearly everything you can imagine.

When bureaucrats aren't directly financing special interest, it's giving out tens of millions of acres of National Parks and Forest to ranchers, mining, energy, and forestry companies for nearly nothing. They lease it for so little it often doesn't even cover the cost of running the program. Meanwhile, private interest is giggling in pure ecstasy. If the knuckleheads charged fair market value there wouldn't be a federal deficit!

Some lobbying group's team up for the really monumental projects like the Keystone XL pipeline and just buy their way to whatever they want done. To get this oil project passed, many teamed up with brethren buffoons such as TransCanada, Shell, Devon Energy, American Fuel, Petrochemical Manufacturers, BP, and our favorite earth destroying company Koch Industries. Then they went to ALEC, where House Representative and ALEC national chairman John Piscopo of Connecticut presided over a willing group of Keystone XL backed congressmen and senators. Which begs the question: Why is a Congressman ALEC's chairman?

ALEC took it from there by setting up several trips to Canada and around the U.S. They called them "corporate sponsorship opportunities" for the not so paltry sum of $80,000 each! They let the companies pay for all lodging, transportation, meals, and anything else they wanted, including model laws for the states the pipeline ran through, and even some it didn't, like Ohio - where they gave one to Rep. John Adams to push through. Once they had legislators lined up and the bills written, they got them to appoint their own industry people to write the environmental impact studies required by the agencies that were supposed to regulate them and then passed them. To assure that they had millions of people duped, I mean 'convinced', they needed the project for the good of America; they rounded up the TV monopoly's to run their ads in favor of the project and squashed the oppositions telling the truth.

Super Pac's and big business work like a well-oiled machine running the country into the ground and oppressing the 99%ers.

Before politicians were completely hijacked, you had people like the Kennedy's using the Mafia to get what they wanted for decades. Despite John Kennedy's great inaugural speech writer, Kennedy not only used his dad's mob friends in Illinois to secure one of the two states he needed to become president, he sunk so low, he chose Texan Lyndon Johnson as his running mate to secure the other state he needed to win, Texas, despite despising him.

U.S. Supreme Court justice Louise Brandeis said: "Our government teaches the whole people by its example. If the government becomes the law breaker it breeds contempt for the law. It invites every man to become a law unto himself; it invites anarchy." As well as: "We can have a total concentration of wealth in the hands of a few, or we can have a democracy, but we can't have both." Isn't that the truth? With the demise of the Glass-Steagall Act that almost single handedly allowed us to be the most powerful middle class in the world, we regressed back a century to the days of the few... Maybe we really are that stupid!

Despite this seemingly impossible separation of Wall Street, special interests, and the government, we will try to give them the benefit of the doubt that they are indeed separate entities. Hey, quit laughing again!

Let us now look at other government shenanigans that led us down the path of self-mutilation. Somewhere along the line, Congress became convinced we had to have an economy that must perpetually expand in large doses. Certainly this was impossible without exhausting all the worlds' natural resources and polluting the planet into extinction. However, they kept monitoring old economic indicators such as the consumer price, spending, and gross domestic product index's as if never ending growth in leaps and bounds was a good sustainable strategy. The 112th and 113th Republican Congresses (voted the worst in history) led by John Boehner, was unanimous in saying slow steady economic growth was killing America. Never satisfied to let the natural course of the economy play through, politicians continually manipulated the economy in their attempt to look good come election time, and the brainwashed, weary voters bought it every time.

Most of the time the villains simply collaborate with each other in keeping the darkest skeletons in their closet, other times they manage to slip out for a breath of fresh air. For instance, according to the Associated Press, there were 300 oil pipeline spills in less than two years in North Dakota and none were ever reported to the public or the people who owned the land the pipeline ran over. One day a wheat farmer discovered a massive spill on his plantation and reported it to state and company officials, only to have them keep it quiet for 11 days until the AP inquired about it. In one of the spills the pipe was leaking for nearly two weeks before its discovery. It covered seven football fields worth of farmland and groundwater.

Just in 2013 alone, North Dakota had 140 leaks that spilled about 500 barrels of oil. Like other oil producing states, they don't require reporting spills to the public, so what happens to the 17,500 miles of pipeline crisscrossing the state is a mystery. Most people only find out by dumb luck or seeing it in their yard, wells, or waterways.

News Bulletin: Six months after an oil train in Lac-Megantic, Canada, blew the town to kingdom come, two BNSF trains owned by greed-mister Buffett's Berkshire Hathaway Holdings collided. One carrying crude oil exploded into a fireball so intense firefighters couldn't get near it. The town of Casselton, rocked by blast after blast, escaped total devastation, but still had to be evacuated as the deadly poisonous smoke and fumes billowed for miles above the site and into surrounding towns.

This was a tragedy just waiting to happen. As was a string of derailments, including West Virginia's, where 12 tanker cars of the 100 car train from the Marcellus field exploded one by one, leaving nuclear bomb-like mushroom clouds after each and one house incinerated. The trains from North Dakota, Canada, and the Marcellus are so full of oil and gas, it has caused a flood in rail transport and left some auto manufactures unable to get their vehicles to dealers. Apparently, they're not sleeping with their congressmen.

Speaking of sleeping habits, some misguided politicians help government officials from offices like the Ethics Commission and the Federal Elections Commission (FEC) police themselves by voluntarily resigning from office to avoid prosecution. Congressman, Eric Massa, of New York is a perfect example. Accused of sexually harassing some staff members, he claimed he was just engaging in some tickle fights with male staffers. He then got into more hot water for hiring his wife as treasurer of his campaign account and paying her for payroll and accounting services. The FEC wasn't convinced and said she was managing the campaign payroll for a staff of one – herself!

New York politicians seem to be making headlines more than any other state - mostly for sexual misdeeds. I wonder, is it just coincidence or a carryover from the Wall Street arrogance?

In Florida, it was Rep. Tray Radel who got caught using crack cocaine, but was not prosecuted and instead voluntarily went to rehabilitation. And don't forget about Tom DeLay and Bob Ney, who are just the tip of corruption mountain.

On rare occasions, legislators like Illinois governor Rob Blagojevich, who was found guilty of trying to sell the Senate seat vacated by President Obama, are prosecuted for crimes while still in office as a deterrent to others for breaking the elected officials ethics and election laws. But with an army of specialist and unlimited dark PAC money protecting corporate America and our double-dealing, career criminal politicians, it was just too time consuming and expensive for law enforcement agencies to prosecute even a small portion of the violators. This was one reason the too big to fail, jail, manage, regulate, reform, or shrink banks and corporations of the 21st century never had one top executive prosecuted and jailed for their part in the meltdown of 2008 & 2009.

In congressional hearings on the matter, former President Clinton special counsel member, FBI lead investigator, and Assistant Attorney General, Lenny Brewer, who oversaw nearly 600 lawyers, claimed after cutbacks they didn't have enough investigators. And in every case they didn't have enough evidence or witnesses willing to testify and put the finger on top management. Of course, that's coming from a guy who then took the vice chairman's job with his old heavyweight law firm Covington & Burling, and is once again helping those same corporations he was supposed to prosecute, navigate around financial fraud, money laundering, investigations, securities charges, and corruption. That's how they really got to be TOO BIG TO PROSECUTE!

Dan Rather, one of media's best reporters in history once wrote: "What happened was that we spoke the truth to power, and power had bellowed back through every bullhorn it could command."

The National Security Agency and CIA

The NSA is nearly as problematic for us citizens as the special interest takeover, and nearly as expensive. Their operation has never been cheap, in fact, nobody knows what we spend running it because like everything about them their budget is an impenetrable shield of secrecy. But rest assured, after the 9-11 attacks, it got grotesquely more expensive after they started monitoring almost everyone around the world on secret (and what many legal experts in the Justice Department consider illegal) orders from President Bush. In 2013, they finally got caught red-handed with their hands in the cookie jar monitoring everyone through their cell phones and internet connections. And this time they couldn't squash the whistleblower or kill the story! Everything everyone sent by email and their phone conversations was tapped in the name of national security. They had a top secret surveillance operation called "Prism," which illegally tapped directly into the servers of the nine main internet firms and allowed them to monitor everyone's every move.

The NSA may know everything about you and everyone you ever contacted by phone or computer. They may know your favorite color, who you dated, what foods you like, and all your other social activities. Not to worry, though, you're not alone. They wire tapped the Associated Press, Fox News, and countries on every continent as well, filtering out trillions of bits of information with supercomputers. They even tapped into German Chancellor Merkel's cell phone! Friend or foe, it doesn't matter, we continually give everyone around the world more reason to spite us. Didn't I mention the destructive powers of computers talking to each other? The feds have joined Wall Street in abusing warp speed supercomputers and their massive, secret, destructive, powers.

As did those who exposed FBI abuse in 1971, Edward Snowden finally exposed the NSA's once and for all. A documentary by Frontline points out, it was just a matter of time before someone blew the whistle on their operations. Originally, they had a spy program code named

"Thinthread" that in fact had several other whistleblowers come forward long before Snowden, only to have the Bush administration kill their stories when the New York Times wanted to publish them. Then it strong-armed subsequent whistleblowers by getting the FBI to threaten them at gun point and prosecute them, including congressmen. Many top law enforcement officials from the Justice Department, FBI, and the NSA nearly resigned after finding out exactly what was going on. But they stayed on when Bush made a temporary adjustment to the law by dropping the "national spying" part of the program and limiting it to "international communications" and those coming in and out of the U.S. They wanted nothing to do with it and considered spying on every American without a warrant illegal!

Bush claimed he had the authority under the Patriot and Wartime Authority Acts to spy on everyone's communications and got his cronies to enforce it. They were so ruthless in enforcing the surveillance program; they actually broke the law themselves by changing the non-classified documents to classified! They wanted to show the patriotic whistleblowers who was really in charge around there, and anybody opposing them was going to jail for the rest of their lives one way or another. And Bush rewarded them for their abuse.

His main enforcer and old buddy NSA director, Michael Hayden, was promoted for squashing every good, moral person from every agency, including a congresswomen who was aghast by it. Bush, Hayden, and succeeding President Obama knew they couldn't keep it under wraps forever. So why did they try to prosecute the good people and lock them up when they never released any confidential information?

Surprisingly, when Obama came into office, he continued the program despite a lifetime of backing free speech and civil rights. He even proclaimed in his first presidential campaign there would be no more secrets if he was president. So what is the first thing he did? He started a covert operation using college kids from Latin American countries to overthrow the Castro regime. Their mission was to pose as tourist and spread propaganda through social media until there was a revolt.

Once again, this proves here in America good people simply cannot work for the self-serving morons or big shot corporate America. The corruption, spying, illegal activities, and moral conflicts either eats them alive and they quit, or they're conscience drives them to fix the system - making them the enemy.

The CIA was even worse under Bush! Director George Tenant and counterterrorism chief J. Cofer Black, vehemently warned Condoleezza Rice and Defense Secretary Donald Rumsfeld about a massive attack by Osama bin Laden very soon. But the entire administration ignored them, watched 9/11, and contrary to many of his advisors and staff, the furious Bush blessed the CIA's plan to brake every international wartime agreement by torturing many Al-Qaida suspects at secret locations. It was so brutal, many witnesses and staff were sickened by it, including tortured Vietnam senator and presidential candidate John McCain. Once again, whistleblowers that exposed the arrogant abominations were threatened and prosecuted.

Locked in on his vendetta with bin Laden, Bush then ignored all warnings about Abu Musab al-Zarqawi during initial planning for ISIS and refused to allow the CIA to take him out when they had him dead to rights.

On the corporate side of espionage, the founders of Google (Larry Page and Sergey Brin) were the first conscienceless corporate big shot servers to have the morals of Congress and Wall Street. They force their employees to monitor their customers G-mail to push ads on them. Faced with the reality of losing business if they didn't follow, the rest of the industry eventually lost their scruples and joined them. So the NSA took advantage of the situation and hacked into their servers to "keep America safe" from terrorist? Once exposed, corporate America was furious because they wanted to reap the fruit of their labor. They told the feds they can do it but the government can't. It's just that simple people! Did you forget whose king of this castle?

Microsoft is currently battling the NSA over search warrants for their data stored in offshore countries. Microsoft says they have to go through the countries legal system to enforce warrants under the fourth amendment's search and seizure law. The NSA says it doesn't matter where its stored, as long as the company headquarters are here that gives them jurisdiction. It also claims terrorist and drug dealers can hide their communications offshore if done Microsoft's way, giving them ample time to wreak havoc before they can legally obtain it overseas.

This confirms how our out dated constitution has become a liability in the internet era. Originally the data the feds sifted through was encrypted. It wasn't like just any old hacker could retrieve it from their computers. As utterly incompetent and destructive as George W. was to

America, he had a point about keeping America safe. The constitution needs a lot of tweaking if it's to be the shining beacon it once was.

While the government is having no problem spying on us, we're having a horrendous time monitoring them. In 2007, a Boston attorney recorded police arresting someone with his cell phone and was arrested for recording it! He was charged with "violating the states wiretap law." The court ruled he was within his First Amendment rights and was illegally arrested - which cost Boston $170,000. In a similar case; a Springfield, Ma., lady taped her arrest on her cell phone and was also charged with illegal wiretapping, affirming a double standard that allows officials to wiretap and tape us but we can't do it to them!

According to the First Amendment, we are supposed to have access to public records of all government functions, from local boards to the Supreme Court. While technically we have that rite, in reality, it isn't that easy. Public records request by newspapers, magazines, and the public are met with iron curtain tactics of excuses, delays, and outrageous charges for the material far and above the actual cost.

Here, getting the minutes from meetings, especially executive session minutes, is all but impossible. When I was elected to the School Committee, I asked the superintendent for them so I could catch up (which is the law) and he refused. When a prior court case came up for another hearing, I told him I should have been informed about it. He responded in an arrogant, hiding something kind of way: "I didn't think you needed to know!" Years later, we're still in court on the case and I still know very little. When I asked to be updated on our emergency lockdown procedures, he said "it was confidential and I didn't need to know." If people on the School Committee - who by state law are supposed to set school policy, don't need to know, who the heck does!? Every administrator, teacher, and even my daughter knows - but I can't be told? I had to ask her!

Open government is clearly for those few who have the tenacity, money, and time to enforce it.

Elections – Are They Just a Formality?

The Republican reported every candidate who spent the most money running for statewide office won. Pac's know the vast majority of governance is done at the state and local levels: control the states and you control the majority of elections. The best way to do that is quietly gerrymander districts and rules behind closed doors to stifle democracy. Here in our state, they make sure democracy is a two party system in perpetuity. In 2014, Evan Falchuck was able to establish an official third party called the United Independent Party, yet chances of it ever reaching prominence are as good as a snowballs chance in Hell.

Why? Because the two parties controlling democracy have rigged the system so erroneously in their favor, (and illegally in many opinions) scaling Mount Everest without oxygen would be easier. Whether local, state, or national, you need a certain percentage of voter signatures just to get on the ballot – around 1% in our state. In addition, you need to win 3% of the vote to stay on the ballot for the next election. But the most important factor is the rigged financial system.

Individual donations to an Independent can be $1000 and another $500 by establishing a Pac, compared to $5000 to either of the two controlling parties, and another $10,000 to the state party through a federal account. That's $1500 total for the third party and $15,000 for a Democrat or Republican! Not only that, but their over bloated war-chest can give unlimited donations to any individual running for office, while a nonofficial party's Pac can only give $500. Is that a Democracy!? It's as rigged as a communist system!

If donations fail their candidate, they have one final ace up their sleeve to control the grand prize – the "White House!" Both parties primary process is left over from colonial days and is too ludicrous to fully discuss. Some states have primaries, others caucuses, all with different rules and scattered across five months in a mish-mash combination of voters, delegates, and super delegates (congressmen and high ranking party officials) used to pick their representative for the general election.

All delegates should vote for the person who gets the most public votes or risk paying the price come election time, but super delegates can get away with backing their personal choice or Pac's, especially in close races. Ultimately, they back whoever bribes them with a good position in there Cabinet or other governmental entity, making our vote as inconsequential as the later states that vote *after* the party is over. They don't truly consider everyone's vote until the general election.

For those politicians the Pac's are convinced no longer have a chance of winning, they pull the plug on their funding, often leaving even the biggest of players awash in debt. In the 2008 presidential election, candidates like Rick Santorum, Michele Backman, and former House Speaker Newt Gingrich were left owing millions of dollars to dozens of creditors for all the special services they provided.

You can see why the political process became a game for the richest only. Just hiring a company to get enough signatures to get on the ballot cost you well over $100,000 in the smallest states, never mind a heavily populated one like California - or nationally! By the 21st century, campaigns became so expensive only private millionaires could afford to run for political office. With this reality, people became more and more disenfranchised with the whole process, cynicism set in, and the masses became less and less involved. This was a major contribution to our demise because bureaucrats began targeting a few key groups of voters and states. The rest of us in states known as the red (Republican) or blue (Democratic) states that are sure to vote along party lines are spared the ambush of political advertisements and media coverage aimed at these few key states.

This became a double edged sword though. We couldn't be happier being spared the media onslaught, but this further alienates us since we are being treated like our vote doesn't count. As the older people that voted the most died off, it left the country with tens of millions of demoralized voters no longer willing to participate in the most important and fundamental part of a democracy. You can't have a successful democracy unless all participate, especially locally.

For example, in a recent town election we only had a 15% voter turnout in our little town. And only 1.5% of the registered voters came for the town's most important night - the annual town meeting - where all the town's budgets and new bylaws are decided.

A previous election showed how important every vote could be when our incumbent Selectmen lost by just 20 votes. And a large-scale solar bylaw that rated a large-scale system at a measly 4 kW - compared to the state model law of 200 kW - was approved by just 2 votes, despite it being far more restrictive and expensive than other towns. Its sole purpose was simply to keep solar out of town by the all GOP Select and Planning Boards that admitted hating the sight of solar panels - anywhere!

Every new bylaw passes each year because townspeople don't come to the meeting, then we're stuck with the consequences. Only 58 people voted this time around, of which at least 30 were town employees, and really couldn't vote against it with their supervisors and town officials who hire, fire, and pay their salaries at the meeting watching. This left about 28 unbiased people in a town of 6,600 registered voters deciding whether or not to oppose town officials. So you can see why every voter counts and we can't afford to let them become disenfranchised. This is NOT the democracy or founding fathers had envisioned!

Our town government replicated the fed's. They alienated the people and left themselves virtually free rein to do as they pleased. Every town board is a GOP stronghold, though they comprised less than one-third of all voters. So once again, the minority rules, and like the rest of America we are a town with a different version of regulatory capture – one created by disenfranchised citizens. So much so, the town had to start advertising to get volunteers to work with the three self-righteous anti-environmental, over regulating, tax and spend Republicans on the planning board.

Rigging – Oops, Sorry, I Mean Redistricting

By law we have to redistrict all districts after the ten year population census to reflect the changes in each. That's when legislators and Pac's get together and draw up (gerrymander) the boundaries of the new districts anyway they please to assure their parties rule certain ones... Are you having flashbacks to Tom DeLay's shenanigans too? It never matters where people move to. They aren't put together by the population of an area, or even towns next to each other, they're put together like the draw by the dots picture books we did as kids. They scatter towns and different parts of cities into different districts, making this the only time the two major parties actually work together on anything!

They exchange voters like chess pieces. If one or the other wants a district, they trade people in a town, or even part of a town, to secure the votes they need in all the elections until the next ten year census. That's how they create and separate the blue and red districts. The electoral process is literally rigged, resulting in strategically selected areas of towns, cities, and a Congress of Democrats running certain areas and one side of every issue and Republicans the other. The electorate is just a pawn, the system another form of regulatory capture. The sleazy Pac's by not backing the unbiased Independents have created a Congress at complete opposite ends of the political spectrum and it doesn't take a fortune teller to predict the outcome.

The GOP cried foul when they lost the 2012 presidential election in which nearly every black and Hispanic voted for Obama. Democrats that didn't usually vote came out in droves to put him over the top, so they wanted to do something about it for the 2014 midterms and 2016 presidential race. They dug deep into their bag of tricks and "convinced" a handful in key parts of the country to switch over and run for office as Republicans. Get your minds out of the gutter people. I'm sure they never gave them a dime! Will, maybe a few. Then they got their handpicked Supreme Court to knock out parts of the Voting Rights Act that made it harder, and effectively, barred many low income blacks and Spanish from voting - which really makes no sense after recruiting them. This ignited the feud on a new front and further entrenched both sides.

Can we fix the system? Of course we can. Just scrap the electoral system of delegates like Bernie Sanders and millions of others want, then use public financed elections where everyone from individuals to Super Pac's basically throw their money into a kitty and divvy it up equally amongst the candidates. He proved it works when he ran the first serious presidential campaign backed by millions of citizens and out raised Super Pac mega-millionaire Hillary Clinton, despite his $200,000 annual income to her $30 million. "We the people" could also vote on a set number of important bills yearly, think gun control, to limit Pac rule and have independent redistricting committees draw up compact and contiguous boundaries that don't favor anyone or anything.

Then we go back to our original independent system, or formulate elections similar to major league sports in picking their hall of famers. With "ranked-choice" you choose your top pick as the first place vote, then your second, and lastly your third choice. A top place finish would be worth 3 points, second 2, and third 1. That way Independents wouldn't be tempted to vote for the other two parties in fear of wasting their vote on a vastly outspent Independent. Even Democrats and Republicans would often be tempted to vote their conscience and put Independents like Sanders in power, and if nothing else, just to unbind the stalemate we have now. Also, millions of voters' sick of the two party system would join, and in many cases, rejoin the Independent Party in states they dropped out of because they don't allow primary participation. Opponent bashing is also reduced if they lose their vote.

Trump's election because of his reality TV show portraying him as a real estate mogul instead of the massive failure he was, convinced me we need a simple facts test about congressional and presidential candidates before voting. An informational pamphlet would be sent beforehand.

Believe it or not, at one time Washington wasn't so polarized. The vast majority of politicians were neither radically right nor left; they were centrist and compromised!

Those nearly Independent centrist were the backbone of government for generations. They were the ones that formed the committees and made compromises between their parties, then created the bills that became the law. In the 1970's and 80's, Capitol Hill was able to hash out compromises on major legislation, and even as recently as 1999 before total gridlock set in. The U.S. Senate voted 100 to nothing for a compromise on when the impeachment trial of President Clinton would begin for lying to Congress under oath about his "alleged" affair with Monica Lewinski. It reached an agreement on how to handle sensitive testimony and carefully picked their witnesses. They said they wanted to avoid the already partisan gridlocked House's example. Sound familiar?

Other good examples of our formally functional government were the Clean Air, Water, and Safe Drinking Water Acts as well as the EPA Noise Control and Endangered Species Acts. Bio systems were being polluted out of control, and whole species that had helped balance the planet's ecosystems for millions of years were being wiped off the face of the earth in an ecological heartbeat.

Congress realized we had gone too far when about two-thirds of all lakes, streams, and rivers in the U.S. were polluted and nearly every fish in Lake Erie had died. I'll never forget that horrendous smell! One of the most important lakes on the planet was nearly void of life and declared dead! Combined with the four other great lakes, they hold about one fifth of all the fresh water on earth and are crucial to the U.S. If Congress and President Nixon hadn't instituted the Acts, big business would have annihilated the great lakes and everywhere else. However, Congress presided over the country before special interest reign of terror and took advantage of the more centrist ideology.

The corporations vehemently protested legislation when they were told they would have to voluntarily implement pollution controls or be levied stiff fines in the millions and shut down if they didn't comply.

Back then pollution regulation fell on death bipartisan ears.

5

Our $69 Million Piece of Pie
Pure Gluttony at its Worst

Don't you just love pie? I could buy 25 million of them with the money our town and state spent on one grandiose piece. In our state, the School Building Authority that's controlled by special interest and fueled by an inexhaustible supply of taxpayer money is a financial "death star" for all.

In this state, .01% of the sales tax goes to a special department for school construction and renovations. I know this doesn't seem like much, but even in a small state like ours it adds up to $400-$500 million a year. With the state paying an average of 50-60 percent of the cost from this guaranteed money, it's often used for unnecessary construction of new schools, enlargement of others, and costly frills to get rid of the excess.

Any logical person would tell you it should be put into state coffers, where the money could be used on other infrastructure projects such as our dilapidated roads, bridges, sewers, and sustainable energy projects (considering we import 100% of our energy). Still, state insiders keep pushing the fallacy that classrooms with fewer than 20 students per teacher do much better than those with more.

That fallacy, like the theory of trickle-down economics, is just that: A theory that survey after survey has discredited. It's hogwash with absolutely no merit and I can prove it! As our student population has gone from nearly 2200 students to 1600, there was no discernible difference in our state test scores - recently they've actually been getting worse! In fact, as our student population has plummeted, our math and science scores have gone with them! My daughter's average class size dropped from 22 to around 14 and her scores, like many teenagers, still slipped from the tougher standards, teenage crushes, and electronic distractions, dispelling any propaganda about smaller class sizes makes for more individual teaching, better test scores, and smarter students.

Class size and old buildings have never made bad students! Lousy teachers, programs, equipment, the environment, and teenagers being teenagers do! Many teacher of the year awards are given to great inner city teachers in ancient buildings with huge class sizes of 30 to 40 kids who bring up the level of their students and graduation rates. This propaganda bankrupts towns, cities, and millions of citizens, leaving all in an inescapable money pit. And "just because you can, doesn't mean you should," once again gets tossed out that small window of sanity. Townspeople are left paying outrageously high taxes from over bloated budgets, and school districts have to fire personal to pay for their grandiose schools that are often used more for storage facilities with lots of teacher lounges and meeting rooms than education.

Let me ask you a couple of questions. When your kids grow up and move out of the house, do you enlarge it and add more rooms? If you were a quaint little town with just three schools that already had lost 15% of your student population, with attendance figures showing you would lose at least 15% more by the time the kindergarteners graduate in 13 years; would you merge with the half-empty (and only) school in the town next door that had already lost 50% of their kids. Then double the classrooms at your high school, add a second gymnasium, and triple your office space with three gigantic additions?

We did, and that's after adding 4 additions to the other schools to accommodate the baby boomers and millennials! Now we've joined the bridge to nowhere and opening day at Denver airport with very few customers and criminal mismanagement of our tax dollars. We not only have their now two-thirds empty school with 50% of the classrooms closed off like a ship in dry-dock, but all our other schools are starting to look just as deserted. Our elementary school has gone from 730 students in 2006 to 330, our middle school from 570 to 390, and their school from around 230 to 78!

Not only did we join the other school districts that built unnecessary additions, but we joined them with extravagant features like massive entryways, rooms big enough to play Frisbee in, and excessively high ceilings and clerestories - all with the blessing of the state. All these extra giant buildings, bells, and whistles have ravaged town finances and us taxpayers. The state and townspeople will not only pay around $20 million extra for the unnecessary construction and engineering on our project, but pay extra teachers and other employees for the next 100 years or more. Then pay their pensions, dental, and health insurance until death do us part: And how about maintenance? Do you know how much it cost to heat and maintain these behemoths for 100 years?

The cost are so staggering, like many school districts, we had to drop plans to update equipment and other promised renovations to existing schools for that 'look at my brand new mega-school' bragging rights. We also had to scrap a top notch 21st century curriculum and all sustainable 21st century amenities the kids could have learned from. Things like food pulverizers for the mountains of discarded food that save literally a "ton" of money on trash fees, solar panels, a wind turbine, and hydrogen or geothermal heating and air conditioning systems. Forget the rain water harvesting system with a catch basin full of native plants and the underground cistern the students could have planted, maintained, monitored, and studied for decades to come that would have paid for themselves in just a few years.

These sustainable features would have saved the district millions in the long run while teaching kids the financial discipline and sustainable living practices other school districts are teaching. Instead, we get to throw out top notch science and robotics programs, sports programs, and everything else beneficial. Fanaticism, hyperbole, and short term thinking rules the day and America's flashy, unsustainable, short-sighted, delusional way of life has struck the heart of our little town too.

The states seem to come up with more ways to spend money on unnecessary projects than Capitol Hill hogs. The Massachusetts's School Building Authority (MSBA) went bankrupt just a few years earlier and put a moratorium on school construction projects because so many of the ones they pushed through were premature, poorly planned, unnecessary, and oversized from unrealistic growth predictions.

Statewide, there is now 1 million square feet in buildings not being used for education at a cost of nearly $300 million! Like ours, 25% of those built had extra space due to declining enrollment, resulting in 80 schools being closed - 40 from lack of students - creating 1300 empty classrooms! An additional 150 schools were turned into something else, like we did with our old middle school, now the town hall. All-toll, the old state building authority was $11 billion in the hole from the shabby system, and far and away the main reason for our states financial woes and the name Taxachusetts!

So why would we, or anyone else, keep adding unnecessary schools and additions, and why does the state keep wanting and approving them knowing they went under doing the same thing just a few years earlier? It's elementary my dear Watson – the usual greed, selfishness, ignorance, arrogance, and thirst for power, combined with extremist running education at all levels with an all but unlimited money supply!

These cancers are incapacitating our school systems too! Although there are still many teachers that are loyal and dedicated to our kids, public education is as inundated with fanatics and obsessive, egotistical, paranoid, self-serving maniacs with blinders on as the private sector, Wall Street, and Washington.

It is badly broken, with entrenched insiders guarding the antiquated system. Anyone with 21st century, common sense thinking not in their clique are considered heretics and must be silenced at any cost, including hiding criticism, suggestions, and logical reforms from the minutes and media. Leaving a stone-age system often decades behind that teaches teachers to obediently obey their masters and then pass this philosophy down to each succeeding generation. As a result, we've taught our kids to memorize and regurgitate volumes of useless information, all the wrong ideals, and destroyed and disenfranchised many great students, parents, and communities. Leaving them so bitter and sickened, they wind up hating the schools, kids, and system they once cherished, then drop out of society rather than contributing there valuable insight to the death and blind machine.

I had always been a staunch supporter of public education and seriously considered teaching. Like many people from our little country town, I loved my childhood, cherished the memories growing up here, and dreamed of one day raising my little girl here. To me there was nowhere else! The town my family co-founded in 1770 even had several neighborhood schools named after us into the 20th century. One alumnus loved his childhood so much he did an unheard of thing and donated $650.000 to replace our 60 year old high school track.

When I brought her here for Christmas at age 4, it was such a heavenly, soulful experience. We stayed at grandmas and went sliding at the high school. When we went in to warm up, I showed her the school my class opened in 1971. First we saw the trophy case with friends and family etched into them, and lots of pictures. We strolled the halls and stopped by my old Home-Economics room where a good friend of my mother's once taught. And to my surprise, the prettiest lady in my class greeted us and was working there. Then we stopped by the old library where we made shadow puppets on the overhead screen before finally returning to grandma's to make snow angles. What a glorious day!

The Battle

Lie, cheat, deceive, break the law, and tell the kids and their parents the most deplorable, reprehensible things you can think of to get what you want. Those are the morals, values, and ethics our School Committee, administrators, and some of our teachers taught our kids to pass the unnecessary triple addition. That's why we couldn't afford the new track on our own!

Led by a couple of highly respected and trusted veterans of our school system, the School Committee did a reverse Teddy Roosevelt and betrayed us townspeople that always trusted them to do the right thing.

Maybe we should have seen it coming when they joined the NRA's propaganda campaign in January 2007. That's when we came back from Christmas break and found they had secretly installed cameras and locked down our schools to the dismay of many - especially after saying it wouldn't stop a gunman. High school kids and parents were furious, calling them prisons. That's when they robbed our kids and quant little town of our innocence, freedom, and small town ambiance that was a major reason many of us moved back here to raise our kids. And many others moved from neighboring cities as well. We didn't move our kids back to be imprisoned, we moved because they were NOT, and we've enjoyed the freedom and small town ambiance for centuries that eludes thousands of communities across the land. I even wanted to buy a house across the street, for the schools were to be my only and very lonely child's whole world. Now, there is no joy in Mudville!

As you may recall, the fearmongers installed an armed policeman before it was mandatory, and refused to sign our State School Committee petition to ban submachine guns and large magazines of up to 100 rounds each, making them look more like a cog of the NRA than administrators: Especially after they refused to give our towns Emergency Management Director the vital evacuation and lockdown procedures. To top off the insanity spree and make it easy for the first bonehead with a grudge, they tore down our sturdy brick two story facade from the middle school that sits about 100 feet from the school and replaced it with an outrageous glass wall. In this day and age of assault weapons, it will be as easy as shooting pigs in a pen.

Oblivious to history and tradition, perhaps the worst and most destructive School Committee in our long history even banned birthday cakes, cupcakes, brownies, and the pizza parties some teachers used as an award for various achievements. Then, with total disregard for what their actions would do to their employees, town, or townspeople, they pulled out all the dirty tricks, smoke, and mirrors in the book to ram the mammoth additions down our throats that tore the heart and soul out of people, turned family, friends, and neighbors against each other, and left people wondering who their real friends were. They ripped the town apart at the seams, left employees bitter just waiting for retirement, and town and school finances in dire straits for decades to come.

In our case, it wasn't easy for the school district's master sorcerers to trick many people into approving the additions through the same old argument of bigger, newer, buildings with more teachers and fewer kids per teacher make smarter students. A good many of us argued, good teachers, dedication, and natural abilities make good students - not huge half empty schools - and our proof was in the pudding. We have a girl from town teaching in a hut in Africa, and most every other country in the world has much worse facilities and equipment than us, yet many outscore us decade after decade on test. In recent years we've had many students go on to Ivy League colleges that do quite well from our supposedly "overcrowded" schools. A girl that graduated five years ago was named Neuroscience student of the year in college, and a neighbor of mine went on to lead NASA's crew responsible for reentry communications during the space shuttle era, despite our allegedly "undersized, outdated science classrooms."

None-the-less, using illusion, assumption, and despicable tactics, they pushed on with their plan and we went to battle over the triple additions. A battle that made some neighbors, employees, and fellow parent's enemies that now hate each other and the schools they once cherished so much, they moved away.

The whole thing started when our town selectman wanted to bring in more business and additional tax revenue to our town coffers. An opportunity seemed to pop up when a couple of large land owners decided to sell their property to real estate developers. The ensuing increase of X-generation yuppies brought those spoiled rich people that force the locals out of town and want their gargantuan houses with everything to match. They did indeed increase our tax coffers and spent lots of disposable money on local businesses. So far the plan was working.

We were able to renovate the town's municipal buildings and build the second largest volunteer fire station in the state.

Still, nothing is enough for this generation. After a few years, their kids started going to school and we decided to incorporate both pre-kindergarten and full day kindergarten into our elementary school. This stretched class sizes to the maximum 22-25 students the district wanted and they were satisfied with those numbers. Many school districts throughout the country, and world, would kill for those numbers! Yet the newcomers and blind fanatics were increasingly dissatisfied with our older schools. They had money and were the main contributor to our town's financial wellbeing, so they demanded we renovate the schools and do something to alleviate "their" version of overcrowding, especially at the elementary school.

To appease them, the school district hired a consultant to access the situation, along with the state and another respected county consultant. For once the state suggested two prudent options, and all three agreed we could do one of two things. We could put a small addition onto the elementary school or have the town next to us (which had grades kindergarten through eighth) join our district. Then we could send our pre-kindergarteners and kindergarteners up to their half-empty school. They even threw in an $18 million financial incentive to regionalize and renovate the schools at the same time. We had been taking their high school kids for decades and they were going bankrupt trying to keep their school running, so it only made sense to do it one of these two ways without incurring any unnecessary expenses.

Several School Committee members were friends of some business owners and these new rich townspeople (some were the new rich towns-people). So they did the unheard of thing and turned down everyone's recommendations, then came up with their own plan. They decided to do one recommendation only and regionalize with the town next to us to get the incentive the state offered. But instead of sending our kinder-garteners to them, they wanted to add the three additions to the high school that would... double our classrooms, add a second gymnasium, and quadruple the administration office space. Plus renovate the elemen-tary, middle, and high school! Then they would make the high school a junior/senior high!

When they came out with a drawing of their plan, many of us almost fainted and had a heart attack! We all wanted the renovations, but we couldn't believe they went against the state and our well paid consultant's professional recommendations. Between the two towns we had already lost about 15% of our kids by the time they rolled out the plan, and the state estimated we would lose at least another 10% over the next ten years. As you know we were already down to 14 kids - and as few as 6 in one of my daughter's classes that's scheduled for 3 this year, to go with 1 in her Drawing II class - her. So we had to bring in kids to try and fill all the empty seats under the state's "school choice" program that allows kids to go to another school in another district. It reminded me of that giant IBM office complex they built for thousands of employees just as the telecommuting phenomenon got under way that turned it into a strangely eerie, empty, white elephant.

Needless to say, many of us townspeople were furious! Why would the school district want to double the classrooms at the high school after losing hundreds of kids and hundreds more coming soon? Taxes had already skyrocketed from the real estate boom of the early 2000's and other town construction projects. And they installed a sewer system in my part of town then slapped us with a $9000 betterment on our tax bills to pay for it. Many people, including yours truly, had to go with the towns 38 year payment plan, costing us $1000 a year extra on our tax-water-sewer bills. Most of us couldn't afford that, never mind an unnecessary gigantic high school that would leave the other schools as empty as the one we picked up!

So the town split into two camps, with most of the people backing the project from the opulent new developments that were ignoring the fact we didn't have nearly as many kids anymore, and weren't going to, and us low and middle income sensible people. The master sorcerers used the logical illusion that all the new houses in town were still adding kids to our school population, and then gave out a brochure containing downright fraudulent future student population and capacity figures. This duped the under 40 parents - and surprisingly many older folks - into believing more houses really did mean a prolonged increase in students. After all, authorities never misinform us, right?

It was a furious battle, with many people shopping in other towns to avoid the enemy! Teachers, bus drivers, and all the other school employees took their positions, with morale and cynicism sinking to depths never seen before. It was no longer about educating our kids, it had grown into an all-out war... led by me!

Going against state law, two of the three principles joined up with the privy parent group backing the project. By law they couldn't speak their opinion or aid anyone pushing the project one way or the other, yet they dove in headfirst anyway. They went so far as allowing the hustlers to hand out propaganda flyers filled with despicable lye after lye in their schools. One even asked if my group was outside protesting their actions, and I received an erroneous email to the other saying they had dropped off their flyers in her office to distribute to parents.

Meanwhile, the superintendent backed them up at public meetings, claiming we had to pass it now or be sent to the back of the line - which there is none. To real them in, he then used that $18 million carrot the state waved at us to regionalize with our neighbor and build the additions... now! Threatening over and over the money would go away if we didn't and we might get nothing.

Many parents and grandparents that came to drop off and pick up their kids at the elementary school were furious when the pushy, young parent group jumped all over them and shoved their flyers in their faces. They claimed the schools were overcrowded, dangerous, we were one of the neediest school systems in the state and a slew of other fraud, including property values would go up if approved. They claimed the state accreditation board had us on warning status (which doesn't exist) because of our "dilapidated, overcrowded schools" and many good tin soldiers bought it hook, line, and sinker.

We countered with nothing but facts directly from the state building and accreditation authorities. Contrary to what they were telling and mailing the townspeople, the state never said we were overcrowded. Why? Because they have no maximum student population laws, in fact, they wrote in their report that our class sizes of 14 - 22 kids was very good! And we were actually in the top 10% of the best schools on the states needy list, with 90% of the schools rated *worse* than us! You read that right! Ninety percent of the school districts were needier than us, and our scores for every category from class size to maintenance to curriculum offered scored 'at or near the top.' We were given the number one rating in almost all categories.

So why was the school district and parent group plugging these massive additions that would bankrupt the town and many townspeople and lying about the project? After all, if we approved it, property taxes would hit stratospheric levels for our share of the additions we obviously didn't need. More importantly, why did the state approve it? We didn't even meet their requirements for the minimum number of students necessary to approve these additions, or any of the other criteria in their needs survey.

When you include the associated expenses that escalate around 3% yearly over the 130 year life cycle, it could easily cost this tiny town 200 to 300 million dollars extra! That would leave us with no money for the things we really needed for a top notch 21st century curriculum many other schools had. Or to properly run the town and school district, maintain them, and offer nice programs and amenities. Even contractors for neighboring school building projects in surrounding towns were baffled. Like the Savings and Loan debacle in the 1980's, we wanted some answers, but like the financial meltdown of 2008 - we got none!

We did know one thing. The school district had a smooth talking, grandfather-like, devious, conniving, pompous, arrogant, bully, veteran outsider superintendent who knew nothing about our town or its people. You know the kind! He wants to be called Doctor, though he's not a medical doctor like my grandfather, who was a pioneer in cataract surgery and delivered babies or anything else when people needed him most. He even delivered the congressman's parents the district was trying to recruit for a TV spot promoting the project. A fact the out of touch outsider and his entourage were oblivious to.

But he did have political and state connections in Boston helping him lead the charge. And the former superintendent that first introduced the project was now strategically placed on the towns Finance Board to finance it and the School Building Committee to build it. They had all the big- shots in town "publicly" on their side, including businesses who knew it would be a white elephant, as well as the town's newspaper spreading their propaganda. They had complete control of the local media that gave them many interviews and TV spots, while illegally denying our rebuttals. However, sanity ruled, and the little people prevailed when we defeated it at the ballot box 55% to 45%. HURRAY! Chock one up for the little people!

This wasn't the first time that's happened here. In 1969, when the high school was first being pushed to alleviate our severely overcrowded junior/senior high with over 1100 kids (now the middle school), the townspeople voted it down. Why? Because the proposal included a pool and we were just a tiny town of around 6000 people that had just built that school and the elementary one in the past 15 years. Then we expanded the new elementary school for the title wave of baby boomers, so we were flooded with debt. Knowing we had 30 or more students per classroom, some with no desk, the School Committee and Selectmen realized another school was more important than a luxurious pool. So they listened to the people, dropped the pool, and the happy towns-people overwhelmingly passed our third school in just 15 years. Ay Caramba!

The Second Time Around

This time the School Committee ignored the victorious majority who wanted the 3 additions dropped and knew the latest baby boom had peaked and was waning. With another chance to get the whole town aboard like in 1969 and renovate all the schools, they ignored history, and the well-off threw their collective weight around. They bullied and harassed the three town selectman (all businessmen fed by these new yuppies) and many town businesses into putting the project back on the ballot a second time. Considering one of the selectman said the pensions alone would kill us, and his wife, along with another prominent member of the GOP joined forces with me to defeat it again, combined with her saying they didn't think the opposition would win - would lead a normal person to think they put it back on the ballot to appease their pushy, rich, clientele. Isn't that how it always works? One prosperous, well know, well liked business went against the moneyed elite one other time and their retribution nearly bankrupted him.

We were devastated, but I didn't throw in the towel against Goliath. The towns GOP members asked me to run for School Committee, and they planned to get a few more members so we could take over and control the committee. After filing my election paperwork, I asked them how many people they had gotten to run. Their response was "none!" "But we don't need anyone else, we have you, and you're almost as good as a Republican." Despite the vote of confidence, I was not happy being David, nor was the 55%.

This time was twice as bad as the first. The school district and the parent group pushing this expansion launched an all-out, desperate, do or die campaign. The high school and elementary school principal's continued backing the Yuppie, young brainwashed parent group, and the results were not pretty.

Suddenly, I got a call from a well-known and respected former School Committee member about the high school. She said some of the teachers were telling the kids they wouldn't graduate with a diploma and would get a general education degree (G.E.D.) instead if we didn't approve the additions. They told them their credits wouldn't count, they would have to go to an accredited night school if they wanted to go to college, and they would wind up with a lousy job at someplace like McDonalds – so go home and tell your parents to vote YES!

Us good parents were shocked! How low could our school district get, and what were they teaching our kids? They even had a plan to get the brownies and girl scouts to go door to door to push this thing until it hit a local newspaper. Would you want to send your kids to school with such outrageous, maniacal, management? To this day it makes many townspeople gut-wrenching sick, but we had to suck it up for the sake of keeping our kids with their friends and teammates.

The next night I went to the district's parents and press meeting at the high school, where I spotted an old classmate that worked there. She confirmed the story, with the details in the exact same order as the School Committee lady the night before. I told the selectman whose wife was helping me I wouldn't say anything in front of the press and cameras about it, though in hindsight wish I had. After confirming it with the high school kids working at the local grocery store and the policeman's son across the street, I did, however, spread the word by way of a flyer we mailed to every home to counter their lies. I was personally there when his son told us the same story, and added they were targeting the ninth and tenth graders because they would be the first ones graduating after the expansion. They specified it was crucial for them to tell their parents to vote yes on it.

It gets worse people, a lot worse! A parent told me they pushed their despicable lies beyond the extreme. They said, one day a little kid they knew came off the bus crying hysterically and latching on to their mom. So the mom asked... Why are you crying? This poor, sweet little kid said, Mommy I'm never going to see you again. And the mother responded... What are you talking about? This precious little kid said he was going to "die" because the school was falling down and it was going to kill him. We were shocked and horrified!

Understandably, those of us good people with scruples and no money to burn on frivolous oversized toys were furious! Disgracefully, his story was verified the day of the second vote. When my daughter and I were out with our sign, we had a group of young kids from the travel soccer team next to us yelling and screaming the same propaganda at cars going to vote. They were all fired up and screaming the school was falling down and they were going to get killed! Believe me; I straightened them and their young mother out in a hurry!

To this day, after 3 years on the School Committee, I have not found out why they wanted this triple expansion. Our Chairman promised to tell me when my term was over but reneged on his promise. It appears the whole scam was about bringing in the junior high school kids to bolster the sports programs with low participation, adding more teams like boys' and girls' volleyball, hockey, and football, then stocking them with school choice kids. Plus, we get paid from the cities that send their kids here: A real win-win for us, right?

Not so fast people! For a second you probably thought it was the right thing to do, didn't you? Well it's not! First the money coming in from the school choice program never comes close to paying for the additions and the decades of expenses that come with it. Then there's the environmental factor and tear down cost at the end of its useful life span, plus we are stealing other school districts reimbursement money.

Also, the state has been pushing us for decades to become a more racially balanced school district. We're 97% white and they want more minority kids from the city to diversify us. When you add up all the boneheaded reasons for the additions, despite student population in a freefall, it almost makes sense! All you have to do is lye your brains out, tell the little kids horrifying stories until they think they're going to die, ignore our true lack of need for it, and brainwash all the young parents into getting behind it - then you can build it. And that's exactly what happened! What's that tell you about our town… and society?

There was just one problem with the "master plan." Remember that little detail about bringing in school choice kids to pay for everything and provide us with enough kids to give us that 'look at what we have' bragging rights and $18 million incentive? Like in the movie Field of Dreams, we built it, however, opposite the movie - the extra kids never came, nor the $18 million. In fact, many kids from our district are going to the other ones that have 21st century curriculums, amenities, and programs we can no longer afford, leaving us with even fewer kids. Everybody else has the bragging rights, and we're stuck with our new '20th century' colossal junior/senior high that's so big the vice-principle may have to get a Segway. The schools are beginning to look deserted with overall class sizes expected to go down to an average of 12 kids by 2018. And we've already proved we didn't need the additions when we closed off half of our elementary and middle schools for construction crews during the three years of renovations and never missed them.

We also had to drop and cheapen many of the renovations promised to the people, of whom many claimed they only approved the project because they were attached to the additions, and claimed they didn't trust the school district to do the right thing and renovate without them. A Building Committee and School Committee member told me, we can't even put solar panels or any other energy device that might be invented in the next 130 years on the roof because we had to go with a cheaper roof that can't take the weight. We can't put them on the ground either because the 3 additions have used up all our open fields. The town and school district are in financial ruin and have no money for anything, never mind environmentally sustainable projects, a top-notch curriculum, robotics club, or anything else for that matter. Our $1 million reserve fund and $3 million left over from construction and renovation reductions have already been wiped out. Other schools are winning awards for everything we can never afford, and I'm a hero to half the town and a dog to the other.

People still aren't talking to each other and the school district brainwashed the kids and taught them despicable things to get what you want in this "age of greed." My only child was ostracized, isolated, and driven out of clubs and after school programs by the principals and teachers that helped sell it and told our kids all those insidious stories. Understandably, her grades are sinking at the time they count the most and her dreams of being an art teacher are going with them. Our school district is so exasperating many of us wake up nauseated and have to force a little food down. I shake every time I think of this crap or having to go to the schools I used to love and have such cherished memories of – not good for a School Committee member! Cynicism is at all-time highs, and many employees who knew more than anyone we didn't need the additions are disgruntled and biting their lips until retirement. We've had 6 vice principals at the high school in the 5 years since this thing was conceived, with the one at the time of the atrocities becoming a minister. Gee... I wonder why?

Policemen who live in town had to choose between doing the right thing and setting a good example for our kids by voting the project down on moral and ethical grounds and lack of need for it, or vote for it because the lady leading the parent charge was running for Selectmen and her husband was a state cop. They had to decide if the brotherhood was more important than the moral and ethical teaching of our kids?

Apparently it was! When I was at the cops house across the street and his son told us all the hideous things the teachers were saying (which should have sent him running to his phone to yell and scream at the high school administration), I asked him if he was going to file a complaint. To my surprise, he shrugged his shoulders and said – no! I think we know who he and the others in town and their families were standing by. It's shocking to see those who are supposed to be on the side of good and set a proper example for our kids, will go against all morals, values, ethics, and logic to support a fellow cop's wife.

Some of us filed complaints with the state ethics commission and inspector general. And my daughter's ex-softball coaches who live across the way, along with hundreds of other fools that agreed we didn't need the additions, voted for it anyway. Many supporters won't go shopping at our one grocery store in town because their afraid I'll see them. And like all the other towns in financial ruin from unnecessary and oversized projects, we closed the school with 78 kids everyone knew had to go and they are suing us. When I went down to the shop to talk to the selectmen who voted to put this project on the ballot twice, and whose wife helped me try and defeat it, I mentioned retiring here in town. Him and his brother broke out simultaneously in laughter and blurted out... "Are you kidding me, none of us are going to be able to afford to retire here!" Especially with our tax rate up 70% in 7 years!

The worst part of all is; the administrators that caused all the trouble and strapped townspeople, their kids, and grandkids with paying for this white elephant and its associated cost for the next 130 years, lived out of town, didn't pay taxes or have their kids in our schools, and are now retired! We gave them all pay raises to educate 30% less kids, and were part of those school employees making over a $100,000 a year our congressman has vehemently complained about. Oh by the way! He pushed this thing too and is on the states Ways and Means Committee, which handles all state finances. Oh, Dios-Mios! I told you at the beginning corruption and stupidity ran rapid at all levels of society. By no means does Washington and New York have a monopoly on it.

Even the rich lady on the School Committee that teaches at a private college in Hartford CT, pushed the jumbo-giant the hardest, and insisted the selectmen put it back on the ballot is leaving the School Committee and has sent her daughter to a private school there, along with some of her friends. That shows you what they think of our schools, plus they cost us our state reimbursement money for all of them. And remember the Superintendent that started this whole thing and then got on the Finance Committee to finance it and the School Building Committee to build it? He moved out of state 6 months after construction began! So following his lead before taxes go up $400 to $500 next year, many of us are doing the same thing - leaving some other poor suckers to pay for it.

Evil has won again. We lost our beautiful little town. It's the selfish, moral-less newcomer's town now, not ours. So I joined the others and put a for sale sign in our front yard. We've had it with the town and school district my family co-founded in 1770. My daughter now hates it here and cries in bed from being screwed out of her arts career from a program that exist only on paper, and sadly, will be the last one ever to attend a school in my hometown we cherished so much.

Looking at the bright side, we did pick up a two-thirds empty school and got to spend about $200,000 fixing it up on top of the normal operating expenses for 78 kids. We now have 7 huge additions, partial renovations, ghostly schools with some classrooms big enough to play Frisbee in, and fewer kids than 1965 for $69 million. And like all the other new, colossal, sparsely populated schools, we added to our states shortage of Natural Gas that requires more fracking and pipelines to heat these unnecessary behemoths. But best of all, the state athletic committees may ban junior high kids from playing high school sports! Oh wait! Maybe that's not the bright side!

I got a breakdown from our business manager for next years anticipated enrollments. They're much worse than expected. He not only listed our figures, but compared them to the state averages as well. It turns out the state never did learn from its former bankruptcy. It has approved so much new construction that we are currently just below the average of 15 to 17 students per class. Apparently, nearly every town and city fell for their con of smaller class size makes everything all better.

6

Education From my School Committee Perch

This is one field I can give you the true inside scoop. Believe me, people running our educational system DO NOT want us outsiders to know the details, and like politicians and Wall Street, hide behind a shield of secrecy. Education is a political pawn and big business punching bag full of pompous, arrogant, selfish, extremist hell-bent on destroying our kids - and thus our future. Politics and K Street special interest have taken over right down to small town America education. With yearly stock market competitions for kids as young as 10 years old instituted in curriculums across the nation disguised as part of the math program, the Street's preaching's have infiltrated our schools... and the brainwashed, hypnotized masses don't even notice.

When I first read about it in our schools monthly newsletter, I was so furious I almost pulled my daughter out of the public school system and home schooled her. To make matters worse, the competitions are sponsored by our district congressmen. I can't believe our society has sunk this low! I actually saw a tip on how to practice math published by "Resources for Educators" in my daughter's newsletter that read: "Encourage your middle grader to play the stock market. Using $1,000 in play money, she can invest in companies that make her favorite products like jeans and cell phones. Have her follow the stocks online or in the newspapers and calculate her gains and losses. She also might try a free online trading game like weeseed.com or hold a family competition to see who can make the biggest profit."

After the townspeople asked me to be on the School Committee in an attempt to restore some common sense, honesty, and dignity back to our out of control school district, I protested this unthinkable action. But we aren't the only ones playing the market, it's the entire country, and they're being sponsored by the ALEC controlled state congressmen. When I searched the web for Wee Seed, I found dozens of other websites similar to theirs. And with people like former Assistant Treasury Secretary Phillip Swagel of the Henry Paulson era, and House Speaker John Boehner (former chairman of the House Committee on Education and the Workforce) who told the banks: "Know that I have all of you in my two trusted hands and I've got enough rabbits up my sleeve to be able to get where we need to," joining yet another revolving door between the government, banks, and now education... what do you think they're teaching our kids?

As long as education follows the values of Wall Street, we will continue our slide into social madness and become even more inundated with drop outs, gang warfare, and cities no longer livable.

Money, money, and more money! One food service company actually made kids throw away their lunches for not having their lunch money, leaving some innocent little kids crying and hungry. Traditional Colleges have caught the cancer as well. We import 10% of our college students from overseas to pay out of state tuition fees that are often two or three times that of in state. And in our state, we have tax credits for landowners and nonprofit organizations, such as colleges, that clean up former environmentally contaminated industrial and commercial sights. The colleges then turn around and sell the credits to the same corporations that contaminate them - think big oil, mining, and chemical - to reduce their taxes.

For years we've educated foreign students for multinational corporations (many with grants on the backs of taxpayers) so they can return to their own countries and push Wall Street capitalism, only to see their greed come back to haunt them. We educated them both here and abroad at our best business schools, then watched them take us from the hunter to the hunted. Those that are old enough to remember the 1980's will tell you of Japans economic takeover of the United States that was fueled by tens of thousands of U.S. educated Japanese. Japanese companies were buying everything in sight, from commercial real estate, banks, and shopping malls to the world wide symbol of Americana - "Universal Studios." It seemed like they were going to buy the entire country!

Now, China, India, and other countries are taking advantage of the country that never learns, snapping up businesses at a record rate. Many we educated are coming back to start their own businesses and compete directly against our own right here on our soil! They no longer have to outsource much of the work to their home countries, instead, they bring their workers here and pay them minimum wage so they can undercut their former employer's prices. This becomes a revolving door of low wages when Americans turn down the low paying jobs and more foreigners come in to replace us. For American businesses to compete; they have to offer the same low wages Americans won't work for, and the vicious cycle of bringing foreigners in at low wages and the perception of a skilled workforce shortage rolls around and around.

Another, possibly deadly side-effect of educating the world, has got colleges across the land screening foreign students for diseases like Ebola and SARS.

We also have a total breakdown of communication in our schools since the dawn of the computer age. I've had polarizing problems with my daughter's teachers wanting to talk via email rather than in person. If I call them and leave a message on their voicemail they never respond. I've never had a teacher respond in nine years since she was in third grade. Even then her teacher was mad at my daughter for not paying attention and wrote me a nasty letter, rather than tell me in person when she brought the class to the school library where I was volunteering. Sometimes I would see her at the grocery store and she would say Hi, and we talked a bit, but she never said anything about it. So it's not surprising to see the kids not communicating after two decades of emails and texting when their teachers don't do it.

I was almost the first School Committee member to sue my own school district communication has broken down so badly. I still have steam coming out of my ears. My daughter, like most kids, is actually a bright girl and in eighth grade aced 7 out of 8 courses, yet like millions of us, she can't understand algebra and struggles vehemently with it. Despite getting high grades that year in Algebra I, part I, she immediately started failing quizzes and test in part II of her freshman year. But I wasn't informed until the parent teacher conference; even then I was assured she was doing better lately. When she went downhill again and wanted to get after school help, she said the teacher would roll his eyes every time a student asked him for after school help. Would you want to ask again if you were a shy 15 year old kid and your teacher did that!? She was too embarrassed to tell me she was doing bad again and wound up not scoring high enough to move up to Algebra II, so she repeated it.

Regrettably, our school is only one of two in this region on the block system, which is akin to college with two separate semesters that doesn't allow any time in between to reset your schedule the second half of the year when necessary. The first semester always ends on a Friday and the second one starts the following Monday morning. So I called the guidance office on the weekend and left a message to reschedule her. I knew they would be busy the first day of the new semester so I didn't bother them on Monday. Although it was crucial she didn't miss any more days than necessary after falling behind immediately the first time around. I did call twice on Tuesday, though, and nobody got back to me or bothered to contact my daughter.

The steam was beginning to build. I told my daughter to personally go down to the guidance office Wednesday and have them call me. I still got nothing! You can imagine how furious I was when nobody would return my calls - and I was on the School Committee! If I couldn't get someone to return my calls, how on earth is any other parent supposed to? Fortunately, when she went down to the guidance office she got back into Algebra before I blew my stack.

I wish this story of the lost art of verbal communication ended there, but it doesn't. Once my daughter got to math class, the teacher didn't even have her stay after school and personally catch her up, but instead had her copy another student's notes!

What kind of teacher does this? What if the other kid's notes from the first 3 days were wrong? Once again I called the school and asked for the teacher but had to leave a message, then another. Finally, after never getting a response, I went through the principal's secretary and left two more messages. I couldn't get anyone to call me back for three weeks and by then she had flunked her first two quizzes, not only from lack of caring on her teachers part, but she was teaching completely different chapters from the first teacher. She was giving her all new algorithms to fail! I was *BOILING MAD!* Is it asking too much for teachers to communicate with parents, give kids extra help when they're in jeopardy, and teach them the same curriculum, especially the second time around?

Finally, at our School Committee meeting, I told the principle and she got the teacher to call me. I told her what happened the last semester and what my daughter needed. When I never heard from her again, I thought she was getting the extra help she needed and was doing great. She never contacted me again until my daughter was on the verge of flunking the midterm report card, saying my daughter was now resisting extra help. Don't you think I should have been called instead of letting her fail and repeat it yet again? Another half a semester was wasted and my little girl was demoralized. Every time she took a quiz or test, she studied for hours until she thought she knew the material inside and out and was surely going to ace the test - only to flunk half the time.

Some of you are probably saying I should have kept my eye on her homework and quizzes coming back with the grades on them. Your right! Except that's another frustrating part of today's computer world. Kids are told to put their work in folders at school and teachers are supposed to list the daily grades on the school district website. The problem with that is they often take weeks to update the site, and by then your kid may have flunked several quizzes and often a test or two, making them too embarrassed to tell you.

Logic would dictate you would do better the second time around, but it would also dictate having good teachers willing to help the kids and communicate with their parents. In our case, when the teacher finally did call, we agreed my daughter would stay after school at least once a week to make sure she stayed on track to succeed. What do you think happened? The teacher let her stay a few times until she started improving, acing one test, then kept telling her she had meetings or another kid was staying after school for help and she only allows one student at a time. Guess what happened on the midterm?

Do you think I was reaching the boiling point or what!?

It gets worse people! I called and asked her to send the midterm home for my daughter to re-dew on spring vacation, along with the answers for me so she would, hopefully, finally get it right. I also asked if she could send her some extra practice work by email over the vacation. She said, "I'll try, but I'm on vacation too you know." Do you think she did?

Believe me! Like many of the younger generation and the country in general – many teachers are not what they used to be! When I was a kid, I had a teacher that was so dedicated, she came to my house when I had my tonsils out and had stopped along the way at our local pharmacy to pick up a strawberry milkshake for me. She also brought a weeks' worth of homework so I wouldn't get too far behind. Now that's a teacher!

Remember, I said in the prologue our expectations have changed dramatically? Teachers are used to being paid extra (a stipend) for every little extra thing they do nowadays and aren't getting paid extra to help kids in danger of failing. I know they have extra work getting everyone's scores on the computer, but what on earth has teaching come to?

What other job gets good pay in our state, a nice pension, medical and dental insurance for life, survivor's benefits, and 12 weeks paid vacation a year? Teachers need to follow that sign my little girl put on our doors... I will help someone today!

Certainly this problem could easily be solved like they do in some school districts to help struggling kids and keep them out of trouble. We could add a half hour to the school day to address the minimum hours of teaching per day requirements and extend lunchtime to one hour. This allows kids to get extra help the first half of lunch with teachers from every subject in the media center (library) or designated class-rooms. Those that don't need extra help get an hour for lunch if they choose. You don't need to pay teachers extra if you do it at lunchtime and they don't have to stay after school. All kids get the help they need or they can use the extra time like a study hall we no longer have here. Not to mention, more kids can go out for sports and other extra-curricular activities instead of studying all afternoon and night only to fail. Do you see any downside?

The Common Core

Forty eight governors have given us more good news – sort of. Apparently, after decades of trying to level the playing field for inner city kids with their own test, to their credit, the minority groups across the country have stopped blaming their failures on a suburban white kids test. Philadelphia inner city kids are actually producing some of the best kids now. West Philly High instantly became the talk of the country with their entry into the government's $10 million challenge called the X-Prize. They took a bunch of drop outs and horrifically failing kids and took on the world's behemoth auto manufacturers head to head to come up with a car that can go 100 miles on a gallon of gas. With the help of a former pro racer, they squeezed in just under the deadline with the possible winner. In 2009, they made it through the first round of 120 cars, and then surprisingly the second round as well, putting them into the field of 30 and allowing them to keep the program going. That success stunned the world's largest manufacturers who had spent hundreds of millions of dollars!

Another Philly high school built an efficient biodiesel generator for third world countries, giving their kids a distinctive advantage over your run of the mill high school education. More and more educators are seeing a need to break away from rote learning and tougher standards, and actually teach kids the skills companies need now and in the near future like we used to do. Precision manufacturers, heavy equipment operators, information technology, building construction, medicine, and the clean energy sector are a few areas that are anticipating a shortage of skilled workers totaling in the tens of millions with the ongoing retirement of baby boomers. They're getting more desperate by the day filling these high paying jobs.

With the success of schools like Philadelphia's, the governors want to increase science, technology, engineering, and math (STEM) skills and implement critical thinking skills by using nationwide textbooks and test to fulfill their vision of the Common Core curriculum. That will give kids a strong basis for these highly skilled jobs. That's right folks, a nationwide test and textbooks, regardless of your race, religion, what you ate for dinner, or the color of your pajamas!

Several states success stories, and some with such easy curriculums their top students were failing college, have prompted this nationwide test. Twenty-one states were field tested, including ours. The PARCC (Partnership for Assessment of Readiness for College and Careers) test, if successful in trial runs, would focus more on the new way of teaching. We're finally shifting our focus to the more useful skills we taught to all our kids long ago and have continued through vocational schools for decades.

Laszlo Bock, Google's senior vice president, recently verified what thousands of firms want, useable workplace skills, such as learning and doing projects while using problem solving, creativity, and critical thinking rather than rote learning. In fact, President Obama recognized a change was needed and set aside $100 million for apprenticeships to bolster the tried and true best way to accomplish our new goals. We're also finally going back to well-rounded students, both mentally and physically - like other countries have done for centuries and we practiced until test taking took priority - through physical education, recess, and the arts, as well as allowing more time to relax and regenerate.

Colleges are jumping aboard too by looking for more community oriented, well-rounded students, who actually tend to do better in most fields... plus they're happier. Another benefit is states with low require-ments have many kids unprepared for colleges across the land, leaving them failing or doing badly, so a nationwide curriculum makes everyone play by the same rules.

But there is a downside to this utopia. First, it's extremely expensive to implement. New York State spent over $2 billion of state and federal money implementing the new common core / PARCC test. Second, and the biggest downside to this new method, is the teachers are leaving the kids that aren't good at problem solving or critical thinking behind. One new method is called reverse curriculum, which gives the kids a little information on a subject similar to an outline, then the kids are sent home to figure out how to get to the end product. The problem is, those that aren't good at it spend enormous amounts of time trying to figure it out and can't participate in any after school activities it takes them so long to do their homework.

The teachers expect a lot of kids will come in the next day with all kinds of crazy solutions - and they do! However, many kids that learn by the old monkey-see monkey-do method are getting hopelessly lost and frustrated. Many of us are great at looking at picture instructions and putting things together with minimal help. My daughter even helped me assemble the entire billiards table when she was only nine, and we built our own patio gate from a picture. If you show people like us how to put something together, or give us a picture, we can duplicate it rather quickly. Make us follow the instruction manual without pictures or try to figure out how the parts are assembled on our own, and we'll get frustrated and give up before we get it right.

Another method is "flipping." This is where a teacher has students watch videos, podcast, and online resources to receive lectures and learn the material themselves. Then do their homework at school where they can answer questions. The common core theory is, if someone figures it out on their own, they will truly have a deeper understanding of the critical thinking and problem solving aspect of the project, therefore, acquiring those skills. The truth is, those like us get too frustrated trying our best only to fail over and over. When a kid's homework and test preparation takes all afternoon, evening, and half of their weekend to do it only to fail when they thought they finally got it right, is a very deep, crushing blow. So they start hating school and quit!

My daughter has one foot in that boat because of that one subject that destroys more dreams and makes more kids quit school than all the others combined – Algebra. Historically, a near 90 average student, I'm desperately trying to stop her from giving up completely after getting the dream of her life by going to a top rated art school in Florida with kids like herself, only to be put into an honors chemistry class she doesn't need for graduation or college. I thought I made it perfectly clear when I talked to the school and gave them her records she can't do algebra after telling them our horror stories before they scheduled her, only to have her put in a class that is algebra based!

Didn't we go through this twice already? Sadly it's an exact repeat, only this time on a subject she doesn't even need! I didn't intervene because I trusted her mom to handle everything down there and I had no idea chemistry was algebra based. Nor did I know her scores were being posted on a school website because the school didn't enter me or her mom into their computer to view them until the third semester - after I found out and called them!

Once again nobody called me and I had no idea she was struggling that badly. Now her dreams, and desire, of going to college and being an art teacher herself are being flushed down the toilet from the school not listening, communicating, and putting her in a subject she couldn't do. After going through the last two years stemming from just one subject, I now understand why millions of inner city kids who live in war zones of drugs and guns with little hope or support for college, or a way out, give up at such a young age and my heart goes out to them.

Not everyone is an Einstein, Edison, mathematician, or the problem solvers the common core demands. And 90% of the job market simply does not require algebra, including nearly every teacher you ever had all the way up to the Superintendent of schools, our congressmen, Supreme Court justices, and the president himself. I understand the aspect of getting kids to think outside the box, but it absolutely should NOT be required for college in majors that do not require any knowledge of it. Kids losing their dreams, shutting down, dropping out, and becoming part of our social problem is not worth the price! Vastly more professions and people use the metric system worldwide, so why do we make it mandatory instead of the metric system? Nearly every man has to buy a metric tool set, yet knows nothing about it!

A good argument against mandatory algebra is yours truly and some of our teachers. We failed high school algebra miserably, but fortunately for me, this requirement didn't go into effect until the year after I graduated from flight school. Even pilots don't need it, just a little fourth grade geometry and your mapping out flights before you know it. If we were going to school today, our greatest and most beloved achievements and memories would never have happen. The common core is a great idea, but the bugs have to be worked out before it shatters our youth's dreams and society with it.

At our School Committee meeting, I was informed the state of Massachusetts is going to push the math curriculum to outrageous levels of proficiency. What was taught under the common core in middle school will now be pushed down to elementary students. And the state isn't stopping there. They're going to ramp up the science curriculum they already ramped up for the common core to match the ramped up math curriculum they already ramped up for – you guessed it – the common core. The good news is (sarcasm warning) the state has launched a kindergarten test too. Hey! Don't blame us; we're not the insane ones!

I'm not surprised by the toughest math and science standards in the country for a well-known college state that is home to some of Wall Street's most powerful investment company recruiters. As you know, all hedge fund and derivative scams require complicated mathematical models using significant science, math, and computer skills like those of Amaranths own psycho Brian Hunter (coming up later) who has degrees in both math and physics.

Being the committee's legislative liaison, I talked to our elected representatives. One of them just happens to be state Rep. Nick Boldyga, who now has three kids that will be among the first ones to suffer this fate. I ran into him at the annual town meeting and he said he voted against the Common Core over the Mass. Comprehensive Assessment System (MCAS) test.

Not that he's totally against it, but Nick's secretary told me he's put in a bill to slow down the implementation to give everyone time to adjust to it. She says congressmen have been getting a lot of furious people calling them and saying they want to make sure the kids that need extra help passing the new standards will get it. I told her our story trying to get extra help, and just because politicians want it and make a law, doesn't make it happen in the real world. They need to experience the new system themselves.

When many of us parents see what the kids are studying in freshman biology class we can't believe it. It's much harder than when we went to school. My daughter's teacher, who is a forensic science graduate, told me they have gone way overboard with the curriculum and need to scale it back to a reasonable level. And our accountant (who loves algebra and has a daughter in high school) said she deals with it on a daily basis and the new algebra being taught "makes no sense." But, as you know, instead of cutting it back, our crazy state is ramping it up one or two notches. Good luck Nicks kids!

Everybody in our school district - and as I recall at the State School Committee level agree - these new methods and standards to satisfy the common core will likely make more kids drop out of school and give them an inferiority complex than build new leaders. Some states have already dropped out and it's falling apart.

In our district they're also killing our kids GPA's with the 8 course block system. It makes kids take an extra 7 useless courses to graduate they don't need, will never use, and don't want. At a time when most of the country is learning we need to teach kids a relevant, interesting curriculum for today's job market, our district is pushing more irrelevant material than ever.

We make the high school kids take 5 English courses as opposed to the state college requirement of 4, 4 social studies instead of 2, 2 applied arts and 2 fine arts where 0 are required. That's 7 extra courses just to fill the extra time slots the block system demands not required by the state for college entry. Since many kids are not interested in these extra classes that are often difficult, boring, and irrelevant to their chosen careers; they don't do as well and their overall GPA's hit the skids. That's crucial, because GPA's are now 75% of the college admissions decision and the leading indicator of how good a kid well do in college as opposed to college entry exams. This puts our kids at a distinct disadvantage when applying for college because they will have lower GPA's then kids in a normal curriculum.

We even offer 21 other courses to fill up the block schedule, make the state happy, and draw in school choice kids that year in and year out don't have enough kids to run them. They're just "paper courses!" Nine have between 1 and 5 kids signed up and the others we combine similar courses to run them. I'm all for offering as many options as possible for kids, but in this masquerade to impress colleges, state officials, and the public, I couldn't get the School Committee members and administration to drop the nine that never get more than a few students or even replace them with more interesting ones! These false promises destroy some kid's career choice, including my daughters.

Between the extra boring courses of the block system and the much tougher requirements already in place, not to mention what's coming next year, more and more kids will drop by the waste-side. We already have dropout rates of 50% in our inner cities, and our local station reported only 25% of high school seniors nationwide currently score proficient on math test and 40% on English test. It would be nice to improve our world ranking in the STEM fields, but let the kids that are the most proficient and brightest in those fields that tend to naturally gravitate to them, rise to the top through our current Advance Placement (AP) curriculum without dragging everyone else down. That's what Renaissance and private schools are for. They're based on a tunnel vision system that says from day one, every kid's going to college, and they implement that strategy every single day until graduation. Most of these schools have a 100 % college acceptance rate year in and year out, so let the brightest go there if they please.

Another problem with pushing kids and schools too hard is the pressure for kids to succeed and the schools do well on state exams. This leads many kids to cheat using the newest technology. Even teachers and administrators are accused of helping whole schools cheat on state test to reach their improvement goals. Usually they're some sort of charter or for-profit school trying to make their schools look like they have a magic pill to many underperforming schools. One example is a Philadelphia school where officials claimed the principal reminded kids to write their answers on their worksheets first so teachers could check them and help the kids put down the right answers. After the scandal broke the kids were retested. Guess what happened?

Then, it was Atlanta, Ga., where 20 teachers and administrators were sent to prison for cheating. And for-profit giant Corinthian College was sued by numerous states, fined $30 million for misrepresentation (fraud) and then shut down all their campuses - as did ITT Technical Institute and Donald Trump's Trump University.

Is it all worth the worry? Is doing great on your Scholastic Aptitude Test (SAT) or American College Test (ACT) to get everyone into the STEM fields and college worth it? Many colleges no longer think so.

Less and less colleges are requiring any entry exam at all, because high school GPA's, your income level, teacher recommendations, college prep courses, family wealth, and race are the best predictors of how good someone will do in college. We've known for years the highest income kids do better over lower income ones, with Asians doing the best, and blacks the worst overall for a variety of reasons. Privileged kids can afford private schools and test prep courses, and both the elite alumni and politician's kids can often legally get preferential treatment... big surprise! Even the test themselves are wrought with problems, such as graders having too many test to correct, essays not being factual, and some of the test answers themselves are wrong or don't have a right answer - particularly essays.

People in Washington speak about education through both sides of their mouths at the same time. On one hand they want to push relevant skills for the shortages in the fields mentioned earlier, on the other hand, they push the STEM courses Obama and the rest of Washington claims there is a shortage of. And as you usual they're both wrong!

As Jia Lynn Yang of The Washington Post points out, many people agree this is just a myth. According to the Economic Policy Institute, the U.S. does "not" have a shortage in these fields and has "more than a sufficient supply of workers available." Kids getting degrees in these fields aren't being hired because of "capitalistic greed." All the lies stem from the fact that companies are paying foreigners who come here on work visas "an estimated 20% less than their American counterparts," leaving only about 50% of the kids with STEM field degrees being hired in those fields. Even in the information technology (IT) field, only 64% have a 4 year college degree, of which only 38% are in the shortage categories of computer science and math. In reality, from engineering to computer science, many companies have left a lot of highly educated American kids standing in the unemployment line or getting lesser paying jobs in other fields to pay the rent and their humongous college loans.

Even if there was a shortage in STEM fields, it's a struggle to get great teachers and all but impossible to get teachers who specialize in any given subject, especially math and science. This makes it very expensive for local school districts to send their teachers for the necessary training required to get the students ready for the new PARCC test. And what if school districts were to send their teachers to special training at the townspeople's expense? They might turn around and go to another school, or state, offering more money. It's expensive enough already.

We had a first year algebra teacher who was the nicest, quietest, small town girl you could get. The problem was she majored in Art in college and was more suited to teach elementary kids and art students. This new generation of 8th graders just ate her up. She tried moving the desk around several times to get the distracting kids under control, yet some of the kids still set personal record low scores on the state test from the rowdy classroom. So she gave up trying to control today's spoiled brats and quit.

We had to have an algebra teacher and did the best we could finding one, but this scenario is repeated in nearly all subjects across the entire system. Many teachers are shifted from grade to grade or course to course to fill vacancies, and others are teaching courses outside their major. Many have general education degrees just wanting to teach anything at any level, but the new state and federal laws are making it necessary to have specialist and very few exist. Even if you could get specialist, can you imagine the price they would command? They'd want nearly as much as many overpaid college professors. If we can't afford what they're demanding now, how on earth can we possible afford every teacher getting those salaries? As I write, teachers are on strike at Maine's most expensive school district, where they average $70,000 a year in salary, stipends, pensions, health and dental insurance. All these challenges have PARCC on life support.

Charter Schools

Some people swear charters are the best way to teach kids, particularly inner city kids, but they've had mixed results so far, despite often having better equipment, refurbished schools, and more money. Overseen by state education officials and paid for by taking about $10,000 per pupil of public funding away from public schools, they're often brought to inner city school districts in an attempt to narrow the achievement gaps between the poor, drug filled, violent, inner cities and the rest of the country. They're usually run by "non-profit" businesses or corporations with a board of trustees that try innovative teaching techniques and curriculum. But I really worry about the corporate part of the equation. Any bigtime Super Pac going under the guise of a non-profit "can and do" run these schools, with one from N.Y. doling out $17 million of the $43 million spent promoting charters in our tiny states last election.

Also, lying and cheating on test scores is sometimes used to look good. We just had a local ex-principle plead guilty for instructing her teachers to monitor the students and help them on wrong answers. Her excuse was not unexpected. She said one of the board members told her this is how we make money (higher scores) and pressured her into doing it. Non-profit my...! Robert M. Hughes Academy was investigated for cheating so principal Janet Henry was replaced by ex-convict Fred Allen.

Some charters are even exempt from taking the same state exams traditional schools have to. Also, kids going to charters are the more motivated students from parents that care the most, help with their homework, and have a better overall quality of life. Some parents don't even putt their kids' names on the list. So you wind up taking the more motivated kids out of the public schools and leave the ones that are morally crushed with no family support in the neighborhood schools. Plus, it leaves them with more special education kids who require interventionist that help the teachers at about $60,000 each. This puts the public schools further behind with less money for good teachers and curriculum, so how do they expect inner city schools to improve that way?

Nationally, about ¼ of charter schools do better than traditional schools in their neighborhoods, ¼ do worse, and a little more than half about the same. What's this tell you? Not much without the details. As we've seen, statistics can be jerry-rigged to show almost anything you want.

First, with a fourth of traditional schools doing better than others in their neighborhoods, charters are not doing any better percentage wise. Second, charters have longer days and more one on one because they're specifically designed to take the kids out of the ghetto for as long as possible and into the school setting with the other motivated kids as long as possible. Third, if you take the most motivated kids and their parents out of the public schools system, they're stuck with the more troubled kids that ruin it for everyone else. This crucial information is always left out by Republicans and their Super Pac's pushing charters and gives them ammunition for more of their Wall Street big business schools and the eventual privatization of all schools.

Another thing to consider is charters are allowed to hire anyone with a high school diploma, as opposed to formally trained college educated teachers. At first glance that may seem a recipe for disaster, but it's not.

Night schools are often taught by people who own their own business or have many years of experience in their field. I think public schools would be smart to do the same if they can get state approval and the teachers union to agree. I had night school construction and real estate teachers at the local college who were experienced owners of their own companies, making them more qualified than any college taught kid. I was also on a cooks apprentice program that was taught by the executive chef of the famous Ambassador Hotel in Los Angeles where Bobby Kennedy was shot twelve years earlier.

That's one plus for charters, plus there's no union. Bad teachers and administrators can be fired without battling the union, and as you know, after what some of our teachers said they should be.

I hope I'm not sounding pro charter in its current form, because I'm not. Without a doubt, if you took the same kids and put them in a good public school or one designed the same way for the same purpose of the charters, like magnet schools, the results would be identical. And I have proof. The inner city kids we bring to our schools through the school choice program are often on the honor roll and maximum honor roll and we're not a charter or magnet school! But certainly some business aspects of charters would stop the massive amount of waste and expense our town and state pushed on us with all our unnecessary additions that have left half of us, and the state, in financial distress. No business could ever get away with that much mismanagement and survive. Only public funding allows for this kind of incompetence!

Are charters even worth it? A study of Boston schools reveals the public school kids actually graduated from college faster than charter kids. Nearly two thirds of public kids graduated in 6 years compared to only 40% for charters.

Similar to charters, alternative schools, like magnets, have been popping up in cities lately to try and get inner city kids on the right path, and they are very successful but at an enormous cost to taxpayers. Generally speaking, they have class sizes of only 10 to 15 students (sounds like us) so school districts must hire a lot more teachers for a very strict curriculum that is geared for college acceptance. Like charters, every kid that leaves a school district in our state cost the sending district about $10,000 in lost state aid and $6,000 for those that use the school choice program. The good news is, it works, but only time will tell if the total monetary cost until death do us part will be worth getting the kids out of the ghettos. Normally I'm a downright frugal person, but in my opinion, I would give it a thumbs-up for trying.

Both public and private schools are bringing in new curriculums at all levels to engage students more. I'm not sure some of them do anything other than that, but they are supposed to be aimed at real life world situations. For instance, one college offers a course called the "Art of Walking." It's to encourage our wired, sedentary kids to get off their butts and outdoors where they can study nature, get cardiovascular exercise, and lose weight.

University of California Berkley has a course under "courses you can actually use" called "Simpsons and Philosophy." For the final exam you have to write your own Simpsons episode... sounds like after 400 episodes, the show's writers ran out of ideas and wanted some free help.

Other colleges offer "The History of Shopping," at Yale; and "Death," which is about the decisions people make throughout life. Another has the "Joy of Garbage," and one a course called "Revenge." Rutgers probably offers the only sports management course called "Yankee Stadium," which is dedicated to the New York Yankees.

Although kids need some fun courses, the theories behind them are similar to the real world experiences many of us are backing. We're in a collaborative with six other towns and cities that allows us to teach trades none of us could individually afford because of the often expensive special equipment and relatively low enrollment figures in each subject. Together, we can teach such courses as automotive technician, wood shop, cosmetology, horticulture, and culinary arts to name a few. Most of our kids are in apprentice type after school work programs and will go directly to work after graduation, or better yet, start their own business! But the best part is most of them are high paying jobs!

Finance

There was over 200 college presidents making over 1 million dollars a year in the state of Massachusetts - the most expensive state in the country. It's 39% higher than the national average for two year colleges and 24% for four. Just this tiny state alone has kids owing $24 billion. So Nick Boldyga filed a bill to limit the salaries of state employees to not exceed the Governors pay. According to Boldyga, about 7,700 state employees are making $100,000 or more, including over 2,500 college employees making as much as $800,000. Not including their life long benefits and other stipends like travel expenses. Actual figures would be much higher if you included county and local municipal leaders, as well as department heads, considering our small town administrator and chief of police with small staffs are close to that $100,000 mark too.

Just locally, all but one principal in our district are over that, as is our business manager, along with the same benefits as other public employees. Our superintendent of schools makes over $140,000. That's more than the governors $137,000 a year, with many of the same perks, and he's nowhere near the highest paid in the state for a school district our size. Shockingly, school administrators and union lawyers from the high priced Boston area think that is absurdly low!

Many public employees make much more than the public thinks, including teachers. Because personal salaries are confidential (except the administrations) and are not reported to anyone, only the School Committee members know how much the other school district employees make. In cities like Boston you can count on many teachers making over $100.000 a year, especially with stipends. To get the various pay scales, you can get around the shield of secrecy by requesting the basic salary scales that show what teachers make at each level based on their education level and experience. It is public information you know!

We also have "tenure" that makes it all but impossible to fire educators after their probationary period – except under extreme circumstances. For better or worse, all educators get raises based on their educational level, years of service, and union contracts that call for automatic increases, normally every year, along with pension increases upon retirement. In as little as just five or ten years they are eligible for a certain amount of money upon retirement based on the number of years worked. In some states, they can even switch to a different field altogether, such as nurse or construction worker and still get it. Small towns like ours really can't change the way things work. If we're not competitive in salaries, insurance, and retirement benefits, everyone will go to a different school district. It's the old catch 22.

After reviewing our salaries and contracts, I can tell you they actually do quite well here until the day they die. The smartest unions even get them a free attorney in any disputes or terminations and paid religious holidays for all denominations, costing us nearly double every time we have to hire a substitute teacher for the day.

Good teachers are the backbone of our society, and if anybody deserves a decent salary, it's them; just not the stratospheric salaries administrators and higher education are pulling in. College was free in California before Governor Ronald Reagan's "reign of terror" but has gone up 1200% the last 30 years, and it's the taxpayers and college students that are getting buried in debt from the outrageous salaries some college educators are commanding. Leaving the price of college dragging down students until the day they die. Nearly two-thirds of students now pay for college through student loans as opposed to just 29% from my generation of boomers, and borrowing doubled between 2007 and 2013 now totaling $1.6 trillion or $37,000 each.

On the opposite end of the pay scales lye the part time college adjuncts and substitute teachers. Although adjuncts often require as much educational training as any college professor and can adequately fill in at the drop of a hat, they usually need to work at several colleges just to scrape by for a living. In reality they help pay for the overpaid full-time professors by getting nearly nothing. Do you see something wrong with this picture?

A September 10, 2013 report by US News tells us how unaffordable it has become for many of the brightest kids from families that simply cannot afford the best schools, enforcing the theory that only the richest kids can get a top notch education. According to the report, Columbia University's tuition topped the list of private schools at nearly $50,000 per year, "not including books, room, and board."

The 10 most expensive averaged about $47,300, making the average of the ten least expensive private schools at $8,800 look downright cheap. Overall, private schools averaged about $30,500 and public schools almost $8400 for in state tuition and $19,100 for out of state. Student loan debt now surpasses our total credit card debt, with over 7 million former students in default! They're inundated with a lifetime of payments before they even graduate. It's completely unsustainable and fast becoming out of reach for many kids.

Politicians are always talking about making college affordable to all, yet charge students "nine times" more for loans than they charge banks, and debt is more than five times what it was in 1999. All this debt has made millennials the least likely to own a home under the age of 35 since they started pushing home ownership in the 1980's. I guess they'll have to downgrade to a chicken in every pot but no car in the garage.

They also tried leveling the playing field for low income and inner city minority kids for decades - though that law was recently overturned by the U.S. Supreme Court. Colleges used to give special treatment in accepting minorities to appease the law and help balance out the racial divide. Now, many minorities want the smartest kids getting accepted, not average kids just because they're a minority. They still think college admissions staff should give some merit to their tough economic and social conditions when choosing their students. One other point might be this – yesterday's minorities are now the majority, therefore dispelling any old definition of who's a minority in our backwards society.

Statistics point out college might not even be worth it. It no longer pays to spend the extra money to get a masters or doctorate degree over a standard bachelor's because it stretches out your monthly payments almost into retirement. A bachelor's degree often leaves a student with twenty or thirty thousand dollars of debt, with payments and interest usually stretching into your thirties. But a doctorate could bring that figure into the half a million range and stretch your payments out into your fifties! The more in debt kids are upon graduation, the less likely they'll start their own business.

A report by the AP claims about 37 million former students have student debt, as well as 40% of households led by someone under 36. The net worth of households without debt is nearly triple that of those with it and embraces the fact that they have more collateral to start a business than their counterparts. The bad news doesn't stop there. Both the amount borrowed and the number of borrowers was up 70% from 2004 to 2012, with about 12 million new students borrowing every year.

In an email I received from Senator Warren, she points out another overlooked factor in this debate. Did you know single moms that have been to college are 60% more likely to go bankrupt?

Is a top notch ultra-expensive private university really better than a cheap state one? Another Gallup Poll suggests we shouldn't measure the student's post college success by the traditional "job placement and income" barometric, but instead on whether they "have had a good life in terms of wellbeing, satisfaction, and career engagement."

That's what I've been trying to get through to people the last 20 years, yet it's akin to smashing your head against a brick wall! As I said in the beginning, we have our priorities backwards in this country. Overpriced, overhyped, prestigious schools are exactly that and should not be the barometer you set your goals over. Doing what you enjoy, not the prestige or pay should determine what direction you take in life! We shouldn't be pining every kid to work for Wall Street! Like those who finally got a heart and fought their former employers found out, you still have to live with your conscience. In an interview with Purdue University's president Mitch Daniels about the Gallop Poll, he pointed out, it doesn't matter one bit if you go to a private or public school because they all come out the same in terms of satisfaction in the end.

This study also links the high cost of going to these prestigious schools to a life "less satisfactory" than going to a cheaper school - not the other way around! Students loaded with debt simply are not as happy as those without decades of it! Most foolishly take it on at such a young age because of that false claim it leads to more pay and a better life. Fortunately, the recession has brought many previous high flying families grudgingly back to the more frugal days of finance, and I would like be the first to say... It's about time!

This year a record amount of freshman have turned down their top choice because of the cost and will be glad they did after graduation. Hopefully, if millions of kids do this it will bring down the cost of college by the theory of supply and demand. The less kids and parents are willing to pay outrageous prices, the less kids the elite schools will have and they'll have to lower their prices if they want to compete with state schools. This will also bring more advanced students to state schools - a real win-win for all!

Another interesting thing this poll points out is it doesn't matter how big or fancy the buildings are or how new the equipment is, proving what many of us have been trying to tell people all along. It's the teachers and their relationship with the students and providing hands on learning and outside work programs like internships and apprenticeships that are the most beneficial aspects of education and makes for a happy student during and post-graduation!

Also, students are growing increasingly pessimistic about whether a college degree is worth the time, cost, and energy. "Times they are a changing," Bob Dillon once wrote, and Googles Laszlo Bock is right in the middle of the controversy. In an interview with the New York Times Thomas Friedman, he raised the bar a little higher on this subject when he insinuated Google wasn't interested in hiring just college graduates. He pointed out "employers today care less about what you know or where you learned it than what value you can create with what you know," and "don't just go to college because you think it's the right thing to do and any bachelor's degree will suffice."

Naturally he recommends more vigorous courses such as computer science, because they help you stand out and make you better prepared for today's technology jobs. They also show one's ability to learn things and solve problems, enforcing what the Common Core is trying to accomplish – careers that don't always require a college degree. In fact, he recently started hiring high school kids on a summer internship to give the most promising ones a head start. So if we're all on the same page, why aren't we getting anywhere?

School administrators across the country are adding to the cost of education with ominous spending on a variety of mundane endeavors, especially at the college level. Often they take trips (purportedly in the name of recruiting kids or services) to faraway places and put the tab on the schools credit card, when in reality they're vacations for themselves.

We have one at our local university that was recently fired for exactly that. His, as are many trips, are overseas and they bring back bureaucrats under the guise of improving the institutions. Sometimes their shenanigans backfire for their schools when they get caught and their prominent alumni and other donors pull their yearly contributions and sizable donations to their endowment funds. Lawsuits and investigations often follow, sometimes costing millions of dollars that should have been used for running the schools and keeping tuition down.

Probably the most famous person involved in a college scandal is our old buddy Laurence Summers when he was president of the prestigious Harvard University. The former Treasury Secretary and deregulation cheerleader got Harvard in trouble for supporting a professor who was caught conducting insider trading with Russian stocks that cost Harvard over $25 million. Then he lost the college another cool BILLION in a derivative scam. Harvard showed him the door and President Obama welcomed him to his team! There's that revolving door again!

Super Pac's Destruction

Ignoring charter and for-profit school failures, and elite private schools are the only ones performing well, with poor inner city schools often dragging down overall scores that give us our low world rankings between 20th and 30th in reading, math, and science; education Pac's push harder than ever to privatize our schools. ALEC introduced 150 bills in 2013 alone affecting public education in 43 states and nearly 40 became law. Some allow privately run charters and other schools to use the little known vouchers that allow kids to get public taxpayer money and go to ritzy private schools.

In the Republican stronghold of Kansas, state bureaucrats gave the well-to-do a huge tax break that broke public schools and taxpayers backs. Rich and poor alike called for it to be terminated, and the state Supreme Court ruled their low spending on public schools was unconstitutional. It ordered the state to spend more money on its schools and restore the programs they cut that helped low income area students compete with the wealthy ones.

We have a minimum requirement to avoid such lunacy here, but it's unreasonably high and led to higher taxes. If Kansas is like us and many states, it won't matter if the money comes from a lottery because they'll steal the profits that are supposed to go to education and divert it to the state's general fund. Then divvy it up amongst any state agencies that need it before they finally give any leftover money to the local schools.

Wall Street has gotten its head in the door and has grand plans for our countries education system. It went all out getting into for-profit schools such as the DeVry Institute, Everest College, and the University of Phoenix. And ALEC was more than willing to help it kick-start privatized education and siphon money from public education with its Great Schools Tax Credit Act of 2013.

For-Profit Schools

Is education for sale? Has K Street been good for anyone other than the greedy moguls involved? Bill Clinton alone has made $24 million consulting for-profits. And Donald Trump was sued by 6000 students, New York, and Ca. for fraud over his $35,000 Trump University and is routinely in court for multiple frauds. With Argosy Education Group, it's there often useless degrees at nearly $30,000 a year - about ten times community colleges. ITT Tech's was $22,000, University of Phoenix's charade is 10 grand and Education Management Inc. has been charged with fraudulently ripping-off students with stratospheric loans for their phony schools so they can sell them to hideous investors as securities.

So the house committee on education held a hearing on for-profits. Why? Because they give $20 billion a year in loans to college students and don't want them to be pawns to Wall Street and proprietary schools that make loan sharks look like angles. Plus they get stuck with billions in unpaid loans! Secretary of education Arne Duncan thought they were practicing high pressure techniques and dishonesty with incentive payments for their sales people. The apex predators were so crooked the government took them to court to stop abusing our kids. They were paying recruiters on the number of recruits they signed up - no salary! Denial Golden of the Bloomberg News concern is, if you bring in low performing students with little or no chance to graduate just so the recruiters can make money, you'll bring in just about anyone.

They'll promise you anything to get you to sign up at prices only top private schools charge no matter how bogus their schools are. They'll give anyone a massive student loan, and you're usually left with a useless degree and up to hundreds of thousands of dollars in debt. Plus they can't be discharged in bankruptcy court, so the parasites sue you, garnish your wages, and intercept your tax refund. You also become ineligible for federal employment or benefits. In Phoenix's case, they eventually settled out of court with the feds and two whistleblowers for $67.5 million. Hopefully this will be a warning to the feeding frenzy.

Rep. George Miller, former Chairman on Education and Labor, agrees it's reminiscent of the liar loans banks gave out without proof people could pay them back. Miller claims the overall average default to be 10-11% but an astonishing 50% at for-profits.

Proponents have brought in some really big guns from the investment world. For them it's just another money making business. The Street proves day in and day out why they are poison. Can you believe they actually bet on their stocks!?

Massachusetts filed a lawsuit against the previously noted Corinthian College Inc. (A.K.A. Everest Institute) for fraud. Like Argosy, Attorney General Martha Coakley said "the students were promised careers, high-paying jobs and lifetime support services, but got worthless certificates and no job prospects." They pushed them into high-interest taxpayer backed loans and lied about their job placement rates to boost their lofty profits. As did other for-profits, they recruited anybody regardless of their qualifications with their usual high pressure tactics and deceptive marketing. So the U.S. Department of Education forgave the loans and is considering shutting down the Accrediting Council for Independent Colleges and Schools responsible for them.

For-profits are trying to force us into their schools by default. The industry's plan is to cut public education funding to a level where public colleges cannot be funded to educate all the students they think will be flooding into them, forcing the government to accept their schools. Now, like the financial institutions, they are almost too big to fail. So President Obama tried helping community colleges with $12 billion, but after fierce debate from lobbyist with their millions in bribes he only got two.

Could Wall Street and their lobbyist sink any lower? They want billions to flow into little regulated education while disregarding our young people's lives they are destroying just to enrich themselves. We can only hope they all burn in Hell, along with junk bond king Michael Milken, who is out of jail now and schlepping cyber schools!

Cyber Schools

Also known as virtual schools, in certain instances through legitimate colleges, cyber schools are useful. Taking online courses can give a teacher, corporate person, or anybody else the extra knowledge required for their position or advancement. Even someone who just wants to learn can benefit from a legitimate cyber school. The problem is when you get people like Donald Trump, Milken, (who became the face of fraud with his junk bond leveraged buyouts in the 1980's) and Ron Packard, a former Goldman Sachs junk bond merger specialist involved.

They're Baaack! – Together Milken and Packard run Knowledge Universe and Knowledge Learning, parent company of such schools as the innocent sounding KinderCare child care chain and K12 Inc. Once again, Milken and CEO Packard have gotten enriched on taxpayer money with yet another scheme. That makes them perfect for ALEX's Educational Task Force with their K12 Inc. So now they're on it helping ALEC push their immensely profitable, public failing virtual schools.

The Center for Media and Democracy reported by 2012 K12 Inc. had around 80,000 students in its 60 or so full time virtual schools. They ran somewhere between 20 and $30 million worth of ads that year to attract students on popular children's TV shows like Nickelodeon and Cartoon Network, along with ads on popular teen websites. Why did they spend so much on ads? You should know the answer to that by now, especially when Milken and Packard are involved. You see, it's elementary my dear Watson.

In 2013, K12 received nearly $850 million, with nearly 90% of that coming from taxpayers for their questionable internet schools. The more students they sign up, the more taxpayer money they can legally swindle for their newest scam. In this nearly unregulated and unaccountable world, they get paid for every head they sign up and then their K12 Inc. kind of does a disappearing act. Teachers around the country came forth with stories of getting hundreds of alleged students assigned to them. But most never attend a class, contact them, or do anything. Those that do try to get an education, find the crooked internet schools are inferior to regular brick and mortar ones in every category. Their test scores are about 50% lower across the board compared to their counterparts, including yearly progress and on time graduations, and only 27% meet state standards. For this dismal effort, Packard was given nearly $20 million for his four years of evading authorities and top executive compensation shot up more than 100%!

Even investors weren't happy about K12's performance. With 50% of the kids dropping out completely, they were just as bad as the for-profit colleges. Packard was eventually sued for securities fraud for making false statements and omissions to investors about student performance and their despicable recruiting tactics to replace those that dropped out - to make it look as if the company was growing. So some Wall Street hedge fund managers known for their despicable lust for money at any cost think Milken and Packard have sunk to new depths and have dropped them.

With Donald Trump, his ruse to turn people into real estate tycoons with his Trump University was settled for $25 million - as was charges of racketeering and 200 other settlements that kept him out of jail.

ALEC, Milken, Packard, Trump and hundreds of other charlatans are preying on the American student and America better beware. ALEC has over 150 demented lobbyists and who knows how many politicians and unscrupulous educational administrators anchored in more than half the states promoting their agenda.

One of those would be former Indiana School Superintendent Tony Bennett, who was accused of changing the state grading system he and ALEC pushed through as model legislation for the country they called the "Indiana Education Reform Package." It was really meant to help one of his top donor's, Christel DeHaan, and his charter school to receive a top rating. The grading system was used to determine which schools would be taken over by the state and which students could get state funded vouchers to go to private schools they were endorsing.

After his school received a C grade, he sent emails to his chief of staff Heather Neal saying anything less than an A would compromise all of their accountability work. He had assured the Chamber of Commerce and legislative leaders they would get one and wrote they could not release it until it was resolved. He was afraid his critics and the legislature would use it against them to undue their work and he needed solutions, not excuses, to wiggle out of the lies. So him and his staff got to work changing the grading system, then got the score bumped up twice to the A he needed.

For their reward in corrupting the system, Bennett got elected out of office in one of the biggest upsets in Indiana history. Wahoo! Not to worry, though, he was then rewarded with the top job as Florida's education commissioner instead, running all Florida Schools for Tea Party Governor Rick Scott and his anti-union, anti-public, pro-charter, for-profit, agenda. And Neal got the job as the governor's chief lobbyist. Are you surprised?

I received a flyer from our state association of School Committees and have been informed ALEC is writing bills to banish all school boards throughout the states. They don't want the local townspeople making decisions about their kid's education or the checks and balances. No more School Committees making decisions or hiring and firing superintendents, and no more negotiating with teachers and adminis-trative unions. They don't want us deciding what's best for our kids, which sports they can play, what subjects we'll teach, or any control of our construction projects that are critical for safe, healthy, schools. As usual, they want the drooling fox to run the hen house!

Unsuccessful with their attempts to privatize the nation's schools, the GOP hankered down to keep the enormous profits the banks and government was making off of student loans. They were making about $185 billion a year, and the bank's profits was anybody's guess. What we do know is; they allowed the student loan interest rates to double from 3.4% to 6.8% before going on their summer vacation in 2013, which temporarily doubled their profits... Ka-Ching, Ka-Ching!

They had a plan to let them go as high as 10%, even though the morons were charged less than 1% on many of the outstanding loans. And they were assured by Fed Chairman Ben Bernanke they would continue pouring $85 billion a month into their Wall Street scheme to keep interest rates at record lows and profits at record highs.

Eventually, Congress came to a consensus and tied the loans to the Treasury bill market. Charging 2.05% above the prevailing T-Bill rate, then put a cap on them of 8.25% and 10% of their after graduation employment income that could be forgiven after 20 years. But that still guaranteed the banks hefty profits off of students and their families. Apparently, the Democrats made a deal with them on this one to get a bill through the anti-public education GOP. They wound up reducing the amount of financial aid they will give to the poor and made grad school more expensive. Do you hear private education knocking at the door again?

I'm sure that doesn't surprise you now that you know how college, politics, and Wall Street go hand in hand. With Republicans and ALEC shifting more money from our public colleges to "private welfare" universities - where only 43% of their income comes from tuition and fees - and the rest from you know who, they'll either squeeze the public system out completely or make it inconsequential. Already about one-third of college kids go to private schools and employers hire them first over other kids for a number of reasons. Unfortunately, those reasons are once again tied to status and who you know, not what you know, your grades, or your abilities.

Several things account for who gets hired, and the name of your school is at the top of the list: Followed by what sorority you are in, what college and sorority your parents were in, and do they work there? And nothing beats large donations by your parents to the school or their company's favorite charity. Going to a public college, or the wrong one, along with missing the other above mentioned priorities, will not only exclude you from many big corporate jobs, but reduce your lifetime pay up to over 50%. Certain sororities virtually guaranty you a position at certain firms upon graduation from the best private schools and that 50% salary increase over someone from a public college.

For instance, if you graduated with a degree from Harvard or Wharton with an M.B.A., no matter what your GPA, 2 years later you'll get $125,000 a year compared to $62,000 from the average state school, and that more than doubles 10 years down the road. That seems fair after non-privileged kids load up on student loans, doesn't it?

There is some good news I suppose. People are not having many kids anymore, and this will put a monkey wrench into the GOP push to siphon enough money from the public school system to force us into their private schools. A shortage of students has already begun, especially in the Northeast and Midwest states. And you know we've already seen it here, so we have more than enough room. All the trouble they went to and put our country through to get our kids into their private schools, and now we don't have enough kids for them... tsk-tsk.

I'd like to point out one last thing about education. In the beginning I mentioned our priorities were a disgrace, we were a backwards society, the minority ruled, and we worshiped Hollywood stars. Here in the liberal capital of the world, Hampshire College brought in an actress, producer, and reality TV transgender star to give the commencement speech this year. In my opinion, regardless how nice the former man is and what he went through to become a lady, that doesn't make her a role model. College is not supposed to be about New York and Hollywood sensationalism. One shouldn't be giving a commencement speech because of some people's warped vision of a hero. She's not a hero of impeccable accomplishments our kids should look up to for changing sexes, she's just another media sideshow and they're a dime a dozen. Smarten up America!!!

7

Immigration
Is it Out of Control?

Welcome to flight training! The first thing you need to know as a pilot is drug runners will try and hire you to smuggle drugs and coyotes illegal aliens under the radar screens into uncontrolled airspace in the desert. That's what our instructor told us the first day in Southern California!

Immigration policy, or lack of one, has contributed to our demise in a number of ways, despite the fact we stole many other countries brightest people to advance our own. Union Democrats want strict border controls because they want to keep their union jobs, medical insurance, 401's, pensions, and decent living wages. Liberal Democrats unrealistically want to give everyone a chance for a better life. Republicans want low minimum wages and literally no immigration policy: Along with an open border with Mexico so they can hire both the legal and illegal workers for their factories, plants, and farms for next to nothing, with few, if any benefits. They also need the tens of millions of Latinos and their kids to boost Christianity's dwindling numbers.

Ignoring mother nature, our own history, and Europe's, they force-fed Americans with a deluge of uneducated immigrants in thousands of communities who rarely speak English and no longer have any intention of ever assimilating into our society as past immigrants had. They don't vote, run for office, or volunteer on community boards, leaving the business of running our towns and cities to the same few people who always step up to the plate and sacrifice their time and money. By the 21st century, we had completely lost our identity when recent immigrants went from being the vast minority to the majority. They fractured the country until we no longer had an identity and separated us into a nation of ethnic enclaves. We became a country of sectarian groups from all around the world going our own separate ways. Even businesses are forced to carry the local ethnic group's food and clothing or go bankrupt to those that do. We've lost our national cohesion and social fabric.

As a result, dozens of groups now celebrate their own individual religions and cultures, complete with parades and festivities. The blacks now have Kwanzaa instead of Christmas, and ironically, Martin Luther

King Day on January 19th but black history month in February - effectively giving the media both months to cash in on their history. The Spanish have Cinco de Mayo, pride marches, and October; Muslims Ramadan and Eid a-Fitr, the Chinese their own New Year's day and calendar, Hindu's have Diwali and hundreds of others, and the Irish have St Patrick's Day... that seems to span the whole month.

Still living in his imaginary Hollywood days, Ronald Reagan told us: "I believe in amnesty for those who may have come here some time back illegally." Then gave amnesty to tens of millions more Mexicans than the official 3.7 million, when he, the INS, and the two Bushes used executive power to give their spouses and children amnesty as well. Reagan told us he was bringing them here to contribute to society by doing the jobs Americans didn't want and pay taxes for schools and infrastructure projects. They would keep the economy moving forward his economist told him - and that was his trump card for reelection. Since then, the feds have brought or allowed foreigners in from every country, with an emphasis on those with religions that don't believe in birth control and procreate like rabbits.

This economic theory may be how it worked in Hollywood, but in the real world the vast majority of Mexicans didn't work and few paid taxes. Most were illegal aliens, and those that legally worked overwhelmingly claimed tax exempt and then sent much of their money back to Mexico. None-the-less, Reagan gave them amnesty, got reelected, and to this day they've been draining government coffers while we deal with the resulting crime, poverty, and unprecedented destruction from drug and turf wars like the Bloods and Crypt's in every major city across the land.

Most Spanish immigrants from south of the border were either illiterate or had very little education, and wound up being just another ingredient in our recipe down the path to third world like status - not the savior Reagan and a lot of "go with the flow" economist claimed they would be. Not only were they sending much of the estimated $1.5 trillion a year in buying power back to relatives rather than spending it here, he opened the flood gates to nearly unrestricted illegal immigration - infuriating legal immigrants such as my wife, the Sanchez's, and millions more from impoverished, ruthless autocracies.

Perhaps, Republicans have finally realized their beloved party has lied and betrayed them ever since when they kicked out their House Majority Leader Eric Cantor for his immigration reform efforts - despite wanting to give all illegal immigrants a path to citizenship that would have been much tougher than Reagan and the Bushes virtual free passes. The GOP knows Reagan had bipartisan support from both houses of Congress to give them amnesty the first time around and overwhelmingly passed it. So why is the party opposed to this latest immigration reform bill they're calling amnesty when Black's Law Dictionary actually describes it as "the 1986 Reform and Control Act?"

Because this time it was a democrat in the White House, and not just any old democrat, but a half-white half-black one whose father is from Kenya. Tea Partiers even consider him an illegal alien not eligible for the presidency, and Republicans are afraid of their Tea Party members so they didn't follow through with their proposed reforms. It's not like other presidents haven't used executive powers for immigration reform. Eisenhower did it 3 times from 1956-1960 - followed by Kennedy, Johnson, Nixon, Reagan, H.W. Bush, and his son G.W.

The Amnesty bill of 1986 was passed because of the "manufactured illusion" of farm and factory labor shortages. Of course there never was a shortage of legal temporary workers willing to come north of the border for harvesting time. But the farms and factories the immigrants work for are some of the largest in the world, comprising vast swaths of land in the Midwest states, as well as California, Arizona, Texas, and Florida, and they want guaranteed cheap labor.

The huge processing plants love illegal aliens because they're just a piece of disposable equipment in their abusive capitalistic machine. They're so big and powerful, they are literally self-contained Super Pac's that virtually make the laws of the land themselves. Rarely are they raided by law enforcement agencies because "they are the law." The massive corporations can hire illegals for minimum wage, an amount they themselves construct for the legislature to pass, saving billions of dollars annually while boosting profits for their Wall Street brethren.

They can also get rid of unions who want decent plant conditions such as safety equipment, an 8 hour work day, 40 hour work week plus overtime pay, a very solid living wage, paid vacations, sick days, and pensions.

With illegal aliens, or those with work visa's (Green Cards), these huge corporations can get the cheapest possible labor in the country, then use and abuse them almost without limitation in the name of Capitalism. They fire workers after a few years to avoid promotions and higher wages, leaving tremendous turnover at their plants and sky-high unemployment rates in the area from these unskilled laborers - putting hordes more on welfare!

Plant and farm conditions can be horrendous with despicable housing conditions. Like many poor people in our country, their houses might not have heat or sit on contaminated wells full of heavy metals and pesticides. So, they and their kids get a gauntlet of debilitating medical conditions, including cancer, organ, stomach, bone, brain, and lung diseases. Wells run dry or are so contaminated the EPA makes them bring in outside water. And the companies give them barely enough bottled water to drink, never mind any extra for showers and laundry. Have we learned nothing from the Love Canal?

When people do have disputes or complaints about their treatment, some shameless corporations are known to shut off the electricity, leaving them without heat, ovens, or refrigeration. They brutally control all aspects of life, and no dissent is tolerated because they know they can get thousands of replacement workers the same way they got those.

Very little immigration law enforcement leads to many unintended consequences as well. Employers large and small that don't hire illegals are at a severe disadvantage. They can't charge customers the same puny fees because of their higher payrolls and moral and ethical beliefs. Also, businesses that get used to paying very little don't want to pay much, even for jobs requiring college degrees, knowing they can get a foreigner cheaper. This raises our unemployment rates and discontent for them.

I myself have felt the long reach of companies that hire cheap labor over us Americans willing to work and get paid the going rate for any given industry. While in college back in Reagan's open boarder years, I was a sauté and broiler cook. I worked at a gourmet restaurant in the business district near John Wayne Airport in Newport Beach, Ca. The restaurant was considered the best in the area with the largest menu in both L.A. and Orange County. Unfortunately, for us employees, the owner got in trouble with the IRS and disappeared.

I wasn't too worried, though, because of our reputation. So I applied at a brand new restaurant that was going to open up just down the street. It was beautiful, with an island theme; plants everywhere with lots of large, grand windows and natural light giving it that tropical atmosphere. It was pretty exciting to know I was going to work there.

The chef told me he would call when the restaurant was finished and we would do a pre-opening test run on the employee's relatives to work out the kinks. When opening day approached, I was miffed as to why I didn't get a call. So I went down to see if everything was OK. When I got there, the restaurant was buzzing and I had been replaced by a bunch of Mexicans! The only American was the boss at the wheel, flanked by all Mexicans!

It was appalling and didn't look good for me. I didn't know any other line of work except factory work and farming, and I was still working on my air transportation-commercial pilot's license at school. But in the end it worked out alright... I even got well-deserved justice!

My roommate knew a guy who owned his own landscaping business and he was making over $10 an hour. That was perfect for an old farm boy like me. I had taken care of a local rich guy's landscaping when I was in high school during his two month summer vacations, so I knew what it entailed.

I immediately got a $500 loan from my mom for some equipment and flyers, and then proceeded to go door to door handing them out in Newport Beach and Costa Mesa. The very first house I went to, the old lady next to our apartments hired me, then another, and another, and another. I must have dazzled them with my natural charm - just kidding. The biggest reason many hired me was their gardeners were Mexicans that were usually hired by white owners and they refused to speak English. They couldn't get them to do anything they wanted them to. They all used those two famous words every Mexican uses no matter how much English they know when they don't want to do something – No Comprenday! Before long word got out there was actually an American landscaper who didn't send out a crew of Mexicans to do the work, and I picked up enough of their customers to run a business.

Go figure! I couldn't get a cooks job despite my experience and working in a highly regarded restaurant because I was an American, then got to own my own business because I wasn't Mexican.

Other Major Problems

There's the out of control and very expensive social problems, both from an economic standpoint and a social one. In areas of large immigration, real estate values plummet and communities are drug ravaged, crime infested places with high unemployment and squalor living conditions. Police estimate 99 percent of home invasions are drug related.

In a few short decades we allowed 3 out of 4 illegal aliens (90% from Mexico) to avoid the hopelessly thin border patrol agents along the nearly two thousand mile border. This inundated our country with approximately 100 million illegal aliens, including their kids. Out west, Mexicans, who still despise us, true to their claims, took back their former boarder states of California, Arizona, New Mexico, and Texas: Florida soon followed as the next victim of the Spanish occupation. "Sanctuary cities" like Boston are now swamped with the largest population of Brazilians outside of Brazil, due to being in one of the friendliest welfare states in the country and the Spanish Catholics belief of unlimited procreation. The Haitian population is exploding, and Boston, Springfield, Worchester, Holyoke, and surrounding communities have been taken over and flooded with some of the largest populations of Puerto Ricans outside Puerto Rico and New York City in the Northeast.

I know the Catholics and other religions that don't believe in birth control will be screaming from every orifice of the world, but religion played a huge part in our demise for a number of reasons. First, Muslim's and Hindu's are steadfast in living their traditional lives one generation after another based on their religions and have no intention of ever assimilating, therefore causing public dissent, alienation, and questionable loyalty to America. Second, the Catholic belief of being cleansed of all their sins and then getting a free pass to heaven, allows them to commit murder and mayhem without any concern of being banished to Hell for eternity. Few people dare walk the streets of an average Mexican neighborhood at night, and NEVER in thousands of ghastly ones with waring gangs in control!

Drugs became a paralyzing problem when drug gangs popped up everywhere, particularly in major cities. They now control thousands of neighborhoods throughout the country with their ruthless beatings and murders. It seems more innocent bystanders get killed in the cross-fire or are shot by mistaken identity than the gang members themselves. Mexican drug cartels and gangs such as the Bloods and Crypts took over Californian communities and others throughout the west. And like Mexico and other drug producing countries, nearly all murders and violence is drug related. Many city cops don't even bother trying to stop them after they get out of control. The country is being held hostage right in their own neighborhoods, with cartels and dealers getting enriched off their polarizing, addictive products while the rest of the country falls into ruin.

Mexicans don't have a monopoly on terrorizing neighborhoods though. Washington Heights in New York City is a good example of a good city gone bad from new-age immigrants. Hundreds of thousands of Dominicans moved there in a short period of time, and the city went from a decent place to live to a hell hole. What used to be a nice German neighborhood was turned into another one of those crime ridden drugged-out communities.

The Dominicans took over in every way. Some are good citizens, owning their own little shops and stores, but they never assimilated into America as did past generations of immigrants before them, especially Europeans. As did my step-grandparents from Germany and Poland, the Germans of Washington Heights taught themselves English when they arrived here after World War I. It wasn't easy, yet they made it on their own without anyone's help. Like many recent immigrants, the Dominicans don't even try to learn our language. This, along with their passion for crime, makes them easy targets for the rest of us to despise them, and eventually, that often turns to hatred and prejudice for many people.

Every city from Boston to Los Angeles experiences similar problems. In Long Beach, Ca, its Cambodian gangs holding their neighborhoods hostage. And as far back as the 1970's, Mexicans told us they were going to take back everything they lost in the Spanish American War and the 1848 Treaty of Hidalgo. However, this would be a bloodless revolution done by flooding into the Border States. What little border patrol we had was a joke to them, and they knew if they were caught crossing the border they would be deported for a few hours and come right back the same night. Most of these people were uneducated and lived like rats in squalor conditions that never had any intention of learning English or assimilating. Instead, demanding we learn Spanish and conform to their way of life.

A typical example of their ominous lifestyle would be an experience my neighbors and I had with some tenants in California that typified their way of life. For years we never had any cockroaches in our small apartment complex until some illegals moved in and left food scattered all over their house. Their walls, ceiling, and every orifice were covered with the hideous little varmints. Once there, they exploded in numbers and went looking for food in all the other apartments until it became an epidemic.

I was told by the painter (who coincidentally was a legal Korean immigrant himself) that he hated doing apartments after Mexican's lived there. He said they always trashed them and left them covered with cockroaches. Some actually fell on him as we spoke while he tried painting under the kitchen cabinets and he jumped up cussing at them faster than the speed of sound! Rumor had it they ate them so they purposely lived that way to attract them. Some countries consider bugs a delicacy - perhaps they do too.

This lifestyle baffled me. The only Mexicans I knew were from work and the girls from Mexico City who used to come up for a month every year on vacation. I didn't realize the tremendous difference between the educated ones, who usually stay in Mexico, and many in our country. The girls refused to even talk to the ones I knew or any of the uneducated ones. They called them "bad people," but I ignored them because some of them were my friends. As it turns out, they knew their own people better than I. For example, they constantly kicked in our fence boards to get to their friends apartment instead of walking around the block, and then said oops, sorry, accident. And I had to paint my equipment polka dot pink to work in Mexican neighborhoods because they were stealing it. Eventually I quit working in Santa Ana.

As are most people, I was fooled about their plight. Like the bleeding hearts media always projects, I saw many Mexicans gathered in the park looking desperate and as if they were in need of a job and wanting to work. I felt sorry for them and tried giving many of them a steady job 50% above minimum wage. After taking Spanish classes and associating with colleagues and the girls, I figured I knew enough Mexican Spanish to communicate with them, and they could use the opportunity to learn English - a real win-win for all.

Me being a soft hearted guy, I tried hiring them. But I quickly found out literally none of them wanted to work more than one or two days a week. I even tried picking them up at their house each day and they still didn't want to work! They liked living like cockroaches with six to twelve people in an apartment and only worked a day or two a week to earn enough money to help out with the food and rent, but mostly for drugs and alcohol. It turns out they didn't gather in the park to get full time work, they liked their meager, lazy lifestyle. They gathered in the park to cover up the drug deals being conducted right under our noses and got a cut!

They huddled in the middle of the park so people, and especially the police, wouldn't see the dealers exchanging drugs and money. You should have seen how nervous they got when police cruisers passed by. That's when hordes of them would literally run up to your truck and jump in, then say... "let's go man!" It was like a miracle! All of a sudden they spoke English and wanted to work too! Dios Mios! One guy even fought off the masses and jumped into my truck, then came down the street with me looking all fired up and ready to change his life. After about one minute he figured the police were gone and said he didn't want to work and wanted to go right back to the park. He even wanted me to drive him there! Do you know what I said? Sorry, no comprenday amigo!

Believe me! I never tried helping them again and gave up any further attempts to expand my business beyond a one man show.

I learned very quickly this country was being separated by cultural, ethnic, and religious differences, and they weren't about to assimilate like past immigrants. All immigrants now have their own newspapers, TV shows, magazines, and holidays. America made sure there was no need for them to assimilate, and it cost both us trillions paying for their medical bills, feeding and educating them, and providing housing. And we spend large sums of money on hundreds of other smaller things, such as publishing information brochures in many languages and paying for security at their parades. We're so accommodating and have so little border patrol, kids' form countries in the heart of Central America are passing through Mexico without their parents and sneaking into our country, where they meet up with family or friends. New Mexico even gives kids visas and busses them to their schools.

The illegals can have their kids here and don't have to worry about medical bills or getting a doctor. Federal law makes it illegal for hospitals to turn away patients, whether or not they're illegal aliens or can't pay the bill. This makes the U.S. heaven on earth for them. Not only can they receive free food, medical care, and give birth here, but when born here they are automatically citizens as everyone around the world now knows.

While we're on the subject of medical care, immigrants are notorious for carrying certain diseases and starting epidemics here. When I lived in California, a school nurse told me many Mexican kids come here with the Tuberculosis (TB) virus and spread it throughout the community. This problem was later verified by the state, which set the overall figure at 50%. And most recently we've had a measles resurgence, along with the deadly flesh eating Ebola virus from Africa, to name just a few of the diseases immigrants, especially the illegal ones, bring with them.

According to Republicans - who seem to have contacted some sort of amnesia and are using them as political propaganda toys - those that are being caught are staying at government facilities and adding to our burden. Of course they're right, but after Reagan's amnesty and the two Bushes added 100 million of them, they know we'll do it again so their numbers have exploded.

Religious groups are as fooled as everybody else about their plight and set up daytime kitchens for these so-called "poor innocent people" unable to get a job. In the 1980's, Costa Mesa was on the list of sanctuary cities for illegals to go when they crossed the border because they had free food and cloths. They could stay with friends or family indefinitely so neighborhoods were overrun with them. Property values plummeted, and people wanting out couldn't sell with their underwater mortgages. Now, there are riots over Donald Trump's wall.

In other states like Massachusetts, they actually pay for homeless immigrants to live in motels. This, they reason, in combination with other state aid, keeps them off the streets and gives them a path to a better life.

Ethnic religious organizations from different countries such as India, and even our own Jewish community also get preferential treatment. These special organizations bring in people with stipulations that will help them get a job and become good citizens. It's a much more desirable way from the government's perspective and it helps their image amongst our own citizens.

Other immigrant groups, the Chinese in particular, actually started their own industry by bringing in pregnant mothers on travel visas to have their babies in often small, run down former motels with one or two midwife type personnel to take care of 10 or 12 kids and their mom's. It's like a highly profitable underground railroad that puts tens of thousands of babies, and often their parents, into our welfare system.

We also have social differences amongst themselves different ethnic and religious groups bring. Throughout history religious squabbles have caused nearly 90% of all wars, and if they're killing each other in their own countries, why would they get along any better here? This holds particularly true for Middle Eastern and Islamic groups. After centuries of hating each other, a hard core Shite will never get along with a hard core Sunni and neither one will ever get along with a Jew. After all, isn't this why many of their countries were destroyed and they were forced to come here?

The Japanese added to our environmental problems no amount of money will ever undue when a Silver Carp fishery spilled thousands into a waterway that ran into the great Mississippi River. The massive fish, weighing up to 40 pounds, have completely decimated all other species in it and its tributaries, and are expected to wipe out all native fish of the Great Lakes in the near future. Not only that, but they are such a dangerous fish nobody can safely fish them because of their nonstop 30 foot jumps out of the water that cause dangerous collisions with fisherman from all angels. They are turning every waterway in the central U.S. into a "no humans allowed zone."

Regrettably, most of the illegal - and many legal immigrants - are not good citizens, leaving a dragnet of despair for a very high percentage of places. We are not being picky enough about who is allowed in; as long as it's cheap labor we let them in. And in the long run that attitude cost society immeasurably!

The Great Illusion

As we discussed earlier, politicians want as many immigrants as possible for a number of reasons. More people means we need more houses and apartments to live in, thus stimulating the housing industry - which accounts for about 80% of our economy. Every worker, from miners' digging iron ore for steel used in construction and other businesses to those making finished products like furniture, electronics, appliances, and linens will have jobs and money to spend on everything that makes a house a home. More people, more grocery and home improvement stores, shopping malls, restaurants, and infrastructure projects. With millions getting jobs working in and building them, including the immigrants themselves, it should cause that trickle-down effect – Right?

Wrong! It's for fat corporate profits, CEO bonuses, and self-serving lawmakers. When they aren't offshoring work to foreign lands, they give them H-1B guest visas and make us train our own **lower paid** replacements for such highly skilled positions as engineer and computer programmer. Many other jobs are temporary and low paying service jobs. We're just collateral damage to them, disposable machines.

Unfortunately, mass immigration is only a temporary economic boom and not the slow natural expansion necessary for sustained growth over many decades. Starting in the 1980's, everyone became too greedy, bureaucrats want to win elections, and a good steady natural growth is no longer tolerated. Policy makers want the economy to be ratcheted up to unsustainable levels forever and unlimited immigration is their way to achieve that goal. In reality, many that do work drain government coffers by claiming tax exempt and often work under-the-table (jobs paid in cash to avoid taxation). Since most unskilled labor jobs - construction, landscaping, and some large corporate jobs pay this way, very few pay any taxes. Therefore, not contributing to coffers as the dreamers in Washington think they do.

Out of control welfare is another social burden. Hospital emergency rooms are seriously overcrowded with nonpaying or government paid patients, especially pregnant ones, and food stamp use is through the roof to feed these new unemployed masses. They're often unemployed and penniless in their own countries, so coming here and getting everything for free is as though they died and went to heaven, especially many of those that landed in decent neighborhoods. Why should they assimilate if they don't have to?

And how about the free education we give these people? Once again, the laws are quite clear about educating their kids here. Like medical care, the cost to educate them is staggering and cumbersome. The Republicans point this out as our biggest deficit producing problem with illegals, with Reagan actually promising to abolish the Department of Education in his campaign speeches. Isn't it ironic they court them and then complain about the money they cost us? But don't get me wrong, the Democrats know how to ring-up the cash register too with such things as the vastly lower instate tuition rates if they go to public college.

Here, we have very few non English speaking immigrants. Those we do have, we must provide special teachers for and it's very costly. They're called English as a second language learner (ESL) student. I can't imagine how costly it would be for a city with hordes of students coming from homes with parents, friends, and relatives living there that don't care if they ever learn English and don't teach them before reaching kindergarten. The time lost teaching them English is nothing compared to the time other teachers and students lose while trying to teach them other subjects. It's so overwhelming in some cities, the kids only learn for half the class in English and the other half in Spanish, essentially learning only half as much as they normally would.

The downside of economist theories on immigration and economics is always the same. They never acknowledge the taxes not paid that are supposed to pay for all the overlooked social services. Things like schools, roads, water, and sewer systems that drain far more from government coffers than they bring in - even bankrupting school districts in California - and hospitals shutting down emergency rooms in the 1990's from millions using them. They never tell you about the environmental aspects of uncontrolled immigration, from natural resources used to trash disposal. Have you ever heard an economist proclaim if you bring in more immigrants, you will consume all your resources in direct proportion to the number of immigrants you bring in and run out of them that much faster in the long run?

Do they tell us we'll drain our aquifers, lakes, and rivers of fresh drinking water or that for irrigation and food? Or about polluting our air, water, and land for perhaps hundreds of years? Do they tell you about the algae blooms in your lakes, rivers, and bays from the extra fertilizer used, or the extra chicken and cow feces runoff kills many species as in the Chesapeake Bay disaster. Or what caused the devastating dust bowl, and the Oligalla aquifer used to irrigate those states is running dry?

It's reckless over immigration and those five hideous attributes we live by that causes all these problems! In fact, many deserts throughout the world started out as tropical forest or prairie lands before man arrived. The over consumption that came with immigration turned them into deserts... just like our dust bowl years.

Non-the-less, our government courts them with special low interest business loans and EB-5 visas where well-to-do ones can buy their way into the U.S. through sociopath businessman. If a prospective immigrant invests in a business that creates jobs (Donald Trump charges 500,000 dollars from mostly rich Chinese) or has at least one million dollars and starts a business that hires at least ten people, they get a free pass to citizenship.

Is There a Difference in Immigrants?

Definitely! Particularly the ones from Europe, India, Japan, China, and South Korea. Most of the ones from Southeast Asia assimilate much better than the Spanish or Muslims. They are not only shop owners, but are more likely to get a college degree (often a bachelor degree or higher) and become scientist, doctors, or other professionals that pay their fair share of taxes. They are much more education minded than the drug dealing Spanish and black gangs from Latin American countries.

Thinking back, I would say the oversized Wall Street banks in partnership with the feds was the main reason the illegal immigration boomed out of control starting in the 1980's. That's when they started making it easy for Mexicans by having special check cashing lines where they could cash their paycheck without an account. As I recall, they charged a small fee somewhere around $1.50 for the service and around $5 for bank checks or money orders, which allowed them to send all that money to relatives back in Mexico. It was a good deal for both the banks and immigrants - and still is.

A few extra bucks here and there might not seem like a lot, but I know from running my small business, the smallest customers can be your biggest asset if you have enough of them. For the banks, these small fees from millions of aliens were a gold mine for the first ones who established loyal customers. Like clockwork, they came every week to cash their checks and buy money orders.

Eventually, like European countries that have started rebelling against their own immigrants, many people didn't want any more here as they assimilated less and less, plus we now have the Muslim terrorist threat. Like European countries, every time the people scream for border control, the politicians play their games and attach other pork barrel legislation to it. Once again, as with the stock market, nothing gets done so some states start taking border security into their own hands.

With no hope of ever getting help after decades of asking the feds to secure the borders, they put their own laws into effect. California's Governor Wilson sued them in 1994 and then passed proposition 187 outlawing aid to illegals, and Arizona passed their own version a couple years ago. Not surprisingly, the Supreme Court stepped in and continued their destructive ways in our totally dysfunctional system with their politically motivated opinion and ruled against them. They claimed Congress is the only one who can make and enforce immigration laws.

Blacks Legal Dictionary should list Reagan's amnesty as the beginning of the United States of America becoming a Spanish colony. The occupation started on his watch, now they expect us to learn their language and let them run-amuck instead of them assimilating to us. That's when all the Spanish demands started, and Wall Street and our government couldn't have been happier to oblige. That's when Mexicans and now Guatemala, Honduras and El Salvador, started pouring over the border in basically an unobstructed illegal mass immigration that persisted for the next four decades. That's when we lost our identity as a nation!

A border patrol agent in San Diego told me in the late 1980's, there was three million Latinos (90% Mexican) a year coming across the border, with 2 million getting through and blending into society after that first amnesty. That opened the floodgates throughout the country and especially in the southwest. With no fear of being permanently deported, very little border control, free food, medical, and housing; and an invitation to stay directly from the president of the United States himself - there was no reason NOT to come. And that's why we have Donald Trump's three ring circus in town now!

A second mass amnesty is at hand after George W. gave them more reason to stay after failing to control the borders in his eight years of office. But it looks like something might be done along the Mexican border. As are other countries, we have built nearly 700 miles of wall in the most abusive places and it has slowed the flow. However, I'm confident the new GOP Congress will keep their slaves coming in. despite Trump's delusional sociopathic rants and promises. I'm counting on those stubborn right-wingers to derail reform with another 1930's style repatriation under FDR, and Eisenhower's 1954 "Operation Wetback," when millions were deported, and we will continue our slide into Spanish colonialism. After all – we never learn!

8

Environment Versus Energy Hogs

Newsflash: January 28, 1969, a massive 3 million gallon oil spill off the coast of Santa Barbara, California, covers 800 square miles of the Pacific Ocean with the thick crude - suffocating dolphins, seals, and everything in its path.

That spill led to the establishment of Earth Day through the efforts of U.S. Senator Gaylord Nelson and conservative co-chairman Republican Paul (Pete) McCloskey, who led the environmental movement in Congress and the country into a 20 million person protest of our polluted country. Sen. Nelson's environmental stance eventually ended with President Clinton giving him the highest honor a civilian can get – the Medal of Freedom.

Our former bipartisan Congress and the extremely wealthy titans of industry were united in doing something to protect our planet and joined the rest of us on that first earth day April 22, 1970. In an interview with NBC's legendary newsman Hugh Downs, McCloskey said: "Well I can only speak for the industrialist and congressmen that I have seen, and in the last two years, I've seen all resistance evaporate. There's no one in Congress today that will say I'm against the environment." He claimed politicians knew if they weren't on board, the young people would vote against them - an environmental revolution seemed inevitable.

Republican Richard Nixon was in the White House and pollution was a severe health threat nationwide. Power plants were spewing out enormous amounts of carcinogens and toxins like heavy metals into our air and water, while farms poisoned our wells, aquifers, and waterways with pesticides like DDT and atrazine. Many streams, rivers, lakes, and everything in them was dead or dying and the fish too poisonous to eat. Lake Erie was declared a dead zone, its fish belly up, dying by the millions and stinking up entire towns for miles. The Salton Sea in California's Imperial Valley went from a vacation playground for the stars, to a putrid salt-marsh deprived of life sustaining oxygen. Even those living hundreds of miles away from power plants, farms, or industrial factories were inundated with acid rain, water pollution, and dead fish. Every creature in the U.S. was being poisoned from the top of the food chain to the bottom for more than a century.

The Love Canal is perhaps the most famous polluted sight. It all started when a chemical company had left tens of thousands of barrels of toxic chemicals in the ground in a neighborhood near Niagara Falls and a developer decided to build a subdivision over the sight. This was not unusual back then, and in fact was the normal way of covering up a toxic sight and repurposing it for little or nothing. Though the cheapest way to build low income housing, it came at a horrific price to those who bought homes in these developments. The Love Canal, like all the others, was a death trap that was so contaminated the chemicals leached up through the cellar floors, yards, streets, and streams, causing obscene amounts of gruesome birth defects. Over 50% of the kids had them (including extra body parts).

The entire neighborhood protested vehemently all the way to the Jimmy Carter White House until they got him to send an EPA administrator to investigate. Once there, they locked him inside one of the contaminated houses until he gave them permission to be relocated and put it on the fed's tab.

Jimmy must have learned something that day, because he's been championing the rights of the poor and their battle of being duped into, or unfortunate enough, to be living near Superfund sites and polluted areas around the globe.

Congress was less corrupt back then and had learned from history. They knew back in the 1880's, the San Francisco Harbor was almost destroyed when settlers and the timber industry clear-cut every oak tree in Oakland they could find. Giant sequoias (redwoods) up to 30 feet in diameter and more than 1000 years old were almost logged into extinction, and strip mining along with hydraulic fracking was used for the first time. Fracking the Sierra Nevada Mountains caused so much silt and heavy metal poisoning throughout rivers and bays in the area Congress ordered it stopped!

With industrial capitalist obliterating our beautiful country since its inception, President Harrison and future President Theodore Roosevelt, realized there was only one way to save our country. In 1891, they worked to establish what would become the National Forest Service (NFS) through the Forest Reserve Act of 1891. Then as president in 1905, Roosevelt finished the job and officially established the Forest

Service, which became the NFS two years later. He then added the National Parks, Sanctuaries, and Monuments to his accomplishments. Roosevelt's good friend and fellow Republican, President William H. Taft, followed that up by expanding federal protection of the countries indescribable beauty by authorizing funds to purchase lands on watersheds of navigable streams.

After nearly 100 years of thwarting industry and stopping them from taking everything back or completely demolishing the environment, you would think the country had learned from its mistakes and was ready to clean up the environment, reduce, reuse, and recycle with the world's leading environmental technologies of the time. And indeed Nixon joined Nelson, McCloskey and congress by expanding previous legislation by enacting the National Environmental Policy Act on January 1, 1970, then the Clean Air Act and Environmental Protection Agency (EPA) later that year. They followed those with the Clean Water Act and Noise Control Act of 72 and the Safe Drinking Water and Endangered Species Acts of 73. Democratic president and peanut farmer Jimmy Carter continued the bipartisanship by declaring the Love Canal an environmental disaster too dangerous to live in, and then putt solar panels on the White House in a hail of media coverage.

When Reagan, a former Rock River lifeguard, liberal left democrat, ranch owner, horse lover, governor of the environmental leading state of California, and recreational environmentalist at heart was elected, further progress looked like a sure thing. But as the old saying goes – "Looks can be deceiving."

After corporate behemoth G.E. hired him as their spokesperson, not surprisingly, the liberal democrat did an about face and went to war against the people and the planet while leading the anti-environmental, pro big business GOP you see to this day. Eventually, he took down those dreaded solar panels that were a shining beacon of light for the environmental movement, blinding the people with the truth about green technology and jobs - the leading enemies to their oil and mining operations.

During the 1970's Capitol Hill was more the model of bipartisanship and democracy our founding fathers had envisioned: one that worked to promote a great and prosperous nation for all its citizens, not just the privileged few. But under Reagan, we gave away our environmental technology and the movement slowed to a crawl, even though, like

Nixon, he started out with a promising bang by enacting the Comprehensive Environmental Response Compensation and Liability Act (CERCLA), commonly known as the "Superfund" his first year in office before his corporate alter ego fully kicked in.

Ever since then, Congress has been bought and hog-tied. Oversized mining interest, especially in states loaded with natural resources, started throwing their weight around Capitol Hill, and the revamped GOP killed as much environmental legislation as possible while pushing over consumption. Through ALEC, they now have gotten half the states to push through anti-solar legislation that either limits, fines, or taxes it.

Mining companies weren't satisfied with the record profits from our own absurd consumption; they had to export it too. Without conscience, they claimed then, as they do to this day, it's the best way to ratchet up the struggling economy at any cost to the people's health, environment, and the world - despite the solar industry alone now employing more people than oil, gas, and coal combined. The personal wealth for many Americans expanded as the computer age dawned, and we selfishly became accustomed to frivolously wasting cheap energy. Self-indulgence and borrowing drove the economy like a bobsled on a fast track and many went along for the ride.

We gobbled up this new way of life like it was our divine right to consume everything on the planet and the heck with the rest of the world! We consumed between 20 and 25% of the entire world's energy and goods for the last hundred years but ramped it up to unprecedented and unsustainable levels for the last two generations. As a result, we're still paying cleanup cost from companies abandoning their polluted sites. Logging companies are still drooling over those thousand year old redwoods and beating politicians over the head with money until they get their chainsaws into them. And everything else environmentally and economically correct is being shredded by every Republican in Congress who continues to ignore their own history as far back as Lincoln.

Men have to have their big boy toys - $15,000 Harley Davidson motorcycles, boats, snowmobiles, and ATV's to go with their oversized trucks, SUV's, and Humvees equipped with the largest most powerful engines available. Ordinary passenger cars such as the Chevy Corvette, with its gas guzzling V8 engine that puts out both 450 horsepower and torque, pales in comparison to the 2018 Dodge Demon with its 6.2 liter V8, 840 horsepower and 770 pounds of torque. That's insane folks!

About 20 years ago before gas mileage was a factor, the most powerful truck engine available was the Dodge 10 cylinder at 300 horses and 440 pounds of torque, and that was designed for towing horse trailers and heavy travel trailers. I know because I had them. What on earth good are these cars with such immense amounts of horsepower and torque? None! There is no legitimate function to these gas hogs, just another earth devastating toy for their spoiled, self-centered, owners who could have donated that money to charities instead.

Even big boy toy automobile racings NASCAR gets in on the act, going through 10,000 gallons of racing fuel for their 500 mile races that last for hours and using one barrel of oil for every one of their hundreds of tires used for every race.

I have to admit, when I was a kid growing up on the farm racing around the corn field I wanted to be a race car driver, even writing to Richard Petty and Dusty Baker for advice. I also loved the top fuel races that lasted just a few seconds and used to go to the Winter Nationals in Pomona, California. Personally, I think they're much more exciting than NASCAR. While millions of people still love it, and it's a very relaxing way to kill a weekend, as I got older and my priorities changed, watching race cars burn enormous amounts of fuel going around a track for hours on end while everyone got drunk struck a nerve.

I don't know which are worse, men or woman. Women have to have dozens of pairs of shoes they seldom if ever ware, to match there dozens of outfits they seldom if ever ware. Then slaughter miners and animals so they can wear jewelry, perfumes, and makeup to complete their ensemble. And their cars have to be the most fashionable one of the year. As far back as the 1930's, the auto industry said they had to give people a good reason to get rid of their perfectly good 3 or 4 year old cars for brand new ones, so they decided to sell people on the latest styles and amenities. By the 21st century both men and woman had to have them equipped with the latest, most expensive, distracting, deadly, technology available to keep up with the fashion police. I've seen people whose brand new vehicles that are nearly as expensive as their tiny dilapidated homes - but it looks good in the driveway!

Overall, houses have doubled in size, with air conditioners and heating systems keeping the utility companies burning fossil fuels and nuclear power at record levels. According to the home remodeling and fashion industries, they have to be remodeled every 5 or 10 years to keep up with the latest designs. So we became a wasteful, disposable society of perfectly good products in the name of fashion and keeping up appearances. Giant home remodeling centers sprung to life from this new $275 billion annual home improvement industry. Home Depot moved to a neighborhood near you, closely followed by Loews.

Perfectly fine kitchens, bathrooms, and everything else have to be thrown out and remodeled with the latest high tech gadgets in the latest styles they make up to push their products. Even your pillows and bath towels have to be right or you'll get kicked out of the snob club. They're sometimes remodeled with still older things people get at used home furnishings stores that popped up from the latest trend and overflowing landfills. Often called building recycling centers, they are a good environmental choice for the echo conscious. But old is new, and many customers are just buying things to be trendy and throw away their perfectly good interiors.

With a great big push from the government and its partner in crime, the banking industry, the staple of our economy - the housing market, burst at the seams by the 21st century. President Hoover's old saying of having "a chicken in every pot and a car in every garage" had been up-sized significantly to having a house for every renter with expensive furnishings and two shiny new cars in every garage to match. And we all know how well that worked out after the disastrous 2008-09 financial collapse.

Let us explore some of the destructive things we gluttons of the world have to do to power our energy wasting ways and other ecological calamity in the name of having the highest living standards, largest houses, most frivolous and wasteful country the world has ever seen. All piggybacking on our...

Antiquated Systems - As our power grid becomes older, more blackouts will come from our antiquated delivery system. Like everything connected to Wall Street and politicians, the grid is just another toy for the rich, powerful buffoons and record profits are more important than infrastructure. They thwart renewable energy that requires no distribution system (think home wind and solar systems). And along with America's usual short term thinking and political gridlock, it will be our downfall when the power grid, roads, bridges, railways, and airports fall into disrepair beyond help. While the greedy, selfish moguls wrestle for power and profits, the rest of us are left with a clock set back to the 1960's, with them dumping "70% of their industrial waste and 1.2 trillion gallons of untreated sewage" into our waterways annually. Now nearly half of all waterways are once again "polluted to unsafe conditions," sickening and killing us, with "an estimated 60% of U.S. waters and tens of millions of acres of wetlands losing federal protection in just the last few years."

We should have gotten a hint way back in 1925, when Chicago became the world's leader in electrical consumption and Thomas Edison warned us about our gluttonous use of fossil fuels that we would soon lead the world in energy usage. The United States now has 450,000 miles of aging high powered electric lines strung across the land. We have to have thousands of electrical technicians and helicopter pilots risking their lives every day to keep the power flowing above ground, and an army of miners, oil, and gas workers to keep it flowing from environmentally devastating sources underground.

Above ground, some of these poor guys actually go up in helicopters to inspect the power lines, flying within just a few feet. Extremely skilled pilots with nerves of steel are accompanied by a technician sitting on a bench-like seat outside the chopper. Working together like clockwork, the chopper pilot flies along and between the rows of power lines as the technician looks for damaged lines or those dangerously close to trees. If even one part of the chopper touches a line, they'll both be electrocuted with the 230,000 volts of electricity and a certain nasty death. As a pilot, I can assure you, it's probably the most difficult job a pilot could have.

If the technician misses just one frayed wire or potentially hazardous tree limb, disaster could strike in the blink of an eye. That disaster came on 8-14-09 when a power line sagged and came into contact with a tree in Ohio. Many of you will recall it caused transmission lines throughout the area to shut down, and in turn overloaded the other lines in the nearby grid, causing them to go offline like dominos. The chain reaction shut down power from the Midwest to New York City, leaving us without power during a hot summer week. All infrastructures shut down - hospitals, emergency shelters, gas stations, and transportation centers, including airports, bus depots, and subways... along with communications, factories, and Wall Street. Everyone had to rely on backup generators for days and sweat it out, all because of one tree under the powerline that wasn't trimmed back.

Fossil Fuels - We'll start our environmental train wreck with a look at the non-sustainable use of fossil fuels and nuclear fuel we must mine, transport, and use to maintain our position as the most gluttonous energy hogs the world has ever known.

Coal - One of the best ways to satisfy our greed is coal. About 100 years ago it supplied a majority of our power and everything from steel mills to homes relied on it. The problem is it's an environmental disaster of epic proportions. And at 10 times the pollution of the second worst polluter (oil), it's the world's greatest day in and day out air and water polluter. With its famous coal miner's lung from underground mines to the newer mountaintop removal operations and sludge lakes, nothing has, and still does, poison, kill, and cripple more humans and other living creatures than this ancient plague.

The toxins from processing this cheap energy source are hard to dispose of. If you're lucky, you live upwind from smoke and the toxic coal ash is mixed with water and buried in pits lined with heavy gauge plastic that become giant lakes when filled with the sludge. If you're not, you live downwind, they don't line pits at all and it seeps into ground water and aquifers you drink from and streams, rivers, and lakes you swim and fish in. With decades of having insiders running the EPA, it hasn't gotten around to regulating where and how to safely dispose of this stuff that could fill a train from the North Pole to the South Pole every year. So big coal does whatever they please.

It's so poisonous, humans handling the ash and sludge have to wear "hazardous waste suits," complete with respirators to protect themselves from any of it touching them or inhaling it. When the Kingston, Tennessee plant had 5.4 million cubic yards burst through a dike in 2008, 300 acres of riverfront property was buried with sludge full of arsenic, mercury, chromium, lead, and selenium. More coal ash spilled than oil did at the Deep Water horizon catastrophe, and it contaminated homes and streams so badly it still isn't cleaned up! Like nuclear fuel waist, there is no safe way to dispose of it and nobody wants it within 500 miles of them. So coal plants decided to ship it to a landfill in Alabama that contains municipal, industrial, and the most poisonous "special waist" from 16 states. Believe me! You don't want to know what's in that stuff! I just know I'm not going there any time in my lifetime.

Black Thunder! – The king of sludge. This colossal coal mine in Wyoming, along with about 15 other mining companies along the Powder River Basin that stretches up into Montana, is the largest in the world. Owned by Arch coal, Black Thunder opened in 1977 and is still the largest producer of coal thanks to their buyouts and mergers with local competitors. At the heart of its behemoth mining operation is a fleet of Liebher and Komatsu haul trucks standing over 20 feet tall and weighing in at around 200 tons and over half a million loaded. Filled by enormous back hoe like buckets called draglines weighing up to 6,700 tons, and buckets capable of lifting 70 cubic meters of coal, these goliaths are filled in just 3 scoops and could heat the average home for over 40 years. Then they haul the coal to the dump and crusher station nonstop with swift efficiency and into the trains it goes by way of a monstrous state of the art filling station.

Anybody who has been to the area will never forget the trains up to 1.5 miles long. I was spellbound when I first saw them. Filled with coal that is often hauled to power producing facilities thousands of miles away, they stretched as far as the eye could see across the landscape. Just the mind-boggling train loading facilities at Black Thunder alone can load up to "25 trainloads a day without trains ever stopping," filling each car in seconds.

Coal at black thunder and the Powder River Basin are lower in sulfur then most coals, which allows companies to claim it's environmentally friendly. What they won't tell you is most western fossil fuel mines are under federally owned property the feds lease to them. This makes us the owners of the vast amounts of coal that is reportedly being sold to them under the federal leasing program for about $1 a ton and then shipped to Asia for about $100 a ton: Talk about the fleecing of America! The leasing program is sold to the public as an economic job bonanza. Still, logic dictates we the people are allowing them to go in and blow up and under every mountain, valley, and prairie to release these toxic chemicals and extract these substances so mining can maintain their outrageous profits. Unfortunately, with 100 years' worth of cheap coal left in just this one area, there's no incentive for them or their crony politicians to switch to true environmentally friendly sources of fuel.

In the western mountains of the Appalachia's, they have to go underground in many areas to get to the coal. For more than a century they've mined the stuff in dangerous methane gas filled mines deep underground, where periodic explosions rock the mountains. More often than not, the lucky miners are instantly killed, and the unlucky ones either die a slow torturous death buried in their mountain graves or escape to go back in again.

There's been a few such explosions in recent years hear in the U.S., with one company making most of the headlines - Massey Energy. They own mines in Sago and Montcoal, West Virginia, that exploded from improper venting of methane gas. Massey had been fined $380,000 for "450 safety violations" earlier that year and was responsible for 12 deaths. After the 2009 tragedy in Sago, a rules committee was established and they recommended equipment tracking, among other things, that only 8% of the mines instituted. It was soon tested, when again in 2010 an explosion at the Montcoal mine killed another 29 miners for the same reason, but this time Massey was fined a whopping $210 million. Although Massey did have tracking and survival containers installed, the miners never got to them.

Sometimes an environmentally friendly politician like Mayor Antonio Villaraigosa will get into a position of power. In this case it was mega energy hog Los Angeles, home to every form of over consumption you can imagine. At first glance, the city looked like a hero to environmentalist when they announced they were going to get completely off the super-polluter two years earlier than the state mandated 2027 deadline. The mayor had hoped to get off it by 2020, but a long term contract with Utah's Intermountain Power (which they owned 21% of) was a major obstacle. Sadly, the real reason they were trying to sell their share of the power plant was it would have cost the city much more with the future proposed EPA requirements then selling it. With a new plant costing 11 billion big ones, it was simply a matter of economics - not environmentalism.

Mountaintop Removal - Mountaintop removal is as repulsive a polluter as underground coal and probably worse. It poisons everything both above and below ground to such an extent whole towns in its way have to be abandoned, leaving modern day ghost towns in its wake. Conned, desperate individuals and towns have turned over their land, and by association, everyone else's for hundreds of miles to the destructive and powerful mining machine.

Another industry without conscience, it brings in its earth rattling explosives to blow up whole mountains, dig into them, and haul them away, causing deadly poisonous drinking water, streams, lakes, air, and land for hundreds of miles. Previously pristine waterways are so deadly from coal dust and sludge; fish are losing their eyeballs and dying a horrific mutant death. Now, both miners and innocent citizens alike are getting lung cancer from the toxic dust that covers their towns and suffer the same slow, excruciating deaths fish and wildlife do.

Poisoning the local water is just the beginning for big coal. Its processing facilities ensure they spread their obnoxious air to all states downwind from their plants. Coal burning plants in states like Kentucky and West Virginia have indiscriminately spread their deadly toxins across the entire northeastern United States for decades. Former air pollution free states are at the mercy of the wind with no way to protect their own people from the distant plants. Lung diseases such as asthma spring up everywhere, accompanied by acid rain that stunts and kills all vegetation.

When plants do try doing the right thing and be a good neighbor, the coal industry won't let them. When a Kentucky plant called Big Sandy, capable of burning 90 railroad cars a day, tried to convert their aging operation to the much cleaner gas, it pressured them into continuing it. It controls everyone to such an extent even the U.S. Army Corps of Engineers insist it has no responsibility to protect children's health.

Nuclear Power - Nuclear power is the most dangerous form of energy we brought to fruition in an attempt to satisfy our never ending thirst. It is the most expensive to build, bring online, decommission, and deconstruct of all energy sources, and is so dangerous, it needs its own set of safety regulations throughout the entire process. The Nuclear Regulatory Commission (NRC) requires a 10 mile radius be maintained for emergency procedures during decommissioning, with the total decommissioning of the Yankee Power Plant in Vermont estimated to cost over a billion dollars alone.

Nuclear energy starts out as a very clean energy, but in the end is far and above the world's most toxic. None-the-less, the government and enthusiastic pioneers were dead set on bringing this most dangerous form of power online. The first plant was built in 1957, and was billed as a clean, safe, and best of all "inexpensive" power source. About 100 more were built across the country after Nixon signed the 1970 Clean Air Act in an effort to curb air pollution from coal plants.

But the world got a major warning about what can happen downwind from a nuclear meltdown at the Three Mile Island power plant near Harrisburg, Pennsylvania, on March 28th 1979, when a cooling pump malfunction caused a partial meltdown in the #2 reactor. The world waited on pins and needles for the world's first nuclear disaster. It was the top news story in every corner of the globe. In every office, school, factory, and everywhere in between, the world listened to the unfolding scenario, waiting for a total meltdown. If you didn't know how a nuclear plant functioned before this - you did now.

People within 50 miles were scrambling to get away as emergency crews in nuclear hazard suits attempted to stop a radiation spill of epic proportions. The emergency response team was the only thing between a Hiroshima type radiation explosion and tens of millions of people downwind from the crippled plant. Fortunately, only a small amount of radioactive gas was released, but the near catastrophe put the nuclear program on the back burner for decades.

Environmentalist and scared citizens had warned us for years what a total meltdown would do, but Wall Street and its cronies smelled money in this Russian roulette form of energy. Even after the gargantuan 1986 Chernobyl meltdown in the former USSR and Fukushima, Japans, our greedy mining companies, and one from Canada - Energy Fuel Resources, pushed the US Forest Service (another agency of regulatory capture) into letting them mine the ever dangerous uranium on the south side of our Grand Canyon. Despite a uranium ban only a year earlier, they used the arcane Mining Law of 1872 that gives them priority over anything else on public lands to justify their actions.

We all know it's archaic and needs abolishing, so Interior Secretary Ken Salazar banned mining in the canyon, only to have the US Forest Service do an about face and put the water supply of 30 million people in our biggest cities out west - Los Angeles, Phoenix, and Las Vegas in danger of radioactive drinking water.

Every creature on the planet, including humans, already has radiation in their tissue due to leaks, meltdowns, and atomic bomb testing. As radiation rises in the atmosphere, winds carry it thousands of miles over land and oceans, settling and raining down on every square inch. Even though domed, Chernobyl could spread it for thousands of years and Fukushima is still out of control, despite heroic efforts to contain it.

Also, the waste product produced, although relatively small, is the most concentrated, toxic, dangerous pollutant known to mankind. There's nowhere to store it, or for that matter, any safe way to transport it to a storage facility. Even with the best technology and security available, you're still talking about a material that cannot be safely handled or released into the environment for 10,000 years.

So Congress spent tens of billions on a depository storage facility at Yucca Mountain, N.M., and then shut it down after decades of local resident and environmental protests. Other suitable sites close to plants have been closed down by the powerful politicians living near them. What's that tell us about the danger of nuclear waste? It's not coming to a terrified politician near you – SO MOVE NEXT TO ONE! Or roll the dice like every other sucker.

Oil - had been the cornerstone of the American story of rags to riches ever since its discovery, then transformed by Henry Ford for use by the common man. It gave us a jump on the rest of the world by allowing us to easily transport goods and services nationwide. We had a vast supply and before pollution reared its ugly head it seemed at first a gift from the heavens. As the effects became apparent in congested cities like New York, we were too stubborn to change our newfound way of life and big oil slowly but surely infiltrated our government. Never was it more apparent who was running who when Reagan ordered those solar panels torn down after President Carter's grand speech on leading the world in this new technology or fall behind. Big oil and coal has been in control since the Reagan years with president's and their crony cabinets - and disaster reined with each one.

March 24th 1989, a day that will live in infamy to environmentalist, fisherman, and animal lovers around the world. Exxon's supertanker Valdez had left the Alyeska Pipeline Terminal about three hours earlier on its way to Long Beach, California, when it ran aground in Prince William Sound, Alaska. Nearly 11 million gallons of North Slope crude gushed out of eight cargo tanks in its belly into the pristine Artic Sound and onto the equally pristine beaches and shoreline for 1200 miles.

It was a complete catastrophe in every possible way. Lured into complacency over their prior success's, the crew ignored company and federal policies, so when they ran aground Exxon had literally no cleanup crew or plan in place for such remote areas. Oil was absolutely everywhere in quantities even the 11,000 workers brought in could not contain, never mind clean up. They tried everything to trap and contain the heavy crude, but the spacious sound was not an easy place to do so. They scoured the beaches for months with everything you could imagine, from high-pressure hot water jets to paper towels. But Dawn liquid dishwashing detergent became the hero for droves of workers and volunteers cleaning the birds, seals, dolphins, turtles, sea otters, fish, and other marine creatures. If you didn't know Dawn could get rid of the grease on your dishes before the spill - you did now. I have to admit, the spill convinced my whole family to switch to Dawn.

Eventually, it's thought 100,000 birds and 1000 sea otters died and millions of crabs and shell fish were poisoned. The $100 million a year herring fishery business and salmon industry had to be cancelled, with no one knowing when it could safely resume, or what the long term environmental and fishing prognosis was.

The cleanup of the 1200 miles of bays and inlets seemed to do more harm than good in this harsh artic environment. After spending one billion dollars on the cleanup, Exxon seemed destined to be the poster child for doing everything wrong. The high pressure hot water washes killed most of the beach organisms. It would seem the violent Artic storms and rough seas were better at cleaning both the sea and the shoreline than anything they attempted. Once again Mother Nature was the best cure, as it had been in previous spills around the globe - but at what price?

With mining running the Department of Energy for decades without conscience and George W. with his oil, gas, and other favorite criminals in the White House leading the parade, who do you think won this battle - the environment or the capitalistic abusers in power?

By 2012, the Interior Department had allowed over 37,000 wells to be drilled in the Gulf of Mexico. Sooner or later they had to know something would go wrong again, and when it did, it was just about the worst possible case scenario you could have dreamed up.

Deep Water Horizon - On April 20, 2010, the 40th anniversary of Earth Day, a monstrous offshore drilling rig called the Deep Water Horizon, owned by British Petroleum, didn't heed the warnings about methane gas escaping during drilling and it blew the massive Gulf of Mexico platform to kingdom-come!

Only one other time do I remember anything even close to this explosion. It was in the Middle East off the coast of Pakistan and it rocked the sea like an earthquake.

At the Deep Water rig, eleven men were killed and scores of others were either blown or leaped into the sea to escape the engulfed rig and 300 foot flames that burned so hot it melted steel into pudding. As fireboats rushed to the scene, the oil covered, burned, and injured men floating in the sea were nearly crushed by emergency boats and firefighting equipment. It was a scene straight out of a horror movie. Promises of fail proof rigs and safety equipment echoed hollow to those who later found out they were risking their lives on a daily basis for corporate greed.

Under the rig it was catastrophic. Oil and gas was spewing out of the blown out emergency containment valve at a rate never seen before. An estimated 80,000 barrels a day was mixing with the sea creatures and floating to the top. They tried everything to stop the leak or cap the blown out well. First, BP tried using the emergency shut off valves (blow out preventers) that had failed during the initial blast. Then they tried to hook up a pipe and pump it into ships by putting a dome over it at the bottom of the sea floor, but at 5000 feet, it was deeper than ever attempted before. Lastly, they tried drilling a relief well into the ruptured one to divert the oil flow. No one knew for sure how to contain it, let alone stop it.

But nothing worked and the oil spread into the Gulf before heading for the U.S. coastline. They got hundreds of miles of booms to the site with little success, and then tried pumping what they did collect into an oil tanker. When they finally conceded it was almost useless they tried plan B. Using chemical dispersants, they tried breaking it up at the source by pumping it down the well to where the oil was gushing out instead of on the surface. The dispersants were supposed to stop the oil from forming tar balls but billions formed and got through anyway. When they tried the dome (which was more of a giant concrete box) they failed when ice unexpectedly formed on it.

With the coast guard commandant and everyone getting more and more upset at the failures the industry claimed would work in a situation as this, BP called in a converted supertanker from Taiwan they called the

Whale. It was rigged like the Titanic, with bulkheads floating just under the surface of the ocean, which allowed the floating oil to flow over them as they skimmed it off and captured it in the holding area. Meanwhile, they could return the cleaned seawater to the Gulf, unfortunately, after the second test run - it too failed.

After a couple of months they finally got it capped, and slowly shut the valve while praying the pressure wouldn't blow it off. Several weeks later it was finally plugged with heavy mud and sealed with concrete. By then it had leaked an estimated 172 million gallons of oil over a vast region of the Gulf Coast, killing and poisoning everything in its path for years to come. More than 7 years later dolphins are still dying, wildlife's getting hammered, fishermen have lost everything, and businesses are bankrupt.

Many experts asked, why didn't BP do what they did off the coast of Pakistan after that blowout? In that one they brought in supertankers and loaded them up with oil that had floated to the ocean surface at the scene, then took it to shore, separated it into storage tanks, and returned the water to the sea while capping the well.

Many people thought BP was trying to save the expense of bringing in the tankers the first few days, and then everything escalated out of control to a point where they no longer had that choice. If our media had covered Pakistan, they probably would have demanded them here, but it was a third world country they rarely cover if it doesn't have something to do with war. There was no finger pointing, high profile meeting, or presidential visits. They just went in and quietly sucked up the oil, then took it ashore. That was too boring and unsensationalistic for our over-the-top media.

The Deep Water Horizon spill was the worst man made ecological disaster since Sadam Hussein blew up thousands of wells during the first Gulf War. Beaches, estuaries, and river banks along the coast were covered with oil and tar balls. Thousands turned out to clean it up, but it spread along thousands of miles of coastline and inlets, making it hopeless. Too this day some waterways are still recovering.

BP was sued, and rightfully so, by thousands from coast to coast affected by the blowout that had stifled their businesses and revenue. They had failed inspections both at Deep Water and other oil rigs, yet the warnings from environmental and labor groups was ignored or buried. This tragedy was just waiting for the inevitable so lawsuits were filed by everyone from individuals on the rig to the state and local governments whose economies were ruined, as well as the fed's own Justice Department on criminal charges. Louisiana was especially hard hit because it was still recovering from Hurricane Katrina in 2005, but fortunately, by way of the Oil Pollution Act, all environmental damages were covered. BP paid over $45 billion in clean up fees, restoration projects, and claims, with another $18.7 billion going to claimants, which include murder charge settlements. However, there's still more problems cropping up to this day.

Many believe the broken system of emergency laws was to blame as much as BP. It was illegal for the Coast Guard, National Guard, or any other government agency to help out because the law only allowed for the company itself to contain, protect, and clean up both the land and sea. Once again we must ask. Did Congress or big oil learn anything from this environmental disaster of legendary proportions? I think the next story well answer that.

In late June, 2013, the Republican house voted unanimously to once again lift the drilling moratorium imposed after the Exon Valdez fiasco. Then voted unanimously to allow deep water drilling contracts to be exempt from the transparency rules of what was left of the desecrated 2010 Dodd-Frank Act, going back to their secret drilling deals with the governments of the U.S. and Mexico in 1.5 million acres of the Gulf. The ink was barely dry when another rig caught fire in the Gulf in July, 2013. Not the tragedy the Deep Water horizon was, but it was another confirmation that even in calm seas mother earth has other weapons up her sleeve to protect herself, and anything can happen on these inherently dangerous rigs.

Shell didn't care though. With the gulf tragedy fresh on everyone's minds, the huge oil company immediately got a lease to drill in an even more dangerous location - the Beaufort and Chukchi seas in Alaska's Arctic Sea. They then set out and built the two largest oil drilling platforms ever. The rigs didn't even get started before they were battered by the unforgiving Arctic Seas and sustaining major damage. Still, the industry and feds learned nothing after this attempt to rob the earth of its resources? With their blessing, if you can believe it, Conoco announced it would attempt this trick next, followed by Shell again.

Keystone – Big oil's next brilliant idea commiff by land. One of their most famous shenanigans of the early 21st century is the Keystone Pipeline XL. Owned by the Koch brothers and a few U.S. oil companies, yet run by TransCanada, it is the key component linking The Great Canadian Oil Sands in the Boreal forest of Alberta, Canada, to our Gulf Coast refineries.

The tar sands are full of heavy thick crude that is almost impossible to separate from the sand and ship to a refinery. Even the Canadian government doesn't allow a pipeline to pump it to refineries in Canada it's such a dirty, labor intensive, environmental calamity. Yet here, Capitol Hill bent over backwards to get it to ours, even exempting them from paying into the cleanup fund all mining industries must pay into. Worst of all, President Obama signed a law allowing us to ship light oil products overseas to get around our ban on the oil itself. Do you suppose the $50 million the Koch brothers gave the villains or the $100 billion they may make has anything to do with it?

To convert the tar filled sands to the finished product, they have to clear the old growth forest above it, dredge it out of the earth, and bring it to the separation facilities with the same massive equipment and monster trucks as mountain top coal mining. To separate the bitumen laced oil, it has to be heated with substantial amounts of water, which in itself, is heated by large amounts of natural gas to melt the oil from the sand. Then chemicals are added and it's pressurized. At that point it's capable of being partially refined at the onsite refinery. But to get it to flow through a pipeline, it also has to be turned into diluted bitumen with hydrocarbon liquids. This costly labor intensive way of extracting and refining the tar sands is "twice as polluting as normal underground oil and uses triple the energy to do it!"

This kind of oil production releases almost double normal levels of CO_2. The International Energy Agency and NASA scientist claim if they extract more than 3 million barrels a day they could tip global warming beyond a safe level. But this project has been approved for 5 million. The Canadian Association of Petroleum Producers claim CO_2 pollution from Alberta has already increased 36% from 2007 to 2012 - and that's without adding this ludicrous project.

The feds tell us, the new pipeline is part of a plan to pipe in oil from Alberta to refineries in the U.S. and alleviates the need to get it overseas or drill more wells in the Gulf. In reality, with our enormous oil glut that has storage tanks bursting at the seams, they're really going to export it to countries in Europe that depend on Russian oil. Two of the five proposed pipelines are already built and being used. And this one to the Gulf over the gargantuan Ogallala Aquifer is also finished over the southern portion because it didn't require the Department of State's or the president's approval. But the oil glut has caused the industry to temporarily pull the plug, and they are going to ship it by way of Warren Buffett and his Berkshire Hathaway's railroads west to China.

Environmental groups fought hard to stop the third line through the heart of America for numerous reasons. First are the obvious reasons like the huge Michigan and Arkansas spills… coming next, and dozens of smaller spills (12 in 12 months on one pipeline), the 25 mile 1000 barrel gusher into the Yellowstone River, and in Mayflower, Arkansas another 85,000 gallons of tar sand crude spilled into the streets. Second, it's over the Ogallala Aquifer, which took millions of years to form and runs under most of the states along the way. This is the same aquifer that allowed the Midwest to go from the 1930's dustbowl to the agricultural center of the world. Without its water, there are only savanna lands teetering on the brink of becoming a desert again and the next dust bowl. Third, the oil that will jeopardize our entire Midwest isn't meant for us! It's meant to be shipped to overseas markets in the name of pure greed, politics, and shift overseas markets reliance to us instead of the number one oil and gas producer and supplier – Russia!

If they're running it over everybody's property, does anyone get any say in protecting their property? You're supposed to have the right to protect your property from anyone you don't want on it and have the mineral rights to anything under it. If you put up private property signs in our state, that gives intruders and trespassers legal warning to stay off, or you can shoot them like my grandfather did Mike. The people think they have that same right, but the powerful industry says you don't!

They went on everyone's property to lay out the 2000 mile route of their pipeline through the Midwest all the way to the gulf. If you told them to get off your property, they responded with threats of lawsuits that would bankrupt you or they were taking your land under emanate domain. One farmer and their fellow townspeople sent them and Washington a message by building a barn right smack in the middle of the pipeline route through their property and vowed they weren't going anywhere… and neither was the pipeline on "their property!"

Needless to say, TransCanada is not our government or anyone's. They are a private corporation with no emanate domain powers, but they do have billions of dollars to push you around and threaten you until you either have a nervous breakdown, you go bankrupt fighting them, or you give in. They made it look as though they were operating under federal authority in the interest of national security (energy independence) but have no legal right on people's property. Thousands of people found corporate surveyors on their property staking out the route with total disregard for the law or them. They wouldn't have gotten away with this on our land when my grandfather was alive!

Every farmer and millions of acres of farmland along the way is most at risk, along with the largest food supply in the world! Then there are the thousands of small businesses that will go under in the event of a major spill. How about terrorist attacks? How do you guard 2000 miles of pipeline from a terrorist attack, or even kids playing what they consider a funny prank on the oil company? Then there's the tornadoes, I haven't seen any above ground pipeline yet in my lifetime that can take on the most powerful tornado nature can brew up. Did I mention earthquakes and hurricanes? What happens with the next hurricane Katrina? The next disaster could dwarf the 30 inch split in Kalamazoo, Michigan.

The aging burst pipe at the much smaller tar sands project to Kalamazoo should have affirmed the dangers of piping this crap 2000 miles and was undeniable evidence of its destructive powers. Piped in from the same tar sand mines in Alberta as the new pipeline would, about 1,000,000 gallons of the highly volatile, chemical laced, tarry slush leaked out into a creek that flows into the Kalamazoo River from a little 30 inch split in the pipe.

Normal crude oil floats to the top of the water and is more easily cleaned up, but this stuff is so nasty it took years to get the job just partially done. Toxic orange and yellow algae blooms lit up the river at night and swimming, boating, and fishing was banned in streams, lakes, and the river for more than 100 miles. The bottom was worse still! The oil sank to the bottom everywhere it went and choked out everything in the waterways. The air was laced so badly with benzene and other toxic chemicals, homes around the spill area had to be evacuated! Some never could return and were bought out by Enbridge - the company that owned the pipeline.

The EPA said it was the largest spill in Midwest history and they've never seen anything like it on earth. To this day they've tried every normal clean-up technique available to no avail and have no idea how to get the oil off the bottom.

Despite a domestic production glut by 2013, do you think that stopped our crooked politicians? President Obama actually made it easier to export the extra refined oil products overseas! And the Republican house killed EPA review laws across borders, and then refused to protect the great lakes and crucial Ogallala Aquifer beneath the eight critical farming states in the Midwest from more routine oil spills.

The energy department claims the other pipes are not running at full capacity, so what hair-brained scholar would build the biggest pipeline of them all over the worst possible place in the country? It's like IRA's where the people take all the risk for Wall Street profits and politics. Perhaps worse is our famous short term thinking of profits above all else regardless of the repercussions! If we ship our natural energy products to other countries, won't we run out of them that much faster? Then what? You can start your chant now… U.S.A.! U.S.A.!

Natural Gas - N.G. first became a popular energy source in the early part of the 20th century. Although it's been around since the mid-19th century when it was first used for street lamps, it wasn't until the 20th century that it became more widely available when extracting, storage and pipeline technology became more efficient and safe. Its main attributes were it was cleaner then oil and coal, yet inexpensive, and we had vast supplies that must have seemed nearly inexhaustible at the time.

The problem is the 170,000 miles of 100 year old pipelines crisscrossing the country are leaking, blowing up, and what's left is not easily accessible. What is left has to be fracked from underground shale formations to release it so they can pump it out and transport it through the system of old deteriorated pipes. Replacing the pipelines would take 100 years and the cost would make the price of gas completely unfeasible, so people living near one are playing Russian roulette.

Because new larger pipelines are too expensive in the eyes of gas companies, cities often have to import L.N.G. (liquefied natural gas) to help outdated and undersized pipelines on cold days when energy demand spikes. Not only do you have the added problem of depending on imported gas that is highly explosive, but it's an easy target for terrorists while still inside colossal tanker ships when docked and storage facilities - including leaky, exploding, former salt caverns near towns.

Hydraulic Fracturing – "Fracking" is nearly as polluting as coal, yet like everything else, the industry got it exempted from most of the Clean Water and Drinking Acts during the 2005 oil stained White House. Now 90% of new oil and gas wells are fracked, with only 4 in 10 being inspected on public and Indian lands they drilled at such a rapid pace. So dangerous is it, for years it was kept secret in California, and some companies disguise their operations with environmentally friendly names in our 'land of illusion.'

They are also drilled both vertically, then horizontally, resulting in thousands of wells running under neighbor's property without getting the mineral rights from them. Wells have to be loaded with millions of gallons of water, sand, and very dangerous chemicals, and then blasted underground at extremely high pressure until it fractures the underlying shale-stone. Now, earthquake free Oklahoma is leading the country with nearly a thousand quakes in 2015 between 2 and 6 on the Richter scale, with dreadful consequences.

So much water is required it often sucks wells, streams, and natural springs dry for miles around and releases the toxic chemicals, diesel fuel, and heavy metals into those that are left. Since the 1960's, it's been proven how destructive to the human body and brains these toxins are. If one person is desperate or greedy enough to sign over their land to the mining machine, they inadvertently doom all their neighbors and everyone else downstream.

Many people that have been tricked into selling or leasing their land for the rights to drill and frack now regret it. Sometimes whole towns will be pressured into letting them come in under claims of high paying jobs in areas with some of the poorest people and highest unemployment in their states, only to become mutant carriers of the toxic pollutants themselves, then passing it on to their children. Those kids living in these areas can count on a shortened lifetime of painful physical diseases and often mental retardation.

Some people turn on their water faucets and have flammable chemicals come out, starting the faucet on fire, similar to the rivers of fire before the Clean Water Act… not a real good way to take a shower or bring up your children. This highly toxic and flammable water poisons not only everything underground, including microscopic bacteria needed by plants and trees to process their nutrients, but everything in the food chain. From birds eating the underground bugs and worms to fish, livestock, and us - nothing escapes.

The good news doesn't stop there, 40 states have passed laws that force pooling of underground rights and eliminate the need to get individual homeowners to sign off on fracking under their property... Ka-Ching, checkmate!

With all these problems, you have to wonder, why are these bully's allowed to continue fracking oil when they only squeeze 10% more out of the ground? I think you all know the answer by now. However, I'll give you a few specific details about how the morons control everywhere they go. They even got the Bureau of Land Management to allow fracking on "600 MILLION acres" of our publicly owned land since our body George W. and his cronies took office. And they drilled about 2000 wells a month until they created the oil glut, with 100,000 on public lands that are rarely inspected. All exempted from the Clean Water and Safe Drinking Water Acts.

This industry is so nauseating, some people like former BLM field officer Dennis Willis have defected to fight it by doing consulting work for environmental and conservation groups. He upholds their claims of widespread spills, leaks, and burst pipes, and the loosely regulated industry is just a disaster waiting to happen.

Fracking lobbyists get their racket rolling by corrupting the higher education system and sponsoring studies at respected colleges and universities around the country. They achieve their desired results by paying some of America's most prestigious universities to study the impacts of fracking, including (MIT), Penn State, Texas, and SUNY Universities. With the MIT Energy Initiative co-founded and funded by them, you know whose side they were on!

The head of the initiative at MIT, Ernest Moniz, took a position on the board of an industry consulting firm immediately after the study and an advisory board position on another. Two other authors of the study were also working for the shady industry. They were betting everything on the MIT study, and with everything now riding on the study, they went after the president of the United States himself to sell their environmental destroying policies on a president that ran as an environmentalist. And it worked! They got him to nominate their own anti-environmentalist Ernest Moniz as Energy Secretary for the entire United States!

After corrupting our higher education system, energy conglomerates went to work hustling politicians with their voluminous donations and partnerships in organizations like ALEC. With everyone in cahoots, they personally attacked the EPA and other government agencies assigned to protect Americans. In 2013 alone, ALEC pushed 77 anti-pollution control bills, of which 17 became law, including the Electricity Freedom Act, which repeals state renewable portfolio standards.

The Marcellus – The most famous and fought over gas field in the eastern U.S. is in western N.Y., Pennsylvania, and West Virginia. It's estimated to have enough gas to supply the U.S. for 20 years with its 500 trillion cubic feet of gas. Companies have already fracked hundreds of wells in the Marcellus by doing what they do best - lie, cheat, steal, bully, take advantage of poor people, and bribe local, state, and federal officials… not to mention enriching the government agencies that are supposed to be regulating them.

The Marcellus Shale Advisory Commission (MSAC) claims since 2009, they have created 72,000 jobs at $73,000 dollars a year average, and the industry has paid over $1 billion in tax revenue to the state of Pennsylvania. A Penn State study claims it may employ 200,000 people by 2020. Still, Governor Tom Corbett, leaning on the side of caution, issued an executive order for a study on fracking and said many times "no amount of economic benefit would justify the degradation of our land, air, or water."

The study recommended tough new measures to protect the states environment and conserve precious resources with a permanent committee, and new laws to address it. Plus more details on promoting natural gas and its impact and byproducts to maximize the economic benefits of fracking, as well as ways to train workers, fire, and emergency personnel to better respond. They want information based on "science not emotions or profit," and they need to work hard to separate facts from fiction. The governor said Pennsylvania can become a national leader in energy independence and "We must not lose this moment. It's the economic cornerstone of the commonwealth's recovery from the recession."

Our National Parks - 100 National Parks are threatened by tens of thousands of fracked wells near them, with deadly chemicals and sediments leaching into the pristine air and waterways in and around them. Still not satisfied, mining companies push nonstop to do their dirty work in the parks themselves. The new anti-Teddy Roosevelt GOP and their ALEX allies control the states where most of our natural resources are located, and they make sure protecting our most prized lands since the days of Roosevelt, John Muir, and John Audubon will be a losing battle everyone and everything will be touched by.

Everglades National Park – is one of the world's largest ecosystems. Poisoned almost to extinction and home to some of the most rare and endangered species in our country, such as the American crocodile and West Indian manatee, as well as being the home to the largest mangrove forest in the western hemisphere, the park has been under attack from chemical runoff of sugar plantations, farming, agriculture, and industries hundreds of miles upstream for decades. The slow flowing waters and marshes that have filtered the everglades for millennia have become a gigantic chemically induced algae bloom that chocks off native species and are predictably replaced by unforgiving evasive ones. Poisoned fish deprived of oxygen die off in mass episodes, poisoning birds and anything that eat them. All wildlife in the park or migrating through it has been poisoned, along with its waterways and marshes - dooming some species to extinction.

Elsewhere in Florida, algae blooms kill off the last of the lovable sea cows (manatees) from coast to coast and everywhere in between. They are as sensitive as sea coral and need the almost perfect conditions that existed before the white man came down and started raising cattle and farming. Like the everglades, the fertilizers, manure, and sewage has run into the Gulf of Mexico, the Atlantic Ocean, and their main home the Indian River Lagoon, causing the mammoth algae blooms that choke off the native sea grasses - leaving only algae to eat. That clogs their intestines and causes an excruciating slow death. A record 766 died in 2010 along with 250 pelicans, which naturally ate the poisoned dead fish.

The everglades and everywhere throughout the country is screaming out to a DEATH, CORROPT Congress for help! But does it listen?

Once again, everyone all at once this time – NO WAY!

Have We Learned Nothing?

Did we change our ways, and what are the results of our unending assault on nature over the decades?

At the time of the Clean Water Act, two-thirds of all waterways were polluted. Despite the landmark act, a great start, and hundreds of billions of dollars spent nationwide, Republicans continued to chop down the Endangered Species Act and all EPA legislation, because, as Senator Whitehouse pronounced, "they partner with oil companies and create propaganda to continue polluting for profit." So now we're back to square one with the Chesapeake Bay and Gulf of Mexico having huge dead zones and Lake Erie 50% dead.

We use disposable products over reusable ones then dump 3000 million tons of non-biodegradable plastic products into our landfills every year instead of recycling it. Our antiquated sewer and storm water systems still get overwhelmed time and time again. Throughout the nation, billions of gallons of raw sewage and storm water continues to flow into our waterways and oceans from archaic sewage systems, leaky bursting pipes, and storm water runoff - causing severe health treats. Swimmers are banned, fisherman can't fish, and pets get sick from the untreated sewage. The EPA listed nearly 800 communities from coast to coast that released sewage into our water - usually from heavy rains the systems weren't designed for.

Old water pipes cause a quarter million leaks a year from coast to coast and constantly contaminate our drinking water. Boiling alerts like the May 2-4 2010 one for 2 million Bostonians are rather common. Problems with the ancient infrastructure came to a head in mid-July, 2013 during one of the hottest, longest heat waves in Maryland history.

One town had to shut down the entire drinking water supply for a week because of a decades old water main that had to be replaced immediately. People filled up their bath tubs and bought bottled water until stores ran dry. Some hoarded it; others bought multiple shopping carts filled with nothing but water. Then, in the new American spirit, sold it at outrageous profits to the very same desperate people they left high and dry at the supermarket after cleaning them out.

In Flint, Michigan, they had so much lead contaminated water they brought in bottled water for months and are still fighting lawsuits. Then it was Corpus Christy, Texas, then, then ...

Supertankers and cruise ships continued using a disastrous fuel called bunker fuel (a nasty tar-like fuel with heavy metals and 1000 times more sulfur than regular diesel fuel). In just one day a cruise ship can emit as much as 13 million cars. And Carnival illegally dumped greasy sludge into the oceans for years.

We continue to use pesticides and other deadly chemicals that pollute our waterways, wells, and bays - killing off millions of pollinating honey bees and thousands of species. At first it was smaller microscopic species, including coral, but quickly ballooned to threaten small creatures like honey bees and then large mammals like the loveable manatees... and of course, man himself!

The special interest media keeps fossil fuel companies singing all the way to the bank with their incessant preaching's about using air conditioners when high temperatures approach the upper 70's (25c) for a few hours, instead of opening your windows at night for some cool, fresh, *free* air.

And lastly, the Tea Party governor of Florida, Rick Scott, fired some of his Florida EPA staffers that were enforcing the law and replaced them with the farming industries top people so they could keep on polluting.

You would think after 60 years or so of this crap, even the stupidest person on earth would get it. Where is the GOP conscious? How do these people live with themselves? I'm sure their constituents don't want to have two noses, three eyes, both male and female organs, and other mutations all their lives. Or die excruciating slow deaths as disposable commodities. Do people really want to glow in the dark until death takes them? Can someone please explain to me why people keep voting for these same people over and over again knowing they operate Pandora's Box?

Tens of thousands of cases of pollution from the onslaught of corporate greed have been silenced by industry titans, with the people, country, and planet paying the price. After all, Congress could easily solve all our energy needs a thousand times over by simply claiming eminent domain in the name of national security on the land running parallel to the 12,000 miles of coastline - where 80% of the population lives within 100 miles. Then install the much smaller oceanfront wind turbines that Europe and other coastal countries do to catch the nearly perpetual breeze.

MAYBE WE REALLY ARE THAT STUPID!

9

Our Dysfunctional Government

You would think with the stock market booming and President Clinton putting out the first balanced budget in two decades under the new Balanced Budget Act, along with the U.S. being the last standing Superpower, it would be as impossible to conceive us imploding into 'third world like' status as it was the collapse of the mighty Soviet Union. Yet here we were, just ten short years later doing just that with 536 master thespian special interest proxies at the helm in Washington D.C.

With most Democrats becoming radically left and Republicans right, House Speaker John Boehner started complaining about, and picking on, his own Tea Party members. Republicans abused every trick in the book to derail the Obama express and used the previously seldom used filibuster so many times (about 500) Democratic Senate Majority Leader Harry Reid said, "It's so bad around here that they filibuster their own bills." And President Obama had to use Executive power to fill key positions in order to circumvent their frequent short recesses used to stall appointments to agency's they didn't like, nor want. Things in Washington had gotten so extreme, Reed proclaimed, "Working with my Senate colleagues reminds me of chasing one of these little pigs in a greased pig contest." People are so disenfranchised; the former theatrical pro wrestler Jessy Ventura won the governor's seat in Minnesota over his experienced opponents.

President Reagan and the two Bushes with their big oil, big business, K Street White House agendas, along with the shifty, slippery Bill Clinton could take the blunt of the blame for the entrenched political climate as they partnered to systematically shred our country into oblivion.

I knew George W. was a conniving little rat the minute I saw his beady, little, sinister, eyes and a smile that nearly shattered his diabolical face. His insider guilt was stamped all over it and he reminded me of Hitler. Like most people, I knew little about him. But I did know after interviewing roommates for 13 years I was pretty good at picking out the deceitful ones - and Eric Snowden proved my suspicions correct. Being a Texas Republican, I figured he was a religious zealot and corrupt to the bone. So when he was elected I told everyone to invest everything they could into his oil and gas fraternity.

And *OH-BOY* was I right! The first thing he did was convince the power companies to convert to natural gas. Immediately, and predictably, there was a shortage and the low cost relatively clean source of fuel skyrocketed, leaving George W. sitting pretty in the driver's seat down the road to unabated fracking and his oil and gas company holdings setting record profits. Unfortunately, I didn't have any money to invest.

Bush and Reagan's tax cuts, along with IRS deductions for the elite, which included huge cuts for the top 2% on earnings and reduced dividends and capital gains taxes from 70% to 15%, combined with Reagan, Clinton, and Jimmy Carters deregulation of the banking system was catastrophic. George W., with blessings from Alan Greenspan, brought us to levels of financial disaster not seen since Warren G. Harding had us on the brink of an oligarchy and finally imploded the country in 1929. Blindly ignoring the same forces that caused the great depression and internet bubble, he personally abused them, and then partnered with his cronies to stifle investment bank and special interest reforms, leaving many people, including my favorite political comedian, Mark Russell, to call him a "Moron." When someone asked Russell if he had to make a joke out of everything, he responded – "It's cheaper than taking Prozac."

Ironically, the 1929 crash was manufactured by three consecutive GOP presidents Harding, Coolidge, and Hoover. This time around, it was the three GOP amigos – Reagan, H.W. Bush, and George W., with help from that questionable character Bill Clinton rigging the system.

For the most part we'll talk about our over-bloated federal government in this chapter because they were ultimately responsible for our demise. Like all countries, they are at the top of the food chain and control the actual food chain. Along with expensive farm subsidies and insurance that control both the growing, and in many cases, not growing of crops that dates as far back as FDR's "New Deal" during the dust bowl years. It controls the pork and cattle business from birth to slaughterhouse and the inspection and interstate transportation of all foods. That's just a few of the thousands of responsibilities they take upon themselves. They have dozens of agencies with hundreds of programs, and ultimately, power over the states. It was the complete and utter moral and ethical failure of the federal government that trickled down and embedded itself into the masses. They had the authority entrusted in them to either make or break us, and they chose to follow the treasure map.

Wall Street Strikes Again

Once again, the Street would play the leading role in forcing both the state and national governments to grow far beyond what they or anyone else would have liked. As they were forced to protect citizens from corporate America, they became albatrosses, larger and more expensive to run, and akin to corporate America, fraudulent and radically less efficient. They became stretched, over bloated and weighed down by too many liabilities, such as the outdated constitution, environmental protection, and a democratic form of government both Roosevelt's wanted changed because it was completely dysfunctional for the times - and that was over 100 years ago!

As you know, George W. Bush was one of those Wall Street inside oilmen manipulating the system when he became governor of Texas, then brought that agenda to the White House. What you don't know is his grandfather Prescott Bush, the seedy, possibly treasonous patriarch of the presidential family, seemed to be in more scandals than the whole Street combined back in his day. His wealthy investment banker father-in-law, appointed him manager of and one of the seven directors of Union Banking Corp (UBC), which had its assets seized for aiding and abiding the enemy – Hitler's Nazi Germany! He was suspected of being part of the Nazi war machine because his bank was an offshore hiding company for German coal and steel magnet Fritz Thyssen - who financed and supplied Hitler's rise to power. UBC bought and shipped millions of dollars of coal, steel, fuel, gold, and US treasury bonds to aid the German war build up using concentration camp slave labor.

Like his grandfather, many people thought George W. should have been investigated and prosecuted when he ran for president for his shady oil connections, bookkeeping, and deals with businessmen such as Osama Bin Laden's brother - who invested in his oil company Arbusto Energy, which was later changed to Bush Explorations, then Energy Corp., and finally Harken Energy. Would you trust anyone who had changed company names almost as often as Donald Trump?

As director of Harkin and its predecessors, G.W. was tied to many political and business people involved in serious crimes and scandals. And six of the top ten lifetime contributors to his political doings were oil or oil related businesses, including Saudi Arabia's most ruthless, powerful people. As did his grandfather, G.W. helped teach corporations how to get around tax laws by setting up shell companies, and in Harkens case, to hide oil related losses from investors. But usually it was to hide from the Internal Revenue Service (I.R.S.).

For generations, his family has been members of the secret influential skull and bones society, and like every Republican president since William Taft, he is in the San Francisco Bohemian club. I know what you're thinking, but I'm sure it's just coincidence... and if you believe that one I have some swamp land in Florida I'll sell you! Richard Nixon said the speech he gave at the Bohemian club before his nomination was more important than any speech he ever gave and launched him to the presidency.

Special interest was the premier factor in the government's economic policies down the path of doom, as it followed a legion of corporate hired economist that are often admittedly mostly useless. Appearance wise, they're intellectual geniuses, yet their political and business affiliations make many of them as useless as rubber gloves on a greased pole. They work mostly for large business universities like Harvard that are funded by the financial sector, which would explain why virtually none of them predicted the crash of 2008. Their job has nothing to do with the economy as their title would suggest. Their job is to keep Wall Street humming right along for as long as they can keep fooling the fools. By 2013, the market was again primed for disaster and sitting in record territory on the strength of the Fed's infusions with earnings 50% higher than they should have been. Once again, many economists wouldn't budge and continued singing a happy tune for their employers. They stuck to the theories they wanted to hear – mainly trickle-down free market snake oil. For sure, in the real world with people this greedy, this never works and never did!

Going as far back as the late 1800's and early 1900's, when oilman John Rockefeller, steel magnet Andrew Carnegie, car manufacturer Henry Ford, banker J.P. Morgan, and railroad magnet William Vanderbilt, who proclaimed "the public be damned," were literally gods to the country, and especially the investment world, the captains of industry confirmed they really didn't give a damn about the little people making them rich.

Carnegie worked his way up from peasant to steal magnet and publicly preached the need for labor unions, only to use them as slave laborers with low pay and long hours, leading them to the famous strike of 1892. In response, he locked them out and hired the Pinkerton Security Agency to bash and kill them, then turned around and gave his money away to higher education and libraries.

John D. Rockefeller was perhaps the most brutal of the power hungry robber barons. He brought in hordes of people from around the world to slave away in his mining company, literally stealing their pay many claimed. This led to a brutal strike that tragically ended with exterminators Pinkerton Security burning down the tent city in Colorado he forced them to live in - killing and severely burning dozens of woman and children. The country was so furious even his most ardent supporters wanted to prosecute him, especially President Roosevelt, who called him a "law breaker," then broke up the murderous titan's monopolies. Fortunately, he gave his son and grandsons his fortune and they became philanthropist, giving away hundreds of millions of dollars before his death. Still, it never could make up for his heinous greed and atrocities.

Henry Ford then carried the torch of union paranoia and insanity against people who wanted a fair days pay for a hard day's work. In 1913, the Michigan Copper Country miner's strike saw someone from the Calumet and Hecla Mining Company yell "Fire!" in a building the miners and families were having their Christmas party in. After the ensuing stampede down the stairs, 70 children lay dead, proving many years ago the psychotic wealthy do NOT participate in the theory of trickle-down economics.

Running the Federal Government

Something as immense as the United States government under the best of circumstances is almost impossible to run effectively and efficiently. By the 21st century it had become impossible to do so as it was forced to take on an ever increasing larger role when industries became more and more influential in every aspect of our daily lives. Like Eisenhower's Interstate highway system that laced the country together, our entire infrastructure system, from highways, railways and waterways to airports and schools were forced into disrepair. Often with deadly consequences when politicians became more concerned with Wall Street than our streets.

Even when they have systems like the gas tax in place to pay for public projects they're asleep at the wheel, letting decades go by before updating the laws. For instance, the federal gas tax set at 18.4 cents per gallon in 1993 was never increased to keep up with inflation until this very day because every year is an election year, and Congress never makes the hard choices in an election year. They just keep kicking the can down the road year after year, putting all infrastructure projects farther and farther behind.

They also give energy credits to automakers and energy companies to help them meet their fuel efficiency and pollution control requirements rather than collecting millions in penalties. As a result, automakers have barely raised the average fuel efficiency to 23.6 miles per gallon, a far cry from the goal of 54.5 President Obama imposed by 2025 And companies from mining to power plants are getting away with murder instead of paying hefty fines, leaving us unable to afford enough inspectors for everything from bridges to international cargo. Bridges are collapsing on both our highways and railways, rail lines are outdated, old equipment is failing, and food and construction inspections are minimal. All are causing unnecessary suffering and death from misman-agement, misappropriated funds, and inaction.

A case in point: When the House of Representatives approved the fiscal 2014 annual budget, someone noticed the Appropriations Com-mittee gave the Pentagon $3.6 billion more than it had requested. When a bipartisan amendment was attempted to correct the error, it was defeated and the Pentagon got to keep the extra money. Giant defense contractors celebrated all year when another $70 million was approved for an east coast missile defense installation neither the Congress nor the Defense Department had authorized and the Pentagon hadn't requested. The Pentagon said the current system was sufficient to defend the entire country, but when an amendment was attempted, it too was defeated, despite Congressman Jerrold Nadler D-NY arguing they "can't afford to spend money on a program the military says it does not yet need or work." Not to be outdone, Capitol Hill, with heavy pressure from defense contractor Lockheed Martin, is currently embarking on a new F-35 defense system that's expected to cost up to $1.5 trillion all-toll.

The annual budget was three feet high from all the corporate pleasing amendments and exemptions known as "pork barrel politics" way back in Ronald Reagan's day, and it's only gotten worse. I'll never forget Reagan bringing in stack after stack of the federal budget Congress had sent him to read and approve at the last minute, piling them on the table for the entire world to see in protest of the system. Now, we have a $21 trillion deficit and have lost another $12.8 trillion in the 2008-09 collapse from the corporate capture of Washington. It is thought special interest donated $6 billion dollars to control the legislature and Presidency in the 2012 and 16 elections, with 75% coming from just the 100 wealthiest people and their organizations. The results were $1.5 trillion in annual tax cuts for the loaded, and combined with pork barrel spending, left the nation unable to pay for infrastructure projects, especially those that were constantly over budget like the Big Dig in Boston.

What was the Big Dig you ask? It was the largest most expensive public project since the interstate highway system. It took the freeways running through the heart of the city from above ground to underground tunnels similar to the Chunnel between Great Britain and France. Originally estimated to cost somewhere around $2.5 billion, with interest, it will be over 24 after underestimating the difficulty of going under rivers and on top of a centuries old garbage dump the city was built on. It not only drained the national government but bankrupted the state. For a state the size of Massachusetts, it simply couldn't handle such a massive overrun, even with the feds paying 80%. It really was like the Chunnel!

In 1995 Denver, Colorado, experienced a similar project people were calling the great White Elephant in the Rockies. It was led by former Denver Mayor and then Secretary of the Transportation, Federico Pena, who decided to move airport traffic away from the city. So they built a monstrous airport 25 miles away with a famous tent-like roof that mimicked the surrounding mountains. After many delays and spending $500 million, including $7.2 million for Art of the total $4.8 billion - nearly triple the original estimate of 1.7 - they opened the largest airport in America with scarcely a soul in sight and a state of the art baggage system that didn't work. To top it off, it was the most expensive airport in the country at double the national average. Unlike the movie Field of

Dreams, this was another case of build it and they **won't** come. Eventually, it became one of our busiest airports - but that's because it's Denver's only airport now.

Did they learn anything? They turned around and built the Mid America Airport to relieve congestion at Lambert-Saint Louis with a staggering four flights a day for $300 million!

Another project the feds tried to push through was the famous Gravina Island Bridge "Bridge to Nowhere" in Ketchikan, Alaska. For a "measly" $320 million, they were going to connect the town of 8,900 people with its airport on the Island of Gravina, which had a whopping 50 people. That's 360,000 grand each people! The handful of folks who occasionally took the fairy trip of 15 to 30 minutes thought the stratospheric fee of $6 was too much, and it was too much of an inconvenience. I'm just pulling your leg. Actually, the people of Ketchikan were incredibly embarrassed by Congress's insane authorization. They blasted the airwaves with apologies and asked it to give the money to the hurricane Katrina victims and rebuild New Orleans.

There are thousands of public, private, and military sites used over the years that are so contaminated with heavy metals and toxins they're designated as "Super Fund" sites because of the enormous amounts of money necessary to clean them up. The original Stapleton Airport in Denver couldn't add a runway that would have eliminated the need for the new airport because the former military site was so contaminated they could not build over it. It seems to me it would have been cheaper to clean it up and build the runway than a whole new airport! Daaa! The government will still have to pay to clean it up, along with all the other sites that sit on city, town, county, federal, and private lands throughout the country that are often abandoned and nobody else can afford to clean up, especially ex-military bases.

Those examples are only the tip of the iceberg for our out of control self-serving politicians and their double-dealing pork barrel projects that have destroyed our chances for infrastructure repairs and replacement. It's estimated it will cost us $3.6 trillion by 2020 to bring the most important infrastructure projects up to snuff and our grade point average (GPA) up from the current D+. We simply cannot afford anymore pork and white elephants.

Not only does corporate influence make government too large to manage from a logistical standpoint, but an honest one as well. It became impossible to finance all the private industry request and ventures it got into, from either supporting it or stepping in where it refused to go. It has their own private flood and disaster insurance, mortgage and bank deposit insurance, owns 90% of reverse mortgages, and as you know runs its own bond fund - buying and selling its own treasury bonds and mortgage securities. We even bribe other countries with hundreds of billions of dollars to be our allies and let us steal their natural resources and basically run amuck around the world.

Let's Talk Social Security and Medicare!

According to Parade writer Paul Taylor, they are expected to cost nearly "half of our entire national budget" by the time every baby boomer (those born between 1946 and 1964) is retired. He further points out, "both the Social Security trust fund and one of Medicare's two trust funds will be broke and the ratio of taxpayers to retirees will have fallen to its lowest level ever, about 2 to 1, from the previous 20 to 1 at inception." All-toll, the five merciless gorillas - Social Security, Medicare, Medicaid, interest on the debt, and defense spending, will chew up "77% of all government expenditures by 2025."

One reason is our over generous Congress. On top of the previously mentioned public welfare, they allow anyone who has never worked or paid social security taxes to collect up to 50% of their spouse's award after retirement if the spouse worked and paid taxes, and they get 100% if their spouse dies (survivor benefits). You can also collect social security and unemployment at the same time in 19 states if you go back to work and get laid off. Worst of all, the richest Americans only have to pay taxes on earnings up to $118,000 – the same as anyone else, no matter how many millions or billions they make a year!

Other snafus have the Federal Reserve controlling every aspect of our lives by artificially pumping up the economy with never ending manipulation of the stock market and money flow. Economist and Wall Street call it "easy money" every time the Fed throws more money into the market. Officials call it "quantitative easing." Referring to the theory of economics that proclaims if the government infuses cash into the economy by selling and buying its own T-bills and mortgage securities, it will keep both short and long term interest rates near record lows and allow businesses to buy new equipment, expand, and add workers to reduce the unemployment rate. You know, Reaganomics! Sometimes it just prints more money and infuses more cash, but mostly it bought at least a trillion dollars' worth of its own treasury bonds and mortgage securities a year for about six years after the latest financial collapses.

Buying their own mortgage securities was supposed to do the same for the housing market and solve that problem as well - killing two birds with one stone. In reality, when they lowered the huge government moneymaker, interest rates, down to nothing to stimulate the economy, they further added to the deficit through unlimited borrowing while making crooked banks giggle in ecstasy as record profits rolled in from the cheap money they used for their hedge fund and derivatives schemes. And as you know, they achieved record profit spreads by not lowering interest rates they charged us nearly as much as the Fed reduced theirs. Remember people, trickle-down economics is a good theory - but it's just that.

In 1979, Fed Chairman Paul Volcker cranked up interest rates and put strict credit restrictions on both banks and consumers to fight inflation. When it didn't work, President Carter asked the country to stop borrowing. Combined, they brought the economy to a screeching halt so Volcker reversed course and lowered them again. When Reagan was elected, the economy had recovered but inflation was still high, so Volker cranked them back up to record highs. This caused defaults here and around the world not seen since the great depression.

After realizing the devastation to all, he lowered them again. The prime lending rate he was charging banks had hit a record 20% and they were passing it along to us, bankrupting my largest customer. When Mexico defaulted on their loans, he finally lowered them enough to get the economy going in the right direction, though not before doing great damage. Isn't it amazing how the vultures pass high interest rates along to us but not the low ones equally?

It seemed the Fed tried everything that didn't work in prior recessions that resembled this one. During the great recession of the late 1970's under President Carter and early 1980's under Reagan, things had gotten so desperate when unemployment topped out at 11% and jobs were scarce, 15,000 people applied for 150 openings at one place. Defense spending went through the roof, inflation was out of control, and air traffic controllers walked out on strike. So the former actors' union president fired his brethren and replaced them with less experienced ones (mostly from smaller airports) and made managers work long hours until he could train enough new ones. He cut taxes in record amounts to lead the way for his trickle-down economic policy, only to have to do an about face and raise them again in record amounts when his theory only got us in worse financial condition. Reagan and Paul Volcker didn't seem to do anything right his first few years for the American people, yet amazingly he was reelected by the largest landslide in history. Like a powerful, mystical sorcerer, he had Americans under his spell.

Reagan had publically told the American people he was sticking to his campaign promise of smaller government. But when family farmers went out of business in record amounts (two to three hundred thousand under his watch), he started increasing the size and scope of it by substantially increasing the farm subsidies that FDR started and ramped up military spending. Many experts agree, his out of control military spending, tax cuts for the ruling class, and increased subsidies on things like farming, oil, gas, and mining have been dragging down our economy and adding to our deficit to this day. All these subsidies have contributed to the citizens of the United States being amongst the most spoiled in the world from underpriced goods and services. Reagan hadn't made government smaller – he made it bigger! Yet, he was still a hero to the party despite the 18.6% debt increase to a record $1.86 trillion.

'Reagan-world' policies and Volker nearly imploded us into another great depression. They left us with a record deficit, rampant Wall Street abuse, near monopolistic hostile corporate takeovers not seen since Rockefeller, and 2000 banks insolvent at a cost of $150 - $200 billion and others with unpayable loans on their books. The rich got richer and the middle and lower classes got hammered with stagnant wages and high unemployment not seen since the 1930's. Manufacturing and capital investment dried up, enforcement jobs at the Justice Department, Federal Trade Commission, and four other important watchdog agencies had personnel and fines cut in half - including food safety and inspections. Sound familiar George W. and fans?

The feds expanded into many other private sector businesses as well, eventually buying nearly every home mortgage in the country: a financial catastrophe of epic proportions, when the housing bubble they themselves had created - burst. It had created its own mortgage and homeowner's insurance companies, insuring most of the very same houses they foreclosed. Then they had to pay for all the homes and businesses flooded or destroyed in natural disasters time and time again because they let everybody rebuild in the exact same dangerous locations.

By 2013, the flood insurance program run by the Federal Emergency Management Agency (FEMA) covered $1.3 trillion worth of property nationwide, with just five states along the coast - New Jersey, Florida, Louisiana, Texas, and California comprising two-thirds of all policies. Not only did they insure the most likely homes to be wiped out by Mother Nature, they heavily subsidized the homeowners and actually *paid* the vast majority of their premiums! When it finally looked as though FEMA was learning from their past mistakes and increased the premiums on the 5.6 million high risk homes in flood zones to the proper unsubsidized amount, Congress halted them and put a four year moratorium on the price increases, effectively killing reform. Total cost to the taxpayers was nearly a 'trillion dollars' added to the deficit over the next five years.

The feds also continue insuring bank deposits and stock market speculators, as well as paying for our nation's medical needs, including most of the 100 million illegal aliens that migrated and stayed here. Many are on Medicaid sucking the life out of government coffers by going to hospitals at many times the cost of a doctor's visit, especially pregnant woman and those bringing their kids with minor medical problems as routine as the flu. And the law not allowing hospitals to turn anybody down, forces them to pass the buck to the paying customers through higher insurance premiums. It seems like there isn't anything our legislators aren't into or subsidizing, including Medicare Advantage, which is "private-corporate" versions of Medicare.

We don't just subsidize everything in America, we subsidize most of the world to achieve our foreign policy goals, including international businesses, banks, and governments we want indebted to us.

Meanwhile, on the Street, the government (people) takes all the risk so big business can reap the rewards at a cost of tens of trillions of dollars. I don't think anybody truly knows how much money Congress has invested in Wall Street and the U.S. economy. What we do know is, over the six plus year period after the collapse of 2008-09, they put $85 billion a month into the financial system. That's more than the entire country puts into mutual funds each year for a total of over $6 trillion. That's in addition to all their other endeavors and the existing deficit that was financed mostly on borrowed money from China, Japan, European banks, and itself. Our interest payments alone under Trump are a record staggering $376 billion a year after he added $6 trillion to the deficit.

The Internal Revenue Service

As time went by, the IRS became as dysfunctional as all the other federal entities. By the 1990's, Wall Street, corporations, and Congress had taken over to the point of even controlling the most powerful and feared agency. It was necessary in order to shield there massive tax deductions, reductions, profits, and bonuses during the internet boom of the 90's and make sure it stayed that way: And what better person to have in office than oil tycoon George W. and his anti-business tax, anti-regulation party.

Even before G.W., the 74,000 pages of regulations had become as impossible to follow as bank scams, with enough corporate loopholes to drive a Mac truck through. Senator Elizabeth Warren says the "fortune 500 companies often don't pay any taxes at all and actually get a refund." They hide their profits in offshore tax havens in places such as Switzerland, Bermuda, and Cayman Islands with just a post office box. And the rest of the world reciprocates by hiding their fortunes in our banks and then buy trillions in commercial real estate and things like precious art in cash to avoid messy paper trails.

Here, politicians like Mitt Romney personally test their own laws. According to a January, 2012 report by Foreign Policy – Romney had $8 million stashed away in 12 accounts in the Caymans, and more in Ireland, Bermuda, and Luxemburg to go with his $100 million in IRA's. And there were 19,000 companies using off shore tax havens to hide that $32 trillion. Although the Republicans are the ones who cut taxes for the upper class, Democrats don't put up much of a fight. As Washington attorney and offshore expert Jack Blum put it when speaking of Romney: "His personal finances are a poster child of what's wrong with the American tax system."

Although he makes millions every year, his tax bracket is reduced from the highest level of 40% to only 25% by the time he is done "doing it" to the American people. He justifies his actions by claiming he plays by the rules as written in the tax code and is just taking advantage of the tax breaks like everybody else... sounds like Trump. I guess that's why he has another $5 and $25 million investment from his personal fortune of $250 million in the Caymans nobody's supposed to know about, and his private equity company Bain Capital has 138 more secretive offshore funds their also. Seems to me they could use some new hiding places. Thanks to our historically low rates, he and Bain can also charge higher management fees and receive higher interest on their holdings from the Caymans than they can here.

The trickle-down affect works great 'backwards' when corporate chieftains and insiders hide money offshore. It substantially lowers government coffers and reduces the abusers to a lower tax bracket - further reducing its income. The corporate share of taxes has gone from 30% of federal revenue, to just over 6% since the 1950's, and not surprisingly, the deficit has gone in the opposite direction with every penny they stole from us. This leaves mom and pop businesses and the rest of us that play by the rules making up for the conscienceless captains of industry.

American multinational corporations undoubtedly abuse offshore tax laws the most. Very few pay anything made by their international subsidiaries. As Mark Shields of the Washington Post points out, all they have to do is renounce their American citizenship, pretend to be bought by a company in another country, and move their headquarters on paper – known as inversion. They just get a Corporate Service Provider to set it up and registered agent to take calls. It's just that easy! Not only can they hide their profits in other countries, they can shift it around within their own corporation. This makes their accountants far and above the most important person in their operation. You can always get another chief executive officer or board of directors, but a great accountant that can legally hide billions of dollars annually from government coffers is as good as gold.

Facebook, for example, had profits of over a billion dollars in 2012, yet paid no taxes, in fact, got a refund instead. As long as Wall Street and large corporations are allowed to legally evade the I.R.S., trillions of dollars will go to the affluent rather than helping the American people.

There are actually tax exemptions and write offs for both rich and poor - most for the rich of course - like the previously mentioned IRA's that just happened to help the middle and lower income people. Gifts to relatives or charities are a huge one for the well-off that trickled down to everyone else. They can be something as sizable as real estate or as small as clothing for the poor. Employers often get involved with matching contributions of various amounts, not only to help lower their taxes, but it's a good publicity stunt as well. Some crazy things like donating your flight rewards to charities is allowed, as are your minimum distributions from IRA's for people over 70 ½. Why 70 ½? Don't ask me! That's our crazy and complicated IRS's.

Reiterating, the different forms of IRA's alone are quite complicated for the average person and most people need a financial advisor. For instance, a typical one allows you to contribute pretax income to it with withdrawals taxed later. But what if your income rises over the course of your life - as most do? You will be taxed at the higher rate on your withdrawals. If you have a Roth IRA it's the opposite scenario. You're taxed first, which often allows you to be in a lower tax bracket when you're young and not making much money, therefore paying less tax. This is the advantage over the popular taxable CD's, but as you know your money also goes into the stock market. Also, there is no minimum withdrawal at 70 ½ like the typical IRA. These are just a few of the complicated rules governing them.

Marriage brings in as many complicated scenarios as retirement accounts, which is one of the main factors behind the gay marriage push. They want the same tax rights and social security benefits married couples have enjoyed for generations.

Every year politician's talk about simplifying the tax code and closing the loopholes for the moneyed elite, yet always give them more. As verified by the code climbing from 40,500 pages to 74,000 between 1995 and 2015. Corporate executives continue to receive hundreds of billions of dollars in stock options that are written off as salary deductions. And billionaires lower their capital gains taxes by carrying the interest from their egregious, ill-gotten gains while writing off the broker fees and commissions.

Super Pac's are also predictably allowed to write off their contributions to everything they put their blood money into. When combined with literally thousands of other legal deductions, the Citizens United ruling, and a part of the tax code that allows them to hide their donors; a great accountant can make a company, large non-profit, or tax-exempt organization making billions of dollars in profits suck us dry! They make some of them look as though they are actually non-profits and others tax-exempt to keep their legal tax statues as 501©(4) tax exempt corporations.

Karl Rove's Crossroads GPS and the Koch brothers Americans for Prosperity are perfect examples. They're listed as tax exempt 501©(4)'s, which by law clearly does not allow political organizations this designation, yet they spend tens of millions of dollars on political ads for their buddies. On the Democrats side, former advisers and campaign aides for Senator Reed and President Obama countered with their American Bridge 21st Century Foundation and Priorities USA. They all claim they are not political organizations and qualify as tax exempt "social welfare" organizations. Even the National Football League with its billions a year in profits claims to be a non-profit. How are they non-profit? By law, a tax exempt non-profit is supposed to be a neutral organization plugging nonbiased good will.

Another IRS statutory provisions states, "organizations exempt under IRC 501©(4) may not allow to have any part of their net earnings to inure to the benefit of any private shareholder or individual." But so far, donations by these organizations are on pace to triple again this year to $1 billion. Economist claim the tax laws put into effect since Reagan has allowed the richest 2% to control 90% of the wealth ever since. After inflation, the other 98% was still making the same or less income in 2016 as they did in the late 1970's! Are you surprised?

There are other issues plaguing the IRS that takes its toll on the agency when trying to limit tax cheaters. In May of 2013, the ultra-conservative Tea Party (so named after the original Boston Tea Party that led to the colonial revolution against England) claimed they targeted them to keep them from getting the tax-exempt 501©(4) designation because of their political ambitions. They claimed the IRS ordered its employees to red flag any organization that had used certain references that might make them look like a political group associated with them. The claim against perhaps the most hated government agency was a gift from the heavens for them after all but disappearing from the radar screen. Everyone had branded them too radical and obstructionist to want anything to do with them. With their claim of prejudice, they were once again plastered all over the news with interviews and a blitz of media coverage.

Just as everything on a slow news day here in America, the media descended recklessly on both the Tea Party and IRS like the Apocalypse was here. And as usual, they never stopped to get the main fact that the 501©(4) tax exempt designation clearly states its primary reason is "not for politics and influencing elections." It was designed for non-political organizations, who through the generosity of their hearts wanted to do something good for the country or their community. None of the major networks I watched the night the story broke mentioned this crucial fact in defense of the IRS. Only our local Public Broadcast System (PBS) station bothered with the facts. The simple fact was, the Tea Party, like many others, was unquestionably a political party that was trying to cheat us from paying their share, and it was the IRS's duty to stop their constant filings to skirt the law. They were properly targeted for their nonstop attempts to cheat the American people because that is the law and it's their job to stop them!

They would prove to be partially right though. The government did target smaller organizations they could easily control rather than the powerful Pac's. The two Super Pac's, Crossroads GPS and American Crossroads, spent about $175 million on mostly GOP ads influencing the 2012 elections. Since the Citizens United ruling in 2010 opened the floodgates for the "social welfare" tax-exempt 501 ©(4) designated groups – the filings mysteriously doubled in just 2 years.

To stop non-profit abuse, the IRS is trying to get rid of the loophole that contradicts the regulation. The new law says a 501©(4) provides an exemption for civic groups that operate "exclusively" for the promotion of welfare, instead of "primarily," which allows groups to donate up to half of their spending on politicians. The new law will make it clear "promoting social welfare does not include candidate related political activity!" In 2012, the Center for Responsive Politics estimated there was over $250 million donated to election coffers under the radar screen by nonprofits, compared to just $3 million in the 2004 election period.

If legislators ever did the right thing and slithered out from under the giant foot of special interest and reversed the corporate tax rates, special rates for the privileged, and closed loopholes to pre-1980 levels - it could fix the country's infrastructure, add millions of high paying jobs that additionally bring in more tax revenue, and start that trickle-down economics they constantly talk about. Some congressmen, particularly

Democratic Senators Sanders, Warren, and Sheldon Whitehouse pushed for campaign finance reforms, and Carl Levin (D) Michigan and John McCain (R) Arizona led a senate investigation, but you can guess how that ended. The new GOP Congress further cut IRS funding to make sure they cannot afford to go after the big shots now!

States

States do just about as many outlandish things as the feds do. They went bankrupt trying to enforce its laws on top of their own problems forced upon them by big business jerry-rigging. The fracking industry, for instance, is required by all states oil and gas target to hold both public and private hearings, conduct surveys, and according to the Washington Post - in Illinois, hire "50 engineers, inspectors, lawyers, and other experts" to set up a regulatory system. Then there's years of expenses and possible delays from lawsuits, protest, regulation, and enforcement. Towns and cities in their way also have enormous additional road and bridge repair and replacement cost on top of pollution problems they will have to pay for; all because mining companies have politicians in their hip pocket.

In cases where private industry wants to drill, blow up, clear cut, or whatever else they want to do on your land, they have to buy out the landowners or lease it, right? Yea right! What about eminent domain? By law, and rightfully so, the government or corporation (depending on who's taking it) has to pay the fair appraisal value (just compensation) for every grain of sand the project runs over, under, or through according to the Fifth Amendment of the Constitution. Even then, this can still only be done if the project is for public use or benefit. This applies to all governments.

But now that we have an all GOP government, it would appear the feds will take a piece of thousands of people's property for the Keystone pipeline and the two or three subsequent lines TransCanada wants to build under the guise of energy independence. What the total cost would be, especially if it's litigated for years, is anybody's guess. They might even get an easement, in which case they'll pay property owners nothing. Or, they might take just the land the pipeline runs over, which has been allowed by some courts in the past, costing only the meager court proceedings.

In one of the most outrageous eminent domain projects ever, the state of Massachusetts took three whole low lying towns and flooded them by way of a dam for the city of Boston. They claimed Boston's need for water to accommodate their expansion was more important than the three towns, people, and their history.

Sometimes municipalities take people's property for corporate profits disguised as benefiting the public. In New London, Connecticut, they took over some houses and tore them down so a hotel, condos, and a club could be built, claiming it benefited the town. The "unbiased" courts actually upheld it but it was never built. They made the people go through hell fighting it and move for nothing, leaving just a block long empty lot after they bulldozed everyone's homes down.

With many new laws come unintended consequences that add millions to state and local budgets. Municipal projects are often caught in a catch 22. For instance, new laws stipulate if you renovate any portion of a public building or other project, you have to upgrade the entire building, or at minimum, the portion of the building or project being renovated to the most recent building codes.

In our town, we had sidewalks installed as part of the street renovation project that was funded and owned by the state. Any laws associated with state projects are expanded to adjoining publicly used properties along the way. One law requires updating handicapped access to them. In our case, it was a war memorial located about 50 feet from the new sidewalk on the church grounds. We had to install a sidewalk across the church property to connect the memorial to the new state sidewalk at our own expense. And when we renovated the town beach and built a new bathroom, shower, and snack facility, we had to build handicapped accessible ramps to the beach, water, and the new facility. The state may reimburse us, but either way, one of us will be paying for it with our tax money.

Sometimes you run into a project where you just want to upgrade a town building - such as a school. That kicks in requirements to upgrade that portion of the school you renovate. To expand our science classes, for example, meant we had to meet the new minimum 60 square feet of space per student requirement for new school construction and upgrade the mechanical systems (plumbing, electric, and heating systems) in that portion of the building, along with a slew of other requirements. This always cost both the state and us much more than we anticipate.

By law every public project, from small town to giant federal ones, has to be awarded to the lowest bidder. At first glance one might say politicians finally put a law in place to control cost, but as we all know, first looks can be deceiving. Many projects under this system come in over budget because the bidders often lowball the bid to get the work, costing everybody much more in the end and putting governments deeper underwater. Rather than driving prices down with competitive bidding, it often increases the lying of how much a contractor can do the project for. Then they add the true cost onto the project later when you're too far into it for the government agency to drop it... or get someone else. This routinely happens on the largest projects like the Big Dig and airports, with perhaps only one or two companies capable of doing such enormous undertakings. Lowball estimates are the easiest way to get it approved, but that can set taxpayers up for shabby work that barely passes inspection and using lesser quality materials than originally planned (like we did our schools).

When states aren't going under from national laws and unintentional side effects of their own, they're doing boneheaded things that only make matters worse. They ultimately invest their pension money into the crooked market, and we all know how well that works out every time the market invariably collapses. In Massachusetts, they stopped collecting tolls on the western end of the turnpike used to maintain their roads and bridges, which put them in worse financial condition. So they had to add another tax onto a state that is already called "Taxachusetts" with a new tax on computer and design services, then add an additional three cents per gallon onto the gas tax to make up for it. To top off the stupidity spree, they reinstated the same turnpike tolls they took away that had made a small deficit into a larger one, then took the ones in the Springfield area away again and rescinded the computer and design tax. Way to go guys!

We also give the kids of law enforcement - i.e. police and corrections officers - free college educations, as well as firefighters, prisoners of war, and those killed in action.

And you know California went bankrupt from too many Mexicans not paying taxes and sending it to their home country instead of it going into public projects. Schools had no money, and one of the largest projects in state history, the new Oakland to San Francisco Bay Bridge that opened in 2013, was billions over budget like the Big Dig before it.

Even when they tried doing the right thing (making the state the leader in green technology and sustainability), they didn't have the necessary tax revenue, putting them in such a deep hole they had to tax everyone to death - and for once that included the rich. California now has the highest top income taxes in the country, rivaling European countries, but also has a $4.2 billion surplus that's expected to reach 10 billion by July, 2018 - mostly from proposition 30's sales and income taxes, which includes capital gains taxes from the booming market. They are now able to pay down previous bonds, increase school spending, and add to pension funds thanks to Governor Brown.

Note to Washington: LISTEN TO JERRY BROWN! ... Occasionally.

One of the most controversial policies all states have is giving tax breaks to large corporations. Many states give tax breaks to Hollywood movie studios if they bring in their operation to film a movie under the assumption it will boost the local economy while they're there. And the subsequent tourist that will invariably follow will add more to their coffers. States always get into bidding wars over movies, automobile plants, and other large corporate facilities. Hundreds of millions of dollars in tax revenue is given away in shaky deals on the promise of thousands of jobs and a stable economy for many years. States have to carefully weigh each proposal and counter offer to "guesstimate" if they'll make or lose money, after considering such things as what the expanded infrastructure projects will cost (which is never cheap) and what kind of environmental destruction it will bring in the long run, to name a few.

Cities and counties often go bankrupt nowadays too. Starting with Orange County, California, in 1994, when they lost $1.5 billion gambling on "over the counter derivatives." The financial world acted shocked... even though they caused it and knew it was inevitable. Others slowly followed until the financial crisis of 2008, when the pace rapidly ac-cellerated, and one by one many towns, cities, counties, and states went down the drain. Many lost tremendous amounts of money on flagrant schemes, others couldn't pay back the substantial debt piled up after municipalities across the country ran into similar difficulties with expen-sive projects and severely deteriorating infrastructures. They didn't stand a chance with the Street and government pushing more leveraged debt at lower rates to get out of the same debt they had gotten everybody into using debt in the first place.

On July 19, 2013, the city of Detroit filed bankruptcy. Once the industrial capitol of the world and richest city in America, it too fell on hard times from 60 years of neglected infrastructure, mismanagement, corrupt politicians, colossal pension obligations, and the big three auto makers moving operations to cheaper locations to satisfy Wall Street's unquenchable thirst for higher profits. Basic services had to be cut when repair or replacement became impossible from freefalling tax revenues. Unemployment slowly rose until it reached a never before high of 30%. Schools went under, crime skyrocketed after police, firefighters, and emergency personnel were laid off, and whole neighborhoods were abandoned when response times hit one hour and made living there a party for crime. Nearly two-thirds of the people moved out, leaving about 80,000 abandoned homes and businesses behind.

Like other municipalities, Detroit became unsustainable and continued to borrow to pay off their creditors, municipal workers, pension plans, and bonds. Banks allowed it to keep borrowing until they reached an insurmountable debt of $18 billion, which included 9 billion to city workers and 600 million to their pension funds. They owed a total of approximately 100,000 creditors, and Mayor Kwame Kilpatrick went to jail on charges of racketeering and other crimes. As usual, the banks came out much better than anyone else, with Detroit offering 75 cents to the dollar for creditors, and the people getting pennies to the dollar on the municipal bonds they held in retirement accounts they probably didn't know were invested.

Pension funds eventually reached $3 trillion in unfunded systems in every town, city, county, and state. And the federal government is insuring all of them! Detroit's pension at 83% funded actually looks pretty good compared to some others. In all of Massachusetts only one pension fund is funded 100%, and that's a small school district in Lexington. Twenty-Five funds are at less than 50% and some under 40%. Our third largest city, Springfield, is the lowest in the state at just 29% funded, with a liability of $652 million. It put $37 million into its fund this year, but will add to its overall poverty by skimming services elsewhere and adding on more taxes - or both. They hope they can add 6% a year until it's fully funded in 2037. Residents won't be happy, but at least city employees will.

Will this be another Detroit? As do state and federal budgeters, they relied on the stock market for an 8% annual increase and revenue forecast that was merely wishful thinking, or outright fraudulent, to keep the people satisfied until reelection time. A white collar manufacturing downfall and a middle class white flight, replaced by a rapid boom of poor minorities has led to the same poor schools, housing collapse, and flight problems as Detroit.

There's a thousand ways for governments to go bankrupt from special interest annexation. Despite Reagan and his Republican Senate's stand against guns, the new GOP and NRA's solution to all the mass school shootings is for legislators to give us more money to buy their guns and arm everyone from our teachers to the grounds crew. Can you imagine every teacher, principal, custodian, cook, secretary, bus driver, and groundskeeper with a six shooter on their hip? Better yet, the NRA could arm them with assault weapons! That would scare the living daylights out of kids, and getting caught in the crossfire would probably kill more than the gunman would. And how about the tension it would create and life lessons that would teach them?

The NRA also wants us to supply all our school employees and kids with chairs draped in bulletproof covers you can wear like a vest and give the kids bulletproof backpacks! Arming our educators and supplying them with bulletproof everything so they can get into Wild-West like shootouts is supposed to protect our kids they claim. I think the only thing it protects is the gun manufactures profits!

None-the-less, our state has bought into the NRA's rhetoric and made it mandatory for all school districts to hire cops.

10

Two Bank Meltdowns in Twenty Years
and
Other Scams

What caused two massive investment bank and dozens of corporate meltdowns in just twenty years? Did America learn nothing from the near meltdown of 1907 that was only avoided by the intervention of J.P. Morgan and led to the establishment of the Federal Reserve six years later? Did it learn nothing from the 1929 crash, how about the 1987 one, or the Savings and Loan disaster in full swing at the same time? Oh yes! I almost forgot our bailout of hedge fund company's Long Term Capital Management (LTC) in 1998 and Amaranth in 2006, the forerunners of the Bear Sterns, Goldman Sachs, Lehman Brothers, Washington Mutual, and American International Group's (AIG) titanic failures.

Once again, I'm sure you all know the answer. Still, I thought you might want to know some of the details to the latest one, and believe me, it doesn't take a crystal ball to know – IT WON'T BE THE LAST!

By the second quarter of 2014, banks had lent as much money ($8.11 trillion) as they had just before the gargantuan collapse of 2008-09 and mortgage lenders were even worse. With mega-banks renting out New York City offices in their corporate headquarters to the very same government agencies that are supposed to be regulating them, do you really think this isn't going to happen again?

Those of us that can still think for ourselves knew this second collapse was coming when President Clinton completed deregulation and the stock market pushed into record territory on a near daily basis throughout the late 90's. Like major earthquakes that occasionally rock California, the NSA spy-gate, or the cataclysmic Super Volcano eruption waiting under Yellowstone Park that's 40,000 years past due - it was just a matter of time before all hell broke loose again. The string of cataclysmic corporate failures that followed LTC were... Enron, which blew up in 2001 from one bogus deal after another that were hid by their giant crooked accounting firm Arthur Anderson. Anderson eventually went down with them, making them bedmates in prison. WorldCom followed in 2002 because of the shady accounting methods they used to hide

CEO Bernard Ebber's margin calls on his own stock he was using to finance other businesses: And lastly, the implosion of Amaranth in 2006.

For those of us who didn't have our heads buried in the sand, these devastating failures didn't just set off bells and whistles - they set off "AIR RAID SIRENS!" Then, finally, the "BIG BANG" came in 2008 with the failures of Bear Sterns in March, followed by Lehman Brothers, the government's own subsidiaries - mortgage lending giants and insurers Fannie Mae and Freddie Mac, and mega insurance company AIG (who was insuring the derivative scams of everyone else). These failures were immediately followed by the near collapse of Wells Fargo, Bank of America, JPMorgan Chase, Citigroup, Morgan Stanley, Goldman Sachs, U.S. Bancorp, and several other behemoths, that were only averted by secret loans set up by the Treasury's Hank Paulson to Bank of America and Wells Fargo. Then Timothy Geithner stepped in to save his old bank JPMorgan and the rest of the barbarians of banking.

Fed Chairman Ben Bernanke claimed it was "the worst financial collapse in global history and 12 of the 13 most important financial institutions in the U.S. were at risk of failure within a period of a week or two."

When President Reagan partially deregulated the industry in the 80's with a big push from Walter Wriston, his economic advisor and CEO of First National Bank, now Citicorp, it didn't take long for people like Wriston, Charles Keating, and his partner in crime, junk bond king Michael Milken, to realize they could get as rich as Joe Kennedy had in the 1920's before someone made it illegal again. As did Reagan and Greenspan, Wriston, the father of modern deregulation and age of greed, hated regulations, and his laissez-fair economics fit theirs to a tee. Getting Reagan and Congress to lift the limits on interest rates for savings accounts and CD's, and merging commercial banks with savings banks, which allowed all banks to issue credit cards and give out loans of any type, wasn't enough for Wriston. He continued to lead the charge around and through what little regulation was left, all the while handing out more bogus loans as if they were candy.

Meanwhile, like other varmints with ties to politicians, Milken and Keating, the face of Lincoln Savings and Loan, led a group of bankers and investors down the old junk bond and Ponzi scheme trails that very quickly brought the Savings and Loan industry to near extinction. As I recall, Keating's purchase of Milken's junk bonds was the major blow for Lincoln and got him over four years in jail. Milken got ten for being the junk bond king and almost singlehandedly causing the meltdown and recession of the late 1980's and early 90's. Unfortunately, he only served two years after cooperating with investigators.

Back then, the people were asked to bail out the banks when the Federal Deposit Insurance Fund couldn't and we wanted answers and justice. We got both! Around 1000 top executives and employees were found guilty and went to jail in the Justice Department's response to reign in Wall Street's immediate abuse of the new lax regulations. And some prominent politicians barely escaped the same fate back when we had a reasonable democracy.

Junk Bonds wouldn't play as much of a roll in this meltdown. As you know systemic hedge fund and derivative schemes were a huge factor in the 2008 world financial collapse. Yet they may have gotten away with it if not for the second bank meltdown in 20 years caused by the same over leveraging by both Wall Street and the public. According to the Wall Street Journal, U.S. households had borrowed 10 times more than they had in 1980, and financial corporations doubled their borrowing in the 8 years leading up to the collapse. Does that tell you anything about borrowing money? It was frowned upon just two generations ago!

The Bloomberg News reported Morgan Stanley took out $107 billion in Fed loans in Sept. 2008 alone. Citigroup topped out at 99.5 and Bank of America (B of A) 91.4 billion in Jan. and Feb. of 2009 to avoid a colossal meltdown for the umpteenth time under the Wriston and Milton Friedman theory of economics. The Morgan Stanley loans, along with Congress rejection of the TARP bill, ignited the Dow Jones to its biggest single day drop in history – 733 points.

If it wasn't for Bloomberg LP, we may never have known just how much the banks had borrowed in their conspiracy with the Federal Reserve (most of it while under the helm of Greenspan and Bernanke) or for how long. Bloomberg had to sue it all the way to the U.S. Supreme Court under the Freedom of Information Act to break the cover up. It didn't tell anyone which ones were in trouble and wound up committing '$7.77 trillion' to them from 1985 to 2009, culminating with the $1.2 trillion bailout on Dec. 5, 2008. That will bankrupt a country in a hurry, won't it?

Bloomberg also reported, on Nov. 26, 2008, just as the meltdown got underway, B of A's CEO Kenneth Lewis wrote shareholders a letter stating he headed "one of the strongest and most stable major banks in the world." I guess he accidentally left out the part about them already owing the Fed $86 billion, and they had set up 11 lending facilities by the end of 2008 for banks, security firms, and corporations that couldn't get short term loans from their usual sources to keep them afloat. Also hidden was the fact that nearly half of the top 30 borrowers were shaky European firms.

It was just like old times. As usual the high rollers were rolling the dice, but this implosion had a new twist to it that was led by Citibank, Bear Sterns, Goldman Sacks, and Countrywide Savings Bank. Like Lincoln Savings was in the 80's, they would be the new face to the ultimate bank fraud of the 90's and early 2000's. The difference was that they would use the federal government directly (us taxpayers) as their biggest sucker. By 2008, Bear Sterns would emerge as king of securities fraud tied to subprime mortgages, though most of the other parasites were heavily engaged in mortgage fraud, recruiting and approving just about any loan that came to their office. Then they bundled most of the $10 trillion market and sold them to the government and any other fools ignorant enough to buy them.

Goldman Sacks own Fabrice Tourre was found guilty of securities fraud when he bundled bad mortgages into CDO's (collateralized debt obligations) and sold them to two different large investors. He then let one bet they would go up and the other they would go down. The one that bet they would go down was famed Wall Street billionaire John Paulson, who was allowed to help choose the ones he bet on... Gee, I wonder how this guy got to be a billionaire! Sacks wound up paying a $550 million settlement for being morons.

When Bear Sterns stacked deck collapsed, they were rescued by a deal between legislators and JPMorgan - who had been bailed out by us taxpayers - in a buyout the equally fraudulent Morgan couldn't resist at $2 a share. As the market was collapsing, Congress blamed Morgan, who then passed it to Sterns for fraudulently covering up the bogus loans.

During the meltdown of 2009, with few rules to stop them and betting Congress would bail them out, the top twenty five whales of Wall Street - the biggest hedge fund managers - made a record $25 billion. Leading the way was David Tepper at $4 billion, George Soros with 3.3, James Simons at 2.5, and John Paulson at 2.3 billion, making his $40 million home seem like chump change.

Back then Countrywide was the number one mortgage originator in the country and had commercials everywhere. Everybody knew who they were after their seismic media blitz, especially those businesses and individuals with bad credit, low to no income, and small independent businesses with unprovable income. Countrywide didn't care though, like Citicorp, they had no intention of keeping them. Loan originators, bankers, appraisers, businesses, and individuals alike falsified their applications to get them approved, then top management rubber stamped them. Most of the people pushing the loans were getting paid by commission and executives were becoming billionaires, so it doesn't take Sherlock Holms to figure out once again greed was the special of the day on the Street.

Fraudulent loans were being identified left and right, with 60 to 80 percent of them "not meeting company underwriting policies," leaving approximately one third of them underwater. Chief Underwriter Richard Bowen of Citibank tried for two years to get Board Chairman Robert Rubin - yes the same Robert Rubin who was Secretary of the Treasury — to stop the fraud and get an outside investigation going, but was instead demoted and quit. Alayne Fleischmann, Managing Director for J.P. Morgan, and many others who mirrored Bowen's actions, were outright fired. They should have known there is no place for morals and honesty on Wall Street and it is rewarded with severe repercussions.

President Obama, who inherited this mess from George W., signed the Fraud Enforcement and Recovery Act and appointed Senator Ted Kaufman to lead an investigative committee. He promised heads would roll like after the 1980's bank failures. Despite his heroic efforts, rather than hundreds of top management being prosecuted and sent to jail - not one was! The CEO's screamed their innocence with arrogance and ignorance, and Lloyd Blackfein, CEO of Goldman Sachs, claimed their victims "were professionals who knew about their deals and what marketing strategy was all about. Basically you sell your crap to get rid of your risk," he proclaimed. Blackfein, Rubin, and the other CEO's who sold the bad loans, then made billions more for themselves and their banks by betting they would fail. And guess what happened to the loyal employees who made them ultra-wealthy? They were laid off by the tens of thousands!

The Justice Department, led by Lenny Brewer, Chief of the Criminal Division, then threw a smokescreen at the betrayed public. He claimed they couldn't prove beyond the reasonable doubt a jury needs to convict the top executives that any of them knew about the fraud. But the truth is: First, millions of people throughout history have been convicted on circumstantial evidence alone. Second, the witnesses were highly educated whistleblowers, not some drunks or drug addicts off the streets. That makes their testimony credible well beyond a reasonable doubt. And third, Jamie Demon was one of Obama's biggest backers during his run for the presidency. So it didn't matter if an honest loyal American bank regulator like William Black wanted to throw top executives in jail as they had after the S&L prosecutions - the immunity deals were closed long ago.

The arch villains of democracy and the world were never charged. They even got to keep their billions in pay and stock options in exchange for some relatively minor fines considering their crimes against humanity. Two Bear Sterns hedge fund managers did eventually go to trial, but with "18 defense attorneys" and purportedly "no whistleblowers" to testify against them, they too were let go.

Everyone was furious, executives were laughing arrogantly, and Wall Street got away with murder in every sense of the word worldwide.

When Citibank was questioned by Kaufman and his Senate Committee, whistleblower Bowen testified "there was clearly risk taken that could only lead to substantial losses" and he notified all the top management personally. Oblivious to the intimate relationship the bankers had with the Obama administration, and confident they had the evidence they needed to put CEO's behind bars, the committee turned over the prosecution to the Justice Department, only to come away with a guilty plea for failure to do due diligence. Once again no heads rolled and the blame was shifted to Clayton Holdings, a due diligence company for many criminal banks who fraudulently claimed the mortgages were O.K.

Documentation brought up in civil trials clearly revealed the fraud and Mr. Bowens assertions of up to 80% of the loans being defective at Citibank. Other testimony verified those at JPMorgan and Lehman Brothers was nearly as deplorable. The civil suits and successive whistleblowers revealed there was massive cheating at Bear Stearns as well, and it went all the way to the top executives.

Isn't it ironic that presidential cabinet cronies like Robert Rubin that move back to Wall Street can get away with murder and mayhem around the world?

A Little Know Secret

There is a little publicized, nearly secret, monumental voice controlling all stock market activity. So seldom mentioned, and kept hush-hush by the major TV networks, I myself forgot about their existence, even though they are the underlying force behind the entire market. Some of you have probably heard of rating companies like Standard & Poor's (S&P), Morningstar, and Moody's. They rate everything from individual stocks to the whole country.

Hypothetically, "independent credit analyzers," they are anything but. Handcuffed to all the markets, they are constantly under pressure from Wall Street and international markets to keep all ratings on everything as high as possible. Nothing is more coveted by the Street, municipalities, and international capital and credit risk management professionals than a strong recommendation from these overly powerful market movers. Bankers and investment firms lend all the money necessary for municipalities to do infrastructure projects based on their ratings. They are literally the investment manager's best friend.

You can see why the roar of corruption is so easily attracted to them, and for that same reason you almost never hear a word about them. You would think the world's economies and banking systems that ride on their every rating would put them on the front page of every newspaper and broadcast, but the stifling corruption keeps their intertwined business practices as silent as a tree falling in the woods. Their raters almost never downgrade any funds or large players no matter how unstable they may be, and are often forced to do quite the opposite or be fired like veteran analyst Marvin Roffman was by Donald Trumps. Which is also why S&P paid a $77 million fine for what the SEC said was "fraudulent misconduct" and "they loosened standards to drum up business."

Moody's rater's alone convinced banks to gamble over $1 trillion of unsecured debt in the past year, claiming increased clarity on the risk return profile of the instruments "made them safe." Isn't that what they told the Titanic investors? With pressure from the powerful financial institutions and bureaucrats, credit analysts are about as honest and accurate as the mostly useless economists that reside in their hip pocket. Even when they get a little honest streak going, it still doesn't make them right. For example, while they were downgrading the market and hundreds of companies like Netflix to a sell position in 2013, their stocks and the market shot up. They also hated some international markets like Japan's in 2013, but it too spiked. Wrong again guys!

Their silent control of the market reached so deep, the Treasury Department was trying to figure out why small and medium sized firms couldn't compete on Wall Street for access to capital like the larger ones. In their study of decimalization brought about by the supersized traders, they concluded the popular electronic trading at low cost favored the highly liquid big shots at the expense of peons because of raters.

Decimalization reduced the spreads that helped fund the analyst and reduced their profits substantially from 25 cents a share to 1 cent! So only the heavyweights with their extremely high volumes were worth underwriting. That put pressure on them to rate only the largest corporations. The volume from peons was just too low for the commission bounties they wanted. As a result, the Global Analyst Research Settlement of 2003 made it illegal for research analyst at ratings companies to be paid through investment banking revenue. The last couple of decades had seen the tick size on trading reduced to half of what it was for generations. So bringing it back to where it was would "allegedly" reduce the short term quick profit investing and make it more worth underwriters time to help out the little guy, spread the money around, and help avert the cataclysmic failures everyone knew was coming. My guess is – IT DIDN'T WORK!

Exchange Traded Funds (ETF's)

One of the "safe instruments" analyst rate, these funds can be relatively stable funds with low management fees, or they can be BIG losers with outrageously high fees. Some are highly speculative and carry risky instruments, such as junk bonds, that make the fund managers giggle all the way to the bank while draining your wallet.

One of the low coast index funds, like those tracking the S&P 500, for example, will nearly always beat a higher cost actively managed or specialized one. To reiterate, you only pay about a 1% onetime fee compared to the larger upfront and annual fees of actively managed funds. Some ETF's have done real well the last few years, but what hasn't since government started sleeping with Wall Street and pumping trillions of dollars into the market after the crash, on top of the trillions they put into it since the 80's.

This is why I tell people, never go into the stock market in any way shape or form. You would be better off burying your money in the back yard then putting it in the market... but that's from my honest little bubble in a world that no longer seems to exist. That's why I just love crashes! I finally get vindication from the crooked system and get to say things like – In your face! I've been warning you for years! How are your fraudulent profits doing now? Regrettably, I only get to say those things every 10 years or so, and those smarter than me invest their money into parasitic corruption knowing it's just a blip on the radar screen.

As with mutual funds and IRAs, most of the time you have no idea exactly what you've got your money in, and even if you think you've picked a winner, the entire stock market is speculative and controlled by powerful forces beyond your control and often anyone's. Everything is affected by these outside forces and rackets. And if you're in any of the popular target date retirement funds, you probably own lots of flimflam rip-offs. Considering the people investing your money get paid by commission, DO NOT count on them picking the ones with the best returns and least cost to you!

One fad to hit the market is fundamental indexing funds. Rather than the 'highly specialized' index funds that often don't do very well, these funds weigh certain fundamental aspect of the companies in it, such as earnings, dividends, or sales. This is supposed to be a better way than a lot of index funds that use market capitalization (share price times shares outstanding) in weighing the funds. But like index funds, a fund with a few exceptionally large heavyweights on a hot streak can unrealistically carry the entire fund on their backs as in the first 7 months of 2017, where just four jumbo Dow company's accounted for 98% of the gains. This can cause obvious problems if they suddenly turn sour. Some of the largest players still standing from the 1990's bubble have done just that and to this day drag down the whole fund.

Like millions of others, I myself used to own top flying internet stocks from that era that are doing significantly worse all these years later than in their high flying market leading days. Many were absorbed by other firms and hundreds of others have vanished off the internet bubble face of the earth. Can you imagine how much money the poor suckers who invested heavily in some of these unbelievably high flying stocks and funds loaded with these losers lost?

Payday Loans

This mostly big bank scam didn't start out as their own personal ruse, but morphed into one when the robber barons just couldn't resist the enormous profits of the smaller operations that numbered in the tens of thousands throughout the country. This rip-offs been around since the 1990's and is opposite most Wall Street con jobs because these prey on the poor, just as predatory home mortgages did. Although predatory lending was "purportedly" banned throughout the country, pay day loans have only been banned in 15 states and outlawed for military personnel nationally. Once again, the top dogs reap the obscene profits while crushing any further regulation.

Remember when payday loan stores first started popping up? They didn't get much attention until the press was notified about these predators by people losing everything, including their homes, from their paralyzing short term loans.

You see, there's millions of desperate people who can't pay their rent, usually in poor neighborhoods, but sometimes middle and even upper class families who are living that opulent life they can't afford. Both are living from paycheck to paycheck when they see an advertisement on TV or a sign along the street that says something like "CASH" or "LOANS." These places prey on the poor and desperate, and when you call or go in, they tell you nobody will be turned down and act like your fairy godmother. But they are completely unregulated businesses who claim they aren't banks so they don't have to follow the banking regulations or truth in lending laws. That allows them to get away with anything they want... and *OH-BOY* do they get away with anything they want!

They start by telling you the basic way pay day loans work. It's exactly what the name says it is. It's a loan until you get your next paycheck. You can get a short term loan for perhaps two or three weeks by writing out a check to them in advance of your pay check, using your next check as collateral. The lowlifes will even set up automatic withdrawals from your checking account to cover the "non-loans." If you're lucky, they will explain the terms of the loan and how much interest you'll pay over the short period you'll need it. But since the vultures are usually dealing with relatively uneducated, desperate patsy's, they can get away with murder.

Despite always starting out with an exorbitant fee of around twenty percent of your pay and ending with interest rates that could kill a rhino (usually around 200 to 300% annually), the desperate and foolish come back month after month for more punishment. So you can see why the unscrupulous jumbo banks didn't want to miss out on this highly profitable no risk scam. It's like being a legal loan shark. These outrageous rates are a death trap to almost all who take out these never ending economic death spirals. Even the loan sharks themselves admit their biggest money makers are the people who can least afford them! Still, with the two largest newspapers in the country (the Las Angeles and New York Times) pushing for pay day loan reform - we got nowhere!

It never ceases to amaze me what these scoundrels will do to pad their wallets with millions and billions of dollars in a never ending cycle of greed. They are the hierarchy that set the morals, values, and ethics bar most of society now follows.

Do you remember when we had a decent society? Sometimes it's so discouraging I can hardly continue telling you about all the crap that got us into this predicament. You all know what I'm talking about! How many times have you been screwed over? Sometimes your life has to be in danger before many people will do the right thing over money nowadays. I had to get two different heating companies and pay each one twice before I could get one to replace the faulty ignition switch on my furnace boiler we all knew was bad. Yet, like everyone who must rely on their integrity and experience, I got screwed paying them for years until they finally did the right thing *after* the boiler blew its stack!

Debit Cards

Thanks in part to the government's policy of promoting both long and short term borrowing as a way to improve one's standing in the world, we've become a nation of debtor's. But we know whose standing is really improved! Across the land, debit cards became a forced fed way for banks to replace credit cards for millions of people. After having virtually no requirements of any kind for as long as I can remember, even sending applications to kids like my daughter, they claimed they came up with a solution to the tremendous debt many people and banks were getting themselves into.

In a move to shift the inevitable and mounting credit card fraud caused by the banks continued use of the cheaper magnetic strip cards to the unsuspecting public, they use their loose ways as an excuse to shift hacker losses that total in the billions, including some high profile cases. Normally, credit card theft and hacking are restricted to just a $50 loss to the consumer, with the companies that were hacked into and the banks taking the other losses. Previous cases resulted in firms biting the bullet for hundreds of millions, but in cases where negligence can't be proven, the bank eats the losses. Why do you think they push nonstop to get us to buy their unnecessary credit card insurance? We aren't the ones that need it - they are! So the Consumer Financial Protection Bureau finally did right and got them off our backs with a case against Bank of America that made them pay a whopping $772 million in consumer refunds and civil fines.

Although companies are not usually liable for mammoth breaches like the 40 million credit card one at Target in 2013, debit cards are always the consumer's loss if the bank chooses not to take it and reimburse their checking account. In individual cases, they can place the entire burden on the consumer to prove the charges are fraud. Even if hackers don't steal your money directly, they get you by adding little expenses to your overly long cell phone bill if you're not paying attention. Some foolish people pay hundreds, even thousands of dollars in extra charges because they never check them.

As you all know, it takes a lot of willpower to deny these con-artist because they ruthlessly push you until you give in – henceforth the B of A fines. When they call you, they titillate you saying there are no hidden fees and you'll get free overdraft protection. If you try to turn down the free overdraft protection, they insist it's critical and bug you until you cave in or go to that place with the big guys and strait jackets.

Yah right! Wake up! This is America people! They actually call it a free service to avoid the Fair Credit Act, and often you can't drop it according to that tiny fine print in your agreement nobody can read. The fact that your debit card is tied to your checking account is *their* free prize. That fine print gives them permission to cover any overdrafts you may accidentally incur in any order they choose, and you'll be charged around thirty dollars each time!

At first glance, this would seem a relatively fair way to do business considering their other monstrous scams, but you know American banks don't do anything fair anymore! There are strings attached to this whole racket. They don't notify their customers immediately after making the mistake. And there is no reason for you to suspect you made an error unless you carry your checkbook around with you and keep tract of every purchase. So the scheisters are taking advantage of two things: First, nobody has carried a check book around with them for thirty years, and second, people are now used to using a credit card that will automatically be denied if you're over the credit limit. If you're like me and do all of your shopping in one day, the thieves can charge an overdraft fee over and over every time you make another purchase. So in essence, fees can actually amount to tens of thousands of percent of your original purchases...Ka-Ching!

The scavengers have one more ace up their sleeve. To make really big money on debit cards, they pay the merchant, and then charge you each overdraft in order by the smallest purchase to the largest in order to charge you more fees and interest. With banks in cahoots with Washington, there are no laws requiring them to pay the overdrafts in order by date of when they receive them from the merchants. So they hold off paying the larger ones that often come in first and pay the numerous smaller ones instead.

Huge firms such as McDonalds are helping banks also. For some reason - I'm sure you can guess why - they started paying their employees by making them open debit accounts with certain ones and depositing their money into their accounts, rather than giving them a check or directly depositing it into their normal account. As a result, these same low educated, low income employees have to pay monthly fees and penalties associated with misusing the debit card. Do you hear another Ka-Ching for the banks on the backs of the working poor?

It wasn't always this ludicrous. I remember back in the late 1970's, before deregulation, when debit cards were first introduce. Banks used them to give the mostly young people an opportunity to establish credit before issuing them a credit card. They weren't out to get as rich off of everyone as they are now, and didn't have all the fees and penalties. They wanted to help you establish credit with them and hopefully keep you as their customer for life when you moved up to their money making credit cards and home loans. That's not to say they didn't charge a lot of interest for those who didn't pay in full and on time, because they did. It just wasn't the stratospheric profit rates of today's thieves.

Undoubtable it takes two to tango, so like payday loans or any other predatory lending; one can't blame the banks alone. What we can blame them on is their nonstop bloodthirsty ways of preying on the poorest, most desperate, and often least educated citizens: Those that often borrow unwillingly to stay alive, pay the rent, and have food and a roof over their heads. Then there are the yuppies and millennials that for one reason or another are perfectly comfortable borrowing large sums of money they probably can't pay back in the long run. For them it's a much more selfish reason. They want it all at any cost and don't care how they get it, that Wall Street commercialism mentality the imbeciles love preying on. What better customers can you abuse than those who are desperate, or selfish and greedy with no financial self-discipline?

The 2008 collapse finally made the scoundrels tighten up their uncontrolled lending ways to the poor, so they once again outflanked the regulators and picked on all of us loyal, dependable, credit card holders instead.

In everybody's contract, it says in tiny print the banks can change the rates and terms at any time without your permission, and often without notice. So after the meltdown they themselves created, they took advantage of that little detail. They sent about 50% of the people, including their most loyal and trustworthy customers, a notice in the mail that said they were lowering your credit limit to around one fifth your previous limit. Then they raised the interest rates on those with a balance in an attempt to make up for the tens of millions of those bad credit risk people they courted so willingly before the crises.

As did millions of loyal on time paying customers, I called my behemoth bank and asked them what the heck was going on. They told me for the past year I wasn't spending enough money on a monthly basis, so they were only going to allow me what **they** considered the maximum I might spend in a month. Like most people, in previous years I had emergency car and home repairs or airline tickets that were quite sizable in any given month. But I was finally getting lucky and had no major purchases for the past year. I told them I was getting older and had most of the things I needed for the rest of my life and claimed this was a good thing, and they didn't complain when I was making large purchases in the past! They still insisted on lowering my credit limit. So I insisted – You're Fired! Guess who it was? That insidious varmint JPMorgan who bought my bank Chase and became JPMorgan Chase.

I told them to cancel my credit card immediately and I would take my many years of loyalty to someone else. And you should too!

That's how they operate after deregulation. Their attitude changed and use you when their profits are good, then spit you out when they no longer think you are profitable enough to keep, even though you were a loyal customer for many years. I hope tens of millions of you fired their butts like I did.

To get back at legislators for the new regulations in the Credit Card Act and go where the most money was, for the next several years the vultures tightened up credit to everyone from individuals with excellent credit to small businesses. They made sure almost nobody could qualify for a loan or credit of any type except for their usual wealthy buddies and institutional brethren that supported them.

Perhaps in an attempt to make up for his past associations with the banks, Senator Dodd told them they were responsible for the countries financial crises. He acted furious they weren't lending the money the Fed was lending to them at near 0% interest rates. With the Office of the Comptroller and Currency backing him, he finally attempted, at least publically, to stand up for the little guy by trying to push through regulations controlling the massive heist. But once again the government agency put in place to protect us hopped aboard the gravy train and said they failed to see how regulation would help.

Secretary of the Treasury Timothy Geithner, who had previously backed deregulation when he was working at the Fed, ripped into his former boss and current chairman Ben Bernanke. At the Department of Treasury meeting with regulators that were supposed to be protecting us, he bellowed: "You should put the interest of the country ahead of the bankers!" Was the tide changing for the good guys? Did the 99%ers actually have a high ranking federal official controlling the treasury on their side, or was this just another sideshow for the media?

Whatever it was, he appeared to want reform, but the Republicans weren't about to tolerate his mutiny no matter who he was. They had him outnumbered in that meeting and told him bluntly he was literally the ringleader of a liberal scheme and "there shouldn't be any consumer protection system at all." That's the new GOP way! Just let the free market do its thing and run hog wild as it had throughout both eras of deregulation! That's why Trump is pushing to get rid of the Consumer Protection Bureau and all regulations.

Without a doubt, this crap went all the way to the Democratic White House too, and none of them have the guts to bite the hand that feeds them like Teddy Roosevelt. Their version of a free market economy now goes something like this. The banks borrow their money from the Fed at around .5% interest, and then charge their customers 30% interest rates on credit cards, 300 to 400% on pay day loans, and whatever they can get away with on debit cards. The mind-blowing profits are then used for their proprietary scams. After all, that seems fair, doesn't it? Take everyone from the lowest, poorest person to the federal government for everything you can. They call it *"Capitalism"* and a *"free market economy."*

Banks and investment firms had lost so much on their stock market sorcery; they actually caused the successive attempts to regulate them. They now penalize all us good people by demanding enormously high credit scores and down payments. Qualifying rules are so impossible, even Ben Bernanke was turned down for a loan in 2014. That's right, the same guy who 3 paragraphs ago was defending the morons! They said he hadn't been employed long enough after he stepped down to qualify. His response: "The banks have goon overboard in their qualifying rules." No, Really? I guess the word *former* Fed chair carries about as much weight as you and me.

Both individuals and small businesses are punished in the name of self-serving regulation. Banks punish many small businesses by lowering the credit lines they rely on to pay their employees. Often forcing them to max out their high interest credit cards instead, or use cash when purchasing materials. This further deteriorates the economy when many go under. As Mr. Bernanke proved, only the wealthiest tycoons of industry and big business can get credit. And I'm sure you already know what they do with such privileges.

You guessed it! After the 2008-09 meltdown Warren Buffett, for example, sent an army of realtor's to buy every foreclosed and short sale house in Florida he could from the Orlando area to Tampa Bay my real estate agent told me. He personally forced the prices up with every purchase he stole from under us little peoples noses. Homes he targeted, which were almost all of them, were sold to him and under contract before they even hit the areas multiple listing service... and I personally witnessed it. Only his hand-picked army of shady realtors could receive the commissions, and all competition in our "free market economy" was squashed like an ant under the giant foot of "Buffettlism!"

Prices shot up 30 to 50% in months, and with banks not lending to those of us with great credit who couldn't meet the new outrageous underwriting requirements designed for the plutocrats - we were forced out! His monopolizing army then reopened the escalated houses for sale to the public (more formally known as flipping). He then wanted us patsy's and all the realtors he left out in the cold to sell and buy his often stagnant, mold filled, roof leaking, broken window, run down homes that often cost tens of thousands of dollars to bring back up to building code he never personally new existed.

Florida had so many bad house's being sold by unscrupulous agents, they came up with a standard short sale and foreclosed homes "As Is" sales contract. This holds the real estate agents harmless from anything wrong with the houses, and once again the people were left carrying the burden. We were supposed to buy back these houses at Buffets self-made inflated prices and his army would be kind enough to let us bid on them. This fed the panick machine and pushed prices substantially higher by what people perceived as a housing shortage. So naturally, a buying frenzy sprang up with the usual skyrocketing prices in his self-made speculative bidding wars. Does that guy know how to manipulate the markets or what? His agents loved it! They could once again collect an even larger commission on each dubious sale!

When I tried to buy a house, realtors told me every house I tried to buy had multiple offers on it but they couldn't legally tell me how much the highest offer was. They often said it would probably take so and so price to get it and I should make an offer at or above that price. Nobody else had any idea what the other offers were, or if there even were other offers above the listing price, never mind tens of thousands of dollars above it. Was this a scam from the realtors or banks? Either way, it doesn't matter. The only thing that matters is the same thing all magicians count on to fool the audience – ILLUSION! People had no choice but believe the realtors when they told us there was a shortage of houses, when in reality, guys like Buffett and the banks were hording them to force up the price - and still are.

Where Buffett and his Berkshire Hathaway go, so do institutional investors. Following his lead, Hedge funds started investing in real estate in Las Vegas and other depressed housing markets. They were actually buying the same foreclosed houses and short sales banks forced people out of and had already been reimbursed for from their fully insured government mortgages. Now, they were not only joining Mr. Buffett in shutting out the rest of us, but making double the profits and billions doing it!

Banks came up with dozens of smaller ways to steal our money as well, such as charging a nonrefundable fee for a home mortgage application, like they did me. After assuring people with excellent credit you are preapproved for a mortgage, they charge a nonrefundable fee - in my case $155 - to send it to their underwriters who often turn them down for an income to debt ratio that's too low in the first place, and they know it! Being cautious, I did the math myself before forking over the money. I told the lady with decades of experience handling it I didn't have the income to debt ratio they required for the loan, but she disagreed. So I trusted her opinion and lost my money. It doesn't take a genius to figure out turning down a million loans is an easy $155 million in their pocket.

They also get low income people and those that want to buy a much larger house then they can afford to take out "adjustable loans" that at first glance look like a way to make your dreams come true. They start out with a lower interest rate than a fixed rate loan, and then artificially lower them further to what most people call a "teaser rate" to get you qualified. Still, these can balloon upwards if interest rates rise dramatically as they did in the 1980's. Most can go up about 2% a year with a cap of about 10% over the life of the loan. A traditional rate of around 10% can go to 20% in five years. As they did when Paul Volcker, used high interest rates to stop inflation, resulting in many real estate investors like my former customer and homeowner's alike going down the tubes.

Then you have "balloon loans" that set a specific date - usually ten years until the whole loan is due. My line of credit is one. You make low monthly payments and on the due date you usually refinance at the current rate, which is good if rates go down, but could be tragic if they shoot considerably higher. That's why I pay down the principal early. Adjustable and balloon mortgages are one of Wall Street's favorite instruments – speculative gambles. And as usual, we are their vehicle.

Not satisfied, banks also control the board rooms of publicly traded companies. Small shareholders are furious they have no say in whom or what their corporations spend their money on. Banks, for example, are heavily spending their money on everything from dirty fossil fuel projects to political ads. Remember, the Street's never picky about where the money that feeds the beast comes from.

The little people realize their one or two votes don't mean anything when it comes time to having a voice in the companies they partially own and started rebelling. A case in point would be Google, where the two largest shareholders control 16% of the votes. So someone came up with the idea of running them the same way they elect officers and get rules they want installed controlling the financial side of the equation. They believe the fairest way to run a publicly traded company is to run it like public elections and the U.S. Senate. Each and every voter has equal weight, regardless of how many shares a person or entity owns.

Every shareholder has the same right to put regulations they deem appropriate on the ballot. Since they have no idea what politicians or Super Pac's their money's going to, they need a fair way to control the corporate budget. So they go with a simple majority vote, with non-voters considered a no vote. As of time of publishing, the battle for corporate control is still being waged.

By now I'm sure you realize the kings of chaos exist for one reason only. Despite record profits for years, they prove to be greedier than ever with one proprietary scheme after another. The only question that remains is - when will the rest of the American people smarten-up and revolt against their own moneyed oppressors?

11

New York City and the Media

New York, New York – so bad they had to name it twice! It was summed up best in the movie "Ghost Busters II," when Vigo the Carpathian came back to life and Dr. Peter Venkman told him "Only a moron would come back and choose New York City!"

Sadly, other movies and TV shows such as "Welcome Back Kotter," "All in the Family," and dozens of others have accurately portrayed it as the axis of evil and main cog in society's great downfall. Originally our young nation's capital, it has been on the threshold of Hell with flames licking at its feet for more than a century. It's the birthplace and center of the oligarchy, and everyone from the richest scheisters to street hustlers, drug dealers, gangs, and prostitutes peddle their evil wares. The place we worship its richest and poorest is a bastion of pestilence, spreading its tentacles across the globe. It's been the most crime ridden, varmint infested, fraudulent, sleaziest, low life, blood sucking, cockroach infested city in the country for generations.

Both rich and poor scavenge off of each other, devouring and digesting their prey. New York's led the country in every despicable health problem, from the recurring rat infestations and their diseases, to the unsanitary conditions caused by tens of thousands of horses before the invention of the automobile, to the choking and destructive air pollution after. It even had our country's only outbreak of bed bugs in over 100 years. The little critters took over the city, investing every orifice from hotels to the Empire State Building.

Anything deplorable, destructive, or despicable can be found there. From tax dodge "Billionaire Building," where you're not allowed to see your up to $100 million condo until *after* you buy it, to Wall Street, investment banks, rapist, murderers, kidnappers, shady politicians, drug dealers, terrorist, poverty, street peddlers, the media, assault weapons, gangs, and of course the Yankees. Yes, even the Yankees play in a ghetto and have bought every championship since they bought Babe Ruth from the Boston Red Sox. When they recently built the new Yankee Stadium, they invariably built it right next to the old stadium in the same ghetto that was rated the poorest in the U.S. People have feared going into that neighborhood to watch a Yankees game for generations, especially tourist and visitors, so who would be foolish enough to build it in the same place?

New York led the country in murder and mayhem for decades. In the 1970's, arsonist burnt down so many neighborhoods they put happy looking cardboard scenes over the charred and broken windows. It's the number one money laundering and drug trafficking distribution center in the U.S., and dwarfs anywhere else with the life destroying chemicals that have strangled our country's youth and created carnage of our streets. Drug gangs instill fear and terrorize neighborhoods while battling for supremacy, leaving dead and wounded bodies scattered across the city like a war zone. Ton after ton of cocaine, heroin, and marijuana is rushed in by plane, train, ship, and highway as if in short supply on the New York Mercantile Exchange.

Fleeing New Yorkers then spread their pestilent ways across the country, bringing their fears, paranoia, and way of life to all. It's so despicable there; native George Carlin made his living telling jokes about life in the city where some places never see the light of day and people are holed up like Bonnie and Clyde, with blinds closed, shades drawn, and up to five door locks on impenetrable steel doors.

Combined with our government in Washington D.C., have there ever been two cities more joined at the hip in controlling every facet of society? The 9-11-01 terrorist attacks would verify this extremely close partnership.

That's New York City though, a real gluten for punishment. No man or beast in their right mind would want to live there, never mind pass through it. And who can blame them? Humans of different races and cultures never could get along, so they decided to mix 8 million misfits from around the world to see if they would kill each other. And on April 7, 2014, the city police and fire departments tried doing just that at a charity hockey game that broke out in an all-out donnybrook. Only two of them didn't throw at least one punch.

Only New York would take the largest media, banking, fashion, and financial center of the world and mix it with some of the most violent, drug dealing slums in the country. It's as notorious for its crime, ghettos, and famed Mafia as it is Wall Street, hotels, restaurants, and the high fashion entertainment and media world we live so vicariously through.

What little good does come out of it is born from its own pestilence and need to forget and escape. Nearly everyone ever born there moved out or wants to. Even refrigeration giant Clarence Birdseye said he had to get out of there way back in 1912. Those psychos that work on Wall Street and the financial sector who can afford to live elsewhere do, with most not even going into the city anymore. They now live anywhere in the country and run their fraudulent scams out of their home offices. The once jam packed, insane, bustling, trading floor of the New York Stock Exchange now resembles a ghost town. And most of the other people in high paying or high publicity jobs that have to be at the office or studio move to Long Island or Southern Connecticut.

Who can blame them? They only suffer the excruciating long commute to satisfy their greed, publicity, and the high life. Those wealthy enough, or crazy enough, to both live and work in this axis of evil, stay in the most expensive, often tiniest, little apartments per square foot in the country.

New Yorkers are a strange, fad driven, cliquey breed that spread their warped lifestyle around the world. The newest fad is to actually live in tiny apartments called "micro-pads" in upscale neighborhoods that are smaller than most ghetto ones. That lifestyle has sprouted a tiny housing industry cult that pushes extremism to the max. People who used to live exact opposite yuppie lifestyles in huge, plush, apartments, condos, and houses, blew a circuit and now live in these places sane people wouldn't live in for all the money in the world that are more fit for squatters and the homeless. As I sit here in my home, I have to wonder... Why would anybody want to live in something the size of my living room?

At the other end of the scale, are the richest and greediest New Yorkers who live in extravagant Manhattan apartments and penthouse condos overlooking Central Park, with concierges and other superficial personal amenities costing in the tens of millions of dollars for the more luxurious ones.

Another fad New Yorkers champion is telecommuting to stay out of the city. It's an excellent way for employees of Wall Street firms to get their work done and just about anyone else who work on computers most of the day that don't need to be in the office. However, this brings up as many problems as it does solutions. While employers can save money on many things such as phones, office space, and equipment, like everything in the cold electronic world, they can't meet person to person for conferences and teams never personally meet face to face. You can't sit and relax at lunch chatting with your co-workers, so they now make friends and alliances via electronic communications. There is basically no real socialization with any other humans. From a society standpoint, can this be good?

Other tradeoffs include problems with oversight - think a teenager with a computer or cell phone trying to do their homework. And the cost of supplying employees with the necessary equipment needed at home is worse than supplying that teenager with school supplies. Like anyone, adults can also get lazy and lose focus from electronics, kids, and other family members - resulting in shabby work.

From an employee standpoint, many enjoy telecommuting because they don't have to put up with the rush hour crush. They save money on gas, repairs, and insurance, plus they have more flexibility to go to their kid's activities and can babysit or take care of their sick kids.

Led by N.Y. and Hollywood, we've become a society of fanatics, fads, and clicks worshiping all the wrong ideals, from Hollywood stars to fashion, Wall Street greed, and Washington hypocrites. It's so ridiculous a gold and white dress at the 2015 Oscars spurred a record number of responses on social media about what color it was. And a lady wore a dress made out of pearls that cost $150,000 and was - not surprisingly - stolen immediately. Out west, the home of many Hollywood stars, Newport Beach, Ca. even has a giant shopping mall called Fashion Island shopaholics have adored for 50 years. Brainwashed, mesmerized, and delusional, people are unable to think for themselves anymore - doing whatever the N.Y. media, Hollywood, and the government tells them. From the richest to poorest, New York, especially, dictates our perception of who we are and our social values. Like a sheep to a Sheppard, we obediently follow it into moral and financial extinction.

In the city where 1 in every 22 people is a millionaire, reality has completely disappeared for many. ABC morning news reported New Yorkers give their kids over $13 for every tooth that falls out. That's 13 times more than my daughter got just 8 years ago at the age of 10. Others claim we have to give our kids $1 dollar allowance for every year of age every week, regardless of the fact that most kids do nothing to earn it anymore. Some actually say earning it is bad! That's $8,901 by the time they're 18 and $26,703 for 3 kids. You would need a second job just to pay their allowance, or be one of those millionaires. Even some weddings cost 30 grand or more, causing nearly half the guests to decline the more extravagant ones they simply cannot afford to attend.

We have to have the newest gizmos and gadgets to go with the latest expensive fashions to satisfy the fashion police, that more often than not, break our bank accounts just to sport the look of some model, Hollywood star, athlete, or singer. Fanaticism's run-amok and kidnaped the country to such an extent, fashion trucks have popped up similar to the ice cream man, and Yuppie parents are bringing in interior designers for some of their kids' college dorms. Everything from electronics to automobiles has to seduce us and be as sexy and sleek looking as the models that showcase them. Perception and disillusionment has reached such horrific extremes, advertising and marketing are the highest paying jobs outside of Wall Street, contributing heavily to that 1 in every 22 millionaires.

Those millions upon millions of mindless drones worshiping all the wrong ideals are dooming themselves to a life based on gimmicks and illusion. Poor people that can't even afford food for their kids buy drugs, lottery tickets, and sport shoes with famous athlete's names attached for hundreds of dollars a pair, then rely on our over generous government to pay for their food. They no longer seem capable of thinking for themselves. Somehow, and for reasons I cannot contemplate, people get sucked into the most irrelevant, frivolous things for entertainment, convenience, and that "keep up with the Joneses" appearance.

I saw one family on TV who symbolized the typical middle class New York City yuppie family that spreads their mindless, discipline-less lifestyle throughout the country. They, like millions of copycats, have made my 'what's wrong with America list.' Having absolutely no knowledge of the value of a dollar and craving everything they can't afford at their convenience, they set about stacking their credit cards with debt at enormous interest rates, piled up huge cell phone bills, and ate out all the time. Apparently brainless and nearly broke, they decided to spend more on a money manager who claimed he could save them nearly $200,000 dollars with a little work and a lot of discipline. After giving them a clue about the real world, he cut out most of their extravagant lifestyle, refinanced their mortgage, and changed their insurance plan. They wound up saving about 16 grand a year, and to their astonishment, still enjoyed their commercialistic, frivolous, yuppie lifestyle.

We all know people like them. They're programmed by capitalist hogs and the media into believing they have to have every new, and most assuredly, expensive toy. They often bankrupt themselves trying to live high end lifestyles and wind up with a garage full of things they eventually tag-sell or auction off on the internet to eat and pay the rent. I had a tenant that did exactly that.

These people are a dream come true for everyone from corporate executives and their fleets of salesman to drug dealers. Corporate executives can sell them anything, no matter how expensive, impractical, or immoral, and drug dealers can sell them their life shattering poison as if it's candy. All they have to do is convince them it's the newest fad, they can't live without it, everyone is doing it, or it's cool.

How many times do they push their latest electronic device, drug, fashion, diet, health food supplement, or any number of a thousand other things you don't need: Or as the salesmen like to say – things you didn't know you needed. As you know, even as far back as the early years of the automobile industry, the top brass said they had to constantly come out with a different looking or functioning product to give the people a reason to throw away their perfectly good three or four year old cars.

The Media

Breaking News: The Koch brothers might buy The Tribune Company - owner of the Los Angeles Times, Orlando Sentinel, Hartford Current, Baltimore Sun, and the Chicago Tribune newspapers!

As is just about everything in the United States, the oversized, overhyped media is as legitimately suspect as everything else. Billionaire owners turned it into Super Pac's, and with the Citizens United case, the media became completely one sided. Much of it's owned by radicals schlepping their goods and promoting their agenda, which is usually politics, money, religion, or social manipulation. You see what *they* want you to see! Did you ever notice the news is slanted to get the owners personal views out, and that Wall Street guru the "Nightly Business Report" (NBR) has a rather obvious background of hundreds of blue oil barrels lined up in unison? Obviously a subliminal message! Is that our old buddy George W. and his cabinet schlepping their product through one of his shell company's?

One supersized company or conglomerate often owns a kaleidoscope of news outlets, thus controlling the entire spectrum of media. Google owns YouTube, and the largest cable TV company Time Warner owns the major TV and news network CBS, the largest book publisher Simon and Schuster, as well as other media outlets. The New York Times bought their major competitor The Boston Globe and Disney owns ABC and ESPN. The same company bought our local ABC, NBC, CBS, Fox, and Boston station in this area, then like all private equity firms, fired staff and combined the news crews, televising the same broadcast on three channels.

I think Comcast tops the cake though. The king of internet providers bought the major network NBC, which already owned the famed Universal Studios and theme parks in California, Florida, Japan, and Singapore. Then bought Netflix, the famous content company who was worried Comcast and the other major internet providers would purposely slow down their TV broadcast, movies, video games, etc. So they paid Comcast what amounts to a bribe to ensure they would smoothly stream their content and speed it up.

The Federal Communications Commission (FCC) wanted their piece of the "funny money" and agreed the immense corporations should be able to squash the little guys by paying bribes to speed up their broadcast over the "last mile." But for once the U.S. Supreme Court sided with of us little guys and ruled against the FCC's plan. Do you think Comcast gave Netflix their money back? Comcast didn't stop there though; they wanted to buy Time Warner, which would have given them two of the four major TV networks and the largest cable provider. Fortunately, this time the government remembered what the word monopoly meant.

If billionaires can't get the owners to sell their radio and TV stations, magazines, or newspapers to push their agendas, they get them through hostile takeovers. Often just paying a media owner more than they can refuse (called a bear hug) will get them what they want and avoid the embarrassment of a hostile takeover or media frenzy. A quite backroom deal is much more preferable than any alternatives; and in the new world of near zero interest rates and every deal being completely leveraged - no price is too high! Whatever way they do it, you have to ask yourself, how honest and partisan could any of the media be that's owned by these monsters?

The Koch's are the perfect example. So hated are they, reportedly, about half the people at an awards ceremony for the Los Angeles Times raised their hands when asked if they would quit their jobs if the Koch brothers bought the paper.

Could you imagine being so hated, half of your new employees would rather quit and suffer the consequences then work for you? That would almost certainly include losing your home to foreclosure, possibly making you homeless and ruin your credit. Some employers use your credit scores to determine your fitness for employment on the theory that someone who is a responsible credit risk will be a responsible employee. Therefore, if you quit working for the Koch's, you might be committing employment suicide as well.

While some media owners are hated, others like Robert Murdoch, chief executive of News Corp, get into hot water because they stop at nothing to get what they want. Mr. Murdoch was charged with ordering the hacking of people's phones he wanted to get secret stories on for his firm. He probably did nothing any other media mogul didn't... he just got caught!

There's no doubt about it, the New York based media and Tinseltown has been taken over by people who have an agenda to push. All they have to do is wave a little flashy tinsel and then watch the mesmerized, obedient, thongs chase it as if they're in a hypnotic state like a kid in a candy store. They tell us what to wear, eat, watch, and think. How much sleep we should get, which toothbrush to use, electronics to buy, what our dreams mean, which sex we should be, and most of all - where to put our money. They tell the world what they should do and feel in every facet of their lives from their warped perspective in the city where some places never see the sun shine.

Speaking of sunshine and perhaps jealous from their sunless offices, did you ever notice the media attacks tanning salons and going outside on sunny days year-round? Despite being rare, you will get skin cancer if you even sit near a window in the middle of the winter without sun screen they incessantly preach on every station. I heard my first warning this February here in Massachusetts.

Do you think sunscreen manufacturers have anything to do with this assault? Marilyn Preston points out, some sunscreens actually give you cancer, and not just skin cancer, but ovarian, breast, and prostate cancer too, and melanoma has tripled since the big sunscreen push started in the 1970s. How's that for honest media all these years? In reality, many studies have shown there's nothing more beneficial both mentally and physically than a good old fashion dose of that life sustaining orb in the sky on a regular basis - without sunscreen! After all, how many Africans or Native Americans do you see slopping it on? Through regular exposure they built up enough melanin to prevent "sun related" skin cancer and passed it down to succeeding generations.

The special interest media has played their part in our downfall by bombarding us into obedient submission. They have some New Yorkers so delusional - probably from lack of sun - they claim New York is the best place in the world to live. The hippie flower child years of the 60's living without materialistic, frivolous things and shunning Wall Street pressure is long gone thanks to the New York media.

Like most countries, the major propaganda companies are used as a powerful brainwashing tool. Whoever controls it, controls the information we receive and how they want to shape our society. President Johnson hated the Smothers Brothers attacks about the government and Vietnam War so much, he had his friend at CBS cancel them, despite being one of the top rated shows on T.V. And President George W. ordered the entire country to switch to High Definition (HD) T.V. to make us buy new ones and throw away our perfectly good ones to boost the sagging industry and stock market. Do you wonder how much stock he bought before his order?

Every station throughout the country was forced to through away their perfectly good broadcasting equipment and buy all new H.D. equipment. Causing bankers to once again giggle in ecstasy as the industry was forced to borrow heavily to convert their operations. This cost billions to implement and nearly bankrupted all (PBS) stations. It also forced those of us who refused to through away our T.V.s to rent converter boxes forever just to view basic cable stations! And to make matters worse, H.D. isn't nearly as reliable as the old underground cable. The picture flickers and we're constantly losing at least one station for anywhere from a few seconds to hours. And the new screen size ratio infuriates people, especially sports fans, by cutting off the names of the teams playing and the scores, even on the newest big screen T.V.'s.

The major network NBC seemed to have a political agenda or was pressured from someone in the liberal camp to include two gay reporters throughout the 2014 Sochi Olympics in protest of the Russian anti-gay laws. And they unsuccessfully tried hiding the true meaning of a heartwarming story about a Russian girl that was adopted by an American couple missing the lower part of her legs, which seemed more about protesting Russia's political ban on American's adopting Russian kids.

Fox news is known for being a Tea Party station, and ABC seems to be owned by them at times. It had what would otherwise be a nice PG13 show starring Tim Allen - who most kids know as Santa Clause for his three great Santa Clause movies. Always a clean cut excellent family actor, he pushed Republican rhetoric nonstop on his show Last Man Standing. And all three major networks push as much transsexual, transvestite, and gay news as they can cram into their broadcast.

Others use statistics and the media in very imaginative ways to discretely push their point of view or hide reality. For instance, when the Wall Street Journal wanted to make the economy look good in 2013 after the great recession, they printed an article proclaiming household wealth was recovering and the net worth of US families and nonprofit organizations rose 1.8%. What they didn't tell us was the top 1% racked up 95% of the gains! Then they reported mutual funds in 2013 had attracted more cash ($76 billion) than any year since 2004, but they also withdrew $451 billion from 2006 to 2012. Do the math people!

In his Jan 14, 2014 State of the Union address, President Obama bragged about our farmers shipping a record amount of food overseas, which helped our trade deficit. But didn't tell us shipping it overseas produced a shortage here that caused food prices to skyrocket and millions to go hungry! The same happened with our record amount of gas production they boasted about that actually caused a shortage here and nearly doubled the price after they shipped it overseas. It was reminiscent of the coal miner's strike a century earlier, forcing people to wear coats and hats indoors to keep warm during one of the coldest winters on record.

My favorite media illusion is the so-called "blockbuster sales" you see advertised every week - like buy one get one free, or 20%, 30%, and even 80% off! During the ABC show "The Doctors," they have actually peddled mostly woman's products at "enormous discounts." Have most Americans become so gullible they really think companies can give you these kinds of discounts and still stay in business? Sadly, yes. They flock to stores without even considering it. They get so taken by the snow-job that they buy themselves bankrupt with their "great savings!"

Sometimes in partnership with the government and sometimes against it, the wishy-washy media has a profound influence on politics. For example, in partnership with the Federal Reserve, it roared with approval every time they announced it would keep buying $85 billion in bonds every month to stimulate the economy after the meltdown. They bellowed the "great news" from every resource available. In reality, its true purpose was to pump up the market, CEO bonuses, and the banks fraudulent borrowing for their Wall Street schemes until it reached record levels by 2014. That, they said, was good for the economy, but as we all know was only good for the bank executives and top 1% and another nail in the coffin for most everyone else. Somehow, even with an $18 trillion deficit and whistleblowers coming out of the woodworks, the Fed just kept giving it away and the banks were allowed to keep on gambling.

The media induced election of Donald Trump and the situation in Syria are perfect examples of it controlling White House policy. It insisted Syria crossed a red line and pushed the president for war instead of peace like the Russians and the rest of the world wanted. What is this red line? Simply put, it was an imaginary line used by the U.S. after WWI in our opposition to the Anglo-French Sykes-Picot agreement between Great Britain and France over the divvying up of the Ottoman Empire. The media has been using it in disputes ever since as a threshold that can't be breached.

When Iran elected a new president, they immediately went on attack with the first question being about its nuclear aspirations and did the holocaust really happen. No wonder everyone hates American media. I wouldn't want them in my country either, and believe me, that sediment is nearly as unanimous here as it is anywhere.

When I lived in California, I went to a city meeting on what to do about the swarm of illegal aliens from south of the border after Reagan's amnesty. They were causing numerous social and financial problems for the city. Yet, when a bleeding hearts TV crew interviewed a furious Italian man whose parents waited decades to legally immigrate here about the open border, they made him look as if he was 'for' the illegals free pass and services they were getting by the time the station was done editing it!

In the N.Y. mayor's race, the media blackballed a former congressman for doing what millions of people naturally do and is on everybody's mind but are afraid to act after the woman's liberation movement - sex. Heaven forbid the guy liked woman! What a crime! He had an affair and propositioned some ladies as hundreds before him had. So the moral police, led by the Tea Party's Fox news, banished him from politics as they had all others who openly showed their affections. The media has pushed sexual harassment to such extremes Dartmouth College instituted the first mandatory sexual violence class.

This book would be thousands of pages if I got into every cultural cancer. However, the media's relentless coverage of the woman's liberation movement is worth honorable mention for its part. Like anything else that starts out as an honorable cause in our country, it became inundated with extremist, spurring the song "American Woman" and Arianna Huffington's book "The Female Woman." It pointed out how the majority of woman felt and they were being bullied by the separatist "woman's libbers" (now called feminazis) to live life their way.

Smelling publicity, the media jumped all over them and made us all pay the price. The hard core ones, as do many fanatics, became that two sided sword that isolated and separated society in their thirst for power. Men are their enemy, especially guys such as Playboys Hugh Heffner. They protest every job that requires a lady to look like a lady. And employers with outfits such as Playboy's Bunnies and Hooters are swarmed down on akin to locust on a feeding frenzy. They constantly use the media to ram home their message, leaving the majority of woman, including world famous chef Giada De Laurentiis - who wants a husband, family, and a chef's career - confused, embarrassed, and often playing the game of life their way.

Using the words "Independent" and "Empowering" like a Decepticon, they badger ladies into feeling guilty about raising a family and convince them they don't need a man or family in their lives, just a career, where preferably, they are the boss. Then tell them you can have it all after your career is established. De Laurentiis was one of the few who successfully achieved balancing all three, and like most of us, doesn't care if the feminist disapprove.

The movement banned fun and left both men and woman frustrated, single, and often childless when ladies chose the career path only to regret it later in life and we became a very lonely and frustrated society.

So lonely, tens of millions joined social media websites to get attention, now 75% of singles look for love from perfect strangers on fraud ridden dating sites. Independence became their battle cry, the leading cause of divorce, one parent poor families, and a negative birthrate requiring massive immigration to "theoretically" keep the economist ball rolling and politicians looking good.

ABC seems to be the woman's liberation channel because of the overwhelming amount of time they spend on woman's issues and talking about empowering woman. They even led the charge against a Barbie book because two guys helped her fix her computer, spurring her to realize she could be a computer wizard too. But they wanted woman to help fix it instead.

Empowering woman, dominating men, and the ladies are in control is their message. They had GIANT woman on their Good Morning America show; all in four inch high heels that made them tower over poor little George Stephanopoulos co-hosting the show to ram home that massage. And everything seems to focus on woman's issues, from how to get a position of power and paid sick leave to date rape drugs. Breast cancer and other woman's health issues are a daily theme, and they've had dozens of lady therapist tell us they want equal everything; equal pay, equal satisfaction during sex, and equal house chores, including time taking care of the kids.

But there is a dark sinister side to their empowerment movement. There's an old saying: "Be careful of what you wish for." They wished to be more like men and they got their wish! Liberated woman became alcoholics, drug addicts, heavy smokers, and terrorist. Now they beat the crap out of each other, including in cages, just as the men they used to call animals. They join gangs to kill and beat each other up, and sometimes buy guns to commit bank robberies and murder. One girl was arrested for joining the boy's 'fraternity of assassins' when she said she was going to kill everyone in her school. Women have become a big part of our overcrowded justice system, and they're as ruthless and corrupt as men in both politics and the business world. Highly educated female politicians and business woman now know what the inside of a prison looks like and get arrested when they don't pay their alimony.

With everybody using the media for their own personal gains, we no longer can trust it to report the truth so we have no idea what to believe. It often silences critics, truth tellers, and whistleblowers. For instance, did you know we have one of the highest poverty rates in the industrial world? And you know many people tried to expose Wall Street and the NSA before Eric Snowden. Even politician interviews are pre-staged, allowing only those questions they agreed to discuss.

Hip-Hop and Rap Music

This is an example of the country idolizing the lifestyle of the poor, violent, drugged out ghetto and their music, fashions, and destructive power that exemplifies all the evil that festers deep within the bowels and darkest alleys of New York City.

The ghetto music known as "hip-hop" and "rap" dumbs-down our kids and teaches men and boys nothing but destruction. It teaches them a lifestyle of violence, guns, gangs, money, and girls are nothing more than a punching bag. One rap group is even called Performance Thug, and like drug dealers, education is their enemy and pimping is cool. With their usual class and visions of treasure, the New York music industry wasted no time jumping on this lucrative bandwagon.

By far the worst of the hip-hop music is rap. When rap came out of the ghetto, many asked, how can anyone call this music? It's just talking to a beat and has no resemblance to real music. There were no notes to play and the so-called "lyrics" sounded more like a really bad poem without earmuffs, so how could it be classified as music? We were sure it would quickly fade away as do all fads. Unfortunately, ghetto fads often explode into main stream society and this was no exception - nor fad.

The more violent the rap and rappers got, the more the ghetto teenagers liked it. It took generations of good black and Spanish people's efforts to be viewed as more than killers and criminal thugs, then rap took that perception right down the drain in the blink of an eye. Every mother and father who desperately spent every minute of their existence teaching their kids not to sell drugs, join gangs, carry a gun, murder, rape, or beat woman lost the war to rap. Rap has young people still embracing everything destructive and makes sure education and kindness is defeated in their blood stained neighborhoods they call "the hood."

Violent Hip-hop shaped and formed our ghettos by first spreading its evil wings to the semi-illiterate, dumbed-down, inner city hoods, then spread like a cancer to people of all races throughout the land; all in the name of - **corporate profits.** In the hood, and to stunned parents around the country, kids and teenagers act, dress, and emulate the rappers in the videos. Being in prison has long been a badge of honor for these kids and many that follow the crowd wind up there themselves. Hip-hop, gangs, and the biggest drug cartels in America make ghettos so dangerous blacks are 15 times more likely to be killed than any other race. Why the lowlifes from the hood dictate our young people's lifestyle, slogans, and fashion is beyond my comprehension... and worse, their evil has spread around the globe.

Phone and Cable TV Monopolies

After the breakup of AT&T's monopoly and deregulation of the media, smaller phone and cable companies quickly popped up and then just as quickly were gobbled up by the few remaining behemoths. The thought at the time was there would be more competition in the free market system, resulting in less cost to the consumer.

At first everything looked rosy after the government struck a deal with AT&T that broke up their nationwide network of baby Bells - as the regional ones were called. In exchange, AT&T would lease their telephone lines across the country to new startups such as Sprint and MCI. This would save the startups the immense cost of installing new lines throughout the country that had taken AT&T nearly a century to build up. They could still serve all their own areas, but only for local calls, or as the lowest bidder in the newly formed competitive long distance market. Bidding for market share was done similar to any other government bidding process, with the low bid winning the contract for that municipality.

However, the task was too much for the few upstart's that came up with enough capital for such an enormous undertaking, and AT&T, Sprint, and Verizon came to control the cell phone, internet, digital technology world: With just two companies for all practical purposes - Time Warner and Comcast emerging as the big winners monopolizing the television world.

This was good for them but questionable for consumers. To seduce more people into buying their expensive full service cable, they put many of the most popular shows on it. They even shanghaied us by switching major sporting events from the major networks to cable if we want to view them. But it also has hundreds of channels full of junk most of us don't want - nor need. Plus, we don't want our kids growing up on all that mindless garbage and then become coach potatoes like my generation. Besides, it's a big enough challenge to control their computer time and websites, why would we need all those channels and On Demand pay per view too?

But as usual, I highly underestimate the values of this nation's people. Here in the media capitol of the world and land of frivolous desires, there's just a few of us left who think the cheapest basic form of cable with PBS stations broadcasting quality shows such as Frontline, Independent Lens, Bill Moyers & Company, Nova, science shows and excellent kid and nature shows is good enough for us. It comes with both local and national channels for the news and more than enough sports programs for us. We pay a reasonable fee of around $9 a month and are happy. But the 90% of people the cable companies prey on for their obscene profits are not so happy with basic cable and they pay through the nose for more – much more!

For the hundreds of channels the obsessed have to have, they can pay hundreds of dollars a month. They are perfect examples of spell-bound corporate pawns played like a violin. Some are so hypnotized like a dog to a bone, paying for electronic entertainment siphons their income to a point where they actually lose their homes!

However, we're a nation that serves our masters, so we watch everything they can think of for hours on end while many get drunk and others pad their already mighty girths. Millions line up to see every violent, bloody, explosion filled, ear popping, overhyped, movie. Both at the theater and then again the minute it's released on DVD or pay per view on their 50 or 60 inch big screen TV's. We have to have our food, fashion, jewelry, and electronics channels. We want our workout channels to pump us up or slim us down, then yoga to relax us after getting pumped up and slimed down. There are Spanish and other foreign channels, soap operas, adult movie, and funky courtroom channels just in case you weren't watching the home shopping and furnishing ones that sell you anything from crappy ankle jewelry to expensive electronics for "unbeatable prices" all day and night.

There are hunting channels with shows like Duck Dynasty, starring a former drug addict from the 60's and 70's and his family, who as millions before them, turned to god. We even have to have channels that broadcast the news 24 hours a day, and believe it or not - a dog channel. That's right! In 2013 they actually put on a channel specifically for the entertainment of dogs. It isn't bad enough we lead the world down the destructive path of sedentary, self-absorbed people; we have to have the laziest, fattest, most spoiled pets on the planet too!

The morning shows have all kinds of things that can bore you to death. Originally on during the weekdays for an hour, they expanded to the entire morning, including weekends on two major networks. They have their daily cooking segment, where celebrity chefs come on and show you how to cook almost everything you will never cook. Some show you how to make healthy snacks or meals, others something more fun, especially the deserts they sell in their restaurants.

During Super Bowl week in New Orleans we were inundated with cooking segments about Louisiana bayou and creole style cooking. Then there is the wine expert or Hollywood celebrity to tell us what they enjoy with what foods, the fashions they wear, and all the latest gossip. There is advice about relationships and enough psychological mumbo-jumbo for ten thousand lifetimes. Gee, aren't we lucky?

The media thinks nobody can live without the daily updates on Hollywood celebrities, the days fashion segment, or the over-hyped, over-broadcast, news of the day. They have everything you can think of day after day, week after week, year after year and pull more crazy stunts then there are ants at a picnic to keep us under their spell. Some people are so addicted they can't function and literally lose their lives to New York and Hollywood illusion.

If the morning shows don't fill the void in your life, you can tune into dozens of soap operas and courtroom T.V. shows in the after-noons, along with even more talk shows - if you can stand it! If those aren't your style, maybe you want the gazillion music channels with everything from symphonies to rock and roll to heavy metal and everything in between.

At night you can watch comedy, cop, or drama shows and dozens of reality shows. When you're sick of those you can watch hordes of talent shows - mostly about singing or dancing. Maybe you prefer shows about relationships or romance, no problem, this is America. You can actually watch a show called "UGLEY BETTY!" The poor girl, I told you we would do anything for money, fame, or fortune. To tell you the truth, she isn't that ugly.

How about some of the relatively useless shows New York puts on the air for an increasingly dumbed-down, ignorant, anti-intellectual, America. Shows like Jerry Springer, Doctor Phil, Maury, Steve Wilkes and dozens more. Then there are a slew of courtroom shows that have mostly semi-illiterate people come on with cases between friends, family, roommates, or small business. They even have a show that puts both guys and girls in a giant cage beating on each other like animals until one or the other is too bloodied and beat up to continue.

With the Jerry Springer show, we're talking about an extremely popular show that brings on the most illiterate low lives and rednecks from around the country to show the world just how dumbed-down America has become. Some women are strippers who do their thing on a stripper's pole and all are uneducated. It seems to center on mostly young, infantile people who slept with their boyfriend or girlfriend's brother, sister, boyfriend, girlfriend, wife, husband or some other relative.

They often start out by getting their story on why they're there and then bring on the instigator of their bad feelings. Usually they get two girls on stage that yell at each other until a bell rings like at a boxing match. On cue they fight a little, sometimes pulling each other's shirts off. Springer also has a more sexually explicit R-rated show where the girls can pull off each other's clothes and show their breast and booties. He often gets drugged out, gross people nobody in their right mind would ever fight over. Jessie Herzfield of Cleveland says "they are actors," others losers trying to get their minute of fame, and as usual, the American public is being duped.

Lastly, they bring out the object of their desires and argue and scream a bit more until the bell rings and another brawl breaks out. Some now call the hopelessly violent city streets of America "the Springer affect" because people in real life argue over something relatively minor that escalates into violence, murder, and prison. When Springer gets sick of his normal routine he brings in one of the three "trans" - transsexuals, transgenders, or transvestites to add a little flair. Now there's a special treat!

Talk about why American society failed. This guy was mayor of the major city Cincinnati, Ohio! Was this the best they could come up with for a mayor? Could you imagine that guy running a major city? I think they would have done better with the Three Stooges!

Give Springer and the spinoffs a lot of credit for their part in the criminalization and destruction of society.

Day after day we're pulverized into submission with the same stories. Murder cases such as OJ Simpson's, George Zimmerman's, and mob boss Whitey Bolger's are the worst because they can drag on for years. It's worse than the Chinese water torture! I'd rather have my finger nails pulled out or fifty lashes - anything to stop the torture! And it seems as if every show is based in and about New York City. If I see one more show based there, I swear I'm slitting my wrist! You have to turn off your TV or those guys in the white coats with strait jackets will come and get you.

Social stories like the British royal family and their kids are driving us to drink. What was once a novelty for the media became an obsession. They probably told us more about them than anyone on the planet, despite surveys showing about two thirds of the people didn't care about the birth of one of their kids and thought the media was overhyping it. None-the-less, the morons bombarded us with excruciating updates on the pregnancy, birth, and first few days of the kid's life. Then they crammed our brains his entire first year on the planet!

Tiger Woods was nearly driven out of golf after the media harassed him for months about his affair that inundated every facet of the media nonstop. They followed him everywhere! They went to his house, his garage, his barber, and his favorite stores! They checked his telephone, computer, and iPod records, and then chased his dog and ex-wife! They chased his family, friends, and mistress, then he himself to the courts and rehab center they put him in. Eventually, they chased him full circle all the way back to the golf course.

And Michael Jackson was chased around the world when he was alive. However, his death was plastered around the world until they got his doctor in jail for his murder. It didn't matter if he was guilty or not. The police didn't even consider him a suspect after their initial investigation.

One survey asked us which celebrity we wanted to see on TV or in a movie the most. Tom Cruise was pushed relentlessly on all the daily shows, but as I recall, finished around 450th by the people. The media often has no idea what's going on, yet have to put something on the air to fill the tens of thousands of time slots for our ever increasingly illiterate, ignorant, and simply bored society.

Electronic Media and Advertising

This world is also controlled by a few bigshots courting millions of spellbound customers. For those that want instant gratification at their fingertips, the newest gadgets, and highest speed internet with all the bells and whistles, they too pay the highest premiums "and more." Like TV behemoths Comcast and Time Warner, the digital media companies couldn't be happier having all these addicts playing their role. They even track them to keep them spending. That's why that location request pops up when you're on the internet. You accept… and *they've got you!*

They push every electronic gadget you ever heard of, and then send special offers and coupons when you're near a store you frequent or are in a competitor's store to lure you away. They know impulse buying has always been human's Achilles heel and those special offers push many over the top. With America's addiction to the newest gizmo that comes out every few months, and things like iPads, computers, and giant screen TV's costing from $500 to a grand or more, mega media giant Comcast was selling their XFINITY Internet Extreme 505 plan for about $4800 a year, plus taxes – which should have come with some land, a wife, three goats, a cow, and some chickens!

Why wouldn't they push all their crap? After all, we're so gullible we buy billions of gallons of bottled water every year up to 8,000 times the price of tap water - although nearly half of it comes from tap water. Verizon sent emails to sign up for a ludicrous service that would bombard you with email and internet advertisements. They wanted to know almost everything about you so they could send it to advertisers that target your likes and dislikes and try selling junk you didn't want or need. How gullible do they think we are? Sorry, dumb question.

Advertisers seduce and brainwash us with home improvement and remodeling shows, pushing products such as high end outdoor patios, furniture, roofs, and decks. Don't forget the fancy new sidewalks, driveways, and landscaping to complete your outdoor remodeling project. Indoors, it's counter tops, cabinets, appliances, fixtures, fireplaces, and new bathrooms. However, we have to tear down or move half the walls in our house for all this expensive new fashionable merchandise we probable don't need in the first place. If it doesn't fit in the old house, we're supposed to expand our already oversized houses even more, often leaving immense houses fit for a king and his staff. My favorite useless outdoor furnishing is the classic Adirondack chair. Have you ever known anyone that could get out of one of those things without an ejection seat?

Pet owners are targeted with pet care products, a $60 billion industry that includes food, nutritional supplements, oils, creams and shampoos of every sent; along with brushes, toys, pillows, little tiny clothes, sweaters and booties for the winter months. Prescription insect, worm, and larvae control is pushed by Veterinarians and medical and funeral insurance by the insurance industry. One Sunday, I opened our small local paper to a flurry of advertisements about allergy, poison ivy, heart, hammer toe, bunions, arthritis, and other pain relief medications and gadgets, as well as laundry fresheners, protein bars, hair removal, and a special pad that's supposed to help sciatica pain. Yeah Right! From personal experience I can tell you, it's bogus!

Even the biggest ticket items are fraudulently advertised! Have you ever seen an automobile advertised for the same price you were told when you got to the dealer? Time and again we call about them, only to get there and have the dealers tell us there was only one at that price and it was already sold. Then they try selling us the same model for thousands of dollars more. And when you're looking for a house and tell the sales person you are interested at the advertised price, they often tell you they have been offered more by someone else and it will cost you thousands above that price to buy it. When I went to get a key made at the Ford dealer, they made the wrong one and tried to charge me $82 to diagnose **their** mistake and exchange it! Do we have signs on our backs that say "SUCKER?"

Financial advisers push their latest Wall Street scam, the fashion industry their latest wares, and makeovers that usually make the poor sucker they pulled from the audience look worse than before. I've even seen segments on what to wear on a first date and who was un-dateable by what they wore and how they looked. Year after year, the greedy industry makes jeans so tight most girls can't actually wear them without starving themselves half to death. Is it any surprise we have so many anorexic, bulimic, screwed up kids? And for what? One newscaster wore the same suitcoat for a year and the fashion police didn't noticed! And shows are always having look-alike contest where nobody can tell the difference between designer outfits costing hundreds of dollars or more and off the rack brands.

The slimy degenerates even have little kids and babies pushing their fashions. I bet you didn't know babies and toddlers cared about wearing the latest fashions did you? And last but not least, the most frivolous, deadly, and expensive of all fashion aphrodisiacs - jewelry, jewelry, and more jewelry! Do you know how many people die for those shiny trinkets for a pittance of pay? And there's a shortage of diamonds brewing like never before that are critical to industries because people are frivolously wasting them on themselves! Things like diamond tipped saw blades and mining drill heads are just a couple of critical items necessary in today's world.

Woman and teenage girls are preyed on and preached to far and above the most. One survey claimed nearly 90% dress up in the latest fashions to look good for other woman, not men! And oddly enough, gym cloths emerged as one of the biggest and most lucrative segments of the industry. Advertisers know how much women love shopping and crave the latest fashions. Want $700 jeans or $200 purses and shoes? No problem girl. This unscrupulous industry often gets away with charging females double or more that of males even though nearly all fashions are merely retreads of the past. You know the old saying - "If you wait long enough, anything will come back in style."

In the past, junkies had slaughtered tens of millions of animals for their fur or feathers, leaving the Great Plains with less than 1000 Bison, homing pigeons extinct, and Florida's egrets and other birds with striking plumage nearly extinct. It got so barbaric poachers didn't hesitate to kill National Park and Forest Rangers protecting our national treasures for the lucrative industry.

The saddest part is, like everything else, America never learns! Once reserved for the elite only, fashion was spread to the masses at any cost. You have people such as Carolyn Rafaelian schlepping her jewelry collection Alex and Ani on the impressionable, spellbound, teenage girls simply because she always wanted to be a millionaire. Companies like Luxottica jumped all over the mesmerized masses, going from a mom and pop operation to dominating the entire eyeglass industry. Originally making sunglasses for the most fashionable high end firms, they bought out Ray Ban and other competitors, including Lens Crafters, where they can personally push their high end products. Low end non-cool ones can go for as little as $10 but escalates up to $200 - $400 a pair for the elite brands!

Speaking of pairs - let's talk shoes. Talk about the ultimate, irresistible female addiction. Many women buy up to 100 pairs or more, and have special closets built in their homes just for their shoes, including those painful and physically deforming high heel ones.

Sometimes there are other consequences for the spellbound that fall for the industries shinny trinkets and sales pitches. The luxury retailers Barneys and Macys of New York City were accused of profiling its black customer's by accusing them of stealing items they bought, then having police detain them. One guy was accused of stealing a $350 Ferragamo belt from Barneys, and an actor was detained by police at Macys about possible credit card fraud. Hey! If you're foolish enough to pay $350 for a belt in the name of fashion, no matter how loaded you are, you deserve some sort of consequences!

Advertisers actually got TV stations to speed up their shows by secretly editing them so they can squeeze in more ads — especially with extremely lucrative popular shows. And telemarketers bombard us with so many calls the government has a "do not call list" for anybody who wants to stay sane. But that doesn't stop many of them. Some people go mad from all the calls! One guy actually went down to the office and tried strangling the telemarketers! Really! And I'm next in line.

I think without a doubt, the best example of how far the New York media goes in pushing big business products is their commercials on the nightly newscast of all three major networks. They plaster the airways with ad after ad the giant pharmaceutical industry is pushing for various medications that are supposed to help your ailments, yet have warnings that could leave you with serious physical problems or "kill" you! Some say they cause severe infections, multiple cancers, nervous system disorders, depression, thoughts of suicide, allergic reactions, dizziness, liver and heart problems that are fatal, hepatitis type symptoms, fever, stiffness, rashes, shin reactions such as hives and blisters, internal bleeding, swelling, and confusion... to name a few.

Buying all those life threatening things being pushed not only can drain your life savings, it tells the networks and advertisers what you're gullible enough to buy and watch. This information is carefully monitored because it tells them how much stations can charge advertisers. The more popular and successful a show is, the more the station can charge, and it tells them where they want their ads for the most exposure. The Super Bowl is the ultimate proof of their game plan.

Back in 1957, when Andy Griffith was young, he played Larry Rhodes in "A Face in the Crowd," a cantankerous, egotistical maniac who went from a nobody to having his own TV show with politicians courting his endorsements in mass from his convincing snow jobs. He told us his audiences "were morons and he could sell them fertilizer as caviar, dog food as steak, and they are like caged guinea pigs." Then he calls them "stupid idiots and trained seals that he could make flap their flippers by tossing them a dead fish."

I have two neighbors he would have loved. To save my family and friends lives, I finally paid to have their towering dead trees removed after losing sleep over my daughter and her friends being crushed. For years they said they would do it, but got full blown home remodels instead. One got 2 satellite dishes, new architectural shingles, triple pane low e-windows, and new siding. The other added a pool, deck, Jacuzzi, a second story to her house, 2 central air conditioning units, and new siding. Commercialism is so entrenched in our psyche, killing your neighbor's takes a back seat.

12

Electronics
Environmental and Social Genocide or Savior?

Newsflash: Google hires Wall Street insider Ruth Porat of Morgan Stanley as Chief Financial Officer for $70 million a year, as the exodus from Wall Street to Silicon Valley continues.

The United States had for all practical purposes brought the world into the electronic age by the 1990's with companies like Apple, Intel, and Microsoft leading the way. Larger mainframe computer capabilities of the 70's from corporations such as IBM and Digital Equipment Corporation were shrunk down to a homeowner's version we're all familiar with, personal computers (PC's). Then within a couple of decades, they were shrunk down again to mind-blowing miniature sizes that merged with and fit into a cell phone. But are quite honestly too small for some of us to easily use and cause many people a variety of mental and physical problems. Computers also brought about miracles in technology never dreamed possible, from medicine and robotics to outer space and the Nano world. Even wars are fought from comfortable bunkers that save thousands of battlefield lives, leaving enthusiastic manufacturers blindly seeing themselves as saviors, while ignoring the Pandora's Box they opened but could not control.

They have a dark sinister side though. Full of some of the most toxic substances on earth, electronics manufacturers joined the most prolific environmentally destructive mining and chemical companies extinguishing and poisoning hundreds of species - including us. Millions of mostly poor people around the globe are sickened, poisoned, and killed for hundreds of miles downstream from landfills and recycling centers that ignore and plunder there precious but toxic materials. The industry and Wall Street are in ecstasy with every new electronic thingamajig they create, but, as does the nuclear power industry, they selfishly ignore their responsibility to safely dispose of their creations. And anywhere the giants of the cyber world and their millionaire employees go, local townspeople and businesses are forced out of their homes and shops by sky-high real estate prices of epic proportions, leaving everything unaffordable for the locals and homeless people in their wake.

The Internet

Invented in the 1980's by the CIA, the internet burst onto the public scene in the 90's and quickly became a social and political tool with billions of users. But it became a double edged sword with its volumes of information and knowledge, along with the ability to make learning interesting and fun. Drastically underperforming inner city schools with horrendous attendance were turned around with soaring scores, reduced truancy, and violence. Unfortunately, it seemed to cause more harm than good. At the college level, all areas of reading and writing took a nose-dive and attention spans went down the drain. Kids from elementary school to college level are texting and playing games in bed instead of sleeping, leaving themselves too exhausted for school the next day. It's gotten to the point where some high schools try reversing the starting times with the elementary ones in hopes the high schoolers will get more sleep.

It also brought about severe bullying and video websites that have mostly kids and teenagers trying to outdo and dumb-down each other for attention and their minute of fame. One social media craze had teenagers dousing themselves in flammable liquids and then setting themselves on fire! Things quickly got out of hand when they couldn't put it out and they get horribly burned. Fraud's run amuck, including hotel chains that rate themselves on sites such as Trip Advisor by giving themselves 5 star ratings and rave reviews. Whole industries that had been around for millennia from toy stores to auctions get wiped out, as do beloved digital pictures with every replacement technology.

Free speech is abused and anybody around the world can lynch anybody they want. It's used for political attacks from unidentifiable sources, leaving victims without any way of defending themselves. Politicians get hammered, cyber bullying is rampant, and hackers are everywhere stealing our identity, bank account, and investment money. But Muslim terrorist are the worst. They spread their evil philosophy around the world to recruit new members and show everyone with internet how to make bombs to carry out attacks. And nobody can do anything about it in the completely unregulated, unidentifiable world of "cyberspace."

The WSJ's Priya Anand took on some of the problems the internet has caused. She pointed out, "in 2013 there was a new victim of identity fraud every two seconds and fraud complaints increased more than six fold between 2001 and 2013! More than 867 million records have been stolen since 2005, and credit cards fetch $20 to $45, but the price falls by half that in a flooded market."

For those who want your information but don't know how to hack into it can just buy it. Even mega-bank JPMorgan Chase had 76 million customer accounts hacked into, despite some of the best safeguards money can buy. Target, Home Depot, and hundreds of others, including the government are routinely hacked too. Anyone banking online or buying products over the net, especially in public places, are in reality "holding a steak in front of a hungry bear."

When hackers from around the world aren't stealing everything from us, they hold us hostage by hijacking our computers and demanding payment for anything and everything they consider important to us. They hack into your webcam as well! Some hackers in Russia watched people get undressed - and whatever else they do within view of their webcams - without anyone ever suspecting a thing. Then they stole over 2 billion passwords a few months later as well as hacking into our 2016 presidential election.

Sony Pictures was hacked, and everything from famous actor's social security numbers to sometimes embarrassing executive emails were stolen and spread around the world. They may have even stolen their movie script from the "Interview" just before its big debut.

Like millions of people, when a hacker broke into our computer disguised as a Microsoft security employee, I knew about hacking scams but couldn't figure a way out of buying his fake 3 year security contract. I tried shutting down the computer but he wouldn't go away, so I semi-believed and hoped he was really a security company hired by Microsoft who claimed he could clear the dozens of viruses that were popping up. With our screen frozen and him in control of it, I sort of panicked and grudgingly gave him my credit card number for what I thought was a very reasonable offer of 3 years security for only $89.

Even if he was a fake security company, I could always call the card company and immediately cancel my card and get a new one. I didn't want to pay the $300 my daughter's friends parents paid to fix their infected computer, so I paid the money. Fortunately, he immediately started deleting the fake viruses he installed and restored my confused computer.

I then followed my plan and called the credit card company to get a new card and we were both temporarily happy. I thought I had a real anti-virus company monitoring my computer and he had my $89. The next day I called Microsoft security and was told I was scammed. However, I did eventually get him to reimburse me after pursuing it with our police department and the detective contacting him. Fearing he was still monitoring my computer, I got two real security companies. One monitored the computer for free and the other removed them for $39 a year. Naturally, I had to turn down the many upgraded products they were plugging for more money, but hey, $39 a year was worth the peace of mind. It proved to be well worth it when we got hacked into again about eight months later... probably by the same guy. They expediently cleared the viruses and kicked his greedy butt off our computer just as they promised.

Cyber Bullying

Online bullying, harassment, and identity theft became one of America's biggest threats to our kid's health and safety. Kids use the unregulated social media to be downright mean, bully, and get good old fashioned revenge for squabbles, such as stealing ones boyfriend or girlfriend. The first amendment, which includes free speech, has become a cruel tool for evil intent.

It all came to a head when Phoebe Prince was bullied into committing suicide while attending her local high school. Originally from Ireland, she was cruelly harassed and bullied both at school and online at all the social websites. At hearings to get to the bottom of what caused her to go over the edge and possibly prosecute the school district, one parent said, "Social media is everywhere and you can't get away from it."

Phoebe isn't the only one in this new era of electronic abuse that gives bullies a fist that reaches around the globe. It's just too easy now to do their damage without ever laying a hand on their victims. Smarter than their parents with electronic media, and able to get around their controls, they do and say anything they want. Armed with cellphones, they use them as weapons with nonstop texting of fabricated stories to embarrass and isolate their targets until they can't take it anymore. So victims often take what they see as the only permanent way out - albeit a tragic one.

In Phoebe's case parents were split on who was to blame, but in the end, it was probably a little of everyone who was ultimately responsible. Some yelled at the school district employees that were put through hell for months. They admitted they missed some important signs, while others claimed parents in general, especially those of the bully's, needed to be real parents and were the ones responsible for their kids being monsters. Hurray for them! One said her daughter had lost all her confidence and spirit. It was so scary in their school most of the kids didn't want to talk to the media for fear of retaliation.

In Deerfield Beach, Florida, one girl was beaten to a pulp by a large boy over a text massage she sent, and another kid was doused with alcohol and set on fire for stealing a bike and a video game! The girl was so beat up she was put into a medically induced coma! Kids across the land are easy prey in this new world of technology and nonparenting. For the most part it has disappeared and their kids are in control. That's not a good thing people! According to a report by WWLP in May, 2014, 1 in 5 kids claimed to have been bullied. Electronics has hijacked our normal way of life, spreading like a cancer. Desensitized by gory video games and no longer communicating in person or by voice telephone, our kids have lost all the social norms of the past and no longer know how to communicate properly.

Many people want social media websites held responsible for what they allow on their sites, in fact every other media source is. But rather than holding them accountable, Congress gave them immunity from anything users post.

Other problems have some students getting rejected at college for being internet bullies, and Dartmouth College got hammered by a woman's rights organization called Ultra Violet. They put ads on Facebook and other websites claiming Dartmouth is unsafe for woman, rape is out of control, and the college isn't stopping it. Their unsubstantiated opinion is killing the college's image and some kids are staying away from it. Once again, this not only enforces what I said about the misuse of social media, but the fact a small minority of 1% or less can get whatever they want in this backwards democracy. So now even college kids can no longer be college kids thanks to a handful of radical dissidents. And while we're on the subject of sex; remember Monica Lewinski? President Clinton's mistress is claiming to be the first to have her life destroyed by social media.

In some instances, bullying became an arm of the constitution. In the highly publicize case of Mozilla co-founder and CEO Brendan Eich, he was forced out of his own company by gay rights advocates using the social network site Twitter for donating $1000 to a ballot question in California to ban gay marriage. Some gays called for a boycott of Mozilla, still others said the dissidents were now just as intolerant as those who sought to ban gay marriage. When it's politically correct for the times to agree with a certain point of view, free speech is encouraged as an integral staple of the constitution. When it's perceived as against the times it's an act of heresy.

All these problems started in the 1990's with a combination of new technology, the media, and a surplus of expendable money for many new college graduates. They brought a whole new meaning to the word "yuppie." This generation of graduates, was perhaps the most spoiled, selfish, frivolous, and wasteful generation in American history. They brought electronic media to levels never seen before, and forced the rest of us into their world of pure gluttony.

Those in the computer field, especially programmers and designers fresh out of college, were being offered as much or more money than people on the job for 20 or 30 years. Companies couldn't get expertise fast enough and bidding wars for their services literally sprung up overnight. For the first time in history they held all the cards, and were telling prospective employers what *they* would except for salary and benefits.

A bitter culture war broke out between the older often lesser paid workers with years of experience and the new hot-shots fresh out of college. The internet bubble of the 1990's required people who could push the envelope to new levels. A new era was dawning, and they were the only ones that knew how to use this new technology, but more importantly - create it. After creating it, they bought their own creations for their kids to play with and taught them how to use them at a very young age. By association, our kids wanted, and thanks to them, needed what theirs had or be left behind. So another culture war broke out between these new rich technology nerds and the old middle and lower classes of society that couldn't afford to, and often didn't want to, keep up with this new generation.

The "X" generation then raised the current Millennials or "lost generation," who go to job interviews dressed in jeans, shorts, and flip flops. You know, that 80% who want to be rich above all else. They live with their parents and quit their jobs shortly after being hired, then complain about the company on social media websites, making employers wish baby boomers were young again. They have no concept of reality or responsibility, and are so obsessed with taking selfies of themselves, college graduations had to ban them. Hollywood jumped on this obsession too, creating a T.V. show called "Selfie."

By the 21st century, manufacturers were coming out with new products that they quickly made obsolete and all but forced us to buy their new ones. Millions of us have cell phones only six or seven years old that we aren't allowed to use anymore after phone companies stopped using their relatively new equipment. We have to buy their newest generation of phones and throw out our perfectly good ones - just as the government made us do with our TV's. This also accelerates the environmental consequences. With each new product they invent and we have to trash, they wreak more havoc on the environment, our health, and society.

This wired generation changed our way of life in other ways as well. They don't believe in books or any other traditional methods of working, teaching, and learning or any other traditional family values and social norms. They don't believe in sitting around the dinner table for a home cooked meal with the family chatting about the day's events like previous generations. This generation thinks a family meal (if there even is one) is either bought at the grocery store food court or some take out restaurant and then brought home for dinner. Complete with ignoring each other at the table and kids playing internet games while parents check emails and finish their work while eating.

After dinner, their version of a relaxing family night of watching a movie together is one kid sitting around the living room multitasking, texting while listening to music on a cell phone plugged into one ear while semiconsciously listened to the movie with the other, and another kid playing games on their laptop while the youngest kids play their DS games. As a result, the art of conversation and real world socializing quickly died.

These media socialites don't believe in volunteering on town or school boards either, leaving positions and school sponsored activities and committees vacant. They transformed businesses, homes, schools, and our social lives into a new way of life, one which millions of us agree is not for the better, but for the sake of my daughter I hope someday they prove us wrong.

So spoiled are their kids, an 18 year old New Jersey high school girl sued her parents, alleging they abused her. So she decided to move out of their house and in with a friend, and then demanded they pay her $600 a week for expenses, plus college tuition at a Private School! When they refused, she sued them for child support, the $600 a month, and tuition! She claimed she was abused, and the parents claimed, through heartbroken tears, she was a spoiled brat. The parents couldn't take her demands and living by her own rules anymore so rightfully kicked her out of the house. By law they have to support her so she sued them. When they went to court she acted like the rich, spoiled, little brat that she is and never said a word to her grief stricken parents, even though her mom was crying over her actions. The parents said she had a good home but wouldn't live by their rules and had no choice but to kick her out.

The judge handled the emotional case brilliantly. He was smart enough to give the parents some rights in this day and age of kids and courts that allow them to abuse the system at will. He said they had to support her financially but did not have to pay for her college. Recognizing both the law and her being a spoiled teenager - not the abused one she claimed to be because her parents had house rules. He reasoned he needed to set a precedent for parents that allow them to reasonably control their kids. This is what society has come to in the electronic age of spoiled brats and too much money!

This was not unusual. In fact, it's been happening so much with these kids people are calling it the "spoiled rich kid syndrome."

Their parents are the ones that will do anything for a high paying job that can pay for their extravagant lifestyle, colossal houses with granite and marble countertops, and often 3000 to 4000 square feet of living space. Then furnish them with equally extravagant furnishings, giant screen TV's, surround sound stereos, and a host of the latest and most expensive paraphernalia nobody really needs being pushed by their own corporations and those like themselves.

This telecommuting generation that has moved their offices to their homes even caught the world's largest computer company IBM off guard by this new development. They built a massive state of the art computer center in the 1980's for thousands of workers, only to see it slowly abandoned until there was hardly a soul in the building. It went from a major computer hub to a ghost center by the 21st century.

Before most lower and middle class parents realize what hits them and not knowing how to stop this cancer preying on their kids, they find themselves spending money they don't have for the sake of their kids keeping up with the new generation of wired ones. But a strange thing happens, the parents become as hooked and addicted as their kids, and everyone, it seems, is now going on the web to watch over a trillion hours of mindless videos.

It's so ridiculous; one video attracted millions of viewers with just a dog staring at a TV! That's all! Another saw 33 million watch a baby ripping paper and laughing! Others watch music videos, and millions more play games all day and night. Mimicking real life, hundreds of newspaper and magazine cartoons show people mindlessly texting, talking, or playing games while walking down the sidewalk or crossing city streets with their eyes glued to their little electronic devices. Some are shown bumping into each other, while others have cars and trucks piling into each other trying to avoid them. And in businesses across the land, people often don't talk to each other anymore at lunch break, instead, wasting away their lunch time playing games, watching videos, or texting.

Rich or poor, the old way of life seems boring to them and they flood stores to buy the newest thing on the market, even if that means sleeping on the sidewalks in front of the store all night to be one of the first to get it. Electronic insanity hits the hardest around Christmas time and the first day a grossly overhyped, overpriced, electronic device is made available to the public. Some people die from the stampeding human wall of bodies pressing into stores that first day. And this tragic seen is often repeated for the after Thanksgiving Day (Black Friday) and Christmas holiday sales. You can blame the employees of the major New York networks who are the first in line and push them more than the advertisers themselves. They're so addicted they actually use them while their co-host sitting next to them are telling us about other stories, then gloat about it on camera when they're done.

I had to turn off the news this morning it was so sickening after Apple brought out their zillionth updated iPhone! Once again the media jumped all over it and had the very sick Apple addicts who slept overnight on the sidewalks plastered on every station. They had to be one of the first to get this *slightly* different product with *slightly* different features, so they could through away their perfectly good ones they just bought six months ago for hundreds of dollars and spent thousands more using. In fact, most people get locked into expensive two year contracts, paying nearly $200 a month for cell phones that includes many services they don't need. To pay for them they wind up working a second part time job, with single parents often leaving their kids home alone. Again, that's not a good thing people!

For those that don't have the money to keep up with the wealthy, Wall Street crooks are more than willing to extend credit to their most unworthy customers at their usual 300 to 400% interest rates. Although many can't afford these financial death stars, they and their kids are addicted. Eighty percent of our kids are so addicted they text while driving, causing thousands of deadly accidents to both themselves and their innocent victims. Even some school bus drivers are crashing into cars, trucks, and trains while texting. Not to be left out, public bus drivers, truck drivers, train, and subway operators join the insanity - killing and injuring thousands across the land. A cop here in town said he knew there were fewer kids at the high school now because the morning accident rate had nosedived!

Now kids can kill thousands more with websites like Twitch that have lowered, isolated, and brainwashed them to a level unimaginable just 15 years ago. Kids that are already glued to their chairs and have no life (thanks to game makers and parents that don't want to be real parents) can watch other people playing video games. That's right. It's bad enough they've hooked our kids on their video games, now they can watch thousands of games they don't have or parents can't afford while driving. Hey America! Smarten up and get a life!

Wired Scams

Social media companies have joined gaming and advertisers in the "scumbucket of the century award" for hooking millions of kids on their websites. They know how desperate they are for attention, so they dangle that proverbial "carrot" in front of them and dare them to chase it for their own profits. In this case it's anything juicy teenagers drool over – usually popular singers, athletes, celebrities, or their fashions. But often it's just some unknown stranger with a video of some sort. They put out the word that a teenage idle is going to make some sort of announcement of interest to them that gets them to use social networks and give them a "like" it. The more likes it gets the more advertisers can target the most popular stars, videos, and products they're promoting.

Clicking that like icon tells them exactly who you are and what you enjoy. The kids are inadvertently telling advertisers exactly what they want, henceforth, advertisers know what products to push on them. Companies such as Facebook and Twitter would go bankrupt without using the kids to gather information for advertisers, and without the advertisers, they don't make any money!

Millions of lonely and desperate kids are spending most of their lives watching this mindless crap and telling the world everything they do. Others spend their entire young lives trying to get famous making videos of interest to strangers (such as setting yourself on fire or sexy photos) in hopes of getting a little fame or big corporations to sponsor them. But this slimy, wired, corporate use of our kids doesn't stop here. We spread our misguided evil ways to every country around the globe, resulting in other innocent countries getting as addicted to social media and video games as ours. Some of our own devices even came back to haunt us when they were used against us in several terrorist attacks. And you know; the saddest part of America's greedy corporations pushing this way of life is people are dying in car accidents, sidewalk crossings, and even bicycling while using them.

To remedy this problem, they came up with hands free devices and advertise them as being distraction free. In reality, they're often more so and deadlier. Social destruction and mayhem means nothing to them.

For now, Wall Street seems to have missed out on the latest form of electronic payment. Invented by some computer geeks, bitcoins are used to pay for things using the internet through bitcoin exchanges. Though many consider it nothing but fictional money, in 2017 it was trading for between $1000 and $19,000 on bitcoin exchanges. They claim it's a new form of currency (cryptocurrency), although it's backed by nothing but thin air. Governments around the world attack it as not being a form of exchange, and they can't regulate it. Some want to tax any capital gains from it, and the U.S. considered treating it as money laundering.

But Ben Bernanke claims virtual currencies hold long term promise, and he may be right. It's perfect for small purchases and other business transactions, spurring Silicon Valley and other leaders in technology -

Scandinavia, the UK, South Korea, Japan, Canada, Australia and Estonia to adopt it. It's widely used in Kenya for loans to buy food of $1 or less.

New York announced it wants to make bitcoins legal tender similar to credit cards, but Wall Street banks have other ideas to keep their monopoly. Ye Ha! Way to go Wall Street! And the IRS responded by taxing all bitcoin purchases so it's dying a slow, agonizing death here. D'oh!

Confirming fears of fraud, the founder of bitcoins disappeared when giant bitcoin exchange Mt. Gox filed for bankruptcy after losing the coins of 750,000 investors. Other exchanges are also being prosecuted for money laundering and phony operations, with their value collapsing.

What a perfect con! People give you their money, you take it and put it into an off shore bank account, then say you lost it. When the investigation starts, you tell the authorities computer hackers must have stolen the untraceable money with their conveniently built in non-tracking system. It's perfect!

By the 21st century, parents were being bombarded with electronic devices and rackets of unimaginable magnitude from all sides by everyone from the manufacturers themselves to the state and federal government. Even schools needed to be reinvented for these new highly wired kids. Parents have bought their kids all the latest gizmos from such an early age, by the time they are 9 or 10 years old, they are addicted to a point of never leaving their phones out of their sight. So now kids sit alone on school buses with their new best friend – cell phones. One girl on my daughter's soccer team actually faked injuries at practices just to text her friends.

Some of the worst cases have parents joining their kids, robotically texting in bed for hours, leaving them too tired to work, take care of the kids, or do their household chores. Similar to sleep walkers, "sleep texter's" awaken in a slumber-like trance a couple of hours after they go to bed and text until their conscience allows them to go back to sleep. Akin to drug addicts and alcoholics, night after night they deprive themselves of sleep from their addiction to those little, cold, heartless, devices. Now we get an average of 2 hours less sleep than 40 years ago, and insomnia is at epidemic proportions that require record amounts of sleep medication.

Many school aged children, especially teenagers, are so addicted to their favorite games they can't do their school work and sink into the fantasy world of computer games. They stop playing sports and talking to family or friends, then drop out of school - and society. Some start out doing great in school with promising careers in their future, only to lose their childhood and promising lives to the greedy corporate game makers. There is very little opportunity or chance of success in the real world outside of video game programing and design jobs for the 'lost generation.' Most don't even look for work and live with their parents, and those that do get jobs quit or get fired as their lives slip deeper into the abyss of fictional gaming.

Some gamers go to gaming centers that prey on their addiction where they can play their favorite games all day and night, sometimes without stopping for food or liquids. Many suffer both emotional and physical problems. In an attempt to save the most addicted ones, rehab centers are set up that strictly forbid any electronic devices. Like all addicts, it's excruciating agony for many who simply can't live without them because that's all they can think of day and night. So success is limited and some just can't quit.

As usual, the United States has spread its capitalistic ways to countries like South Korea, where kids are addicted worse than ours. My daughter is a huge fan of Japanese and Korean TV shows with Manga… think Pokémon for teenagers. Some countries like them recognized the devastation to their youngest generation and instituted some necessary reforms in their schools and society overall. As did Bill Gates and Steve Jobs, they teach their kids at the earliest stages of usage to use all electronics responsibly, sparingly, and ethically and always use good manners.

When my daughter was 13 she got into trouble on a Manga website while visiting a relative. She got bored and went on a chat site. A guy claimed he was in high school in Virginia and they started texting each other for several months before I stumbled upon her undeleted messages. I wasn't into the younger generations gadgets and didn't know how to use most of them. I loved our old easy to use cell phone. But her mom had gotten a new phone so she could call her from out of state that I only learned to make calls on, so I never knew the two of them were texting each other.

One day I saw a message on it and thought it was a real estate salesman I was doing business with, so I tried listening to it. Usually I failed and accidentally hit the redial button or deleted it, but on this day I got lucky and got into the message center. It was a parent's worst nightmare. It was loaded with sexual messages from the man, but my daughter listed him under another kids name at school. So I called the principle, vice-principle, and some of the policemen I knew in town. When I called them, I was surprised by the stories they had of their own children getting into trouble on the internet and their electronic devices.

The relatively young vice principle from the 90's internet boom told me his kids were getting smarter than he was with the newest technology and he should go back to school to stay ahead of them... or at least keep up to them. And the cop that came to my house to go over the messages said he had trouble with his teenage daughters at the same age. So he took their electronics away for a while and made them join so many after school activities they were always too tired to get into any more hot water. He then suggested I do the same with my daughter. He said he wasn't the most literate person either as far as the latest technology was concerned, but he did know enough to show me how to look up all her friends and contacts on the list so I could monitor them for a while.

I hadn't paid that much attention to news clips about the dangers of the internet and stalkers because I had told my daughter about them. She assured me she wasn't stupid enough to go on social websites like Facebook - who was being blamed for a murder around the same time she got in trouble. I had confidence I raised her right and trusted her. We both learned a lesson that fortunately did not end in disaster. I learned to educate myself, never trust a teenager with a nearly unregulated internet, and many lunatics are prowling 24 hours a day for victims. She learned people aren't necessarily who they claim to be, so follow the age old warning - don't talk to strangers, especially in cyberspace.

These stories compel me to say a few words about another costly addiction. With millions of Americans being bombarded with advertisements of every conceivable product mankind can come up with; like gaming addictions, many people are addicted to shopping over the internet. As Red Green would say, "It's just that easy." A lot of woman are internet shopaholics and return 90% of everything they order online, causing company's billions in loses every year. It's gotten to the point where retailers have blackballed many customers from shopping online and make them personally come to their stores.

Even for us non addicts, the bombardment of advertisements titillates us all. You can use pop up blockers, but you cannot escape the ads on millions of websites we all use for everything from researching homework projects to banking.

Personally, for years I only bought two things ever online: a dog training collar that only partially worked and a latex foam pillow from Sears that was much smaller than the dimensions listed on their website. After those two purchases, it was years before buying online again. There is no sure way of knowing what you are buying, especially expensive things like prom dresses. You can usually trust the main retailers, but I never could understand why people trusted giving their credit card numbers and money to complete strangers for products that they can't touch, test, try on, and may never get. Plus, you have no way to get your money back or bring them to justice if you get ripped off.

As you can imagine, this new generation lost another important aspect of society other than their privacy - their social skills. Although we have some of the smartest, most wired, students in the world, by the time they go to college many are rude, obnoxious, members of the human race. Common courtesy and manners are taking a shellacking and sanity has been hijacked. People use these devices everywhere they go, and I swear females are the worst. You rarely see teenage girls, and sometimes grandmothers, driving a car who is not talking or texting on their phones. And about half of them are doing it, or pretending to, in stores, parking lots, and everywhere else.

Texting in public has gotten so out of control, a 72 year old ex-policeman asked a rather large man in front of him at the movie theater to stop his texting during the movie. The guy jumped up with steam coming out of his ears and threw his popcorn in his face, then asked him what his problem was! The paranoid, old, ex-cop took out his revolver and killed him on the spot, showing how dangerous our 300 million guns are roaming public places. Now he's in jail for murder. The unfortunate thing is he reacted similar to what many of us have wanted to do millions of times across the country.

This self-absorbed, generation spread its wings throughout society. Everybody seemed to jump on the bandwagon. Neighbors became more hostile and detached from each other and the rest of the neighborhood, often not even knowing their next door neighbors names. This attitude could be expected in city ghettos, but it spread to the suburbs and country as well. We actually have a man like the mayor I mentioned earlier who threw his dogs poop on a guy's doorstep. Only this guy walks his dog everyday on a long 25 foot leash (6 is the law) so his dog can relieve itself and mark all the neighbor's trees, flowers, bushes, and telephone poles in the yards. Now everyone hates him and their dogs go crazy from his being in their yard.

Cyberspace addiction is a severe problem at schools across the country too. It's sickening to see everyone on campus staring at their spellbinding cell phones while walking from class to class with their heads down and ignoring their friends and world around them. Even at lunch time they gather to multitask and text each other about anything that crosses their mind. Occasionally, they look up at their friends that are often just across the table from them and actually speak to them while eating. They don't consider it rude because their friends are doing it too and you're considered "weird" if you don't. Gizmos and gadgets have hijacked lunch halls and classrooms. Kids are so overstimulated with such short attention spans nowadays it's hard to teach them. I know many of our teachers can't wait to retire from this generation.

At colleges across the country, test scores are down and kids simply no longer can concentrate on one thing with a multitude of electronic media at their fingertips. With mounting evidence they are slipping academically from over exposure to digital media in both reading comprehension and writing skills, experts in psychology decided to do some test on some of the worst abusers.

The test revealed exactly what every long time educator has said. Those who are the biggest and most confident multitaskers are actually horrible at it in every way, shape, and form. Their memories are very disorganized and they are easily districted. Their analytical thinking is just as bad, and the fear is these young people can no longer think clearly. Although students think they're experts at multitasking, the studies reveal what I've been telling my daughter... Do one thing at a time and do it right - because people suck at it!

Brain scans show students are "short circuiting" while engaged in different activities, particularly the older more relaxing ones that are boring to them. The hypothesis is they are being overstimulated by the electronic onslaught and especially the internet. Sure enough! The brain is really relaxed while reading a book, yet goes haywire when searching the internet or playing games. At first glance it would appear using digital media is stimulating their brain, but they are actually similar to drug addicts, alcoholics, and smokers who are over stimulated and addicted.

That's why I always tell my daughter to concentrate on one task at a time, and it is sweet justification to those of us trying to install some common sense and sanity into our kids. I know many kids struggle to focus on homework and pass it in on time since we became wired. They're constantly switching to other websites of interest to them, causing many to do worse since books were replaced by computers.

It was almost impossible raising my daughter when all her friends had the latest devices. She had always felt left out and isolated with the exception of the cell phone. She was one of the first to have one and that was a real big deal to the other kids. I've tried desperately to stop her from getting hooked like the rest of society, but once she started playing in the cyber world it got more and more difficult keeping her in the real world around her. Hopefully, as have other good parents who try so hard to keep their kids from becoming a living arm of the industry, I have successfully balanced the cyber world with the real one.

Often it's hard to distinguish between the two. The National Highway Transportation Safety Administration has given the green light for driverless cars (autonomous vehicles), and worse, BIG RIG trucks! High tech computers are used with location satellites like GPS and special sensors to help prevent accidents. Cars from Google have already driven over a million miles on their own. Isn't that great news? Now, our already addicted society has more incentive to play with electronics all night. They can catch a few extra zzzz's on the way to work and get a good nap on the way home! Personally, I'll drive my own car if you don't mind.

We already have dozens of manufacturer recalls a year on vehicles, with Toyota getting fined $1.2 billion for covering up a problem with sudden acceleration, and GM is in deep trouble with ignition switch problems. Can you imagine what will happen while everyone is sleeping on their way to work at rush hour and someone hacks into the computers controlling them or our enemies jam the GPS signals to them? You could get millions of accidents, injuries, and deaths at the same time. And with the smaller and lighter fuel efficient cars these days, it will be that more deadly! These cars are even being pushed to eliminate freeway overcrowding by tailgating every car so they can pack more cars onto the already jammed freeways. I have enough trouble with our home computer going nuts, never mind trusting my family's life to them. No thank you Google!!!

The Military Plays Its Part Too

The military has joined the rush in abusing this electronic addiction. They learned from the gaming houses and now prey on very young kids and their addiction to games. They shut down some recruiting centers that had been their bread and butter since Richard Nixon did away with the military draft in 1972. They served their purpose well through two gulf wars and the terrorist attacks of 2001, but became a little obsolete in the new age of technology. Wars are no longer your good old fashion ground wars with vast amounts of humans killing each other from close range. So like nearly everything else in the 21st century, military recruitment was updated with a new type of recruitment center, a state of the art video game one complete with food courts and lounges.

The use of drones, laser guided missiles, and other high tech weapondry systems have become so automated from remote locations, the military is taking advantage of the best techno geeks available. Their new recruitment centers have games far more expensive and complex than most people can afford - with some popular games free. But those are just a cover. Their theory is, since most boys love playing video games anyway, why not have them do it there and get them hooked on the more realistic war ones. They also build life size simulators of plains helicopters, and Humvees to sell these kids on how fun the military is.

Some people think these poor kids are being desensitized to war and don't even know it. The military has become like any giant corporation selling their product, only this product is a real life and death one if they hook you. As you can imagine, when parents find out about these recruitment centers many are furious!

Does playing these war games really confuse kids? Are they that gullible? No one knows for sure. We do know some terrorist and the mass murderers were addicted to war games and practiced their technique with them. The theory is they can't separate the two worlds and use them to hone their skills with assault weapons, bombs, and strategies they will use for their real life attacks.

This isn't the first time a phenomenon has been blamed for violence. In the 1950's, the superstar of comic books, Marvel Comics, was nearly wiped off the face of the earth from their superhero collection of social justice enforcers known as the Justice League. But after the wars, psychoanalytical preachers began their social takeover and instilled so much paranoia that towns, schools, and churches banned them and actually had "comic book burnings" right there on their grounds!

I know when I was a kid we played cowboys and Indians and made up war games just like the ones we watched on TV. We had toy guns, fake machine guns, tomahawks, and plastic knives, yet we never confused playing with real life. Then we had real guns ounce we grew up, but that was a time before psychology infiltrated every aspect of our society. Kids, especially boys, were allowed to be boys. We didn't all grow up longing to be in the military so we could go out and kill people. In fact, growing up with the Vietnam War on TV every night and our brothers being drafted and coming home in boxes, it was quite the opposite. Most of us didn't want anything to do with the military once Nixon abolished the draft. We had seen enough war, protest, and mutilated bodies.

By the time the 21st century rolled around, the games we played as kids for fun was heavily criticized by sociologists and child psychologist. Now they always have an excuse or explanation for people's behavior and always an expensive fix.

DRONES - The military isn't the only ones using drones. Techno geeks got them down to hobby size and they are also used by small businesses to independent film makers for aerial shots to spying on your neighbors. In 2013, Amazon unveiled a plan to use them for delivery of millions of small packages right to your doorstep within half an hour by setting up hundreds of warehouses near major cities and population areas. UPS claimed to have the same plan but thought it was impractical having a million little drones crisscrossing the entire country.

After the FAA balked about drones in our air space and some spying on people in N.Y. high-rises, the government shut down their plans. So Amazon came up with a new one to deliver Christmas presents within an hour in some major cities for our new, wired, instant gratification society. But this plan has a few kinks too. Eagles are being taught to snatch the small, pesky drones out of the sky.

Bertrand Russell once wrote: Preoccupation with possessions prevents us from living freely and nobly.

13

Medical and Insurance Fraud
Are We Just Guinea Pigs?

THE WORLDS LARGEST DRUG ADDICTS! The headline says it all. We are the king of drugs, both prescription and illegal. We have around 38,000 overdose deaths a year, consume 99% of all the hydrocodone, and 80% of opioid pills despite having only 4.6% of the world's population. We've got the money, and where there's money, there's always someone willing to take it. Like so many things you've read about thus far, 1,350 lobbyist and nearly $100 million a year spent lobbying had our laborious Food and Drug Administration (FDA), doctors, and bureaucrats doling out 227 million opioid prescriptions in 2015, leaving tens of thousands of mothers and their babies addicted.

A Medicare government report reveals 28% of the $64 billion paid out to individual providers goes to just 3% of them. From medical equipment manufacturers and their sales fleets to the pharmaceutical industry, doctors, hospitals, nursing homes, and assisted living facilities - Wall Street profits rein. They're all incessantly in the news for Medicare and Medicaid fraud and are more than willing to join the party with the most profitable con jobs they can brew up. Thanks to the estimated $100 billion a year in fraud (half of our annual deficiency) we spend nearly double that of the highly successful Germans on health care, who have a system based on both the free market and the government working successfully in public-private partnerships. In Germany if a person or family can't afford private insurance, the government steps in similar to our Medicaid, but it's much more willing and successful in controlling incentive based fraud and costs. That's our kryptonite!

When there's a profit to be found, Wall Street pounces on the opportunity, when not, they turn tail and run the other way instead of stepping up to the plate and give a helping hand. That giant sucking sound you hear is shysters siphoning off federal insurance coffers and pumping up expenses, then stashing it in their offshore accounts. Why do you think we pay far more for pharmaceuticals than anyone else on the planet? They're so expensive here, legislators had to ban people from getting them in Canada, Mexico, and overseas. They claim they are protecting us from dangerous unregulated drugs that could be no more than sugar pills - and they may have a point. So why don't they just make the drug manufacturers lower their price domestically to what they sell them for internationally? More than anything else, diabolical profiteers are responsible for driving up the cost of healthcare to the unsustainable levels that have left our system in shambles and people paying $1,000 a month for their family's health insurance!

Pharmaceutical giant Purdue is so greedy they lied about OxyContin to addict the world, but it cost them $635 million in fines. And Pfizer tried buying a British company so they could shift taxes to Britain's lower tax rate. Hiding their outrageous profits in offshore accounts isn't a good enough reason to stay here; they want to take advantage of Britain's nearly lawless financial system like Glaxo Smith Kline did. Chinese authorities caught one of Kline's British executives in a massive bribery scheme of doctors and hospitals that were pushing their drugs, resulting in hundreds of millions in extra profits, but also a $3 billion fine. I'm sure Pfizer isn't planning anything such as that – aren't you?

According to our friend and national whistleblower Al Lewis, "Pfizer has more than $51 billion in annual revenue," and where do you think a huge chunk of that came from? Medicare payments! Over 20 years, it's expected to cost the government $1.17 trillion, with Pfizer and their brethren reaping the rewards. Sometimes, though, firms get caught with their hands in the cookie jar like AstraZeneca, who was fined a measly $7.9 million for kickbacks on their heartburn medicine Nexium.

Some doctors push prescription drugs for kickbacks, especially opiate pain killers like Percocet and the newest one Zohydro. Combined with the current craze, heroin, drug overdose "is now the leading cause of injury related death" says the Centers for Disease Control. Some states are calling the epidemic a public health emergency because of the 38,000 annual overdose deaths, of which 60% come from prescription drugs - mostly painkillers and opiates. Nearly all drug addicts say their addiction started with those such as OxyContin, resulting in us consuming all that hydrocodone and opioids. Fortunately, some crooked doctors are finally going to prison for selling them to addicts, and everyone on the planet knows Michael Jacksons doctor went to jail for giving him a lethal dose of the very dangerous anesthetic "propanol" to help him sleep.

Despite the consequences, manufactures lobby to keep everyone drugged out and give "donations" to those who might rock their boat.

Misusing these drugs, especially with the elderly that can't be trusted to use them properly, really keeps manufacturers pockets jingling. Our mom had been misdiagnosed for years and was put on Percocet when she was in her 70's. She had fallen and smashed her head on the frozen concrete sidewalk, where she laid in the ice and snow until someone found her half frozen. Then she fell several more times in her apartment on the tiled concrete floors, which included smashing her face into the bathtub. All these falls caused what should have been some obvious symptoms of a spinal fluid leak in her neck. Although somewhat rare, its symptoms are obvious. Like everybody with these leaks, they lose their appetite from foods metallic taste or some other unappetizing flavor, and the spinal fluid slowly seeps down into their sinuses, filling them until it creates permanent 24 hour a day migraine headaches. If the person gets lucky, they eject the substantial amount of fluid built up through their nose and mouth every month or so, giving them temporary relief and food taste normal again for about a week before the hell starts anew.

For unknown reasons doctors misdiagnose this condition time and time again around the country and put people on these strong painkillers the rest of their lives. This just causes unnecessary addiction, and mixed with high blood pressure medications and a host of others the elderly are on, makes them more unstable and fall down that more often. Furthermore, they abuse these painkillers by taking them whenever they feel they need them and can easily take a week's worth in a couple of days. Our mom and my little girl's only grandparent went from being a robust energetic grandma, who came over several times a week for dinner, or vive-versa, to a bed ridden invalid who eventually wound up starving herself to death to get out of pain. And I for one have to wonder - was it all for money?

My brother was also misdiagnosed for years that resulted in repeated doctor visits and expensive rehab. He had no hip joints left and was walking and sitting on his sciatic nerves. Many of you know how excruciating a pinched one in your back is; can you imagine it being permanent and walking on it for years at 250 pounds?

He finally went down to Boston General and they were absolutely shocked! The doctor yelled: "You have no hip joints left! Can't they read an x-ray over there in Western Mass?" Was he put through unimaginable pain all those years just for money?

Some doctors push more unnecessary treatments, test, and prescription medications than there are gamer's at an electronics convention. In a report by Marilyn Preston, she points out there is an estimated $225 billion a year wasted on unnecessary and often very expensive test in the U.S. because 95% reveal nothing. Among the most abused are yearly cardiograms, exercise stress test, routine EKG's, annual Pap test, and MRI's for lower back pain. Research by the American Board of Internal Medicine Foundation suggest you more often than not don't need nuclear stress test after heart procedures, yearly electrocardiograms, blood test to measure PSA levels for prostate cancer, PET scans to diagnose Alzheimer's disease, X-rays, CT scans, and MRI's for lower back pain, yearly Pap test, follow up ultrasounds for small ovarian cysts, and yearly physicals. Phew! That's a mouthful.

Fortunately, doctors are finally escaping the steel grip of big Pharma, and like other countries are promoting a holistic, healthier lifestyle of exercise and socializing to combat people's psychological and physical problems rather than drugs. But rehabbing the country won't be easy.

Fraud and insiders have driven up health care cost so high the system is cutting corners to save itself from imploding. But unlike Wall Street - imploding is not an option here!

Speaking of the Street, it has their giant, grubby, blood stained hands sprawled across the board in health care products. Soda is spiked with caffeine and sugar, and energy drinks are double so, leaving about 20,000 people going to emergency rooms yearly with spiked heartbeats, seizures, and monster headaches. And conglomerates such as Coca-Cola force stores to keep shelves stocked or be banned from selling it. We have an endless supply of weight loss schemes and products that promise everyone they'll feel great and look like swim suit models and athletes. Health food stores popped up around the country selling every conceivable supplement to slim you down, build you up, make you look and feel younger or anything your heart desires, including sex. Some have proven health benefits but most don't, yet we still spend billions of dollars every year for unproven supplements.

My Personal Testimony

Like most of you, I can personally attest to all of the wasted doctor's visits, test, and unnecessary surgeries meant more to boost profits than for our own good. Like millions of Americans, doctors used me as a guinea pig for so many years I now tell them I don't want any unnecessary test or surgery and outright refuse to go if they order any.

Although many of you know our system, for the uninitiated who haven't been used as lab rats yet, I'll delight you with a few more stories about capitalistic greed.

In my case, I became a cash register starting in 1996 when I injured the giant sciatica nerve. I slipped while mowing the grass on a steep hill and landed on the edge of the seat with my left hip. My leg instantly went numb. However, being an old farmer and just starting the summer season, I kept working and bouncing around on it for another month until it was burning so badly and shutting down the other nerves I couldn't drag it one more step.

That's when I wound up going to 9 different doctors at 6 different offices trying to get just one to believe me. I told every one of them the same story. I was sure I hurt it under my hip because of the immediate pain and numbness, and my leg collapsed several times. When I sat down, my hip and leg instantly became ice cold, numb, and painful. And every one of them told me I was wrong - "It's your back!"

They sent me for lower back X-rays and wanted to do an MRI, but like tens of millions of people, I had no insurance and had to pay for it myself. I had no intention of paying for an MRI on my back when I knew the injury was under my hip. Finally, the last doctor sent me to the one person I should have seen from the beginning, a neurologist, who only verified what I already knew. After shocking me half to death to determine the amount of nerve damage, he said I damaged the sciatica nerve that "may or may not be permanent." Gee…thanks for the update Doc! How much do you think the electrocutions cost?

Was I being used as a cash guinea pig? After all, doctors love cash? No insurance forms to fill out, no waiting for reimbursements. For years they insisted I hurt my back.

Eventually, I was so beat up from work I couldn't move anything except my left arm without pain. My wife had to dress me and bring our baby girl to my bed, then set her beside me under my good left arm. With tendinitis arthritis throughout, doctors wanted to give me drugs. Desperate, my carpet man told me Glucosamine Chondroitin with MSN cured him, and combined with fish oil and stretching it helped me immensely. Proving some supplemental drugs really do work!

Now you see why I only go to a doctor when I have a serious problem, because once you have insurance you'll be used as a lab rat more than ever. For instance, I've been losing an unusual amount of weight and strength the last few years, and more recently suffered dizzy spells with vision problems. So the primary care doctors in the medical group I was in sent me to every doctor and specialist in their group! You know what I'm talking about! You've been there – done that!

They started out doing the appropriate thing and took blood test looking for some sort of disease or organ problem. But when I started having psychedelic colors swirling around in my eyes, they went a little hay-wire. I told them I thought it was from something simple, specifically, the semi-rancid fruit juice and ice tea I drank a couple of times when I was in a hurry to get my daughter to her soccer game. It always seemed to happen about an hour after drinking them. I know what you're thinking! Why were you stupid enough to drink spoiled juice and ice tea? In my defense, I was in a hurry and guzzled it down before I considered it. Hey, I never claimed to be the brightest pea in the pod!

As usual, they didn't believe me and did a barrage of blood test, then sent me to their neurologist, a cardiologist for an artery scan, then their imaging center for a brain MRI. How much do you think they charged? The neurologist office visit was $170 and the vascular scan was $1,700 for about an hour of their time. The brain MRI was $2,200 for another hour, and two office visits was another $498. That's $4,568 for a few hours at the doctors!

You may have noticed I said that's what the doctors charged the insurance company, though, that's not what they get paid! There's this strange game they play, and it applies to everything they bill them for. Although there is a predetermined set price for every office visit and procedure, they charged over triple the price they knew they would get for the brain MRI and about double the office visits. And the cardiologist that charged $1,700 only got $760. This insane game is played on a daily basis with doctors, hospitals, and millions of patients.

What's the point? Is it greed and our capitalistic system that seems to function on the core belief you should gouge as many people as you can, for as much as you can, as often as you can. I think the eye doctor I went to was one of the biggest thieves in the business. The eye exam I got after the blurry vision cost $545! It included 189 for a new patient,

134 for a visual field exam, 112 for the eye exam, 84 for eye photography and 26 for an echo exam.

Here in America, the patient better beware! Another unethical doctor performed unnecessary inferred hemorrhoid surgery in his office for about $2500. I was instantly worried when he told me he was a general surgeon after going to him based on his false advertisement in the yellow pages as a colon and rectal specialist. He said he could seal the hemorrhoids by burning them with two or three inferred treatments in the office and my problems would be solved "permanently." Needless to say, all he did was create a lot of internal bleeding and unnecessary pain and suffering. When I refused to go on with the second treatment, he sent me across the hallway to the real specialist.

He said my problem was extremely minor and it was just a skin tab left over from hemorrhoid surgery. He wanted to snip it off and use just two external stitches to solve the problem. When I asked him if he could do this minor one minute snip in the office, he said NO! This thief, at the regions award winning hospital that has recently bought all our local hospitals, said it required hospital outpatient surgery with general anesthesia by an anesthesiologist and an operating room - for just two stitches! Give me a break people! We've all had cuts more serious than that! Like all chronically constipated people, after trying a gauntlet of remedies, an honest doctor finally suggested 400 mil of magnesium daily. Voila! Problem solved!

Then there was Aspen Dental, who claimed I needed to have extremely painful and expensive "reconstructive surgery" on my lower gum to permanently stop a blister under the denture! Knowing it was a scam, I went to the local dentist and she ground it down in the bad spot... VOILA! Problem solved. To jingle the doctor's pockets, I've even had unnecessary extra eye surgery, leaving 25 scars in one eye and 12 in the other! And when I got an infection on my ear, the dermatologist gave me a choice of using antibiotics for a week or cut it off. I chose cut it off. After, I asked when it would heal. He said a couple of months, "but we have special donut pillows for sale on your way out that are covered by your insurance." After 3 years, I'm still using a special pillow.

Now, I'm just one person being screwed. Can you imagine how much suffering and unnecessary money is spent all-toll on everyone?

In some defense of doctors, I offer the possibility of lawsuits here in the litigation capitol of the world, and after what they've done to me and my family I can understand why they need medical malpractice insurance!

For years the medical and insurance industries have tried to put a cap on how much a person can receive in a successful malpractice suit. There's a list of different injuries sustained from mild to the most severe in their request for caps. Based on the amount of harm doctors do to people determines how much money they get. For instance, someone who had a tooth pulled out by their dentist, instead of being filled, obviously had very little damage compared to someone that had the wrong kidney removed. Therefore, it only makes since that person shouldn't get nearly as much as the person who is likely to die from having the wrong kidney taken out.

As it currently stands, the amount of money each one gets will either be hashed out between the lawyers or decided by a judge or jury. This leaves doctors and insurance companies at the mercy of unreasonable lawyers, judges, and juries who often give out staggering amounts of money in their awards. This, in turn, causes doctors to do all these extra test just to cover all their bases.

I think one reason the industry has failed to get any maximum compensation awards into law is because they always lowball the awards they want, especially with some of the most severe injuries. What is a life of hell worth to a person that could have been fixed up and winds up crippled or mentally retarded for the rest of their lives as Joe Kennedy's daughter Rosemary was when he gave her a revolutionary treatment at that time - the horrific lobotomy! It left her severely retarded, and he hid her in a mental institution the rest of her life so nobody could destroy the Kennedy image and his egotistical plans for his kids.

Pharmacies are also getting in on more insurance action by offering walk in medical clinics that offer limited services. They may have some merit though. They're convenient for minor infections, colds, vaccinations, and even sports physicals for school athletes, plus they are conveniently open at night and on weekends when everyone seems to get sick and doctors' offices are closed. Still, I think they're in it mostly for the money. There is the economic incentive to take the money and then tell you to go to the doctor because they aren't really set up for your particular problem. As we all know, any time there is an incentive for money – there's incentive for abuse!

The government has been trying for decades to stop fraud in the Medicare system with little success. Forbes reported in 2013 there was nearly a 20% increase in improper payments over 2012 for a total of $49 billion. To combat the abuse, Medicare has recently come out with a list to publicize how much individual doctors are personally getting from them. Some get over $10 million a year. Their hope is, if fraudulent doctors are publicized it will cut down on their abuse by notifying patients they may be using them as Guiney pigs.

Psychiatrist, Psychologist, Psychoanalyst and Therapist

Using our sensationalistic media to instill a feeding frenzy of psychosis and mass hysteria, like a true sorcerer, they rely on gimmicks, gadgets, confusion, and illusion to manipulate and convince us we have every form of mental problem they can dream up. Many people are consumed with and analyze every thought and action until they're paralyzed by them in this era of psychoanalysis. If you are eating, sleeping, breathing, working, married, divorced, unemployed, are bald – in other words if you're alive - you have some sort of psychosomatic problem that needs very expensive therapy, treatment, drugs, surgery or all of them. They pile it on so thick they have some people changing sexes and the vain getting unnecessary plastic surgery. We even have team psychiatrists for our multimillionaire professional athletes when they're in a slump to salvage the owner's investment!

Speaking of investments, the stock market has jumped on the bandwagon by showing people what they will look like in old age to get them to invest and save more for their future through 401's and stocks. They claim people save or invest about double after seeing their future images.

Do you have a dog or cat, bird or pig? Good news, we have animal psychiatrist and therapist for your pig with an attitude!

Our country's been overrun by the industry, from the highly trained at the most expensive medical schools to therapist with no training at all. Half of us are brainwashed into thinking we need their services, especially generation X and their millennial offspring. They prey mostly on those with insurance that covers both prescription drugs and mental problems, while ignoring those without it that can't possibly afford their services - though they're the ones most likely to need real care. At two or three hundred dollars an hour for therapy, I think they invent syndromes and diseases that don't exist!

They relentlessly prey on kids like a mad sorcerer, taking away their childhood for their own selfish gain. If kids are energetic (as most kids are) they have Attention Deficit Hyperactivity Disorder (ADHD) and need to be drugged out on very expensive medications such as Ritalin and Adderall pushed by big Pharma, then brought to equally expensive therapy. One kid was put on BOTH, plus Prozac all at once! Doctors are even giving it to an estimated 10,000 toddlers! Acurian Health actually sent people letters looking for children with "depression, negative thoughts, low self-esteem or feelings of guilt and anxiety" between the ages of 7-17 for clinical trials. Hello! That's nearly everyone! Then they pay them $450 and send them to a therapist for free. The children's mental health industry is getting to be more profitable than us 'highly disturbed adults!' To them we're all ready for strait-jackets and that place with the rubber rooms. It's such a scam the mafia is jealous!

Our most honest and greatest president ever, Theodore Roosevelt, was the most energetic, hyperactive kid that ever lived. And without question would have been a drugged out lump of contentment in this day and age, long before the world realized his greatness was driven by that pent up energy. Dr. Leonard Sax points out the realities about boys being drugged out, being seen as the enemy of woman's rights, and being stripped of their masculinity through the educational system and culture, leaving hordes of them dreading and hating school, unmotivated, underachieving, and living at home well into their thirties.

Psychoanalyst set the social norms, despite the fact they are often the psychotic ones who should be the last ones on earth telling the rest of us what we should do and how we should think and act, especially the dear Abby types who often have no training. They're second only to law enforcement in committing suicide. They have millions of woman convinced they are constantly being raped and abused mentally, physically, or both by strangers at parties, boyfriends, and husbands. And they need expensive therapy, heeling, and that word they've been engraining into our social psych the last 30 years – "closure!"

They've even destroyed the college experience. So many women at college campuses across the country have fallen under their spell, the government investigated claims of sexual violence and harassment at 55 colleges and universities, including Harvard and Princeton.

You can no longer say you're "mad," now you're "angry." And everything has to be "positive" or we'll hurt someone's feelings or make them lose their "self-esteem." Positive makes a happy world and reality or negativity makes a terribly depressed society.

Let me tell you something Doc: I'm mad as hell with a bad attitude and life's not sugar coated, so shut up and give me some Prozac!

Worst of all, they took away all our fun things, especially in sports! High fives, low fives, and celebrating great plays, particularly in American football with the universally beloved touchdown celebrations that now cease to exist thanks to them! The much anticipated end zone team dances brought to Super Bowl status levels by the 1986 Chicago Bears for their super-duper end zone dance rituals, were crushed by the hands of the wimpy psychiatrist, psychologist, and sociologist. No more celebrating a job well done they said, you will hurt the other 300 pound grown man's feelings. They also try making us feel bad about the native Indian names we have used for generations for our sports teams. The Washington Redskins, Atlanta Braves, and Cleveland Indians are cruel, insensitive, and insulting they say, along with Florida States Tomahawk Chop. The last stand for American men has been crushed, and the meek have inherited the earth.

To make us a civilized nation, they womanize our boys from birth through manhood, prompting the show Last Man Standing. That allowed the NRA and gun industry to push their hyperbole to arm every man, woman, and child they could with the weapons of their choice. So men were kicked out of schools and schools were locked down like prisons, even in the smallest, mellowest, towns like ours. After brainwashing the younger generation and their kid's, mental health advocates got us to put expensive psychologist in every school.

I remember the days when schools had real tough guys. Guys from local motorcycle gangs pulled up to the school riding their Harleys (Hogs) with the mandatory biker fashion accessory - a ½ inch chain strapped to their belts for rumbles with opposing gang members. Now parents drive up in there SUV's and mini vans decked out with TV's and other electronic babysitting accessories! And how about the bloody, violent Vietnam War protest? People protest by email and social media now. Don't get me wrong, I'm not wishing for the days of chain wielding bikers and more useless wars to return, I'm just trying to make a point how overboard we've allowed fearmongering analyst to go.

They've even taken over the law and courts. We aren't allowed to discipline our kids for fear of going to jail. Many parents would rather go into financial ruin, giving their kids anything they want then risk their kids telling authorities they are abused. Then when our kids are completely out of control, they make us take them to one of their own for therapy. If we're lucky we only have to pay for our kids. If not, we have to go to therapy ourselves and pay them double.

Many physicians are no better. They too instill fear, paranoia, and mass psychosis in areas such as cancer, and then reap the abundant insurance money for themselves and their hospitals they increasingly partner with and work for. Often woman, including some celebrities, have breast removed for fear of dying from even the smallest of tumors because they don't tell them very few actually developed into deadly malignant (cancerous) ones. Nor do they tell them it could take years to develop to the stage of emergency status and a simple lumpectomy works just as well. Colonoscopies are another huge money maker for quick easy profits based on their lectures that strike fear into our minds, despite most cancers taking nearly a decade for the tumors to develop into a life threatening cancer - if at all!

Most doctors deny cheaper treatments like medical marijuana, which can be used for many ailments, including some very serious and life ending seizures such as Dravet's syndrome. Instead, they push the drug company's overpriced drugs and special pediatric epilepsy centers for treatment. They shun special marijuana low in THC (the ingredient in marijuana that can trigger seizures) but high in CBD (the ingredient that stops seizures). Then ignore the fact it has drastically improved hundreds of kid's lives, but more importantly, stops their suffering and even drawn out deaths. They claim it's harmful for their young brains. Still, I can't see the purpose of not trying it! How do they ignore those kids who are suffering and will die before adulthood without it?

Without a doubt, some people have serious problems and addictions and the industry is there waiting to take advantage of them. Betty Ford was the first famous person I can remember going into a rehabilitation center. Rehab quickly became a lucrative industry after that. Even Mitt Romney's own Bain Capital has jumped on the bandwagon. Although some people have insurance that covers rehab facilities and medications, the government gets screwed through Medicare and Medicaid insured patients. And with the affordable Care Act, all patients under Medicaid are now covered, opening the floodgates for abuse. Gee! I bet Romney didn't see that one coming when Bain bought 25% of the HCA hospital chain!

As much as rehab can help, there are some major problems beside potential monetary abuse. Success rates for completely curing people are limited, and anybody with a high school diploma with no training can be a counselor in many states.

Other addiction's needing real therapy includes shopaholics. Usually they're women addicted to shopping who devastate their families with shopping binges similar to an alcoholic or drug addict. With them it's usually the latest fashions and jewelry. Others are addicted to hording everything that ever comes into their homes, including trash that makes their houses unlivable and often condemned by public officials. They stuff their houses from wall to wall with everything from newspapers and magazines to pets and other animals. Some even have rats. They eat and sleep in filth for no other reason than they can't make themselves throw anything away. Some hoard relatively harmless items like cloths and newspapers. Others are truly demented and stuff their homes with rotting food, animals urinating and defecating everywhere, and never bath themselves - never mind their animals. These people are a party for every conceivable varmint. The mystery of how animal diseases jump to humans loses its mystery with these people!

In defense of hoarders, they aren't usually just lazy slobs. Many are actually out of control shopaholics, whose frontal cortex in the brain is activated when they see these things and get confused. They feel like a kid being punished if they throw them out. At least that's what psychiatrist tell us for around $200 dollars an hour.

Government Insurance

Congress tried fixing our medical system with the Affordable Care Act (ACA). But, unlike other previous beneficial acts, the new radical GOP continues trying to abolish it for one of the most profitable industry in the world – private insurance companies! As Paul Thomas, an executive at a major insurance company told me: "We have more money than we know what to do with!" Instead of fixing the parts they don't want, the GOP pulls out every dirty trick in the book to kill it, once again ignoring history and all other industrialized nations on earth.

Back in the 1930's when F.D.R. started the social security system, it too was argued vehemently, but they hashed out their differences and implemented it, then tweaked it until this day. Now we couldn't imagine life without it.

We have been insuring people over 65 and the disabled ever since Medicare first came out, so why did we only have universal healthcare for the most expensive 40% of our population?

To be unfathomably profitable you have to gouge your customers for everything they have. By robbing everyone under 65, the industry maintains their power over politicians with the resulting hordes of excess money. Otherwise protecting everybody with universal health care would make the most since. It is the highly profitable under 65 group who keep universal health care affordable in all other countries. Theirs weren't perfect when they were implemented and never will be, but they're sure a heck of a lot better than ours! Once again, the most technologically advanced country in the world has fallen flat on its face in the name of Capitalism.

To make sure the Affordable Care Act is as expensive as possible to people with preexisting conditions; insurance companies are retiering their most expensive specialty drugs and charging much higher co-payments. In an effort to dismantle the ACA and discourage those that require special drugs to stay alive, they have jumped on the ACA's requirement of co-insurance to keep their profit spreads among the highest in the world. They're charging some people more than a $1000 a month for a prescription drug (including my late mom before we intervened) and Turing Pharmaceuticals charges $750 for **one** 99 cent pill. According to America's Health Insurance Plans, only 1% of per-scription drugs account for 25% of the cost, so insurers will save tens of billions of dollars if they can get people to give them up. They also seem to be teaming up with GOP states such as Texas and Florida, where they have raised the co-insurance rates to 50% compared to 30% or less in states like California to make the ACA look too expensive.

My other beef with not only government insurance, but all insurance, is it's too complicated with too many rules and scenarios. I'd rather get stuck in the tar pits than try and figure out health insurance, especially for the elderly. A quick example of its complexity would perhaps be one of the simplest things in the system - prescription medications. The best I can make of it is: You have STAGE 1 - your yearly deductible (your share of the cost) until you reach your out of pocket cost of $4,550. That puts you in STAGE 2 (your initial coverage). At this point you're on your own paying 100% of your prescription cost over the next $4,519.25, unless you have a private coverage gap policy, or one paid by Medicaid on your behalf, which is STAGE 3 (the coverage gap). Lastly, STAGE 4 is the catastrophic coverage stage in which you pay nothing the rest of the year. It's just that simple! To a computer maybe!

Speaking of, the electronic age has introduced a new twist. Recently, I had a life threatening injury and had my first hospital stay in 35 years. One of the first things I noticed different was everybody that came to take care of me, from the ambulance EMT to the hospital personnel until the day I left, every little detail was recorded into a computer. Even pictures from cell phones to sonograms went into the data base. This got me thinking about several things. What would happen if a doctor or nurse imputed the wrong information, or hit the wrong key and put me under the wrong name? What if they are in a hurry, which every doctor is, and accidentally copy and pasted the wrong information or delete me completely at the touch of a button. We all know how easy that is!

Were there any handwritten backup notes in a file cabinet? What if hackers steal my records? Also, does a doctor have enough time to input all this information while properly diagnosing and watching me and his other patients at the same time? It seemed to create more work on top of the sixteen hour days they put in. I know I can't function when I'm tired, and I don't have people's lives and family's hanging in the balance. Did you ever notice the computer age was supposed to reduce, or even eliminate paperwork, but seems to have increased it?

All my worries not only seem to be legitimate, but the blasphemous pharmaceutical industry is tracking all prescriptions sent to pharmacies by computer. Companies that collect it, sell it to them for enormous profits! I think they could put pressure on doctors to push their most expensive drugs rather than cheaper ones or generics. The government appears to be doing the same with both doctor and pharmacy health records. Will this create an incentive for more fraud? Sorry! Stupid question!

We already have companies like Mallinckrodt Pharmaceuticals that bought their only competitor so they could raise the price of the 65 year old child tremor drug Acthar *100,000%!*

As you read on, you'll see other private insurance scams, but first I want to tell you about a scam that sent seven owners of a nursing home to jail for Medicare fraud. My older brother had the dubious task of working for them when it was raided by the FBI.

A True Story

My brother worked for a nursing home in Florida for over twenty years as an occupational therapist. Like all employees, he went about his business taking care of the elderly without much cause to think about the management side. Then one day the (FBI) stormed the building asking questions and demanding answers. They wanted the keys to all the medicine cabinets and everything locked down in the building. Naturally, my brother and the patients were as stunned as the rest of the employees and didn't know what the heck was going on, so he just did as they ordered.

After things settled down, they interviewed the employees and decided they wanted my brother on the witness stand to testify against his beloved small time family employers. Talk about shaking in your boots! He was a nervous wreck going over the proceedings with attorneys and waiting for the trial! Although he was a small time landlord with the occasional tenant not paying the rent, he never experienced anything as extreme as testifying for the FBI!

Finally, trial day arrived and he testified. The owners were found guilty of falsifying insurance claims and overbilling the government millions over the years. They are now sitting in prison instead of retiring and wishing they had lived an honest life. Greed people, is the parasite feeding off America! Too bad big Pharma doesn't have a pill for that. It might actually be worth the price and they would get theirs free!

Greed and Medicare fraud comes in another less dubious form. Millions of people are on disability that were at one time disabled but have remained on it for years, even life, despite getting significantly better. They have duped the government out of untold billions for a number of reasons. The first and most important is its lack of oversight in this critical area.

Not too long ago, people that qualified for disability had to get reevaluated every couple of years to continue collecting it, but that requirement seems to have been streamed down to just filling out a form stating your current condition. With no real threat of actually having to be examined by a doctor, there is no incentive to get off of it. This entitlement has gotten way out of hand, especially when you consider everyone on disability gets the same Medicare insurance as retired people on Social Security.

Another reason is, in a roundabout way, connected to the first one. When a person retires and applies for Social Security their payments are calculated on a number of factors. One of them is based on your earnings the last 30 years, and I believe they take the top ten years' worth to set the amount you will receive every month. For instance, if your top ten years averaged $40,000 dollars, they take a percentage of that, along with a complicated formula with other variables, including if you have a pension coming when calculating your payments. Most people are shocked at how little they get compared to what they think they'll get come retirement time.

This leads people who are on disability later in life to seriously think about continuing to stay on it until they reach the normal retirement age, because like welfare, it usually pays significantly more than going back to work for five or ten years. It's become particularly true after the economy collapsed and older people have virtually no chance of getting a job, never mind a decent paying one, and explains the recent 50% increase for people collecting disability.

Other insurance fraud includes people faking being hit by cars or slipping on someone's property, others burn down their house or hire someone to do it. There are individuals who fake all sorts of things, but one company called Precision Builders came up with an igneous way to get lots of unjustified business. The insurance industry calls them "storm chasers." I don't mean the kind that chase tornados or hurricanes for the thrill of it or scientific knowledge. I mean the kind that follows the destructive path of storms for financial gain. In their case, they were a construction repair company ripping everyone off.

If your house was damaged by a storm or natural disaster, they came to you and gave you an estimate to fix it, and if your house didn't have any damage they damaged it for you when you weren't looking. That's right! They put holes in roofs and siding or anything else they could think of, then told you the storm did it. Sometimes they gave estimates as much as double that of a legitimate company or an insurance claims estimator and told people they would do the repair for the price of the insurance quote. That made people think they were nice guys and they trusted them. When they were hired, they put a sign on their lawn and went to another house in the neighborhood, then another, and another. Pretty soon they had enough signs up in the neighborhood to make people think they were a very popular and respectable company. With neighbors not communicating anymore, business snowballed.

Fortunately, greed took over and they didn't know when to stop. The insurance companies got suspicious and set up cameras to catch them and "nailed their butts to the wall." Democracy was once again captured by greed. Sorry I forgot – it's called Capitalism!

When insurance companies aren't getting the shaft, they're shafting us. We've all encountered pushy salesmen, but some take it to a whole new level. People that go price shopping to get the lowest rates are sometimes asked to give a credit card or debit card number to the salesman as an excuse to sign you up with their company without your permission. They claim they need it to check your credit rating so they can give you the lowest price. If you deny their quote, they cancel your insurance with your current carrier, sign you up, and steal your money without you ever knowing it until you get your bill.

Another great scam they are famous for is collecting premiums for decades, then when you have a natural disaster or other reason to file a claim they disappear before your eyes. The list of things they insure often pales to that they don't. Even the ones they do insure, good luck getting your house repaired or replaced, especially in a natural disaster! I think they have more loopholes then the entire ruling class combined. Even if they do pay for the repairs, they jack up your premiums to nearly double the previous rate, or drop you completely, as they did my aunt and uncle after 30 years of payments. So what good is insurance?

For-Profit Assisted Living Facilities

My downstairs tenant works at one, and she warned me they are not the best place to be. Frontline did a documentary on her for-profit assisted living facility that became king of the hill in representing the worst nightmares of our capitalistic medical system. Emeritus Living Facilities, they point out, takes advantage of the mostly unregulated system by preying on and torturing our beloved elderly parents and grandparents into sometimes excruciating deaths.

I have one of their brochures right here, so I called them to see for myself if they were blowing their story out of proportion. The young man I talked to was very nice, and aside from the outrageous price of $3500 to $6000 a month, it sounds great to me. They have substantial help and living arrangements: a program called "Join Their Journey" for residents with Alzheimer's, "Friendship Suites" similar to dormitories, 1 and 2 bedroom apartments, studios, and short term living so you can give it a test stay. They also have home cooked meals, transportation, and a slew of other amenities for an active lifestyle with independence. The best thing is they have one in the most affluent town around here! Could it be as repulsive as Frontline claims?

They say unsuspecting family members are given uplifting, positive sales pitches by salespeople they assume are evaluators who claim they will treat your parents like family. Yep, it's in the brochure! But people are often shocked by their sales pitch that emphasizes their "Memory Care" program, rather than asking medical questions for entrance into their beautiful looking facilities. And that's a red flag they say!

Little do people know, Emeritus facilities scattered across the country have left at least two dozen beloved elderly family members dead in various states from coast to coast. And they have the most complaints per bed than anyone else their size in the entire country. They also reported they prey on the sickest, most demented old folks they can find that can afford their extremely expensive facilities. Then torture and abuse these elderly, fragile people that by the laws of every state they operate in should be in nursing homes.

Emeritus directors and many other whistleblowers came forth to expose them and reinforced the complaints they were running their operations without enough staff or training. They unanimously said they were constantly ordered to reduce staff, fill every bed, and keep the facilities full with these mentally ill people. They said the company told them they didn't follow the required caregiver to resident ratio because they didn't want lawsuits. Those good souls that complained or sent the company letters informing senior management of the deplorable working conditions and tried to help the poor souls were, of course, fired! Others just couldn't stand seeing the abuse and quit.

Driven by shear greed, president and CEO Granger Cobb and top executives, were convicted for having complete knowledge of the way their company did business, as well as instructions by senior members of the company to their facilities directors and sales staff to target those with advanced dementia and the seriously ill.

Emeritus was found guilty of recklessness, oppression, and fraud by a unanimous jury that was sick of all the previous deaths, complaints, law suits, and state fines filed against them. They awarded a complainant $23 million in one case. When Emeritus attorneys filed to have the judgment reduced, the judge was so sick of their operation he gave them a resounding - NO!

This award was a long time coming. And quite frankly, Emeritus was lucky they were let off the hook by states, which like themselves, did not have the staff necessary to fully investigate and prosecute them across the country, resulting in fines of just hundreds of dollars. They also slapped them on the wrist for insufficient staff monitoring the number of residents they had, and bringing in people that were too sick for assisted living facilities for their "under qualified and undertrained staffs." However, fines are so small or nonexistent they continue breaking every law in the book.

In light of all this and considering what my tenant told me... I think I'll cancel my visit.

14

The Legal System

"The Washington Redskins are sued again over their team name and logo!" With a country of over a million attorneys, we have an attorney for every 274 people in the U.S. and nothing is off limits. We became a country predisposed by worry that we'd be sued at any time by just about anyone, from homeowners afraid someone will slip on the ice to municipalities worried they could be sued for kids taking peanut butter and jelly sandwiches to school. Attorneys joined special interest, Wall Street, the mental health profession, and aristocrats in abusing the country at will. Now everything is settled in court. Not exactly the vision our founding fathers had in mind, who couldn't possibly have predicted such abuse in their worst nightmares.

Television commercials for law firms dubbed "ambulance chasers" plaster the airwaves daily. From prescription drugs that may have injured you to car accidents and hospital malpractice lawsuits, we're pushed tirelessly by ambulance chasers to sue everybody. Whether we make a poor decision ourselves or the other party doesn't matter, as long as we can find someone breaking one of the million or so local, state, and federal laws - we sue! Whether we have a legitimate case or even a case at all doesn't matter either! We still roll into courts like wave after wave at high tide and file lawsuit after lawsuit, and then get the defendants to settle out of court knowing 90% of all cases are settled that way. Only about 10% ever make it all the way to a trial because it's much easier, cheaper, and safer to settle out of court than take your chances on an unfavorable decision by a judge or jury. Either way, like stockbrokers, lawyers get paid enormous amounts of money win or lose!

It's actually more profitable for them not to bring a case to trial. I learned when I was a landscape gardener; many small customers in one place are more profitable per hour than driving around town to larger clients for a few more dollars. The same is true for small time lawyers. They can make more money doing many small cases than spend too much time preparing larger drawn out ones that require scheduling, attending court appearances, and teleconferences with judges. Many attorneys won't even accept cases that aren't quick and highly profitable. I call them paperwork cases. Disability cases are a good example. Most people fill out the standard forms and file it on their own. When the government turns them down, attorneys refile it for about 30 percent of the first payment, which includes perhaps a year or more of back pay.

Although mom and pop attorneys comprise what most of us will ever deal with, there are those selfish egotistical maniacs that chase the biggest bucks. Those are the ones that have kept many major international corporations pondering if it's worth doing business in this country. These mammoth law firms make incredible amounts of money rivaling Wall Street by chasing class action lawsuits and large corporate ones, where like the Street, they get rich while the people injured and killed get a pittance of the total reward. One example is General Motors (GM), who was hit with the maximum fine allowed by law for not taking action sooner on their ignition switch problem. Toyota and Honda got hammered as well. How many millions do you think the lawyers made?

The long arm of the biggest companies even stretch into the lucrative sports world. One groundbreaking case was about a lawsuit involving Collegiate Licensing Inc. and Electronic Arts, who used college teams and about 100,000 student athletes' likenesses in NCAA branded video games. That one was settled for $40 million. The athletes got as little as $48 and the law firms their usual 30 to 40%! That's why so many corporations offshore their work to countries where both labor laws and lawsuits are virtually nonexistent or aren't enforced. Just as malpractice lawsuits do in medicine to drive up cost, so do lawyers that chase everything else.

With so many law firms chasing easy money, parents have unwillingly lost control of their kids. They are now afraid to discipline them by spanking them, making them do chores, or the most dreaded torture of all - take away their electronics. Those acts of heresy us older folks call discipline and raising our kid's right, could give the state cause to take your kids. Or in divorce cases, give them to the parent the kids played like a violin that never disciplines them and gives them everything they want. You, the good parent, and sometimes both parents, are then sent to parenting classes and put on probation.

As you know from the Rachel Canning case in New Jersey, millions of kids like her are so spoiled and given anything they want; parents don't know what to do when they misbehave. Kids in public places are ticking time-bombs, prodding and embarrassing their parents, grandparents, and babysitters, knowing they are in full control.

Many times dads are held hostage for fear of being falsely accused by their kids of rape or beating them. Teenage girls have become famous for putting their dads, former boyfriends, relatives, and other men in jail simply because they are mad at them: usually for not getting what they want, which is often drugs, money, or electronics. They aren't always picky though, sometimes they have their mom's, school administrators, and teachers locked up too. Even a kid's friend spending the night on a sleepover or just there for a visit could land you in the pokey. It was so easy to lock up anybody they wanted, many falsely accused dads sat in prison for years with little hope their kids would someday get a conscience until DNA testing came along to free the innocent. You can see why attorneys have parents, school systems, and everybody else walking on pins and needles when kids get out of control.

When they aren't trying to imprison everyone or make insurance companies pay what amounts to a ransom, overzealous police and state prosecutors are now putting parents in jail for their out of control kids they are legally responsible for. Cyber bullying draws the same wrath. When kids get out of control they try locking up us parents, all the while knowing many of us are as technologically challenged as they themselves are.

My daughter and I feel social networks have limited acceptable uses, therefore, we know little about them. But if she were to use one to cyber bully, or is being bullied, I would have no idea it's happening. Lawyers and prosecutors will say I should ask and monitored her activities. However, like most parents, police, and the prosecutors themselves, they know more about technology than we do. And they really don't think a kid is going to tell their parents I'm cyber bullying someone online do they? As usual, it's easier to prosecute the defenseless little people instead of the now immune powerful social media corporations responsible for the website's the kids are abusing.

Many times sweet, little, innocent kids get caught in the frenzy of overzealous law enforcement officials who are often full of good people trying their best. But the fact is; both courts and the Department of Children's and Family Services (DCF) often destroy as many kids and families as they help. Woman abuse the system in mass under domestic violence laws meant to help real cases, then the courts and law enforcement go about like the Wild-West by arresting first and asking questions later.

For years men had no rights and were sent to jail by woman scorned in their own eyes with no conscience, or afraid of losing their kids for what they themselves had done. They let their husbands, boyfriends, or just acquaintances rot in prison while their kids cried for them and withdrew into their own worlds. When the poor kids acted out in anger and despair, officials sent them to those child psychologists who put them on antidepressants and hyperactivity drugs. Adding to the demolition, judges must follow the outrageously high state alimony rates that cause more homelessness, drug addicts, alcoholics, poverty and inmates. There was an actual case wear an architect was threatened by the judge with revoking his professional license for not being able to pay the ghastly alimony after getting laid off from his job.

Often courts give custody to mothers who are drug addicts or mentally unstable and are ordered to undergo psychological evaluations. Thus making officials take their kids away from them as well to what could be described as "children's prisons" in DCF offices. The system is often a pipeline for child destruction, divorce, poverty, and **profiteers.**

When the ladies aren't abusing the system, the system is abusing the ladies and kids without conscience. I've dealt with many people, particularly woman in the system, whose idea of helping the kids is that of radical feminist. Throw away their dad, who is often the good parent and gets full custody, and convince both the ladies and kids they are abused mentally when physical abuse is not involved. This keeps court psychoanalyst raking in the big bucks and rolling in dough. Our families are lunchmeat for them and the attorneys who game the system, never caring about the mangled, tattered, families caught in their dragnet. They leave society shattered and in shambles with their "Instagram" divorces and both single parents broke working two jobs, with daycare centers and others raising our kids.

This long line of abuse and devastation has spurred some men's rights organizations, politicians, and public officials to turn back the clock to the pre-abuse days of old when you were actually considered innocent until proven guilty for the sake of the children.

No sooner than I finished writing the above paragraphs, my former downstairs tenant, who is a severe drug addict and alcoholic, called me and told me she was going to tell the judge in our back rent case that I was a child molester and all the horrible things I did to my daughter. This is the perfect example of any drugged out lunatic trying to put us good people in jail because she didn't want to pay the rent, and instead used her money on drugs, alcohol, and living the high life. The system is so overwhelmed by drug addicts and dealers, we have to build the most prisons in the world for the most prisoners in the world.

Fortunately for me, the judge and police already knew her from previous run-ins with the law. Causing her to lose her husband, kids, beautiful house on the lake, boat, pharmacy license, driver's license, and be ordered to monthly drug testing. I'm very lucky she had such a long list of being out of control, and she was only threatening me because I was suing her for back rent. But thousands of dads and landlords are abused and threatened with such lies that can't prove their innocence beyond a reasonable doubt, and they wind up in prison with theirs and their kids' lives ruined by these very convincing, pathological liars.

When I went to court for our eviction hearing, her best friend that had come over to party with her several times was also there. She was there for the same reasons my tenant was and was brought to court by her ex-husband to renew HIS restraining order. Keeping the kids away from their drugged out mothers didn't come cheap. The husbands went bankrupt lining their attorney's pockets for two years. My tenant's ex-husband said he spent $100,000 to keep the kids away from their mother, and the courts agreed with both of them every time.

I also helped a homeless girl with two young kids. I gave her a great furnished home, and drove her everywhere until she got her car, G.E.D. and college acceptance. When she didn't get free air conditioning, she said she would get me, and then screamed RAPIST! CHILD MOLESTER! in the driveway and went to police, prompting an investigation and a neighbor to tell me to stay away from his 30 something daughter!

Now, do you believe that millions of psychotic ladies are gaming the system? In our cases, the ladies were extremely convincing pathological liars and accused the fathers and me of many horrific deeds. Fortunately, for them, their persistence and deep pockets beat back their lies and let the truth shine through. But if they didn't have such deep pockets, who knows how bad things would be for them and their kids?

Mediation and Arbitration

In the land of lawyers and lawsuits, the courts became inundated with frivolous lawsuits. For example, one guy got caught getting out of an elevator at the Washington Metro station and threw a banana peel on the ground, then pretending to slip and fall from it and sued the transit agency for $15,000! For his efforts, he got charged with fraud and was ordered to undergo a mental evaluation. His was just one of the 225 claims filed against the agency each month - most seeking compensation for slips and falls. While in prison, another guy nearly beat himself unconscious inadvertently in front of a camera, then tried blaming the guards for his injuries. But my favorite is the girl on America's Court who shanked her shot golfing, the ball hit the railroad tracks, ricocheted back and broke her nose, then she sued the golf course. There are so many frivolous lawsuits against municipalities, government agencies, and businesses; there was a television show exclusively about such people.

With all these shenanigans, it became necessary to establish a way to quickly process the sheer volume of cases inundating our courts. Most cases are now sent to a licensed mediator who is required to take mediation training before being trusted to act as an official of the courts. The mediators are sometimes retired judges and almost always someone familiar with the law. They get the two parties together in a less formal, less stressful, more comfortable place and setting than a courtroom - usually a conference room within the court to get the facts from each side one at a time. After hearing them out, they make a recommendation to the parties and hash out a legally binding agreement if possible, making the whole process as efficient, fair, and non-stressful as feasible.

When disputes with corporations you do business with – think Wall Street banks, insurance, and investment firms – come up, that teeny, tiny, fine print in your agreement or insurance policy always requires you to go to arbitration in any disputes.

While most attorneys are small time private practice attorneys, about 20% are expert corporate or government attorneys the average person would never want to butt heads with. Unfortunately, after the corporate takeover, most people are tied to them through those arbitration clauses they usually never read in their little 20 or so page contracts. Investment accounts and insurance policies have similar agreements, but these are a death sentence for people's rights. Every credit card, debit card, or anything you do with these companies is tied to it. The advantages of arbitration always favor them, especially the clause that forbids class action lawsuits. That means they can take millions of people for billions of dollars and we have to face them one at a time!

Many people confuse mediation with arbitration. Arbitration is similar to mediation in respect to who is allowed to be an arbitrator and how they are trained. But arbitration cases are usually about large sums of money, where mediation handles everything from the dog next door that never seems to stop barking to that car dealer who sold you that lemon. Both go to special training, but arbitration cases usually involve major businesses so it requires more specialized training, and you meet in conference rooms at hotels or wherever the designated place is for that region of the country that holds jurisdiction. They also have a three person panel rather than a single mediator.

This set up pits high powered companies and the best attorney's money can buy against the average citizen who often has to travel long distances to the hearing. Perhaps even pay for hotels and meals for both you and your attorney... if you can afford one: Not a comfortable situation for the average citizen. And arbitration is not for reaching compromises. You have to beat the powerful corporations flat out with sufficient evidence that you are in the right and they are in the wrong. The first thing you do is sign papers informing you there is a very limited appeals process and whatever the arbitrator's decision is you're basically stuck with it! You give away your right to appeal all the way to the Supreme Court if necessary or file class action lawsuits before you even get started.

The ability of business to eliminate class action suits is a severe blow to democracy. No longer can many people ban together and pool their resources into a large law firm capable of taking on Goliath. You are all alone and have to take on some of the world's most powerful corporations knowing this. One by one the giants squash every person that comes to oppose them like the ants they are... Checkmate Goliath!

I know because I went to arbitration with Fidelity Investment Corp over loses I claimed were from a wrong quote their representative gave me, which they later confirmed from recordings, and the rigging of the market. That was the day I mentioned earlier when the market opened in a lock down supposedly caused from the finance minister in Brazil resigning.

Shortly before the market opened I called them to verify the price of Amazon. You may recall, I was one of those desperate people that was so beat up from work and injuring my sciatica nerve I couldn't move anything except my left arm without pain, so I borrowed on margin two days earlier. As my brother later recalled, I was extremely desperate at the time, calling him and breaking down in despair.

I had laid there for weeks watching the ticker tape do nothing but blast into the stratosphere and had come to the conclusion our only hope was to double our money on a fast moving internet phenomenon like Amazon or Yahoo. So I sold all our mutual funds that were doing quite well and borrowed on margin. Unlike most people caught up in the market frenzy of the late 90's, I wasn't being greedy and giving up my business and successful "Select Funds" for the risky margin plan because I wanted to. But as I said earlier, sometimes the most conservative tightwads that normally can squeeze water out of a rock can get desperate enough to do asinine things!

When I called Fidelity, I was assured the price of Amazon was indeed the same as the closing price the night before, despite the rest of the market being in lockdown. I questioned this seemingly impossible fact, then nervously sold all of my stock at what I thought would be a nice gain. To my surprise, when the market opened minutes later, it opened about $35 a share less than the day before. I was stuck selling at that low-ball price and that monumental drop triggered margin calls on the rest of my shares. Talk about being a happy camper one minute to losing tens of thousands the next.

Fortunately, I had the tape I mentioned earlier and had brought it to the arbitration hearing. Unfortunately, arbitration with a huge financial company for the average citizen means shocking amounts of confusing paperwork and procedures only a lawyer who specializes in that field can successfully handle, which I couldn't afford.

That's another big catch with arbitrating. On the one hand it's good because each party is responsible for their own attorneys. But on the other hand, the average person doesn't have enough money invested to make it worth paying a lawyer his substantial hourly fee or the thirty to forty percent contingency fee from your recovered money - if you can actually find one that works on contingency. Plus, when you hire a lawyer and lose... its bankruptcy court next baby!

In my case the arbitrators were very nice and one tried desperately to help me but was reminded by the chairperson they couldn't give any legal advice. After the two day hearing, I had time to analyze the hundreds of pages, prices, and facts Fidelity had given me more thoroughly and realized what the arbitrators were so desperately trying to point out without going beyond their legal authority. I had asked their attorneys about the remarkable one hour turnaround of the market and Amazon in particular, but didn't have the proof to bury them in their own deception… or did I?

I was convinced the tape of that day confirmed they manipulated the markets. Combined with their own testimony that I had called just before the market opened to verify the price was still the same, I was sure I had sufficient evidence that I got shafted and they probably partook in rigging the market. But a combination of being tired, in pain, outmatched, and not knowing the law, combined with little previous courtroom experience, cost me the case. Sadly, that's what they count on, and that's exactly why they insist on arbitration! If I could have appealed, I could have presented the crucial evidence I discovered *after* the hearings the arbitrator was trying to point out.

We aren't the only ones stuck with arbitration: Foreign corporations like TransCanada, which sued us over Keystone, use private trade tribunals to skirt the law. Governments in treaties such as NAFTA are at the mercy of international decisions made by just three people!

Arbitration isn't the only thing businesses have up their sleeves. They had ALEC introduce 71 bills in 2013, of which 14 became law that affectively reduced citizen access to courts.

Other problems with the legal system could be blamed directly on the government. At all levels it is inundated with attorneys. Historically about half of the congressmen are attorneys by trade and about two-thirds of senators. Normally it would make sense having some attorneys in Congress. After all, you're constantly making the laws of the land and interpreting existing laws. The problem is having too many, and their role of being public servants has changed to siphoning power, wealth, and influence to themselves and the ruling class.

A case could also be made as to whether so many attorneys in the government give us the separation of the three branches of government James Madison had envisioned in the Constitution. He was adamant about keeping tyranny out by not giving one person all the power, or even a few, like other countries had. But this stacking of the deck blurs the lines. Intrinsically, some have worked for Super Pac's, and lawyers are notorious for writing legal documents that are so confusing and often contradicting, it leaves the parasites with loopholes you can drive an 18 wheeler through and courts baffled when trying to interpret them.

In Texas there are actually instances when you are "required by law to hire a lawyer in the legislature!"

Another problem is the attorneys themselves sometimes get into trouble. Recently a well know Jacksonville attorney was charged with operating a gambling network under the false pretense it was a veteran's charity. Prosecutors claimed the internet cafes his clients were running were actually a front for a $300 million gambling operation, and he was basically guilty by association. Yet hedge funds and derivatives aren't?

In our area, a probation commissioner was charged with... how shall I put it?, taking care of legislator's interest and covering his own back by hiring less qualified candidates to appease the state legislators. The commissioner and two subordinates were charged with mail fraud, conspiracy to commit mail fraud, and racketeering for hiring politically connected people rather than more qualified less connected ones. Then they lied and filed false paperwork to cover it up. Now, they're awaiting jail time pending their appeal.

Even before the legal system became as confusing and nearly as corrupt as everything else, interpretation of the millions of laws, as well as state and national constitutions, made decisions handed down by courts nearly impossible to predict. Time and again a lower court's decision is overturned by an appellate, state, or the Supreme Court itself.

A good case in point would be our old buddy former House Majority Leader Tom DeLay, whose conviction for money laundering based on overwhelming evidence was overturned by the Texas Court of Appeals. Decisions such as these bring into question the validity of our courts. We all know the Bush White House and its cronies have had a stranglehold on Texas for decades. Is anyone surprised the higher court overturned a decision by over 40 unbiased hand-picked witnesses against the politically powerful DeLay... in Texas?

The U.S. Supreme Court

The court was recently stacked with republican presidential nominees' Chief justice John Roberts, Anthony Kennedy, Antonin Scalia, Clarence Thomas, and Samuel Alito who systematically demolished democracy and handed it to Wall Street and the plutocrats on a silver platter. The Citizens United decision was probably the worst and most hated abomination ever handed down by the Court.

It was all about a radical Tea Party Super Pac (Citizens United) that's been trying to get around and abolish campaign finance laws for years. They made a 90 minute advertisement with a 101 reasons why Hilary Clinton was unfit for the presidency and tried pawning it off as a documentary. It united people as few things could because people had already been pushed to their limit by corporate swindlers. Not surprisingly, politicians on both sides got blasted by their constituents, so many actually filed something nearly unheard of - a constitutional amendment to overturn the Supreme Court's decision. State after state rolled in with their petitions, but you know how that wound up.

Hell bent on destroying all democracy, the Supreme Court then handed down their second worst decision in history to stifle democracy. Shawn McCutcheon, an extremely wealthy Republican, wanted to donate the maximum $12,500 to any Republican running for office in the country if he pleased. He claimed federal campaign contribution limits were against the first amendment's right to free speech.

For decades, back when sanity ruled, you were limited to donating just $123,200 total to all national candidates, political parties, and Pac's so as not to have too much influence over too many people. But in this new age of greed, McCutcheon wanted a bigger piece of the pie. He had already donated $93 million in the last campaign, so I don't think he had any trouble pushing his agenda through his favorite puppets. I guess he didn't think he donated enough to shakedown every elected official in the country and wanted to make sure he has all of them beholden to him. The crooked court agreed with him, and you are now allowed to donate $3.6 million directly to an unlimited number of candidates and parties in any election cycle. Sadly, states may have to follow this ruling and lose control of all local and state political donations as well.

They then pushed the country closer to a theocracy by ruling government functions can start their public meetings with a prayer. What this Christian court meant by a prayer was a "Christian prayer." They didn't rule against other faiths, but unless they offer a prayer from every religion they would be discriminating. Not that this conservative court's ruling was surprising, but it does point out the problems when religious beliefs dictate the law of the land and go against the constitution's separation of church and state. If this keeps up we'll have to follow Turkey and institute a constitutional amendment that orders the military to expel any government that becomes a "Theocracy."

In one of the strangest and most contradictory decisions it could possibly make, they voted unanimously to tear down the 35 foot buffer zones around abortion clinics that had been the scene of anti-abortion fanatic's violently harassing workers – sometimes killing doctors and staff. The court ruled buffer zones stopped the protestors from enacting there constitutional freedom of speech, and the public has an unrestricted right to use any public sidewalk. Yet they disregarded the one that is permanently closed off in front of their own court and thousands of others during special events like tonight's independence celebrations. You would have to be death not to hear a mob yelling and screaming at you from just 35 feet away...so the ruling makes no sense.

YEY! Finally they did something right for the people. Lower courts have gone nuts and ruled police can search and seize your cell phone under the 4th amendments reasonable search and seizure law, and it can be used against you in a court of law! They reasoned it follows the current law that allows cops to pat you down and go through anything on your person or wallet for the purpose of identifying you and your address, as well as search you for weapons or drugs. We say no one has the right to go through our email, contacts, etc. without a warrant! We don't care what the guys in the black robes say, and for once, the highest court in the land agrees with us. They ruled there's too much personal information in a cell phone to search it without a warrant.

Elsewhere: In California the people took justice into their own hands and overwhelmingly voted to amend their constitution. It was prompted by a true patriot group calling themselves "Fix Our America." They started running a parody advertisement proclaiming they were live in the Congress with C-Span for the official swearing in ceremony of the newly elected senators. They show Vice President Joe Biden coming into Congress to swear in the new senators and dubbed in the words from Mr. Biden: "Would you please raise your right hand? I'll read the entire oath. I swear to represent my biggest corporate and private donors and political action committees 90% of the time on any and all laws and those passed, so help me god... I do!"

Other states are more and more belligerent of federal laws as well, sometimes outright ignoring them, especially when they conflict with their own. Two perfect examples would be the legalization of marijuana in some states and the Affordable Care Act, which requires all states to set up their own system of implementation. In marijuana states they just outright ignore it. With the Affordable Care Act, every GOP state refused to set up and implement it even though some of them secretly wanted it. Go figure!

In the case of medical marijuana, the states are caught in a catch 22, when people vote to legalize its use for certain ailments in direct violation of federal law. The line is blurred between states' rights to govern themselves and federal jurisdiction. Originally challenged by the feds, it more or less gave up trying to enforce their law when more states legalized it.

Those states that legalize it put more strain on both the state and local authorities in the form of writing up new laws in how to carry out the peoples will. Cities and states have no idea how to carry out the growing and distribution of this easily abused substance they had banned, eradicated, and imprisoned millions of people for over the decades. Everyone from small towns up has bumbled their way through the process, with states giving towns and cities moratoriums until they come up with their own bylaws or wait for them to come up with model laws for guidance.

One thing's for sure, everyone wants to collect tax on the marijuana sales, even if they are illegal under national law. It's allowed under a little known tax law that allows taxation whether something is sold legally or not, though it contradicts the Federal Substances Act. Let's see how the courts handle this sticky wicket!

Currently 80% of states are ignoring national laws on "marijuana use, gun control, health insurance requirements, and identification standards for driver's licenses." The most radical states - as you probably have guessed - are the Tea Party states like Missouri and Kansas. Kansas's governor actually signed a measure threatening to arrest "federal author-ities" who enforce gun laws! Once again, the party of no has ignored and abused the constitution it fiercely defends when it doesn't suit them. Nine GOP states claim they don't have to follow gun laws, despite the constitution being very clear that fed law supersedes theirs and it's upheld every time by their own Supreme Courts.

Millions of laws mean millions of confusing and often conflicting cases. And the Supreme Court is stacked with political nominees from whoever's party just happens to be controlling Congress at the time of nominations. Resulting in a court unseparated from the political and business arena as the writers of our constitution had intended.

The oldest constitution in the world has become a liability and a crucial ingredient in our demise. There are more and more cases that affect the masses in the field of cyberspace. The Federal Communication Commission has been tight-roping around the conservative courts decisions that have shot down their attempts to regulate the airwaves time and time again. They claim the FCC keeps overstepping their power to regulate it under the constitution's first amendment of free speech.

The FCC is trying to implement new rules to open the Internet that "would allow content companies to pay for faster delivery over the 'last mile' connection to people's homes, but enhance deals so they don't harm competition or free speech." The new "net neutrality" rules are hotly debated, because without them, consumer's ability to freely access certain types of content could be constrained by giant conglomerates for business, political, or other reasons such as AT&T did. A federal appeals court struck down their previous attempt in this area and has made them jump through numerous hoops to make a new law that can survive the sure to be court challenges. Once again, this proves how outdated and irrelevant parts of the constitution have become, making it a dinosaur in this day and age.

State Courts

State courts are often stacked by governors and congresses with judges representing big business. The EPA often has the most trouble of anyone from lower courts of appeal, where Super Pac's can position a small percentage of the overall judges where it counts the most. So big business doesn't care about state rulings knowing they have the appellate courts in their hip pocket. Time and again, they turn back EPA regulations from the lifesaving Clean Water and Air Acts in the name of mining, fracking, oil, and gas exploration.

The courts have a small hand in bankrupting the government as well. They often make both the state and federal governments pay restitution for things that happened decades and even centuries ago. Such as paying the families of the World War II Japanese internment camps, broken Indian treaties, and hundreds of other things the courts found them guilty of over the years. All-toll, we pay hundreds of millions of dollars for various things we had nothing to do with except read about it in our history books.

Overall, though, the everyday function of courts across the land goes relatively smoothly and most of the judges and staff do a commendable job presiding over small personal cases and family matters. Still, there is one process of corporate control and big-time trials that's really controversial - picking jurors! Even judges are frustrated about picking them and what evidence will be allowed.

As most of the world knows, here in the U.S. everybody accused of a crime is entitled to the case being heard before a jury of their peers. So people get jury duty notices and go down to the courthouse on the day of their appointment. You sit in a waiting room full of other prospective jurors waiting for the judge presiding over the trial to call you into the courtroom, where attorneys for both the defendant and the prosecutors are waiting to interview you. They ask the people that know the defendant, such as friends or family members, to leave and continue interviewing the rest of the people one at a time until they have enough jurors and alternates to try the case.

That's all fine and dandy, but what gets me is the power of the corporate lawyers and prosecutors to dismiss anyone that doesn't fit their perfect image of the type of juror they want on the case. Sometimes large public and corporate cases can take weeks and a thousand interviews to find people they all agree on. In the Aurora massacre they lined up 7000 possible jurors and reserved months for interviews. This is a perfect example of the money the NRA and gun manufacturers have cost us in the judicial system alone!

In a fair and just trial, anybody that has no preconceived prejudice against the defendant should be allowed on the jury, and the jury would contain a cross section of society. There should be about fifty percent men and fifty percent woman of mixed races and backgrounds to resemble everyday society, but that's not how it works.

In the George Zimmerman trial, the female judge picked six ladies, five white like Zimmerman, and one Spanish lady. Not one black! While she, the prosecutors, and defense attorneys stressed each jurors life experiences would control their decisions, it was strange the judge went with a couple of ladies that were married to attorneys who inherently must have discussed the case the minute they heard about it. One said she recognized some of the names involved in the case and another recognized four names on the potential witness list. So, prosecutors tried to get the first one stricken from the case and twice the second one from the jury. Lastly, for this strange jury, they all had kids. One was a victim of domestic violence and was very emotional about it.

This was an extremely high profile case with the media hounding them nonstop. However, it didn't involve any hot shot corporate lawyers, so the judge seemed to throw anybody she wanted on the jury. They only questioned 58 people about their exposure to the case and interviewed just 40 for spots on the jury. I don't know about Florida law, but in this state, the judge interviewed over 200 people for a wrongful corporate death case to fill 12 juror seats and two alternates I was summoned to.

Picking the jurors is just the beginning of negotiations between the judge, prosecutors, and defense attorneys. All juries are told to base their decisions on only the evidence presented in court, but did you know that evidence is strictly controlled and anyone with knowledge of the subject is disqualified? That's right; all evidence presented is at the discretion of the judge after deliberation with, and between, the attorneys on both sides. Crucial evidence is often disallow or D.A.'s withhold it, leaving many to think people aren't getting fair trials and the truth is being covered up.

In this case the judge didn't allow the audio tape of someone screaming before the shooting. She said it was inconclusive as to who was screaming. Also, everybody must say and use the exact right words in the exact way the judge wants them to be used. She didn't want anybody to use inflammatory or racially prejudice words in certain instances, but could use them in well-orchestrated ways.

In the Boston bomber trial, the prosecutors wanted people who were not biased against the government or law enforcement, didn't question authority, believed the system was reliable, and could hand down a death penalty sentence. The defense wanted people who were independent thinkers, didn't care about authority, were sympathetic, and would only impose a life sentence. Both types of people supposedly fit a certain philosophy that contributes to their decisions.

Also, professionals (hired guns) are paid to testify and some think that sways their testimony. Fortunately, with detectives coercing fake testimony and threats of incarceration, district attorneys constantly honing their skills for highly lucrative private or corporate careers, and evidence often handled like stock market derivatives, DNA testing has given us an almost unarguable method for the courts in some cases.

In one case an ex-policeman was convicted, not once, but twice with murdering his girlfriend. A shirt with another man's DNA was found at the scene yet disallowed in his first two trials, only to be allowed in his third trial. He was finally found not guilty and freed, while the man who's DNA was on the shirt was convicted.

In other cases, the evidence allowed is suspect and can have dire consequences. Bite-marks, for instance, was allowed for years as fool-proof evidence until they discovered otherwise. More than 25 men convicted of murder or rape were exonerated after a judge went against tradition and declared them unreliable scientific proof. In one case, two men convicted of raping and killing two 3 year olds were released when they were determined to be from crawfish. In another, a forensic dentist testified against a defendant that was found guilty based on his testimony, despite three other dentists saying it wasn't him.

Who's Policing the Police?

Every day we seem to be headed more and more toward a Police State as police around the country from small towns to big cities abuse and intimidate the public. As do politicians that are given immense powers, police often can't refrain from using their position to get in trouble.

Thousands of cases of rape, intimidation, drunk driving, child pornography, beating people to a pulp, murder, and stealing drugs and money from the evidence lab routinely pop up - along with the abusive use of guns, stun guns, and Tasers. The civil rights beatings in the 1960's and the Rodney King beating in 1991 are perfect examples of police brutality before the stun gun Taser era. We had one of our best high school athletes from town murdered after the Boston Celtics won their first championship in over 20 years. The parents and some witnesses claimed multiple cops sat on him until he stopped breathing. Then another kid with Down syndrome was killed in a movie theater with claims of piling on top. And a California Highway Patrol officer beat the heck out of a lady with his fist to the disbelief of passerby's.

The four killings that finally woke the sleeping giant came from Ferguson, Missouri, and New York City. In Ferguson they killed a black teenager for just walking down the street! The cop that shot him claimed the guy reached in his car and tried taking his gun, and then shot him in the ensuing scuffle. In New York, they killed another black guy for selling cigarettes on the streets without a license or paying taxes! The whole thing was caught on tape when they choked him and once again piled on top until he stopped breathing, despite him putting his hands up and offering no resistance and saying twice… "I can't breathe." Then they shot a kid with a pellet gun when he exposed it, and another in a stairwell. All were black folks, and every cop was let off the hook after a grand jury cleared them of any wrong doing.

The murderous Albuquerque police department kills people at nearly ten times the rate of New York City cops, as well as each other. I don't know if it's the Wild-West like surroundings, drug smugglers, or what the reason, I just know I don't plan on going there.

One of the most unusual cases of cops gone bad happened in that favorite city of mine - New York. Motorcycle gangs are terrorizing the city. These are not the old gangs like the Mothers, Diablos, Outlaws, or Hells Angels on hogs that used to beat and kill each other. This is a new breed of punks, some of them cops! They ride around the city intimidating and threatening anybody they feel like in gangs of 10 to 20.

One time they surrounded a guy with his wife and kids, forcing him to partially run over one of them trying to escape. This led to a fantastic vendetta chase through the streets. When he finally got stuck at a traffic light full of cars and couldn't escape, several gang members smashed the window with their helmets, dragged him out onto the street, and beat him to a pulp. It turns out one of the gang members was a cop and one witness was an off duty cop that did nothing to help the poor guy!

My favorite story of law enforcement going overboard was down in Arlington Texas. On August 2, 2013, a SWAT team, code enforcement officers, and narcotics detectives stormed a ladies back yard organic garden while they held her at gunpoint. Expecting to find marijuana, they instead captured 17 blackberry bushes, 15 okra plants, sunflowers, and a bunch of tomato plants. Apparently mad about her taste in vegetables, they then demolished her sweet potato patch! Looking on the bright side, she did get her yard cleaned up for free. They cleared out some old pallets, seized her compost, and got rid of her old tires and furniture.

Some think this kind of aggressive stand toward a rumored drug garden is from irrational Tea Party officials and gun lobbyist pushing police agencies and others into a militarized mentality. Everyone is a criminal or terrorist in their eyes! I suppose if anyone has the right to be paranoid about the 300 million guns that include assault weapons and machine guns, along with a stash of grenades, kettle bombs, and small artillery it's them. Despite a 1 in 20 million chance of dying in a terrorist attack, the NRA and weapons manufacturers use that high powered threat to infiltrate their minds and install fear and paranoia - verified by swat team deployments going from 3,000 in 1980 to over 45,000. Even here, our small town built our new police station into an impenetrable fortress with a tiny public entryway and waiting room, complete with a bullet-proof glass counter window. I don't know if it's the militarized mentality or the pressure and power just gets to them after a while.

None-the-less, it's almost impossible to get these incidents under control when cops are policing themselves. Every state I know of has internal investigations of crimes committed by its own officers instead of an unbiased outside agency - such as the justice department or an independent community board. Some places have a community board for input, but the final verdict and punishment is always handed down by the police department itself.

Whatever the reason for police abusing the people and the system, New York has paid out $428 million in settlements the last 5 years and Chicago another $450 million to lead thousands of cities and towns that total in the billions. If a revolution is coming, it will come from these and the ensuing murders and abuse that have kick-started this countries lack of civil disobedience: Was Vegas, the police massacre in Dallas, and Marjory Stoneman Douglas High the spark?

Prisons

As I mentioned earlier, Wall Street is even taking over our prisons. And with maniacal, egotistical prosecutors that could probably come up with a scheme to put babies in lockup, it has become big business. Each inmate cost taxpayer $60,000 a year, plus legal fees, and 70% of juvenile inmates return throughout life. As the Center for Media and Democracy reported, one of the largest corporate run for-profit prison companies is GEO Group, with nearly $1.5 billion in revenue, of which 86% comes from us taxpayers. Run like most private equity firms and for-profit assisted living facilities, they achieve most of their earnings through barebones staffing, pay, insufficient training, and benefit cuts to everyone accept top management.

With a 500% increase in incarcerations and detentions in the U.S. over the last thirty years, along with bed guarantees and lock up quotas that require the states to keep the prisons full or the taxpayers flip the bill for any empty beds; CEO George Zoley was richly rewarded with $22 million in compensation over a four year period. It definitely beats any government run facility for the top brass wouldn't you say?

One other quick note and food for thought about the $70 billion industry: That 11year old that blew away his future stepmother is rotting away in an adult prison instead of a juvenile one where he would get treatment, rehabilitated, and released when he becomes 21. This would inherently seem a better way to handle such young kids than pay for 70 years of incarceration and through away his life. Some states allow this and some don't.

15

Sports

News flash: Miguel Cabrera gets a $292 million 10 year contract, Giancarlo Stanton a 15 year 325 million one and pitchers David Price and David Kershaw punch in at 217 and 215 respectfully. As is par for the course - greed, selfishness, and insanity are at the helm of our $15 billion dollar a year pro sporting world and $7.5 billion college one. Some owners never learned from the Babe Ruth trade and give one player so much money trying to draw in fans they have no money for the other ones, often leaving the team with little talent, years of mediocrity, sky high prices few can afford, and fewer fans.

All major sports have gone mad. Our national pastime "baseball" has taken the most fun event of the year - the All Star Game, and turned it into a winner take all for the right to have the home field advantage in the World Series. I remember when I was a kid, I couldn't wait to watch the All Star Game, and not just because they showed only one game a week back then. I had lots of favorite players on many teams with names like Yaz, Catfish, Boog, and Boomer. I couldn't wait to see my hero's out there joking around and grinning from ear to ear. I think they had more fun than me... as they should have. So who would be delirious enough to ruin such a fun and exciting event many kids enjoy more than anything by making it into a hard core serious competition?

The National Basketball Association (NBA) is famous for coaches being fired from one team and rehired by another within days. And now the Commissioner wants to legalize betting on their games and get a cut of the hundreds of billions illegally bet on sports every year. He claims both the league and taxpayers would benefit from the extra revenue.

The National Football League (NFL) and Major League Baseball have completely lost their sanity. They partnered with the giant fantasy sports company "Draft King" that is by all definitions of illegal gambling a criminal enterprise. Yet owners Jerry Jones of the Dallas Cowboys and Bob Kraft of the New England Patriots actually own a cut of it!

The 2014 AFC conference championship game was again played on a freezing cold winter night in Massachusetts. While the NFC game on the west coast three time zones behind us in Seattle was having pregame warmups after breakfast and played at noon their time. To add to the lunacy, the Patriots, who had a small lead at halftime, were accused of cheating by underinflated the footballs for their offense to make it easier to throw and catch them in the freezing winter rain. Meanwhile, Indianapolis maintained the proper pressure and dropped a number of passes, making it very suspicious. This kind of insanity is routine nowadays, and for what? Money, commercialism?

Although we have always enjoyed our sports, it didn't used to be that way. In fact, until the 1970's, players from all the most popular sports could barely get by on what little they were paid. In Babe Ruth's day people were appalled by his $10,000 contract that was increased to $37,500 in 1934. That was considered unheard of at the time, and that's why the Boston Red Sox traded him. As a pitcher, Ruth only played every four days with Boston until his last two years, when he played both pitcher and outfield so he could hit more often. That's when the wealthy owner of the N.Y. Yankees offered at least $100,000 for him, an offer the cash poor Red Sox couldn't refuse. They figured they could get enough quality players for that kind of money to win the title, but sadly, never did for the next 83 years. Meanwhile, Ruth and the Yankees won nearly all of them, propelling the Yankee success story for decades.

Pay was so low for most of the other players they had to work part time in the off season to support their families. Sports were put into proper perspective before cable TV with its dozens of sports channels and the media blitz blew them out of proportion the last 35 years. Now part time, mediocre, old washed up veterans and free agents are given up to $15 million or more a year for often horrible performances.

For many years sports played a dominant role in our leisure time. People of all ages actively played them with friends and neighbors or were in corporate or city organized leagues. Some did it for the competition and others just for fun. In the 1960's, with any luck we would actually get to see a game on TV. It was a real treat and a special time for the whole family to actually see one of our professional teams play. Although more affordable then, going in person was still either too expensive or too far away, and we only had the three major networks that showed a game once a week, plus Saturdays Wide World of Sports. It showed many sports that were in season at the time. When there was an overlap, such as the baseball playoffs and World Series, with football, basketball, and hockey, the networks showed one game of each.

There was a catch 22 that made it so special. The leagues had, and still have, a 100 mile blackout for all teams that didn't sell at least 85% of their seats within 72 hours of the game to help bring in money for the team. They didn't get many sellouts or the grotesque TV contracts like the nine year $7 billion a year deal the NFL landed in 2013. Back then, people asked each other and called their friends to see if the game was a sellout, because more often than not, you would be all fired up for the game and when you turned on the TV you got an old movie instead. Still, when it was on, being such a special occasion, it got us so fired up we went out and played our own game. But about 35 years ago when cable TV became widely available at an affordable price, people began migrating to their living rooms, stuffing their faces, and drinking alcohol while watching sports rather than playing them.

Within a few years, insanity took the controls and a media blitz targeted at cable viewers, sports in particular, expanded coverage of all types to an insane number of channels. It grew into the extreme you see today where you can watch sports from around the world 24 hours a day, every day of your life. Unfortunately more and more people seem to do just that. Some fanatics are so obsessed they actually have a television in every room, including the kitchen and bathroom. The computer age has made it heaven for the hard core ones, who can now watch sports anywhere, including work and when shaving in front of those new mirrors with a small computer screen embedded in it. With any luck, they can still do their work and not cut themselves shaving.

Let's say you are from another country, which half the country is, and your national team is playing half a world away. You can now watch it on your work computer, personal computer, or phone live. In previous years you probably would have taped it on a VCR or DVD and watched it *after* work.

Some people now realize sitting around stuffing their faces and drinking alcohol while wasting their lives away watching sports isn't such a good idea. Not only have they wasted years watching this thing we used to call the "boob tube" (because many said it would turn you into a mindless boob), but many can't see their feet anymore when they look down. America is not only the world's largest energy hogs, but the world's largest consumer of food and beverages. This years' Super Bowl alone is expected to see us gobble down 1.3 billion chicken wings and 1.4 billion hamburgers.

Once again gluttony has replaced moderation, so some try setting the clock back to the time when they were participating in the same sports they are now watching. But after attempting to get back into them, they realize they are now old, obese, and out of shape. Years of watching, instead of playing, left their new jumbo sized bodies unable to take the physical stress, and they either can't do it anymore or they get injured and face reality. You've heard the old saying – "The mind is willing but the body isn't." Ours isn't! Sports for tens of millions of people, from kids to old men, has moved from an outdoor sport to an indoor one you no longer actually play.

I can give you a number of sports that were affected by this migration to the sofa. Bowling, for example, was played and enjoyed by people of all ages. There were bowling alleys in almost every town and city, now there is just a handful scattered across counties. The same is true about tennis and basketball courts, with tennis courts disappearing completely in many areas. Like most aspects of American life, sports have entered the realm of big time corporate capture… and you know that can't be good!

For better or worse, billionaire owners contribute to states financial woes when states give them hundreds of millions of dollars in tax breaks to bring their teams to whatever city gives them the best deal. But they're not alone. The $7.5 billion college sports industry gets in on the act too, building as many pro-style stadiums, arenas, and track facilities on campus as an entire city normally would, and some colleges pay coaches more than the pros.

Greed and a piece of the pie extended to the kids at Northwestern University - who wanted to unionize and get paid for playing there. They wanted health insurance and claimed they were employees making millions for the school, not just college students playing for fun. They may be right, but with universal health care they are now insured and it's a moot point.

Other greed-misters include a company called Ticketmaster. They established a virtual monopoly on selling tickets to live sporting and entertainment events, and then increased their ransom (I mean handling fees) to exorbitant amounts for every game and entertainment venue they control. Those excess fees have caused many of us to forgo going in person and bring the family, so we now leave it to the hard core fans.

I used to love sports when I was younger. So much so, during my teenage years racing the pickup around the corn field, my family thought I would be a sports caster on the local news when I grew up. Akin to Fantasy Sports fans now, I knew everyone's statistics on our teams and many others, as well as all the race car drivers. I don't know if I'm getting older and wiser or I've seen too many sports over the years, I just know I don't enjoy them nearly as much as I used to. Maybe it's the outrageous salaries and lack of both player and owner loyalty. Or the NFL is more of a big business Super PAC with its $9 billion a year profits hidden away in a tax exempt bank account that has soured me on the sport. It could be the $5 million 30 second Super Bowl commercials that totaled about $350 million this year with the help of the stock market. Yes, I said the stock market! Advertisers stock goes up both before and after the game from the expected increase in sales.

Perhaps, it's the media's heinous power over sports. The NFL actually fines players tens of thousands of dollars to those who refuse to talk to the media. Maybe it's the massively over-the-top stadiums we taxpayers have to pay for every 20 years or so at a cost of hundreds of millions of dollars, with one exception. As is everything in the land of big oil, presidents, and their cabinets, Dallas Cowboy Stadium blew all other stadiums away, costing a whopping $1.15 billion of taxpayer money only the oil barons can afford to go to. Even the more humble state of Minnesota tore down the 30 year old Metrodome for a $555 million new stadium.

Player and owner loyalty is nearly nonexistent now, with owners often offered more money or new stadiums to move. The Los Angeles Rams went from L.A. to Anaheim to Saint Louis, and then back to L.A. in just 28 years. The Oakland Raiders went to L.A., then back to Oakland and now Las Vegas. And every sport has strikes sooner or later that sometimes wipe out entire seasons. Fans never seem to matter to either side; both know they will soon come back in droves. Each time they say we'll have to do something special to win back the fans, yet they know it doesn't matter. Few hard core fans stop watching or coming to games, and major corporations have no intention of abandoning their stake. Fan protests are short, corporate protest are non-existent, and the teams are insured for stoppages. So there's no real incentive to come to terms until someone loses lots of their own money. Even the $3 million 30 second Super Bowl commercials are insured.

The 2013 Super Bowl

The king of all sporting events, television, and media hype is the annual (NFL) Super Bowl. We're bombarded with hundreds of professional and college football games seven days a week for five months, then beaten to a pulp by the media in the weeks leading up to it. It's an excruciating experience for those of us who put it in proper perspective. Instead of a special treat, it's a wretched time for many of us. The media blitz is more staggering then a Muhammad Ali flurry or George Forman punch in his prime. It's on every channel and nearly every show. No television show or station seems to have the guts to put it in proper perspective with the exception of public TV. Even the conference championships to determine the Super Bowl combatants is so extreme in the states the teams come from, many of us have to turn off our sets or watch PBS the entire week - or be sent to you know where!

I think the network people are already there. They brought in a mini football field with puppies romping around with each other that could have cared less about football. Like the baseball World Series, where someone was selling tickets to the 2013 Boston Red Sox vs Saint Louis Cardinals games for $12,000 each, the Super Bowl commands even more exorbitant scalper prices of up to $35,000. Not surprisingly, many hard core fans get taken for thousands of dollars buying what they think are genuine tickets over the internet, only to be stuck with a useless ticket. Some people get so caught up in the game they organize and run illegal betting pools at work that will total about $115 million this year while on company time. Even the two mayors of the cities represented make a friendly bet on the game, complete with interviews and details.

Millions of football fanatics go out and buy giant screen T.V.'s (7.5 million this year) to see everything I don't want to see. It's so absurd, special ads are produced featuring the Super Bowl leading up to it and others are run just during the game itself. Most of the women that watch almost unanimously do it just for the commercials, they say. Some ads flash back to the older games or their players, while others are brand new ads about the current game and players.

Let me give you a small sample of what we go through every year for 2 weeks from the 2013 game. The three major networks that now start at 7 AM, have every bit and piece of information about Super Bowls past and present you might want to know… and everything you didn't.

There are shows about the history of the Super Bowl and shows about the players in those old games. Did you know the site of the 2013 Super Bowl, New Orleans, has hosted 10 games and has a Super Bowl park? For that year's game they started preparations 3 years in advance and had to reschedule the Mardi Gras to the weeks leading up to it, then ending it with the big enchilada. Did you know that year's Mardi Gras had the biggest float in the world, or New Orleans mayor Ray Nagin was convicted for taking kickbacks, conspiracy and money laundering? If not, I'm glad I told you. I wouldn't want you going to your grave without knowing that!

Speaking of graves, we were informed the most popular player on both teams may have gotten away with murder years ago.

The networks had special coverage of the city itself after hurricane Katrina literally wiped it off the face of the earth. However, common sense did not prevail and the government rebuilt it with everyone else's tax money. They said it had too much history and was too important to let it wash into the abyss. This time they claim they have rebuilt it with higher, stronger, and longer protective walls and floodgates at a cost you DO NOT want to know. How much do you want to bet Mother Nature well wipe it out again sooner or later?

The media interviewed every player and found out everything about them, from the time they were in diapers until their lunch that afternoon. They interviewed the two stating quarterbacks and did commercials with them and other former Super Bowl quarterbacks until they nearly collapsed. They did stories on the two Manning brothers, who won previous ones, the only brothers to do so. This interest in brothers was spurred by the two opposing coaches - the Harborough brothers. It would be the first time brothers either played or coached against each other in the same Super Bowl, and believe me, the media never let us forget it!

As usual, the New York based media was the worst of them all. With this being such a historic occasion, it jumped all over the parents of the coaches as well. The poor couples probably wanted to hide in an underground nuclear bunker by the time the game started... I know I did.

Hollywood stars and local celebrities crawled out from every rock and crevice to get a piece of greatest show on earth. One famous chef told us about his great tailgate grub along with a former Dallas Cowboys star. I think it was mutton and sausage gumbo with cheese sauce. He even called in Drew Breeze; the man they say saved New Orleans to try it. They proceeded to talk about how he saved the city with his Super Bowl win 3 years earlier, complete with highlights. He then talked about probably the only good thing to come out of this media blitz, when he discussed his crusade to fight the childhood obesity problem his sport helped create here in the good old U.S. of A.

We were lucky enough to see the 40 ingredient Super Bowl dip. I know I couldn't have lived without knowing all 40 ingredients, could you?

We were given a tour of the famous house of blues and New Orleans most famous musician, then got quotes from Samuel Clemens (Mark Twain) and the weather was compared in both team's home cities. The mayors made their usual bets before an obviously spellbound lunatic proclaimed Baltimore was the greatest city on earth... I guess he didn't read the crime reports!

The media's attention then turned to the star halftime singer, Beyoncé, about whether or not she was going to lip sync the show as she did the presidential inauguration. They didn't have to worry though about her in the headlines for the 2014 game in the northeastern state of New Jersey. For the first time ever, they played in the dead of winter – OUTSIDE! I told you sports have come unglued too!

It could have cost an arm and a leg if they needed the thousands of trucks full of salt they had on standby to melt the ice. Along with massive snow melting machines, snow chutes, and double the usual grounds crew to make sure the game wasn't played in a foot of snow or ice. Some people, me included, said it was the stupidest idea the NFL ever had. UPS had just missed delivering thousands of Christmas gifts on time because of the ice storms that spread across the country. If it had happened at Super Bowl time, both international and national airlines would have been grounded and unable to get people to New Jersey. And those that arrived early would not have had any public transportation running to get them to the game from their hotels.

The rest of the world must have thought playing up north was a stupid idea as well. Hotels near Super Bowls normally sell out months in advance but still had a 20% vacancy at game time, despite being in the media capitol of the world. Even with good weather some people still had problems getting to the game on the N.Y. City area subways.

In that one, like every time they played, the media hype started when New England and quarterback Tom Brady played against Denver and Peyton Manning in the conference championship. Each time their teams play each other the media blitz proclaims its Brady versus Manning. It's as if they have no teammates and play the game all by themselves. It was almost as bad as when the Boston Celtics with Larry Bird used to play the Los Angeles Lakers with Ervin (Magic) Johnson. In both cases the media made up special rivalries above and beyond that of the two teams. It's enough to drive you to drink!

After reading a fraction of what we go through at Super Bowl time, do you understand why some of us want to hide in a nuclear bunker?

In Other Football News

We are in the midst of ever increasing concern over head injuries - concussions in particular. Little kids are now being treated by coaches like professional NFL players in their preparation methods for games and media exposure. Winning has become the only thing for some parents and coaches, and like it or not, coaches are under pressure from the peewee leagues to the high school level to win at all cost. In the most popular sport in America, high school football has reached a level only the professionals were at just ten years ago. That's when a couple of professional players died during practice from heat exhaustion in the deep southern summers. Now it's the high school kids dropping dead down south from demented coaches and those pressured to win at ANY cost.

High school football has always had thousands of injuries each year, with some kids being severally hurt or even paralyzed for life from brutal hits - usually to the head. Now they are pursued and trained like the pros, with special weight rooms, Jacuzzi's, and athletic trainers to bulk them up to enormous size and weights unheard of in the NFL just a generation ago. You read that right, many high school kids are now bigger than the professional players were in the 1970's and early 80's, when someone such as New England's John (the hog) Hannah was ruling the trenches at a whopping 273 pounds and Art Shell tipped the scales at 280. Now the vast majority of offensive and defensive linemen at the top high schools are over 300 pounds, especially down south where football is king.

I was watching a show on high school football that made me turn off the TV it was so sickening. The kids were in full gear practicing in the scorching hot sun with temperatures well over 100 degrees. Some coaches didn't seem to care if their players died or not. "They'll practice until they drop," one said. When asked if they'll keep practicing for hours on end in the summer heat right after one of the kids died from heat exhaustion, he said with a smile, "Yes we will, we have to keep practicing. This is an area with hillbilly pride and they're going to '"lay the wood'" - as they say down south. He kept screaming at his players to lay the wood. All the boys kept saying the coach's stress hitting them again and again as hard as you can. The coach with the biggest team didn't care if kids got killed or crippled for life. He tells his players to hit them and hit them so hard they won't want to play anymore and they'll lose their next game from "brain mush" they'll be so beat up.

The kids are too young and inexperienced to even come close to comprehending the harm they are doing to their bodies or their opponents. And the worst thing is most of the parents don't seem to care either! One kid said he had his whole life to worry about football injuries, but for now he wanted to do it. Believe me, after two motorcycle accidents, he may be haunted the rest of his life from those words!

Aside from the occasional deaths, paralysis, and sever injuries to their brains, there are 60,000 concussions a year in high school football. A simple cognitive test any first grader could pass is failed by half the high school players tested. Brain mush apparently was a good word for these kids, because they couldn't remember one simple letter in a flash test that flashed one letter at a time in one second intervals. Flashing just two letters at a time revealed 50% of the time the kids couldn't remember the preceding letter.

High school football has been desecrated! It's all about money. Winning brings in the money no matter what the cost is to the kids. As that maniac coach said, if any of his kids make it to the pros (where only one in a million does) they will make as much in one day as everybody else will in a year... and probably won't remember it.

It's not just football that has that destroy mentality at any cost. When my daughter was 10 she played rec-center softball for the first time. That's when the coach's older daughter twice the size of the opposing team's catcher crashed into her to knock the ball out of her glove to score. The catcher was a skinny girl, hurt badly, and crying! But the parents cheered wildly for her hard hit that, shockingly, included a very nice mom who completely dismissed the poor little girl. That's when I realized nearly all parents, including myself, had lost it over a 10-12 year-olds softball game. The dad told his distraught daughter it was all right because she played within the rules, though it didn't help much. We all realized the poor little girl could have been seriously hurt or paralyzed and I'm embarrass and ashamed for us parents who cheered!

Continuing America's journey down the path of self-destruction, we now turn to baseball. With the average professional player making around $3.5 million a year and some of the best commanding 20 or 25, it wasn't surprising baseball players and steroids dominated the drugged out late 1990's and early 21st century sports section. Everybody it seemed wanted to get an edge on the other players and reap the rewards.

The steroid scandal started in the late 1990's with Manny Sosa, Roger Clemons, Mark McGuire, and his bash-brothers partner Jose Conseco. All had many accolades taken away from them after they were found guilty of taking performance enhancing drugs (usually steroids). The greatest home run derby of all time between McGuire and Sosa in 1998 saw both players demolish Babe Ruth and Roger Maris's home run records, only to see them stricken from the record books. It was a hard pill to swallow for all of us baseball fans. McGuire had set the rookie home run record with 49 in 1987. Unfortunately, like Harman Killibrew, the greatest home run hitter of all time per at bat, he was beset with multiple injuries over the next decade and took the over the counter supplement Androsteindion in an attempt to stop the injuries. It didn't seem to violate the drug policies at the time, but he lost the home run record anyway.

The next year Sosa broke McGuire's record and he too was stripped of it. It was a crying shame. I've never seen anything so exciting in sports history and I don't think anyone else has either! It was a big scar on baseball, and like other sports, winning meant millions and was done at any cost. Performance enhancing drugs started spiraling out of control as other players attempted to keep up with the cheaters until Major League Baseball put the hammer down on all suspected ones.

In 2013, our team played the New York Yankees. All week we were bombarded with stories about superstar Alex Rodrigues - the former MVP (most valuable player) of the Yankees and highest paid player in baseball. He had just received a 211 game suspension for performance enhancing drugs and encouraging others to go to the same facility where he got them. Two other former MVP's got significant suspensions along with him in a decade long crackdown on steroid use that gave some players significant advantages over the rest. He appealed his suspension, but players and fans alike say he did something wrong for years while the others followed the rules so he shouldn't be playing.

With the latest suspensions, one of the most powerful solidified unions in America was falling apart at the seams. Many players, especially pitchers who got driven out of games and losses attached to their records rather than possible wins, along with their career ERA's (earned run average) swelled by these hitters, were furious. They worked their butts off against these guys, suffering extra losses that may have cost their teams a chance at the playoffs or possibly the championship. The players and fans were divided about what to do. Some wanted them banned for life while others said the suspensions were too harsh.

Almost every player goes to the highest bidder for their services, even if that means playing in that hell hole New York City. Winning championships doesn't seem to matter. We are constantly jolted by our favorite players who go for the BIG MONEY, and that definitely added to my spite and loss of interest. Likewise, 15 year old kids are getting over a million dollars for signing with major league teams. The Archie Manning's, Magic Johnsons, Larry Birds, and Carl Yastrzemski's of the sports world have virtually disappeared into a bygone era, with the exception of a few like Dustin Pedroia and David (Big Poppy) Ortiz. Pedroia took a pay cut to remain on the Red Sox and Ortiz was making half that of other big name free agents, despite all but single handedly carrying the team to the 2013 World Series title with perhaps the greatest hitting performance in playoff and World Series history.

Many of these spoiled brats that go from rags to riches get into all kinds of hot water with both the court system and the press, including Kobe Bryant. The Los Angeles Lakers superstar *sued his mom* for holding a garage sale and selling some of his childhood things to complete strangers. He said she should have asked him first so he could go through it and save the things he cherished. She said "he should have cleaned out his room years ago like a good boy." You can't fight your parent's house rules, especially in court, no matter that you're a superstar mega-millionaire making $30 million a year.

Then there's Lance Armstrong. Most of you know he won the famed Tour de France bicycle race about a gazillion times, then was banished of all his titles and trophy's for drugging (doping). He apparently injected blood boosters instead of the usual steroids America's baseball and football players preferred because his sport required endurance over shear strength. I believe it gave his body more oxygen for muscle use, which would act as an extra-large heart such as Bill Rogers had and some other long distant athletes.

New York Giant football great Lawrence Taylor - who led the Giants to two Super bowl wins - was routinely in trouble with illegal drugs and woman, as was New York Mets outfielder Daryl Strawberry with a cocaine addiction. And boxer Mike Tyson was in and out of jail since he was a teenager and found as many ways to get into trouble as a teenager left alone with electronic devices and social media.

I didn't want to leave out Aaron Hernandez of the New England Patriots. An extremely talented young tight end with hall of fame potential, he threw away a brilliant career when he shot and killed a man. He was convicted and sentenced to life in prison on circumstantial evidence from all the boneheaded things he did, both before and after the murders to cover it up. I guess he figured former fellow football great O.J. Simpson got away with it, so why shouldn't he? Both appeared to have overwhelming evidence against them and prior run-ins with the law, but O.J. proved what the power of an NFL hero and a team of crackerjack attorneys can do. Hernandez could have afforded the best attorneys also except his $44 million contract was voided by the Patriots after his arrest and he was banished from the team.

After Hernandez arrest, Patriots coach Bill Belichick said they would choose players more carefully in the future. But no sooner than the words got out of his mouth, they brought in an undrafted player with seven arrests before he was 19! At least the price was right. If he made the team he would have got paid the minimum salary for NFL players.

In 2013, accusations of bullying joined the list of crimes NFL players were charged with. Miami Dolphins veteran offensive lineman Richey Incognito was accused of bullying his fellow lineman - rookie Jonathan Martin. Both over 300 pounds, Martin a quiet, shy type, said he feared the somewhat crazy Incognito would beat him up. Incognito said he was trying to toughen him up for the battles in the trenches all rookie lineman need to get used to.

Major amateur sports have also joined the band wagon down under. Once considered the last pure highly skilled sports entertainment left, college sports has become nothing more than another high stakes corporate playground. The days of pure college competitions are long gone, and now the two most coveted sports, football and basketball, are vying for the largest paydays. Both have immense pressure to win at all the major colleges. Coaches get enormous amounts of power, wealth, prestige, and pressure for top notch programs. They often become bigger than the institutions themselves as they grow into mega programs even the presidents keep a close eye on.

Football has a four team championship playoff. With hundreds of millions of dollars involved, the players know the pressure is on to win at any cost. Great teams and great players are highly coveted, with multimillion dollar contracts awaiting the best players and millions for their schools. The media circus is as intense as the pros. Some players handle it with dignity, others fall as flat on their face as some of their hero's at the pro level.

Basketball has a more ludicrous tournament than its football counterpart to determine the champions, with 64 teams given a shot at the championship. It's affectionately called "March Madness," and believe me, it makes millions of us want to hide and get away from it. Like the Super Bowl and everything else that is overhyped and over sensationalized, you can't turn on your TV for a month the coverage drives you so loony. It seems though games are plastered on every channel, with highlights and analysis on every media outlet day and night. It's the Super Bowl of college basketball, with 30 second commercials going for well over a million dollars and is worth one billion to all involved. Coaches get paid so much for top notch teams they are the highest paid public employee in 27 states. Capitalism has kidnaped the last bastion of society – SPORTS!

16
Religion

Is the not so "United" States still a religious country? Has it ever been, or is this just a myth? We've always been sold the picture of the pilgrims and colonist getting up early and traveling long distances by horse and buggy to attend Sunday church. Hollywood portrayed it as the day of worship where all families spent most of the day serving god. The truth is; many founding fathers were atheist or Unitarians and only about one-fifth of them attended church. If anyone tells you they based this country on the principles of a religious society - they're dead wrong! Like the misconception that everyone on the Mayflower was a strict Catholic or follower of the Church of England, rather than part of the crew or a trade specialist; they used religion as a uniting force with unalienable rights but were adamant about separating church from state.

Overall, Caucasians are about as religious as they were in the 20th century but more religious than at the time of the American Revolution. In recent decades, many Caucasians have recently dropped out who classified themselves as Christian. In fact, about one-fifth now belong to the party of the "nones," the fastest growing segment of society. Fortunately, for religious zealots, there are millions of recent immigrants replacing them that don't believe in birth control and thus rebalancing the overall percent of those who claim to be religious. The large influxes of Muslims, Hindus, and especially Latino's (of which 52 million are Catholics) have kept us slightly above 50% who claim religion is important. Tea party Republicans and Southern Baptist are the most theocratic of the Caucasians, with blacks being mostly Baptist and Democrats being the least religious with a wide variety of denominations.

Regrettably, a small minority of diehard theocrats infiltrated politics and now set the standards for the entire herd. George W. Bush and his cronies set national policy based on their beliefs - not unlike many countries we call fanatical. The new self-righteous far-right Congress continues pushing Bush's agenda to Christianize America, going so far as inviting the Pope to speak before Congress. And anyone with more than one wife automatically goes to jail, even if your religion allows it or you don't believe in religion at all! Is that any different than a so-called "radical" Muslim or Hindu country... or a Communist one?

How about our currency? "IN GOD WE TRUST" wasn't put on coins until 1861 and paper money until 1957 under President Eisenhower, who also inserted "under God" in the pledge of allegiance - not the founding fathers. And FDR installed the ancient Greek "Eye of Providence" in 1935. It refers to their god Horus, who represents wisdom, health, and prosperity from Gods powerful hand wisely guiding us and the universe. And don't forget it was our hand-picked ultra-conservative U.S. Supreme Court that gave the green light for starting public governmental meetings with a prayer in 2014. With executive branches pushing religion into governance, we should be as skeptical of religion taking over our government as the founders were.

Fanaticism to the point of extremism is becoming a dilemma for the majority of us who the radical zealots call heretics. When you mention extremism, one thinks of renegade Muslims torturing, hanging, shooting or beheading people if they don't denounce their religion and convert to Islam. But Tea Partier's, Southern Baptist, the KKK, and evangelist are explicitly more dangerous and affect the masses much more than the few intolerant Muslims we have lurking in the shadows. They are bold, loud, armed with assault weapons, and donated over $105 billion in 2013 to religious cause's and their agenda - double that of the runner up education and ten times that of environmentalist trying to preserve our life sustaining orb. They've become so radical, President Carter quit his Southern Baptist church he taught Sunday school at for decades.

Numerous religions say God made us in his own image. I don't know about you, but I see God as more of a creationist and can't imagine one who put us here to pillage and plunder our own planet, destroy most of its creatures, is constantly at war in the name of religion and greed, and has crooked evangelist pushing the gospel to a faithful blind who give them everything. If that's your kind of God, you can have him! Maybe the Ancient Romans and Greeks were the only ones to get it right and created Gods after their own image - selfish, bickering, warring ones.

Right-wing Super Pac's seem to be following their version. These demigods are incessantly at war with everyone else and trying to cram their beliefs into everybody and everything, including our public schools, where George Bush's unwavering Methodist wife taught in Texas.

According to the activist group Credo, extremist in control of the Texas Board of Education attacked the science of evolution and actually tried getting textbook publishers to rewrite their books and then install creationism instead. In Florida and the South where Southern Baptist have a stranglehold on some schools, the American Civil Liberties Union (ACLU) has to come in and sue public school districts for implementing their religious beliefs on the public education system. Fanatics have even sent me the magazine "Evangel," and nobody can hide from the Jehovah's Witnesses forever. Then there's the restaurant in North Carolina that gives a 15% discount to pray. Now that's a discount! Are they die-hards or is religion for sale to the highest bidder?

My daughter's Florida public school was taken over by a first year Southern Baptist principle who installed an unofficial church with at least one bible study teacher in every grade. When I told him I wanted to be extremely active in the school and asked him what after school activities me and my daughter could participate in, he replied, Bible study! Not intramural sports or any other normal after school clubs or activities, just Bible study! Shortly after his rein started, signs of all sizes, from small ones to whole sheets of plywood popped up everywhere and in every direction on the lawn blocking the official school signs, with huge letters and arrows that read "Christian Church" and pointed down both the bus driveway and main entrance.

Notorious lobbyist Jack Abramoff was a devoted Christian, who as you know had contacts all the way to the White House. He appropriately gave his speech at the country's oldest Catholic and Jesuit University, George Washington University, in Washington D.C., about his illegal, corrupting ways. Is it just coincidence the university is right next to the Watergate Hotel – the most notorious hotel in the country and perhaps the world? The one and only hotel President "tricky Dick Nixon" had his staff illegally bug in our countries' biggest presidential spy scandal that nearly gave us our first impeached president. Or this religious school has more than their fair share of politicians giving speeches on campus?

We have other minor, mostly regionalized religions that are true theocrats. Mormons, Mennonites, and the Amish are probably the most famous, and for all practical purposes control all aspects of one's life. There's very little decision making to do outside of the church leaders and most of daily life has been practiced for centuries. That's one of the things that attract people to religion. God and his servants have a plan for them and there are few decisions to make. Religion tells them what to do, how to live, and gives them a structured purpose.

The Evangelical World

Abramoff's own Tom DeLay was a loyal visitor to the Capitol's evangelical church, one that is as corrupt as the politicians they bunk with. He's trying to start a new national prayer organization with Ken Wilde, who founded the famed National Prayer Center. Now that he has shone the world what kind of morals and ethics he has, he claims the lord wants him to do other things. Is that the lord speaking to him or his conscience? Has he backed himself into a corner so dark he feels the flames licking at his feet and needs salvation to see the light?

Funny how so many of these despicable people and their brethren legislators turn to religion. I think like everything else they do, they use it to comfort their greedy, moral less souls on the highway to Hell, not salvation. Every major religion condemns their traits, yet it seems nearly all politicians, their staff, lobbyist, Wall Street insiders, and titans of industry abusing the system are all devotedly religious. You would think it would be the Atheist, who they claim have no morals, scruples, or values, who would be the ones leading the parade down under. And I don't mean Australia! What does this say about religion in America? Is it for sale like everything else these guys stand for? Is it being abused by the worst of the worst like Muslim terrorist?

Crooked frauds themselves, Evangelist maniacally abuse the devoted blind in thongs. They chew them up and spit them out, then the faithful follow them right off the financial and spiritual cliff. Can someone please explain this to me, because I don't get it? Can you do anything you want and still get a free pass to salvation? History is full of the most feared and dreaded annihilators of the human species - including Hitler, who turned to Catholicism at the last moment to get what he believed would be a "get out of Hell free pass." Now Muslim Jihadist have joined him with their religious cleansing by claiming they become martyrs for torturing and murdering anyone, including true Muslims. And ghetto Blacks, the most religious of us all, have joined the devout Latino's in being the most violent, sinful, drug pushing murderers of society.

Three of the most famous evangelist were Peter Popoff and Jim and Tammy Baker. Steve Martin did a great movie portraying evangelist in their likes. These con artists push fake healing powers of God on the most desperate people and then clean them out, leading to the song "Would Jesus Wear a Rolex on His Television Show?"

They put on this big production with their own people scattered throughout the massive audience. The scheisters rant and rave about Gods healing powers until it's time to pull a "volunteer" with some incurable disease, broken leg, or other ailment from the audience. Summoning Gods hand and healing powers, they place their hand on the persons head or injured body part and yell something like: *God heal this poor sole and remove this retched disease!* Then they violently push their fake partner away, causing them to stumble backwards and realize they've been healed, or the devil has been extricated from them.

Even legitimate ones such as Pat Robertson and Billy Graham aren't helping public and foreign relations much with their rhetoric… I guess that's why they're so popular with presidents. Pat says Muslims are living in a fantasy world and a lie, stories in the Koran are wrong, and it teaches death and war to all who disagree with it. He claims Christianity is the only true religion and way of life according to God and Jesus, and America and the world are blinded by the enemy (the Koran) to be politically correct and it will be our demise.

Here in the real world, Muslims have preached peace for 1500 years but lived the hatred and Jihadist reality of it. The Koran hints that if one person from another culture is prosecuting Muslims, you can maim, torture, and kill everyone from that clan or country. In reality, a true Muslim, as do all religions, preaches living a clean, modest, noble, life and doing as much good as you can while on earth. They discredit the rich and Muhammad, like Teddy Roosevelt, grew despondent over his wealthy roots as he began to see the plight of the poor.

Pat doesn't seem to realize when he looks in the mirror he's seeing the same fanaticism as those he hates! Actually, all religions are a matter of faith, with more questions than answers, and all have a number of unexplainable and unprovable idiosyncrasies. We've come to learn many passages in the bible are wrong, and others contradict themselves like the story of Noah. And Muslims are basing their faith on Muhammad's wife Khadijah's assertion he was a prophet as well as many other things. He was nearly illiterate and couldn't read, therefore, only God could have given him his ideas they claim. But the thing that mystifies me most is, in his first revelation after a number of days in a cave, he said God told him three times to read. That's all! And each time he responded, I can't read. If god chose him as the divine prophet, why did he keep telling a nearly illiterate person who insisted he couldn't read, to read?

We also have evangelical cults who prey on desperate confused people with their snake oil. The reverend Jim Jones is probably the most famous. Many of us remember him taking a bunch of followers to what he called "utopia" in the jungles of Guyana, South America, which he called Jonestown. He claimed to be the messiah of the Peoples Temple. After killing an American congressional delegation investigating his churches abuse of our teenagers, his house of fraud collapsed and he ordered his nearly 1000 followers to drink cyanide before authorities got there. Some were scared and crying, but in the end, they all obeyed their master – some forcefully.

Then there was Ruby Ridge, Idaho, and the Branch Davidian in Waco, Texas, where leader David Koresh and his followers pulled another Jonestown. After a 51 day siege with authorities that were trying to serve arrest and search warrants for illegal possession of firearms and explosives Congress had banned, 80 people lay dead by the end of the ensuing shootout and fire that engulfed the compound.

In December 2015, Jerry Falwell Jr., president of Liberty University, our largest private religious school, brainwashed his students NRA style to arm themselves and carry concealed weapons everywhere on campus.

Catholic Priest, Bishops, and Archbishops

The big three are incessantly abusing the faithful and are in a pickle with both society and the law. One Archbishop followed in the footsteps of many evangelists and built himself a 6000 square foot mansion at a cost of over 2 million dollars. His closet alone was estimated to cost $400,000. They're in the news nearly every week for rampant child molestation the church has been covering up for centuries. So now, many Catholics are dropping out of religion or turning to other ones to escape the veil of secrecy. Churches hundreds of years old are closing like wildfire from the fallout of a church now seen as being as corrupt and abusive as Wall Street and the government. Europe, the birthplace of Catholicism, actually started the exodus by blaming the churches old fashion ways involving celibacy and non-marriage for all priest (despite the fact the first pope was married) and disallowing woman the right of ordination and equality, as well as the ban on gays. Their thinking is, of course, all people are supposed to be Gods children and loved unequivocally?

Pope Benedict was perhaps the straw that broke their backs. His trusted butler Paolo Gabriele revealed a horror deep in the bowels of the Vatican that went all the way to the pope himself. In fact, he was the one that not only willingly let the mole-stations and crooked Vatican bank continue with business as usual and go unpunished - but ordered it! When several archbishops claimed the one in charge of the bank was so corrupt some European banks refused to do business with them, he ordered them to cease and desist from ever mentioning it again! He then told everyone he was too tired to continue and became the first pope in 600 years to resign. I think he simply couldn't live with his conscience anymore.

Religion never ceases to amaze me, especially with Catholics! With thousands of claims of sexual abuse, cover ups, and priest going to jail in every other town, you would think anti-gay conversion therapy would be the last thing they would want in the press. Catholics actually tried making kids love the opposite sex if they suspected them of being gay at an early age. Naturally, mental health associations said it was incredibly dangerous. And the American Psychiatric Association said the potential risks were great, with side effects that include depression, anxiety, and self-destruction. I don't know if they were complaining or drumming up business. It sounds like their cash registers ringing again to me... Ka-Ching!

Moving on - Muslims not assimilating into our society as nearly all past immigrants had is causing social unrest. Despite the overwhelming amount of radical Islamic individuals and groups that want all Americans dead, those incredibly fortunate ones we do let into our country often refuse to even show their face in public, creating fear and paranoia that they're terrorist and don't want to be identified in an attack. When we demand they remove their Habib's in the name of national security, they protest and say we are discriminating against their religion.

Rapping things up, I would have to say religions main contribution to our downfall is simply this: It's being used and abused as a tool for evil intent. If we stay the course, nothing but disaster well follow if like Molech and the four horsemen, religion disguised as peace and good will opens the gates to the apocalypse as many predict. After all, we're the country that buys billions of gallons of bottled water although half of it comes from tap water. So how hard could it be to get us to follow our religious leaders to the ends of the earth?

17

Our Military Complex

Newsflash: Not heading President Eisenhower's warning, U.S. Army Colonel Lawrence Wilkerson drops a bomb and declares us a country of "interminable war" in the name of "weapons manufacturers, defense contractors, and power hungry politicians." U.S. General Wesley Clark, Ex Supreme Allied Commander NATO, quotes from a memo, "we are going to take out seven countries in five years and nobody knows why."

Believe it or not, even the military had strategic ties to Wall Street way back during the Civil War, when the North instituted a naval blockade of all shipping ports to cut off the South's main source of income - cotton sales to Europe. Unable to sell it abroad, the cotton markets crashed and forced the starving southerner's into surrender or starve to death. It was such a cruel fate, General Grant went against protocol and aided the enemy when he saw the nearly dead soldiers that are now compared to the concentration camp victims of WWII. He called them the "walking dead."

When the Industrial Revolution came to fruition we didn't have much of a military. We were lucky if we could defend our own shores and borders, never mind thinking of being one of the most powerful countries in history. Then Teddy Roosevelt was appointed Secretary of the Navy and built it into a credible force to be reckoned with.

Using the slogan "Remember the Maine" as cover to eradicate Spanish colonialism, he went into Cuba with his Rough Riders, led the charge up San Juan Hill, then kicked the Spanish off the island nation they occupied since the conquistadores. At least that's *his* version! In reality, he was a horribly undisciplined and dangerous military man who ignored orders, commandeered a ship to get there, and just loved killing both animals and people no matter the odds, risk, or consequences. He nearly lost every man and himself in his thirst for blood, excitement, and a high military honor. Regardless of his boneheaded, selfish moves, the Navy still defeated the Spanish in both Cuba and the Philippines to accomplish his and President McKinley's objectives.

His imperialistic side was determined to make the U.S. front page news around the globe and notify everyone the sleeping giant was awake at any cost to live and limb. As president, with the help of his engineer son, he used his naval understanding of moving large construction equipment and materials by ship to successfully build the Panama Canal others thought impossible. For better or worse, we have risen to every occasion ever since on the strength of that Navy he brought to fruition.

After WWI, the Washington Naval Treaty limited armament of the U.S., Japan, France, Italy, and the UK's Navy's. But a mystery for the ages had our entire armed services fall light-years behind that of other industrialized nations. When Pearl Harbor was attacked, the undersized services for all practical purposes didn't exist. If Hitler had invaded us, we may be speaking German right now. But Pearl Harbor reinvigorated the nation, pulled us out of the depression, and united us like never before. We hankered down, and with revenge in our hearts, every man woman and child worked until exhaustion in their determination to end what Germany and Japan had started.

With the blessing of our raw materials and automobile factories that could be retooled for war, along with the invention of sonar, we surprised the world - and dare I say ourselves - with the speed we recovered from Pearl Harbor. Never before, or since, has so many ships, aircraft, and tanks been built and a country mobilized so rapidly to take on the most advanced, and powerful military forces in history.

Despite Germany's impenetrable defenses and D-days initial disaster, using our newest technology, and a little luck and help from the Navajo Indian code talkers, we took control of Europe and the Pacific with our sheer volume of vessels capable of hauling unprecedented amounts of aircraft, equipment, and men. From destroyers to aircraft carriers full of B17's, B29's, and P51's and their cargo full of munitions, we shocked Germany, Japan, and the world with our ability to produce enough equipment and weapons to overcome their hideous war machines and Germany's dreaded submarines in the Atlantic. Using sonar, Germany quickly went from being the hunter to the hunted, then we stunned the defiant Japanese in the Pacific and we haven't looked back since.

Before the ambers from the war had cooled, the Russians made it clear they were going to take as much of Europe as we would allow them to. Despite being the only superpower left and having the atomic bomb, the old warn out FDR, Winston Churchill, and then President Truman, made the undeniable mistake of not using our position of strength to stop Russian leader Joseph Stalin from imposing his will.

The ornery, bloodthirsty Stalin that nearly lost everything to the Germans (including Stalingrad) wanted to surround his country with an impenetrable shield. He demanded, and got, all the countries he liberated known as the Eastern Block. That started the cold war chess match between us, which in turn required staggering amounts of money to outdo each other and control the new world order.

Just as the Soviet's and Europe started recovering, out of nowhere North Korea attacked the south and the nearly 70 year old war broke out. The newly formed United Nations stepped in and was being tested for the first time when Stalin and China's Mao Se Dong took the side of the aggressor. We were one of the few countries left standing from WWII and sided with the U.N. peacekeepers.

With communism spreading, Congressman Joseph McCarthy was so delusional he started an anti-communist campaign to purge our country of what he considered unpatriotic and disloyal communist citizens. His paranoia had half the country questioning their neighbor's patriotism, and the government compiled a list of people they considered possible subversives, including Elvis Presley. This paranoia fueled the cold war tension between us for forty years until Russian leader Mikhail Gorbachev had the wisdom and guts to do as friend President Reagan requested, when he uttered to the world from Germany's Brandenburg Gate those famous words: *"Mr. Gorbachev tear down this wall!"*

How the Military Has Contributed to Our Downfall

You might be asking; how does the United States being the world's last standing military superpower contribute to our downfall? It's elementary my dear Watson – Politics, Corruption, Greed, and Power.

As Colonel Wilkerson revealed, our military is now just a corporate, propaganda spewing, political pawn using us for perpetual war to keep their dynasty. He dropped his bomb on the world, when, like his Wall Street counterparts, his conscience couldn't take it any longer. Like it or not, we are a warring nation that's been at war most of our existence. Wilkerson quotes an investigation by the Boston Globe and Citizens for Responsibility and Ethics that states "2435 former generals have worked for 52 of the biggest defense and weapons contractors, and 70% of retired generals currently do." And they work for and are on both "their" boards and the "governments" at the same time.

He says recruiting and enticing millions of desperate kids to power and keep our empire comprises half our colossal military budget, which stood at $886.8 billion in 2018. It is equal to the next nine countries combined! That doesn't even include the Pentagon, CIA, and FBI's budgets. It far surpasses the other industrialized nations as a percentage of both the budget and monetarily. The military is also the world's largest oil consumer, spurring it to build its own biofuel refineries. And don't forget the cost to care for our 22 million veterans from our warring nation also leads the world. With the formation of NATO and the Truman Doctrine, we spend 45% of our budget on defense compared to 2 or 3 for most countries in NATO - costing our schools, infrastructure, medical, and pension systems dearly.

The colonel says there was never any proof to Britain's MI6 or our CIA of any weapons of mass destruction for George W.'s Iraq war! We waged war in the Middle East strictly for military contractors and politicians jostling for power, and we'll be in it another 50 years unless Congress changes it's corrupt, power hungry ways or there's a revolution. Worst of all, he says the U.S. has heinously tortured prisoners since Vietnam in ways that violate the Geneva Convention, the orders came from the presidents and vice presidents, and those responsible should be charged with war crimes, especially the Bush administration.

This push toward imperialism catapulted in the 1960's when the Russians shot down our most secretive spy plane, the U2. That prompted us to come up with one they would never detect. You may recall a rumor in the 1980's about a plane that was supposed to be invisible to radar: Sure enough, out rolled an F-117A stealth bomber one day for the whole world to see. It had been approved by the Carter administration and used for several years at night to conceal its existence before the government finally caved in after word leaked out that it really did exist. It used both 2000 pound laser guided bombs for penetrating hardened concrete and long range missiles using infrared technology that was very accurate at night.

Guess how much it cost? Each one came with a $2 billion price tag that was astronomical for the 80's… and still is! The military's usual cost overruns and delays were so severe Congress vehemently debated whether to stop funding the program.

Of course the question everyone was asking was, was it really 100% invisible to radar and was it worth the price?

President Reagan thought it was, and like most military projects, Congress had already spent so much money they were in it too deep to scrap it. By then, Reagan's paranoia of communism and unwavering distrust of the Russians had convinced it we had pared down our military too much after Nixon abolished the draft at the end of the Vietnam War and Carter reduced the budget.

He feared Russia's superior subs armed with nuclear intercontinental ballistic missiles so much, he started the Strategic Defense Initiative (SDI) that came to be known as "Star Wars" because of the laser beams we were going to develop to shoot down their incoming missiles. Nobody knew if the system would work or if we even had the technology to build it. But Reagan insisted that a strong military and staying ahead of the Russian's was the only thing they understood... and after what ex-KGB operative Vladimir Putin is pulling in Crimea, he probably was right.

So he decided we would build both of them no matter what the cost. The F-117A was going to be instrumental in our future air raids, and Star Wars was going to defend our country. The threat and insistence by the former Hollywood actor that we were successfully building both, was enough to put doubt into Russian leaders Leonid Brezhnev and Gorbachev, who gladly agreed to the Strategic Arms Reduction Treaty of 1991 that eluded him at the 1986 Reykjavik, Iceland, Summit when Reagan stubbornly went against his advisors and insisted on the right to bring Star Wars from the lab to field testing.

So you see, from that perspective it was worth it. Even though they didn't think it was possible we were that far ahead of them technology wise, they just couldn't be sure. After all, we were "supposedly" years behind them when they successfully launched "Sputnik," the first spy satellite. However, we captured over 100 of Germanys top scientist in WWII, including rocket inventor Wernher von Braun. Who then led our rocket program all the way to eventually building the massive Saturn V rocket that fulfilled President Kennedy's successful challenge to beat Russia to the moon. After that stunning victory, the leery Russians didn't want any more embarrassing surprises!

Those two programs and Reagan's military buildup brought Russia to eventually signing the nuclear reduction treaty, reducing total warheads from over 60,000 to 6,000 each. However, Star Wars failed to be developed into a workable system and the F-117A wasn't quite as undetectable as it was proclaimed to be. Adding insult to injury, they did indeed help bankrupt the nation and propel us into the paralyzing national debt that has grown to the stratospheric proportions of today. From a taxpayer's perspective, and what most nonmilitary people don't consider is, no matter what happens there are always some good things that come out of these programs in the form of new technology and discoveries. Therefore, the billions of dollars spent aren't a total waste.

Despite our cost, we came out smelling like roses compared to Russia - which had spent 48% of their GDP in the four decade arms race, had no food in the stores (or anything else), and lived in squalor conditions of poverty. Their Socialist government that was supposed to spread the wealth became a totally self-serving, corrupt, fragment of what it could have been. The all for one, one for all society was, instead, hording money for themselves, the military, and insiders. Sound familiar?

Farmers had millions of tons of food rotting in the fields and no way to get it to cities with their old broken down equipment and delivery trucks. Millions more rotted along the way to far away cities that were barely staying above starvation. That, and over cramped tiny govern-ment apartments that housed several generations in each, along with sporadic heat, power, and jobs for decades, convinced Gorbachev to finally do the right thing.

Every year since the end of the cold war Congress insist we have to reduce our military budget. And every year the powerful special interest defense contractors easily win the hypocrites loyalty and bribe them to build even more expensive high tech weapons systems by spreading contracts throughout many districts and states (political engineering). Several more versions of Stealth bombers have been developed since the F-117A and cost in the $100 billion range, with no letup in sight. This may keep a few well connected fat cat companies pulling in the money for their employees and CEO's, but it's killing the rest of the country.

To help pay for these state of the art systems, Congress has been closing bases around the country since the 1980's when non-wartime military spending first got out of hand. Don't get me wrong, the military needed some closures, when, like the rest of the government, it became completely over bloated. But I think they may be trying to get it too lean now. It's like a good hamburger or steak, you need a little fat for flavor.

The thousands of jobs and hundreds of millions of dollars the bases bring into our local economies is often money well spent and keeps us safer. Without enough bases in strategic areas, we can't respond to emergencies such as 9-11, the shoe bomber, and all the other wacko's hell bent on becoming martyrs from around the world. We especially need those bases with critical infrastructure, such as maintenance facilities, easily accessible highways, and extra room to expand and mobilize rapidly if necessary.

On the other hand, spending ourselves silly to have the best military and most technologically advanced systems in the world encourages us to be the world's biggest bully, or peacekeeper – depending on your perspective. Going to war has the advantage of testing our ultra-expensive big boy toys and feel as though we're getting our money's worth while stimulating the economy at the same time.

Many argue we start wars simply to keep the economy and our empire going and test our newest killing devices without any proof we need to - or any concern - about bringing the world to the brink of Armageddon. Our invasion of the tiny island country of Granada on October 13, 1983 might confirm that. Code named "Operation Urgent Fury," we went in under the guise of rescuing 800 college students to demolish the new Cuba backed military coup. In reality, Reagan didn't want any more communist countries teaming up with Cuba and we were getting rusty after not being in a war since Vietnam. We needed a tune up for our untested technology that was leaps and bounds ahead of that era and this was a perfect opportunity to get the rust out.

Then there was the Iran Contra scandal in Nicaragua Reagan said he knew nothing about. In that one, the administration and military wound up using Lieutenant Colonel Oliver North as the scapegoat. But it was Reagan who blatantly broke the law after Congress had passed a bill forbidding anyone, especially the CIA, from selling weapons to the Contras. And as North claimed, his orders to funnel arms to Iran was supposed to be for their help in releasing hostages, but was really a plan to circumvent the law and get them to the Contras via Iran.

Unlike the government, the powerful and well connected defense contractors learned from history and know they'll go under without constant federal projects funneled their way, as they did after WWI, when airplane manufacturers, weapons suppliers and part manufacturers went bankrupt in droves. They know they have the biggest stake in international wars around the world that keep their factories and supply chains running full steam ahead.

So after that little test in Granada and unofficial one in Nicaragua, we jumped into the first Persian Gulf War head first. We were able to take back Kuwait and squash Sadam Hussein's previously exulted and highly feared Republican Army in just four days on the ground after weeks of aerial bombardment both day and night had worn them down. With the F-117A leading the way under cover of night, it was an incredible site.

This year it's the new F35 fighter/bomber that can drop bombs, deploy torpedoes, fire missiles, detect enemy aircraft from as much as ten times farther away than any know aircraft... and maybe even cook your breakfast. This capability, along with the highly advanced computer system and helmet that allows the pilot to see the enemy well before the enemy sees them, is supposed to make them win approximately nine out of ten engagements. Like most defense projects, they have been working on it for years, so how much do you think it cost this time. If you guessed $115 million dollars each, $1.5 trillion over the course of the program, and it's already $160 million over budget – congratulations you're right! If you guessed it was beset with problems and years past its scheduled introduction to the world you're on a roll! After reading previous chapters you know the game and probably know the 70 or so planes the military wants will add over $80 billion to our national debt, so there's no since me telling you.

As the latest whistleblowers have shone, anyone can pry open the conspiracy. We now maintain the world's largest Navy, including 10 aircraft carriers, over 60 destroyers, and 70 submarines. For decades now, people have questioned the need for such staggering amounts in this age of technology and wars being fought from comfortable bunkers often half a world away. Destroyers, particularly, have come under attack as being mostly obsolete and being little more than defense contractor's personal bank accounts. In 2009, Katherine McIntire Peters reported the self-proclaimed hater of wars, President Obama, was on a pace to spend more money on defense than any president since WWII, pushing the status que to new heights.

This brings us to another problem we never seem to learn from. We hid the F-117 and its technological advances for about 10 years before the world found out. But ever since then, the media always seems to sniff out our secret weapons and announce them to the world. And if you ever want to know about our most sophisticated planes, ships, missile systems, or aircraft carriers, all you have to do is turn on your computer and you can find out anything you want about them right down to the last nut and bolt. Plus, we sell our weapons and defense system to just about every Tom, Dick, and Harry out there, and then they come back and use them against us as ISIS did.

We don't just give away our technology; we give away where our ships our positioned, our planes and airfields are located, and pretty much anything else an enemy or terrorist can use against us. When the government isn't blabbing about everything, the media tells the enemy when and where we'll attack, giving them advanced warning to get out and hide their weapons and machinery. We all know the old saying – "Loose lips sinks ships." Now it's more like loose lips don't sink ships.

To be fair, I'm sure the military prefers nobody knows, yet the media has its ways of finding out. After all, in the 1950's nuclear bomb test became a spectator sport because the Air Force kept secret - spectators, personnel, and the world were being radiated. And it still covers up the thousand leaks, spills, accidental nuclear bomb droppings and warheads being blown off missiles in silo explosions - like the 1980 Titan II that should have incinerated then Governor Clinton and Little Rock, Ark. Did you know nuclear armaments are everywhere around and above you in silos and planes waiting to vaporize you in another accident?

To make matters worse, recent various scandals have cropped up about dozens of missile operation officers in charge of our nuclear Inter Continental Ballistic Missiles (ICBM's) being drunk, on drugs, and cheating on proficiency test exams. And 50 year old facilities are failing inspection and are wrought with intentional safety violations. If that doesn't make you feel safe - I don't know what will!

Another problem is we gave away our "rare earth" facilities and technology needed to keep the entire military running. These precious metals are used in everything that have computer systems involved - and that's everything! This leaves us dependent on China to keep our military running. Without the rare earths and associated products from China we are up a river without a paddle. Especially in this age of cyber warfare with things like the Stuxnet worm Israel and ourselves used to dismantle thousands of Iran's nuclear centrifuges. The military, CIA, FBI, and all the others will simply wither away if China gets mad at us and withholds these crucial products as they did Japan when they got mad at them. We are both looking for replacement technologies, but until an alternative is found, we have no choice but obey China's every command.

As you know from the Fort Hood shootings, there are also security problems at our military bases. In both instances, they bought their weapons at the gun shop down the street and passed the background checks before going on their rampages. The problem with the military, and country in general, is Muslim Jihadist infiltrating it as Hasan did in the first shooting. Although we're not supposed to discriminate, we have to be realistic about our situation like we were with the Chinese Exclusion Act of 1882 and the Japanese Americans, Germans, and Italians in WWII. Any Muslim could be a terrorist, and considering we are at war with them and life has no meaning to them, except to glorify themselves, we should be especially mindful of that fact. Sometimes profiling is the wise thing to do, even if you have to break a few eggs getting the job done to keep Pandora's Box closed.

Overall, I think most people are satisfied with our military – excess, covert operations, and imperialism aside. But that's what America's all about now, and that's also the military complex's main contribution to our downfall. Even Mikhale Gorbachev blamed profiteers for controlling Reagan's negotiations. It's become more an arm of Wall Street greed and political warlords than necessity, pillaging and plundering oil nations into religious jihadist rule. Russia went bankrupt trying to defeat the U.S. backed Mujahedeen and Osama bin Laden in Afghanistan in the 1980's when it was still a superpower, why did anyone expect our fate would be any different? When the enemy is as unseen as the plague and can bring in new recruits convinced they will become martyrs faster than you can kill them, it's almost impossible to defeat them!

The VA Scandal

A scandal at the Phoenix VA hospital, brought to light the fact that hospitals across the country were putting people on long waiting list for their initial doctor visits that sometimes resulted in veterans dying before they saw a doctor. The AP reported confirmation of the 1,700 veterans that were "at risk of being lost or forgotten" and Phoenix's was just the tip of the iceberg. Back when G.W. was president, he set up a task force that estimated nearly a quarter of a million veterans had to wait at least six months for their first appointment or initial follow up. If this wasn't bad enough, VA hospitals also cooked their books to make it look like the wait times were within guidelines. You see, bonuses are doled out for executives and managers when they meet federal standards, so you can see the incentive to lie and cheat.

Schedulers are supposed to put waiting times on electronic list so they can be monitored, but they didn't in many instances, resulting in months of waiting while people suffered needlessly or died in the name of bonuses. Every study and report claimed this had been going on for years, prompting congressmen to demand V.A. Secretary Eric Shinseki's resignation. After several investigations he finally stepped down.

Congress has known for years about veterans getting the short end of the stick. Still, the heartless, bloodthirsty politicians keep spending precious billions on unnecessary wars and over the top equipment at the veteran's expense. The good news is, they almost doubled the VA budget to a point where the chairman of the House Committee on Veterans Affairs claims the VA "can't spend it all," and its "manipulation and mismanagement" that's the problem. Is that his way of saying corruption? Seedy funding for special interest and other pork barrel projects has caused unnecessary suffering in other areas as well.

Woman in the Armed Services

We have had woman in the armed services for centuries (mostly serving as nurses or secretaries) but not side by side in the daily routine. This has brought about some expected problems in the traditional man's world. I'll never forget the first few recruits at the military academy back in the 1970's. I couldn't understand why any woman would want to be in the service, and it raised a number of questions. Was this just another woman's lib thing? Can they handle boot camp? Will they get frustrated and quit from the hard physical training with the men snickering at every failure? What will their role be? How were they supposed to move up in rank where they would command men that were anything but amused by the idea? They knew they would be sexual objects in a man's world, and what are they going to do when they inherently get pregnant? They would need separate barracks, showers, etc., and they could expect every dirty trick in the book to get them to quit.

Many did quit originally, but for whatever their reasons, those that stayed paved the way for today's recruits. Despite less male chauvinism than in the beginning, most men still see them more as sexual objects and protect them more like sisters in the field than their equals or commanding officers and always will. We're men ladies, get used to it! You know; that same animal you've been trying to change since we were Neanderthals. It's embedded in our genes just like being a woman is embedded in yours. This well never change, no matter how many rules and regulations they come up with "nature will find a way."

Whatever their reason for joining the military, one thing I know for sure. When the moon hits your eye like a big pizza pie – That's Armoire! And you can't regulate that!

This is one of those problems the woman's liberation movement made all but impossible to know what to do. As time went by, more and more woman changed their attitude and nobody could have fun anymore. What was once seen as a nice compliment and some flirting became a treasonous act of chauvinism with criminal repercussions. Although most men still appreciate attention, if a man flirts or shows a little affection to a woman nowadays it could be the slammer for them!

Apparently, woman in the military are as confused as us because they date guys in the military all the time, with many marrying them. How could this be if neither is supposed to be attracted to the other and start the relationship by acting out in some kind of friendly jester or flirting to get the ball rolling? Obviously, like previous examples, not all women feel the same as the hard core feminists do. Undoubtedly, some join to be surrounded by guys so they'll get lots of attention, dates, and maybe marry one. If they get lucky they might even land a high ranking officer. Talk about security with a great pension for life!

Every now and then you get trials of officers and enlisted personnel getting into trouble. There are bar fights here and there or some other disturbance in the force, but mostly it's about sexual liaisons or misconduct. In 2014, the highest ranking officer in history went to trial - Brigadier General Jeffery Sinclair, who was charged with using his position to forcibly rape a lady serviceman. He claims he was having an affair with her and she claims it was rape. To his and many people's surprise, he was court marshalled and released. This isn't the first time and it won't be the last time an officer, male or female, will be charged with rape or using their rank over subordinates for sexual favors. It's been a recurring problem for centuries, but it's been ramped up a few notches since they allowed woman into the service side by side with the men. With Congress letting them get still closer by voting to let them into combat, I don't ever see it not being a problem from time to time.

18
The Presidential Address

<u>"A house divided against itself cannot stand"</u>
<u>Abraham Lincoln (R) Illinois</u>

I love looking back at history to prove nothing ever really changes in politics. It doesn't matter if you're talking about Lincoln's day or now, you'll find nothing has really changed. Let's look at the 2010 State of the Union Address to see if history is yet again repeating itself.

We used to love watching the State of the Union Address. When I was growing up, it was on everyone's watch list, from elementary school kids to senior citizens. People were more involved in their communities and the political process, we even had civic classes. I remember when President Nixon, Ford, or Carter came on TV we didn't want to miss it. It was a big event for many of us, and we would talk about it at school before and after the speech. We loved imitating "tricky Dick Nixon" because of his shenanigans. His jowls would shake when he spoke, and just watching him shake them and giving his famous two armed peace sign was worth it. But in recent years the address has turned into more of a media circus, and 2010's was the most entertaining yet, with posturing on both sides leading up to the big night and cameras placed to show both the president and the Congress at several angles to catch the fireworks.

The speech started off with a rousing ovation for Obama when he mentioned pushing through a bipartisan jobs creation bill. Both houses stood and cheered - though that's as far as the bipartisanship would go. As he got into more of his plans for America, the house became as one sided a joke as I've ever seen for an address. He talked about constant economic expansion, which politicians always talk about to please everyone, despite being an impossibility in real life. He pushed finance reforms, gun control, science, technology, and opening new offshore oil developments. That received a rousing round of applause from the Democrats. While on the other side of the isle, Republicans sat stone-faced, lips pressed tight.

He further upset the GOP with a proposal to take 30 billion dollars of the Wall Street repayment money and give it to community banks so they could lend it to many struggling small businesses the institutional banks refused to. He even threw in a small business tax credit to hire more workers to the delight of Democrats - who stood and applauded vigorously. This same pattern would continue throughout his address, the Democrats cheering wildly and Republicans sitting-stone faced with lips pressed together. Sometimes even shaking their heads in distain and laughing. He did get a rousing round of approval from them when he mentioned his plan for a capital gains tax cut and incentives for both large and small businesses. Then lost them when he said he wanted to build clean energy facilities and upgrades to encourage major companies to stay here by "slashing taxes for multinational corporations overseas." To this day they claim we need to slash these taxes and blame Obama for not doing it, so where were the cheers Trump got for doing it? What a Congress! You can either laugh or cry about it, maybe both.

Next up on the president's agenda was a scolding of the gargantuan banks. He said their rampant speculation cost us 7 million jobs in just 2 years and income declined because of them, before lecturing them about the prior economic expansion that was built on the housing bubble and their speculation. Then talked about the unsustainable health care and college costs escalation, which got a rousing round of applause from the Democrats, while the bank backed GOP... well, you know. The chief did get another solid round of applause from them when he said our goal should include being number one in the world economy, but lost them again when he started back on financial reforms. He blamed the banks for hampering our growth and criticized their recklessness that decimated our economy. "We can't let them take our personal deposits and gamble it away for their own personal benefit," he exclaimed. Sound familiar?

As the camera moved onto Senator Dodd, the president proclaimed the lobbyists were already trying to kill the Dodd-Frank reform bill. That really infuriated the GOP! Steam started coming out of their ears after he said he wanted to create more green energy jobs and innovation. However, they jumped the gun with their distain and almost didn't catch his announcement that his clean energy initiative would include their favorite big boy toys - nuclear power plants, more off shore oil and gas development, biofuels, and clean coal technology.

He asked them to pass a comprehensive energy and climate bill with incentives that will make clean energy profitable. Then thanked the House for passing an insider anti-environmental bill the past year and said "the Senate should follow their example." As well as "the U.S. should lead the world in clean energy technology instead of other countries weeping the rewards," along with doubling our exports in the next 2 years.

Upon turning to education reform, he stressed our need to revitalize our community colleges and make college education affordable to all with a $10,000 tax credit, "because no one should go broke by going to college" and basically colleges must stop gouging the students.

Next, the president got into reforms necessary for the government to operate successfully and win back the trust of the citizens. Like Teddy Roosevelt did when Jay Gould bribed government officials and three U.S. Supreme Court justices, he laid into the Court for reversing the Glass Stiegel Act. Then declared it would open the flood gates to special interests, including foreign corporation's new ability to spend unlimited amounts of money on our elections. I guess he hit the bulls-eye on that one, didn't he? He just didn't tell us he and Mitt Romney were planning to be the beneficiaries in the next election.

Obama continued on the subject by saying he doesn't believe American elections should be bank rolled by America's most powerful special interest groups, or worse, by foreign enemies. "They should be decided by the American people," and he urged Congress to pass a bill to solve this problem... before continuing down the path of ear mark reforms. The chief asked every legislator to post any and all ear mark requests on their websites before there's a vote.

He believes "there are philosophical differences that are deeply en-trenched that will always cause problems about the role in government, national security, and priorities that are the essence of our democracy. And what frustrates the people is that every day is an election day." Did he get some of this from me? "We can't wage a perpetual campaign where the only goal is to see which side can embarrass the other the most. A, you lose I win mentality when every bill is obstructed by the other party just because they can." He did steal my material!

"The confirmation of qualified public servants shouldn't be held hostage by the pet projects or grudges of a few individual congressmen. Washington thinks all the politicking is part of the game no matter how wrong or malicious, but it doesn't help the people, and worse yet, it's dividing our citizens further and causing more distrust in our government. I know this is an election year, but we still need to govern even though election fever is earlier than usual. We still have to solve the country's problems and not run for the hills. If Republicans insist on a super majority of 60 votes to pass legislation, then they must be leaders and not obstructionist. Short term politics won't get the job done. They are there to work for the people, not their own ambitions." Oh- Boy! Did that draw some discontent from across the aisle. To show them he wants to work together, at least publically, he invited them to monthly meetings.

Security was next on the long agenda. "Throughout history we were committed to security both nationally and abroad, and we should be committed to our servicemen and women both during and after the war." He stressed putting politicking behind them and concentrate on supporting our troops. Again he received a standing ovation from the Democrats and a chilly one from the posturing GOP.

The president then took on the nuclear countries. First up was the new treaty with Russia to reduce our nuclear weapons, and work with the 44 countries at the upcoming security summit to secure all nuclear weapons around the world within four years so they never fall into the hands of terrorist. Finally, he received a bipartisan standing ovation and a hoot and holler from both sides.

Another mission he wanted to work on at the summit was the sanctions on North Korea and Iran to further isolate them. He also wanted us to work with the Muslim countries to promote science and education and the G20 to sustain the global economy.

"We are now a leader in climate change," he announced, "and we need to help all the people of the world with food and medical programs, freedom, and human decency. We need a better plan on bio-terrorism and infectious diseases. We need freedom for all here in the U.S. like our constitution proclaims," he said, and he's going to work with Congress and the military to repeal the gays in the military law because "it is the right thing to do." "We need to give woman equal rights to equal pay and fix the broken immigration system." Once again, he lost Republicans but got a standing ovation from the Democrats for things that are at the heart of their values, kindness and human value, lost long ago on the use them and abuse them GOP.

The chief further alienated them by saying the people had lost trust in the government because of big corporations, media, and the government itself. He explained it assisted them by allowing CEO's to reward themselves with huge bonuses for failure, and bankers risking our money for their own selfish gains, with lobbyists and congressmen adding to our distain. "Americans no longer believe in the system and the politicians need to stop cozying up to their Super Pac's and do the right thing for the countries future, not their own:" Then declared the setbacks to democracy because of it - as the camera turned to Patrick Kennedy who would soon leave office after blowing up at the media about these critical issues. "It's a new decade," Obama shouted, and "I won't quit on the people - despite Congress!"

Six years later, Republicans would prove to the world nothing had changed in their party, and they were still hell bent on abusing the American worker. They tried pushing through a law to ban overtime pay, leaving it to the discretion of employers. This, in a year when many large corporations were making their usual record profits; and CEO's were making so much money Warren Buffett himself asked Congress to make the upper class pay their fair share of taxes. So what did Trump do when elected? He cut them further and the stock market responded by exploding into corporate heaven while the deficit skyrocketed.

Obama Can't Please Republicans

On talk shows the next day, they talked to Vice President Joe Biden and Jeb Bush about the speech. They introduced Bush as the former governor of Florida. Who also just happens to be President George H.W.'s son, G.W.'s brother, and a big time insider with massive overseas investment funds as chairman and manager of BH Global Aviation - an offshore private equity fund. He has also worked for the criminal enterprises Lehman Brothers and Barclays and other private equity firms.

Being the Republican from Texas that he is, Jeb went on the attack about not correcting the bad parts of the health care act and energy policies, though the president completely caved in to them on all their energy demands. Bush agreed with some energy parts, and said the party should work bipartisan on the good parts if it was broad based, and Americans "could trust the free market" to increase jobs rather than the government. Ha! In other words, get rid of all government regulations like Trump is doing and let his family, cronies, banks, and Wall Street swindlers continue regulating themselves, eating us alive, and spitting our bones out! Then the scheisters can continue setting policies to give away all our technology and jobs by moving them to cheap labor countries in the name of capitalistic greed.

The host asked if he saw parts of his speech that would help the party take over the State Congresses. He said he thought the focus should be on the state economy and long term growth of 4% a year, not the sustainable 1 to 2% that would give us long term success. He thought there were areas of common ground they could work on but had to choose to do so. And if the president showed leadership in that regard, the Congress should follow. He was then asked about the $8 billion federal grant for the high-speed rail from Orlando to Tampa Bay financed by the American Recovery Act, (which the GOP hated) and would he go to the conference about it if he was still governor? He replied it was more than appropriate for the governor to go because "it was not a sign of support." And that's from one of the most moderate Republicans!

Eventually, Obama caved in to everything the GOP lives for by allowing more mining, oil, and gas wells on federal lands. He offered immigration reform patterned after Reagans, cut inspections in half at critical agencies, did nothing on IRS reform and offshore tax havens, got unemployment down to a normal 5 percent, and continued Wall Street's record profits. To thank him, the party continued hating and blaming him for everything!

It never ceases to amaze me how they stomp on everything the rest of us suggest or do. It's strictly a "my way or the highway" mentality that eventually spread nearly as severely into the soul of the Democrat's as well. Polls reflected this same belief that Republicans were not willing to negotiate and Democrats were. There are no more give and take negotiations like in the past. Millions of jobs were created by the $787 million stimulus package in Republican dominated states, which in a more partisan day would have thrilled the GOP. Yet this toxic post 1990's party would only trash it by publically voting against it while merrily taking it privately. They said it was a complete failure from the party of no ideas, even though the economy was having a superb 6% growth that quarter! As the president said, "they went to a lot of ribbon cutting ceremonies because of it."

Isn't that the truth? The GOP and Tea Party always complain about taxes, over bloated government, and its constant interference and hate for business. But have you ever heard them complain about all the highways, railroads, oil and gas pipelines, water and wastewater plants, and other infrastructure that allows them to be in business and ship their goods from one place to another? Or all the money we spend on their pork barrel projects?

Where Did Lincoln's Republican Party of Social Justice Go?

Starting with Reagan and implemented by G. W., the countries agenda became radically religious and imperialistic. The GOP has no idea what they stand for anymore or what they want. They only know their leaders don't want anything to do with anything everyone else wants. At last count they tried over 60 times to repeal the Affordable Care Act and stop the funding of it, rather than working on a bipartisan fix of the parts they don't want as Jeb Bush recommended. And as you know, they filibustered 500 bills (more than half of our histories total) on everything from confirming federal judges, to their favorite subjects - Wall Street and environmental deregulation. Some positions went unfulfilled for 10 years, especially those concerning environment and labor protection laws. They completely isolated themselves with extremist organizations such as the Tea Party, who temporarily looked like a much needed ally, only to later wish they never heard of them. Then they reversed course when it once again seemed like a political ally.

They decided they needed the Hispanic vote they had always ignored, despite letting 100 million of them flood our country since Reagan welcomed every illegal alien south of the boarder to live and work on their humongous corporate farms, meat packing houses, hotels, and restaurants. The legal ones never voted, so the GOP didn't care what they did politically until after the 2008 and 2012 elections, when the Democrats outsmarted them by courted them first and got them to vote almost exclusively Democrat.

That's when they brought in what few Spanish members they had, such as "Gabriel Gomez," who had never even served on any public board or committee to run for senator of Massachusetts. How could Gomez possibly go from a completely ignorant person about how small town government worked – let alone the U.S. Senate – to a senator?

Now, Donald Trump is attempting this trick as president. People here in town asked me to run for selectmen, but unlike Trump, I wasn't arrogant enough to think I had enough previous experience serving on smaller town boards to properly fill the role.

The GOP was completely divided and falling apart at the seams by 2013. House Speaker Boehner was getting attacked from all sides and eventually resigned from the radical Tea Party's pestilence. Boehner's approach to negotiations with the president in a bipartisan way was no longer what the younger Republicans stood for. Reagan and his Reaganomics, which supported entitlements like Social Security and claimed it was not the cause of our deficit, was useless history in their opinion. And one of their favorite governors, Chris Christie, was blasting Boehner for the party's internal politics for not getting Super-Storm Sandy relief money to the people of New Jersey fast enough.

Super Pac's own David Koch even seemed confused on where he stood, annually donating astronomical amounts of money ($25 million in 2012) to PBS, which traditionally has shows attacking environmental destroying companies, corruption in politics, Wall Street greed, and big business. These shows are in direct violation of party core values. They educate the masses and tell the truth about the hideous things they're into. To add insult to injury, PBS attacked their religious institution, exposing evangelist scams and priest molestations.

The more moderate, environmentally friendly, northeastern ones that love the beauty of nature aren't in line with the mountain blowing up, environmentally devastating oil, gas, and mining industries. The fanatical Tea Partiers apparently are not students of history or they would know ultra-conservative hardliners such as Barry Goldwater, Ronald Reagan, and Richard Nixon were clobbered in the past by the centrist before they learned better. Regardless of history, they threatened to kick out all Republicans for showing a tiny bit of bipartisanship when they agreed to pass a small tax increase on the nation's wealthiest - though we all knew they would never actually pay it with their legion of accountants and tax havens.

Super radicals like Karl Rove, the Koch brothers, and Russ Limbaugh do their fair share of damage in their own ways by blaming Democrats for everything, including the financial crises their own party clearly helped facilitate. And lastly, they pushed the United Citizens decision through their hand-picked Supreme Court.

Nobody seems to be on the same page anymore. Boehner, Governor Christie, and senate minority leader Mitch McConnell all seemed to go in different directions. Senator Rob Portman is perhaps one of the most confused. He vehemently voted against same sex marriage, only to do an about face when he learned his son was gay. Nobody seems to have a central plan that would represent them nationwide, especially Donald Trump. After seeing them run our town, they look the same as what they claim are "tax and spend" Democrats - who also restrict all regulations when it lines their pockets or accomplishes their own personal agendas.

That's where the two other parties' differ from us Independents. We don't aspire to an agenda with a strict set of rules we must adhere to. We don't have anyone telling us what to do or think. That's what the other two parties call "Communism" when they're not doing it themselves. Independents do what we think is best for the country like the Roosevelt's - not our party's.

Former President George W.'s Secretary of Defense, Bill Gates, who stayed on with President Obama's administration, agreed with the majority of Americans when he said "the biggest threat to America's security is our government." He said what we all knew had happened over the last three decades. The majority center congressmen who had made it function since the founding fathers had disappeared and were replaced by extremist. He mentioned the same thing that was going around a lot by the time Obama had been reelected, when he told us the founding fathers had built the government around the principals of compromise. They made sure the only way it would work was by forcing compromise and this simply is no longer what it's all about.

By 2010, the Congress and Supreme Court had once again been completely hijacked by special interest - just political pawns. The 112th Congress was completely useless to the American people, and the 113th was even worse, passing less than half the bills the 111th had passed. Most political analyst blamed the GOP dominated House for no longer being willing to negotiate and compromise as they had through the first 200 plus years. They proved that with their incessant attempts to repeal the health care act patterned after their own presidential nominee Mitt Romney's Massachusetts Universal Health Care law, instead of negotiating for changes like Jeb Bush wanted and they did with other national programs such as Medicare.

The Senate had passed a sweeping immigration bill that overhauled the system, and a farm bill that the corporate farm loving Republicans should have loved, yet the House did nothing except go on vacation for the summer. They even let the interest on the Stafford student college loans double to their delight... Ka-Ching, Ka-Ching! They sure love the sound of enormous record profits being rung up. Who could blame us for putting the countries problems on their shoulders?

Finally in July 2013, soft spoken Senate Majority Leader, Harry Reid, had enough obstruction from their record 400 plus filibusters that had crippled many government agencies from doing their job. They were blocking the executive branch appointments of many officials to lead crucial agencies. Including Richard Cordray for the Consumer Financial Protection Bureau, despite GOP Senator Tom Coburn from Oklahoma saying he was "doing a wonderful job" in carrying out his duties. They blocked Gina McCarthy to lead the EPA, Thomas Perez the Labor Department, and three nominees to the National Labor Relations Board so it couldn't function for lack of a quorum. So Reid finally decided to use an option in the centuries old Senate rules that allowed the Senate to change their rules called the "nuclear option." It would allow the Senate to confirm nominees by a simple majority vote rather than the usual 60% and allow crucial agencies to go back to work for the people. As Elizabeth Warren said, Congress had a simple choice – "protect corporate raiders or regular people." Is she part Roosevelt!

For one reason or another, many good congressmen like Senators Sanders, Markey, and Warren came forth and attempted to eradicate big money influence. Elizabeth was probably the most tenacious. She relentlessly pursued Wall Street thieves and its regulators (of which she became one with her appointment to the Senate Banking Committee her first year in office) and she didn't disappoint the people who elected her. She immediately helped stop the Republican filibuster of Cordray and pushed through confirmation of Gina McCarthy as EPA administrator: Then got back on her horse protecting the people by joining veteran GOP Senator John McCain, Maria Cantwell, and Angus King in introducing the 21st century Glass Steagall Act in July, 2013. Over a five year period, it would ban the government from insuring speculative trading, and once again, separate commercial banks from their investment counterparts. And the too big to fail institutions would be broken up into smaller distinct entities.

I wouldn't bet on a few good congressmen like these righting the American ship, though. Immediately after her initial victories, she and 17 other senators got walloped 81 to 18 on a bill to reform the Stafford student loans. Furious the feds were making billions off the struggling students, she wanted students to pay the same low interest rates as the banks and investment firms. Instead, they were tied to the ten year Treasury note, plus 2.05% with a cap of 8.25%.

Unless America can change the way money, religion, and special interest influences politics, it is doomed to fail. We need to follow the examples of groups akin to the New York Fair Elections Coalition. They support and run a system that allows anybody to run for political office through a public private donation system. It works especially well at the local level where people like me can't afford to run on their own and nobody trusts their government. They take small donations of up to $175 from individuals that are matched at a 6 to 1 ratio of public pool money from the general budget.

This method makes people rightfully feel their small contributions help good people get into office, or at least have a chance to beat the mega-rich and incumbents by leveling the playing field. Even in larger campaigns such as the New York City mayoral elections, which pitted the 7th wealthiest person in the country, Michael Bloomberg, and his $27 billion against Bill Thompson, the election was close and more than competitive. If it weren't for all the polls showing a rout that discouraged a lot of his supporters from voting, he may have won.

Other good things are starting to happen too. The people's opposition to the demigods that write and enforce their own laws and regulate themselves is on the rise. The jury is still out on whether or not politics in America is changing because of a few good people. But I'll go out on a limb and bet they'll be silenced by the roar of corruption and we'll be back in Lincoln's day of a House divided and Teddy Roosevelt's corporate chieftains.

Until we come up with a palpable government playing in coexisting harmony we well sink further into the abyss.

Epilogue
Can America be Saved?

The United States democratic form of government has been under strain and embroiled in turmoil since its inception. Corruption and dirty politics has been rampaging through every orifice of society since the first settlers in Virginia came looking for gold and slowly multiplied in scope until it became the normal way of doing business at all levels.

The Kennedys could very well have been the most openly corrupt of the famous politicians. We talked earlier about Joe Kennedy's rise to power, his ties to the mafia, and his bootlegging during the alcohol prohibition era. But that barely touched the surface of how unscrupulous he really was and what he taught his kids. His son John picked up where he left off in his love for mob bosses and womanizing, and became president through his dad's connections to the underworld and friends like Chicago's Mayor Daily. John's relationship with the mafia continued through his short presidency when he hired them to partner with the CIA to assassinate Fidel Castro. Never before or since has a family of the Kennedys stature been so close to a collection of criminals. Even Kennedy's Vice President and successor Lyndon B. Johnson was accused of rigging votes with the infamous "box 13" in his home state of Texas. Democracy, more often than not, is captured by the greed of capitalism.

Along the way there have been a few great people in defense of democracy. Teddy Roosevelt, for instance, the sickly kid who became a burly, good hearted, hard core environmentalist. Like Hyacinth on the British TV series "Keeping Up Appearances," he knew for most people it was just an accident of birth they weren't important. Part dictator, socialist, imperialist, and progressive democratic capitalist, he declared war on the affluent and proclaimed too big and too much was no good. "You can stand for humanity or stand for the privileged" he bellowed at his Republican Party!

As you know, he stepped in to help the little people, environment, and the country by crushing their monopolies under the Sherman Antitrust Act. And his "Square Deal" reformed the slave labor type workplace through government regulation of industry and consumer protections to help the lower and middle classes. To save capitalism,

Roosevelt believed the relatively new third party of Abraham Lincoln's should be the same progressive party it was then: One with a strong federal government led by the president, who could balance out the polarizing special interest states run by the robber baron tyrants of the new industrialized America. He believed the GOP should be the party of social conscience and human rights - the exact opposite of today's imperialistic, destructive, abusive, capitalists!

Born into an elite family in New York City, with a true American hero of social conscience for a dad - who not only heavily donated his inheritance money but personally worked at those same charities he supported regularly - the Harvard educated Roosevelt worshiped his dad's values and instilled an ethical and moral conscience into American politics unmatched in history. He despised his high society surroundings and sided with country folks and average Americans at every turn. In the 1890's, as New York police commissioner and president of a four man police board, he attempted to clean up corruption in the force and rid the city of street prostitutes, casinos, and drug dealers.

His intervention in the torturing of millions of people who couldn't heat their homes during the coal miner's strike of 1902, and his work on social issues made him a hero to the people. Teddy threatened the mine owners with taking federal control of their mines if they didn't shorten the long workdays and give miners a raise. He didn't give a damn about their constitutional rights, or the crooked U.S. Supreme Court, and answered their threats with brutal verbal attacks and dictatorial like action. Believing the president is the people's counterweight against the privileged who abused our capitalistic system, he roared back at their protest claiming he was abusing and overriding the constitution with rants and rages! They were so scared of what he might due next, they donated heavily to reelect him. Teddy was one wild stallion that couldn't be bought, broken, or defeated!

Roosevelt hated the ruthless, sometimes murderous tycoons and stacked Supreme Court with such a passion he thought the people should be able to veto their decisions through popular vote. So after stepping down, the restless, ultra-high energy Roosevelt declared the two-party system undeniably corrupt and started his famous Bull Moose Party to balance the scales. Ultimately, he failed in his comeback bid for a third term. But not before establishing himself as the greatest, most important, influential, people and environmental president ever.

Teddy was the first American to win the Nobel Peace Prize for his role in the Soviet Union's unprecedented thirst for expansion by bringing the emperors of Russia and Japan - both claiming ownership of Korea - to the White House and making them agree to a compromise that saved face for both nations. Through his Boone and Crockett Club, he was the premier force in getting congress to establish the National Forest Service between 1876 and 1905. Then through the foresight of Iowa Congressman John Lacey and his brilliant National Antiquities Act that gave the president unlimited power to preserve our national treasures, Roosevelt declared everything from bird sanctuaries and Petrified Forest to National Sanctuaries and Monuments sacred grounds. He then ended the greatest presidency in our history by declaring the Grand Canyon a National Monument to keep the mining industry from tearing it apart and established the first and greatest National Parks System in the world.

Despite the richest most powerful aristocrats, murderous poachers, and big game hunter's wishes to exploit and destroy them, he ferociously protected them and their inhabitants. T.R. saved the American Bison and Florida's Egrets by outwitting Wall Street and all those who attempted to exploit and decimate them for their own moral-less greed. An avid naturalist - yet befuddling robust hunter - he learned from his mistakes and realized senselessly annihilating every wild creature would leave no more to hunt and castrate the fragile interwoven natural world forever.

Good friend John Muir, Steven Mather, Secretary of the Interior Harold Ickes, and cousins Eleanor and husband FDR, led the charge in continuing Teddy's relentless campaign for the people over the miserly, psychotic aristocrats by out flanking and maneuvering them for decades. Following in cousin Teddy's footsteps, FDR put the bankers and capitalistic abusers back in their place with his "New Deal" by installing the Glass-Stiegel Act and deposit insurance after the 1929 crash. It convinced people to put their money back into the banks they had just taken it out of - which caused the systemic failures. He forced farm prices back to profitability by instituting subsidies to get Dust Bowl farmers to quit over-farming, and gave unions more bargaining rights. Then followed that up with his own "Square Deal" that put millions of people back to work, as well as instituting the social security system and unemployment benefits to protect their futures.

So far the U.S. has refused to learn from these great men and the tide has once again shifted. Are there any more Roosevelt's, Muir's, Mather's, and Ickes to stop it? Can America be saved, or have the conniving oligarchs finally embedded their despicable greedy ways throughout society beyond defeat?

Once again, the Hudson River and hundreds more are too polluted from sewer and storm water runoff to swim in or eat the fish. Coal ash sludge is still routinely spilling into our waterways with no clean up and disposal regulations. Chemical companies are exploding on a regular basis and trains routinely collide, causing oil and chemical tankers to explode into deadly fireballs that kill employees and townspeople across the country and cause whole town evacuations from coast to coast from the deadly chemicals, smoke, and toxins. And Freedom Industries had a massive spill in West Virginia that polluted three major rivers used for drinking water, swimming, and fishing, causing a ban for weeks for hundreds of thousands of people. In the forest, poachers are hacking up and killing 1000 year old giant sequoias for a few measly scraps of their precious wood.

In response to public outcry, believe it or not, the Republicans refused to pass a Democratic bill regulating disastrous chemical spills and making the companies notify the government what chemicals they manufacture, mix, and handle. They then pushed for deregulating all chemical, oil, mining, and gas companies, and if you can believe it, all power plants, including Nuclear! They expanded fracking in the ocean off the coast of California near the 1969 platform blowout off the Santa Barbara coast and immediately had another spill. Then passed a bill to allow public access to every inch of our National Forest and U.S. Fish and Wildlife Service land, including the millions of square miles under the Bureau of Land Management for recreational use: which included the use of the most environmentally destructive off road trucks, dirt-bikes, and all-terrain vehicles.

Arizona's power company Arizona Public Service, a subsidy of Pinnacle Capital Corp., attempted to kill the largest solar industry in the country and people's right to be self-sustainable by implementing a monthly fee so high nobody could afford it. In Cape Cod, Ma., the wind industry was attacked by the wealthy homeowners and special interest, stopping the first offshore wind farm in U.S. history. The mining indus-try is as relentless as ever, getting permits to mine our national forest, and is still trying to destroy the Grand Canyon and the rest of the country.

No need to worry, though, when we use up all the worlds natural resources and obliterate the planet, we have a plan B. We're going into space and harvest asteroids for their raw materials.

Warlords still rule, guns are out of control, and school shootings are still happening at about one a month using a wide variety of weapons. Republicans are still killing all gun control bills, and worse, they're trying to get guns with silencers in the hands of every person in the country with their kill or be killed mentality. They want to arm postal workers along with teachers, apparently forgetting the multiple post office massacres in the 1980's that contributed to the war on guns. And Smith and Wesson is still throwing veterans parties and preying on them for sales disguised as Memorial Day tributes and charity functions.

We're going back to the drugged out 1960's. Heroin use is as out of control now as it was in the early years of Hong Kong's epidemic and the hippy generation. Even what appears to be good news turns sour! Our 2,000 mile border with Mexico is being secured with a wall but drug cartels are digging tunnels under it, complete with miner rail lines for their drug and gun smuggling operations. They haven't killed any of our boarder agents lately, but still control everything in Mexico, laundering their profits effortlessly across the border.

The financial industry is ahead of schedule in setting us up for their 20 year bailout with record profits every year from their ever growing leveraged scams. And government affiliations and CEO's are being more richly rewarded than ever for implementing them and holding damage control to a minimum. Super lobbyist like Ed Gillespie - who founded former G. W. Bush advisor Karl Rove's fanatical American Crossroads Super Pac - are running for Congress, instead of running it from the outside. Donald Trump and the GOP are repealing nearly all consumer protection laws and agencies, from veteran and elderly ones to the Dodd-Frank Bill and Consumer Financial Protection Bureau. Including the one that requires all financial advisors and brokers to be fiduciaries and put their client's interest "ahead of their own!"

Both Democrats and Republicans teamed up to kill reforms to the federally insured $700 trillion derivatives market that caused our bank meltdown and global crisis that still exist. Speculative trading on the Commodities Future Trading Exchange and New York Mercantile is still mostly unregulated, allowing huge swings in oil and gas prices. Private equity firms are still buying lucrative companies, destroying them by loading them up with debt, firing millions of people to boost profits, and then cashing in. Wall Street is as out of control as ever, with PC manufacturers stock skyrocketing while sales and profits plummet. Corporate greed is so demented, some of the largest gambling casinos - with the blessing of Nevada, New Jersey, and Maryland - opened up gambling sites online to take advantage of addicts 24 hours a day. Then they were caught laundering the extra income. And lastly, people are still bankrupting themselves with record borrowing for unnecessarily large T.V.'s and a cadre of other electronics, over the top homes, vehicles, and monstrous student loans.

It seems though it's still business as usual here in the United States. But is it? Is there still hope? Are we seeing seedlings of change?

What Must Be Done to Save America!

Simply put, we must set the clock back to the Roosevelt Presidencies and follow their common sense intellectual and moral ways more in line with Buda's than Alan Greenspan and Madonna's opulent, over materialistic, individualistic, society. First and foremost, we must reinstall the entire Glass Stiegel Act in its entirety and stop rewarding banks and financial institutions for their corruption, fraud, and reckless bets with ceaseless bailouts. Wall Street must repent like Gould, Rockefeller, and Carnegie. Record borrowing year after year must stop at all levels, and the 400 wealthiest people cannot be worth the 150 million poorest.

Corporate profits and riches for a greedy few must be set aside, tax loopholes closed, and rates raised to pre-Reagan levels. Record profits and destruction year after year from private equity firms, investment banks, oil, gas, and mining - just to name a few - must come to an end, along with their partner in crime - executive bonuses. The Walton's can't be worth as much as all their employees combined and the other "40 million" lowest paid workers in America. Being on welfare can't be more profitable with better benefits than working at companies that make tens of billions of dollars in profits every year while their employees live in poverty as in the pre Teddy Roosevelt years. Greedy corporate raiders like Carl Icahn, who became famous imploding TWA airlines while working his way up to the $20 billion club, have got to be outlawed!

Furthermore, the entire country must stop and desist from being run by, and for, the top 1%. Ninety-nine percent of the economic gain since the great recession can't go to the top 1%. As T. R. realized with nature, the middle class has to be allowed to make a comeback or the top 1% won't have anybody to buy their products and the entire economy will implode to a point of total devastation.

Inherently, we must halt the regulatory capture and political engineering in Washington and the rest of the country by reversing Citizens United, and then replace it with a general fund for all political candidates to draw from to balance the scales. Then shorten the election period, lengthen house terms, and ban backdoor bill tack-ons! Our Attorney General can't say the banks are "too big to prosecute" and imprison the reprehensible morons like in the 80's Savings and Loan disaster.

Companies led by convicted criminals like Mark Rich must not be rewarded for their crimes against humanity by the ethical and moral-less plutocrats by giving them and their executives' record amounts of money for their IPO's knowing what they have done. We need to back the few politicians who care, including Bernie Sanders and Elizabeth Warren with bills like her Truth in Settlements Act, so we know why banks like Wells Fargo paid far less for their fraud settlement than J.P Morgan. Then reinstall free college like California had for decades.

The constitution must be modernized so Super Pac's akin to the Koch's "Americans for Prosperity" masquerading as "educators" for the United Sportsman of Wisconsin Foundation to promote hunting, fishing and trapping can't be given unlimited grant money to promote guns, mines, and other GOP priorities under the false pretense they are nonprofit tax-exempt charities.

Republicans and their Tea Party have to stop being the party of lawlessness. They must stop banning all environmental regulation and exempting drilling and mining companies from nearly every law protecting the environment - and ultimately both man and beast. We need to know how much we receive for drilling and mining our public lands they're making a killing on, by bringing back our transparency rules that contain the most important details of our contracts for the very same public that pays for them and the seas they are decimating. We must shield people from the NRA and keep members out of our national parks and forests that are meant for our enjoyment and relaxation - not "Target Practice." The vast majority must go back to ruling at every turn!

We will have to fundamentally change the way government works and get it more in line with the other countries like Germany and Brazil that have excellent public-private cooperatives. Exact opposite our failed ones, including the Federal Housing Finance Agency that bought the tens of millions of fraudulent mortgages under the more familiar names of Fanny Mae, Ginny Mae, and Freddy Mac. After losing trillions on bad mortgages, they can't turn around and pay the same fraudulent bankers to refinance and lower the interest rates on selected defaults, second mortgages, and lines of credit. That is NOT how successful public-private projects work. Insanity at the controls has got to go!

We cannot continue spending over half our discretionary budget on defense and must reign in spending and corruption everywhere else. Most importantly, the government must stop insulting our intelligence with every word that comes out of their mouths and set a proper example for the nation: Whoopers, such as "the U.S. has never defaulted on its debts," knowing damn well it had after the British burned down Washington in the war of 1812 and again more recently in 1979 under President Carter, when we defaulted on over $120 million in T-bills.

Outsourcing American jobs overseas and to Mexico like the auto industry does to satisfy Wall Street is unacceptable. Something is wrong when our largest auto parts manufacturer Delphi is one of Mexico's largest employers and Dodge Rams are flying off their assembly lines at nearly one per minute while we pay their workers 1/7th that of our own. When states can't protect their own citizens from Super PAC's, the NRA, and the gun industry from a hundred daily murders across the land and anyone can buy as many machine guns and as much ammunition as they please, no questions asked, something is wrong! In cities like Boston where 65% of gun murders are committed by out of state guns from nearby states like New Hampshire and Maine because they have no laws - something is wrong!

The entire country needs an attitude change back to the basics of a civil society similar to the Mari's of New Zealand - who don't need to buy thousands of machine guns every month to stop crime. They stress civil obedience as a normal way of life, and use ancient ways to deal with offenders that bring them back into the community in a one for all, all for one mentality. We need to get the millions of juvenile delinquents out of jail and back into being an integral part of the community and become the kind of communities we had in the 1950's: When people were friendlier, more courteous, helped their neighbors, and actually knew their names. Not the kind where trailer truck drivers intentionally run you off the road in the middle of the night, almost killing you and your daughter you're rushing to the hospital just because they don't want you to pass them.

Corporate digital media needs to help us technically challenged parents and stop addicting our youth at a very early age. They must take a socially responsible position instead of making us play the bad cop that can't restrict and monitor their every move. And parents have to follow the leading inventors of the technology revolution, Bill Gates and the late Steve Jobs, by giving their kids' rules and restrictions to electronics and digital media – rather than kids telling them what they should have and do. Then stop bankrupting themselves by buying hoards of the latest electronics and actually start being parents again instead of joining them in hours of mindless games and social media.

The media has to take a stand on sensationalizing millions of stories like Eric Massa's that compelled Patrick Kennedy to explode on the house floor over the media coverage on him, rather than the barbaric war - when only 2 reporters showed up for that coverage and hordes for the Massa scandal. Both the media and public have to stop being as mesmerized by the shameless Hollywood and entertainment industries as they are electronics: Missing the Golden Globes, Oscars, or Country Music Awards is not a case of life or death.

Immigrants must start to assimilate into society as they did for centuries instead of continuing to do everything the way they did in their old countries. Medical fraud has to be reduced substantially in every area of medicine, from primary care physicians to unnecessary operations and procedures to double billing and padding bills. Like the 31 other industrialized nations and Cuba, a national insurance program must be permanently installed and tweaked until it's as good or better than anyone else's. Insurance fraud from people such as storm chasers must be halted in their tracks.

We must stop our ignorance and arrogance, then partner and assimilate to the rest of the nearly 200 other countries, not use and abuse them for Wall Street psychos and our own never ending greedy, selfish lifestyle. Creating wars in the Middle East and Africa for their natural resources and profit for our psychotic, belligerent corporate executives and weapons manufacturers must come to a halt!

Can It Be Done?

In a nutshell… of course it can! Hope springs eternal and the pendulum may once again be swinging to the better side of democracy. Certainly there are encouraging signs that show a few good politicians, state and federal government department heads, and even investors led by Warren Buffett are on the right track - teaming with other billionaires to donate nearly $500 billion to charities.

The USA's second wealthiest person - who led many investors down the dirty fuel express with his coal, oil, and gas investments, including his coal and oil hauling BNSF PacifiCorp Railroad, leads the country in wind installations, is currently building one of the largest solar farms in the world, and invested over $15 billion in renewable energy. Needless to say, it's highly unlikely he had a change in heart over his role in environmental destruction. Undoubtedly, as he has pointed out, he goes where the profits are, and in this case, fortunately, so does Wall Street and politicians. If Buffett says go green to make money, everyone on the street follows.

He also pushed to get greed-misters to pay their fair share of taxes by saying they shouldn't be paying less tax then his secretary… though I don't recall him ever voluntarily paying a dime more. He believes they don't need to further bankrupt us by collecting social security on top of their billions of dollars and colossal holdings. And after criticizing Coke for their executive compensation plans, they finally did the right thing and scaled back their world devastating CEO stock options and shifted to more cash based performance awards.

Facebook has followed Buffet's skewed environmental ways by flying solar power planes in remote areas of the world. The question is… Is it for social prosperity or profit?

With congressmen like Sanders, Warren, Markey, Tom Harkin, and Pete DeFazio biting the hand that feeds them, the days of Wall Street abuse is facing congressional opposition and legal battles. Harkin and DeFazio reintroduced the Wall Street Trading & Speculators Tax Act that puts a 3 cent tax on the elite's transactions. And the country's largest retirement system (California's) has kicked hedge funds out of their portfolio – starting a domino effect.

Presidents are no longer pardoning investment criminals, as Bill Clinton did with convicted commodities thieve Mark Rich. And more companies are successfully being prosecuted like the former Las Vegas Sands Hotel and Casino, who, like Donald Trump, reached a settlement with the feds for money laundering. Tyco toys former CEO Dennis Kozlowski was sentenced to eight years in prison for his $134 million fraud case. And the "worst patriot award" winner HSBC bank paid nearly $2 billion after pleading guilty to money laundering for "Mexican drug cartels and terrorist groups!"

After failing miserably to prosecute investment banks for years until civil lawsuits were successful, the government filed suits against thirteen mortgage servicers. Including Bank of America, JPMorgan Chase, and Wells Fargo for fraud after selling them tens of millions of home loans they knew were given to people who were all but guaranteed to default. But in a deal to keep many whistleblowers testimony buried, they settled for a pittance of what they stole. It included $4.5 billion from JPMorgan for their part in the financial meltdown, then another 2.5 billion for failing to police Bernie Madoffs activities adequately. A few weeks later they settled another case for 13 billion, B of A paid almost 10 to settle up with Fannie Mae and Freddy Mac and 7 to consumers. Citigroup kicked in 7, Goldman Sachs 5, and Wells Fargo 1. The bad news is, the way the settlements are rigged, the banks will pay very little after tax write offs and crazy bonus credits.

In other victories, SAC Capital was found guilty of insider trading and fined $615 million (over 6 times that of J.P) for receiving insider information on four companies, then buying their stocks before the public disclosers came out. And Capital One was fined $3.5 mil for underreporting $123 million in losses on auto loans in the months before the market collapse.

It was successfully prosecuting some of Wall Street's most abusive scheisters, including hedge fund and derivatives top people. Bernie Madoff was forced to pay $20 billion back to those he stole from. Apple settled a multimillion dollar dispute with the government for anti-trust violations and paid millions to people who lost money when their kids thought they were playing pretend games and accidentally bought products for them. Even the Supreme Court did something right by allowing employees to sue their employers over losses to their I.R.A.'s after allowing them to continue investing in them – despite knowing it was too risky. And they finally made the health care act permanent! Now they need to change the rules making future appointees Independents.

But far and above our biggest hope has come down to the spoiled millennials seeing, and more importantly, learning from their parents misguided values and Wall Street's demolition. After what happened to their parents in the dotcom bubble and great collapse of 2008-09, most claim they don't want anything to do with the market and are living at home longer to save money the old fashion way. This allows them to pay off their student loans and save more than boomers and their X-generation parents. It also dries up the retirement money the market has been feeding on the last 30 years because they are NOT putting it into 401's either. Combined with more boomers cashing in, the market will no longer have that inexhaustible revenue and theoretically bleed and starve to death - then implode! This will force Wall Street back to being just another blip on the news like most of the first 200 years, rather than the overbearing, artificial force it is today. And they and their kids are actually revering 60's and 70's family shows instead of social media crap.

Can you believe it? Unrivaled corporate greed is now coming back to haunt them! With a groundswell of protest from low wage and middle class workers, we are starting to revolt against our oppressors and over rambunctious, abusive, police departments. We may very well be seeing the beginning of the end!

Other great news saw President Obama using his executive right to implement the presidential "Nuclear Bomb" to get around the "zero regulation" Republicans. He banned Pfizer's $35 billion tax break, and after filling some key positions being held up by the GOP at federal courts and agencies such as the Consumer Financial Protection Bureau and EPA, the feds once again started fining corporate America tens of billions of dollars for their unconscionable environmental violations.

The BP Deep Water Horizon lawsuit is wrapping up, with the feds getting up to $18 billion under the Clean Water Act and hundreds of other lawsuits covering thousands of litigants. Anadarko agreed to a $5.3 billion cleanup settlement from its uranium deposits and other contaminates. And after several oil tanker train collisions, the National Transportation Safety Board wants stiffer standards. Big oil mistakenly lowered gas from nearly $4 a gallon to about $2 when their sheer greed and over drilling caused a flooded market and accidentally stimulated the economy, temporarily killing their favorite love child - Keystone!

The EPA, and perhaps the coolest judge in the country, hammered the country's largest electric power producer "Duke Energy" after the

Dan River spill and leaking coal ash at 5 other plants. The EPA settlement makes them pay a poultry $102 million fine, but more importantly, restitution, clean up, capping, and replacement of their leaky sludge pits! And our on again, off again, semi-environmental Obama reinstalled those solar panels, then managed to bring us in line with the rest of the industrialized world by pushing through universal health care. With any luck, and despite Trump blessing Keystone, we'll follow California and order a couple of water desalination plants in the Gulf, then pipe fresh water through it instead of tarry oil so farmers can feed us and the world like Howard Buffett wants to. Plus, it well help lower the burgeoning seas, transfer salt mining to the over salty oceans, and provide cheap salt to every table. Can you see any downside to that plan?

Earth days Republican Rep. Pete McCloskey is so fed up with his party he is actually endorsing democrats for Congress to stop them. And many others finally came aboard, reforming their party by temporarily giving the radically right Tea Party the boot and then actually passed the first bipartisan budget in years. We almost dropped dead after they topped that by passing the budget for the following year days later and renewed Reagans Undetectable Firearms Act that banned plastic guns in airports and elsewhere.

Many states are calling for an amendment to the constitution to overturn the Citizens United case, with over three-fourths of Los Angeles voters in favor of it despite TV ads attacking it. And we're finally taking a page from the Mari and teaching our prisoners job skills and partnering with private business to give them a new life.

You may recall former Indiana school superintendent Tony Bennett, who got rewarded for his lying and schemes to privatize public education with the same top position in Florida. After being exposed, he resigned from backlash over his system and it reverberated around the country. Both the states and feds are changing the way kids learn from a rote memory system to one based on problem solving, critical thinking, and technical skills. We are reinstalling an emphasis on technical schools to bring high paying manufacturing jobs back and fill millions of critical employee shortfalls. Some kids are even starting to realize money and fame isn't everything, and believe it or not, are actually picking more careers they enjoy, including the humanities fields! Now we just have to stop wasting money on radically oversized schools, dump any bad teachers filling them, and give the best ones a raise.

Led by the Center for Media and Democracy, the most destructive Super Pac in history, ALEC, was forced to make its entire library of model congressional bills publicly available for scrutiny, resulting in over 100 corporations dumping them since being exposed.

Lastly, cities and states are installing a $15 an hour minimum wage that is gaining momentum nationally. And revolutionary science break-throughs, from electric storage devices to building origami like cancer fighting proteins may save us from ourselves.

Do you think oligarchs, politicians, and corporations are finally realizing what secretive Super Pac's and Wall Street are doing to the country and they need the bottom 99% after all?

Many people's baby steps appear to be turning into real change. Will they ruin my predictions?

Yeah right! I have faith people! I was just messing with you and giving you hope. As sure as the Stand Pat Republicans that tore the party apart over 100 years ago in the early 20th century could come back as the Tea Party, America will continue to ignore and deny history into super-power oblivion like all the others. It already started when junk bond aficionado Donald Trump and former Florida inside governor Jeb Bush ran for president in 2016. Their massive oversees investments may make Mitt Romney look like a saint, but Bush said he's fine with that. Yep, he's a true Bush all right! For better or worse, the "self-proclaimed" billionaire who ran as a publicity stunt beat the inside millionaire and the others for the presidency.

We all know how well it went the last time a Bush was in the White House. Still, with the ultimate in Greed, Selfishness, Ignorance, Arrogance, and Thirst for Power stocking his Cabinet with the same Wall Street bankers and CEO's that caused the meltdown, and others working for Russia, including National Security Advisor Lt. Gen Michael Flynn for Russia's Kaspersky Internet Security, TV network, and airline, along with the GOP controlling both houses of Congress - can you imagine this all Republican government led by Donald Trump?

You better order some more signs Sam! And make sure they read:

WALL STREET BILLIONAIRES ➡

⬅ DOOMSDAY VAULT

PROLOGUE:

2. 81% of college freshman want to get rich: Jen Wieczner, "10 Things Millennials Won't Tell You" June 23, 2013" Wall Street Journal

2. 19 trillion dollars of which 5 trillion is owed to other countries and 1 trillion to individual brokers: "Here's Who We Owe That $17 Trillion Of Government Debt To" Henry Blodget Oct 11, 2013 www.businessinsider.com

2. Now 90% of Americans are poorer than they were in the 1987: Matt O'Brian "Bottom 90% poorer today than in 1987" Washington Post

3. Using between 20% and 25% of all the worlds' energy: www.eia.gov

4. Pets: Sharon Kay "Pets looking more like their Obese Owners" Sept. 11, 2012 www.earthdayhealth.com

5. Crash test dummies: Oct 29, 2014 ABC news

5. 1 in 10 people have unclaimed property. Mass department of revenue www.ma.gov

5. One guy held four elderly men prisoner: "Houston Garage was Prison for Three Elderly Men" Manny Fernandez The Republican July 23, 2013

6. the guy who locked his sister in her room: "Police say man kept sister in room for 7 years" Robert Rizzuto Apr 27, 2014 rrizzuto@repub.com

6. And another kidnapped three girls for 20 years for sexual favors: "The Fritzl Case" April 2008 en.wikipidia.org

7. Facebook gambles billions: "Three smart Lessons From Facebook's purchase of WhatsApp" Adam Hartung Forbes Feb 24, 2014

8. In this continuing revolving door: Is This the Best Time for Investors? Don't Bet On It. Brett Arends May 19, 2013 and Federal Reserve www.federalreserve.gov

9. And in California: "Students Kicked Off Campus for Wearing American Flag Tees" NBC News Sep 29, 2010

10. A turnout of only 36%: "Voter turnout for 2014 midterms worst in 72 years" Nov 12, 2014 news.yahoo.com

11. General Electric's fined by the Securities and Exchange Commission: March 17, 2013 tellittoal.com

12. The highest percentage of adults under 35 unable to buy a house: June 3, 2014 wwlp morning news

Chapter 1: THE STOCK MARKET AND FINANCIAL INSTITUTIONS

14. 1 in every 22 people is a millionaire: CBS Evening News July 23, 2014

15. Joe Kennedy: In general, see The Kennedy's, (Frontline) and other sources

17. In 1995, John Boehner handed out tobacco lobbyist checks: "John Boehner" www.sourcewatch.com

18. "Shouldn't be intimidated, and everyone can do well in the stock market. You have the skills and intelligence and it doesn't require any education. You only need patience and a little research and you're good to go.": You tube

19. Buffett forces shares up: "A Smart Buy" Dec. 21, 2014 WJS Sunday

19. The dart game: "'Beat the Darts' Winner Shows How It's Done" WSJ Sunday June 30, 2013

20. ($32,000,000,000,000) hidden in offshore bank accounts. "Check Out Who's Hiding $32 Trillion in Offshore Accounts" Greg Madison May 1, 2013 moneymorning.com

20. 1209 North Orange Street: Rupert Neate The Gaurdian "Trump and Clinton share Delaware tax 'loophole' address with 285,000 firms" April 25, 2016

22. "American's hold $4.2 trillion in 401(k) plans" and "an additional $6.5 trillion in IRA's": Josh Boak AP "Fees eating away at some 401(k) plans" Apr. 27 2014 The Republican

22. Romney stashed away $100 million: "How IRA's Can Favor an Already Affluent Elite" Laura Saunders WJS Sunday

22. Complicated IRA's: In general, see "Retirement plans on autopilot" Fran Hawthorn N. Y. Times April 14, 2013.

23. Most people would think paragraph: Paula Dwyer Bloomberg News "Brokers as fiduciaries would boost savings" The Republican Feb 1, 2015

24. Buffets bet: Wall Street Journal Jan 3, 2015

25. A study of over 700 top performing domestic-equity funds: WSJ Oct 5, 2014

25. Some over-exuberant people: "Next Great Bubble Boom" Harry Dent Jr25. He was getting paid $50,000 a pop: "Call It a Boomer Boom" Bloomberg Businessweek March 27, 2000

CHAPTER 2: PROPRIETARY TRADING ON AN EPIC SCALE

34. Newsflash: "Prosecutors accuse hedge fund company SAC Capital of being a criminal enterprise where executives including founder Steven Cohen encouraged insider trading on a scale without precedent.": "Charged" Sunday Republican July 28, 2013

34. Investment Company Act of 1940 www.investopedia.com

34. Unbeknown to public employees: "Hedge Funds: How They Invest Their $2.4 Trillion War Chest" Brett Nelson June 20, 2013 www.forbes.com

35. Obama injured: NBC News Apr 23, 2013

36. The top 1%.: "Wealth gap growing across rich countries" May 1, 2014 The Republican

37. Dan Loeb story: "Yahoo Buys Back Third Point Shares as Loeb Exits Board" Callie Bost July 22, 2013 www.bloomberg.com

37. Junk bonds alone more than double: John Hilsenrath WSJ

38. "More than $6 billion": Susan Antilla "Manipulating markets" Bloomberg News June 2, 2013

42-49. Derivatives $700 trillion: In general is a compilation derived from "Inside the meltdown" Frontline www.pbs.org, Thomas M. Kostigen, "The $700 trillion elephant" March 6, 2009 www.marketwatch and other sources

48. Peter Wallison of the Atlantic claims: "Hey, Barney Frank: The Government Did Cause the Housing Crisis" Peter Wallison Dec 13, 2011 www.theatlantic.com

48. "They made the arsonist the fire chief": Bill Moyers & Company pbs.org

49. "Wall Street is right back to piling on leverage and leveraged buyouts." CBS News

49. That's $22,000,000,000,000 USGAO

50. "The dirty little secret is: The world has no money and the emperor now has no clothes.": "the David Letterman show" May 6, 2010

51. The London Whale: "JPMorgan fails to end law suit over London Whale losses," Mar 14, 2014 reuters.com

51. Banks' lending 5 or 6: David Stockman on Crony Capitalism Moyers & Company March 9, 2012 billmoyers.com

53-54. John Corzine: In general, see Frontline, The Story of John Corzine and other sources

54-56. Bernie Madoff: In general, see Diana Henriques "Son of convicted financier dies at 48" The Republican Sept 4, 2014 and "Madoff" Frontline PBS.org

56. Cay Club Resorts and Marinas: sec.gov

57. "Credit default swaps imploded, complex derivatives blew up and banking stocks plunged or got wiped out.": WSJ

CAPTER 3: POLITICAL ACTION COMMITTEES

58. The elite and corporate interest groups get what they want nearly 100% of the time from the U.S. Congress: Alan J. Lichtman, contributor "Who rules America" August 12, 2014 thehill.com

59. The Tillman Act of 1907: www.historycommons.org

62-68 The American Legislation Exchange Counsel: In general, see "ALEC exposed" Center for Media and Democracy www.prwatch.org

70. President Nixon: "Nixon tapes show opposition to guns" March 10, 2013 The Republican

73. Aurora, Co. murders: "The Aurora Shooting" en.wekipidia.org

74. Gabrielle Giffords: "I'll see you on national T.V." April 11, 2014 www.cbsnews.com

79. Gun statistics: "Meet Americas Gun Owners" Sept 20, 2016 The Guardian

80. Las Vegas: In general, see "ALEC Exposed" Center for Media and Democracy www.prwatch.org

83. Michael Bloomberg fights NRA: April, 26 2014 CBS evening news

Chapter 4: OUR DISHONERABLE GOVERNMENT

85. "I spent $1.5 million a year on sports tickets alone in order to get policymakers to come with me, so that I would have an opportunity to influence them and have them indebted to me in some way.": "Abramoff Talks Lobbying" Oct 11, 2013 abramoff.com

85. He got to "100 congressmen": "Jack Abramoff: the Lobbyist Playbook" May 30, 2012 www.cbsnews.com

85. "Because that leaves 335 offices that we didn't have a strong influence over," Ibid

85. Bob Ney admitted they were in a "culture of corruption": Ibid

85. It was just a "great big shell game." Ibid

85. Delay was found guilty of money-laundering: "Texas court overturns Tom Delay conviction" Sept 19, 2013 www.usatoday

85. As former Ohio governor Ted Strickland told Charlie Rose, House Majority Leader - "John Boehner told me if he couldn't control them" (the republicans) "he was going to let them loose and see what happens.": "Charlie Rose" Apr 25, 2014 worldchannel.org

86. As Sen. Warren wrote in her 2014 autobiography - former Treasury Secretary Lawrence Summers "urged her to be an insider.": "Warren launches tour for her new book" Apr 24, 2014 The Republican

87. Timothy Geithner: enwikipidia.org

87. Henry Paulson: "Henry M. Paulson Jr." www.forbs.com

88. The Federal Reserve Board: "The structure of the Federal Reserve System" www.federalreserve.gov

89. Dimon's $30 billion bail-out of Bear Sterns: "The Last days of Bear Sterns" money.cnn.com

89. Dimon continues to collect his $20 million paychecks and his bank paid $20 billion in penalties to the government: Jan. 25, 2014 abcnews.go.com

90. "The committee to save the world": Time magazine

90. Mary Jo White spent most of her life switching alliances: In general, see Mary Jo White newyorker.com

90. Mary Jo defended Dimon's mega-bank: Management.fortune.cnn.com

91. Wall Street executives richly rewarded: Bob Ivry, Bradley Keoun and Phil Kuntz "Secret Fed Loans Gave Banks $13 Billion Undisclosed to Congress" Nov 27, 2011 www.bloomberg.com

91. Former Fed chair Ben Bernanke: Al Lewis "Geithner's Victory Dance" May 25, 2014 WSJ Sunday

92. Rutgers University: AP "Condoleezza Rice backs out of Rutgers commencement" The Republican, May 1, 2014

92. Top 1% gain nearly half of all income growth: (Wealth gap growing across rich nations" May 1, 2014 The Republican

92 Monsanto: Personal email

93. "John McCain, the Republican senator from Merrill Lynch, Citigroup, J.P. Morgan Chase, Goldman Sachs, Morgan Stanley, UBS and Credit Suisse.": Al Lewis "Barely Biting the Apple" Sunday Republican May 26, 2013

93. Keystone XL and ALEC: In general, see "ALEX Exposed" Center for Media and Democracy editor@prwatch.org

97. Dan Rather: "Dan Rather's 'Rather Outspoken'" The speed read Justin Moyer May 11, 2012 Follow @justinwmmoyer.com

97. Edward Snowden: In general, see "Inside the NSA" Frontline pbs.org

99. Microsoft is currently battling them: "Microsoft fights search warrant" Ellen Nakashima June 12, 2014 The Republican

100. In 2007 a Boston lawyer recorded police arresting someone with his cell phone: "Court case questions wiretap law" May 15, 2014 The Republican

100. The Republican reported every candidate who spent the most money running for statewide office won: "Candidates who spent most won in 2014"Robert Rizzuto Feb 19, 2014 rizzuto@repub.com

101. the two parties controlling democracy: In general, see "Independent Party, Green-Rainbow Party earn official Bay State status" Shira Schoenberg schoenbeg@repub.com

CHAPTER 5: OUR $69 MILLION PIECE OF PIE – PURE GLUTONY AT ITS WORST

106-108. statistics are from the school district and Mass School Building Authority www.massschoolbuildings.org

CHAPTER 6: EDUCATION - FROM MY SCHOOL COMMITTEE PERCH

122. "Encourage your middle grader to play the stock market...to see who can make the biggest profit": Resources for Educators May, 2013.

133. Dropout rates: WGGB Springfield, Ma May 8, 2014.

133. Is it all worth the worry? : "10 Things the SAT Won't Tell You" Cathy Hill WSJ Sunday May 4, 2014.

134. As JIA Lynn Yang of the Washington Post: In general, see "New study says shortage of STEM workers a myth" Jia Lynn Yang, The Washington Post

136 Ex-principle pleads guilty: "Ex-principal pleads guilty in test scandal" Jack Flynn Oct 9, 2014 jflynn@repub.com

138. New curriculums: Today show Feb 10, 2010

138. Nick Boldyga's bill: Monthly newsletter to constituents

140. Getting "buried in debt:" "10 Things Millennials Won't Tell You" Sunday Republican June 22, 2013

140. Columbia University topped the list: Kelsey Sheehy "Undergrads around the World Face Student Debt" Sept 10, 2013 usnews.com

140. All this debt has made millennials: wwlp morning news June 3, 2014

141. A report by AP claims:

141. Single moms: "I can't get there tomorrow, but I can come on Thursday" Personal email from Elizabeth Warren May 11, 2014 info@elizabethwarren

141. Another Gallop poll suggest: "job placement and income" - "have had a good life in terms of well-being, satisfaction and career engagement." Sunday Republican

142. Times they are a changing: "Bob Dylan at Budokan" 1978

142. Interview with Lazlo Bock: employers "today care less about what you know or where you learned it than what value you can create with what you know" and "don't just go to college because you think it's the right thing to do and any bachelor's degree will suffice." "Insider's guide for finding a job at Google" Thomas Friedman New York Times, Apr. 20, 2014 The Republican

143. Laurence Summers: Summers on Student Debt WSJ Sunday May 25, 2014 20.

143. Super Pac's destruction: In general, see "ALEC Exposed" Center for Media and Democracy www.prwatch.org

144. For-profit schools: In general, see Frontline, For-Profit Schools pbs.org and Denial Golden Bloomberg News

145. "Massachusetts colleges sue state" AP Sunday Republican

146. Milken and Packard's Knowledge Universe: In general, see Center for Media and Democracy www.prwatch.org

CHAPTER 7: IMMIGRATION - IS IT OUT OF CONTROL

152. by 2013 much of their estimated "$1.5 trillion dollars": Raul Gallegos "Learn Spanish, it's good for you" May 18, 2014 Bloomberg News

CHAPTER 8: ENVIRONMENT VERSUS ENERGY HOGS

166. Newsflash: January 28, 1969: "How A Massive Oil Spill In 1969 Changed Everything" Ari Phillips June 30, 2014 thinkprogress.org

166. "Earth Day's beginnings rooted in 1970s activism" Apr 17, 2014 Raycom News Network www.nbc12.com

166. The medal of freedom: "Gaylord Nelson: U.S. Senator and Earth Day Founder" environment.about.com

166. In an interview with NBC's legendary newsman Hugh Downs, Rep. McCloskey said: "Co-Founders of First Earth Day Explain Goals of Teach-In" Apr 22, 1070 cpsnbclearn.com

167. The Love Canal: In general, see "The Love Canal: Children and Toxic Waste" American Masters March 13, 2014 www.pbs.org

167. National Forest and Parks: In general, see "US Forest Service" www.u-s-history.com and "U.S. Forest Service" www.u-s-history.com

168. Clean Air Act: "History of the Clean Air Act" www.epa.gov

169. Comprehensive Environmental Response, Compensation, and Liability Act: "CERCLA Overview" www.epa.gov

169. We consumed between 20 and 25% of the entire world's energy: www.eia.gov

170. NASCAR uses 10,000 gallons of fuel and 1 barrel of oil: "Nation on the Move" America Reveled PBS June, 2012

172. 1960's dumping: "70% of their industrial waste and 1.2 trillion gallons of untreated sewage" into our wells, streams, rivers and lakes: email to the author June 3, 2014 Waterkeeperalliance.com

172. High powered electrical lines: in general, see "Nation on the Move" America Reveled PBS June, 2012

173. When the Kingston, Tennessee plant had 5.4 million cubic yards: "5 years after coal-ash spill, little has changed" www.usatoday.com Dec 23, 2013

174. Black Thunder: In general, see "Nation on the Move" America Reveled, PBS June, 2012 and "Black Thunder Thermal Coal Mine, Wyoming, United States of America" www.mining-technology.com and emails to the author

175. It was soon tested when again in 2010 an explosion at Massey's Montcoal mine killed another 29: "W.Va. mine disaster deal could boost safety in industry" Oren Dorell USA TODAY

176. According to the Republican: Editorial, Let Vermont Yankee Pay the Republican 27 Apr. 2014 masslive.com

179. Deep Water Horizon is a synopsis from an onslaught of live news coverage

183. Keystone: In general, see Center for Media and Democracy www.prwatch.org

183. Do you suppose the $50 million the Koch brothers gave to congress: "Building Keystone XL Pipeline Could Mean Roughly $100 Billion in Profits for the Koch Brothers, New Report Reveals" Koch Cash kochcash.org

185. Kalamazoo River Oil Spill: In general, see Kalamazoo River Oil Spell en.wikipidaia.org

187. Hydraulic Fracturing is based on: "4 in 10 higher risk wells aren't inspected by Feds" Hope Yen AP June 12, 2014 and emails to the author

189. The Marcellus Shale Advisory Commission: Governor's Marcellus Shale Advisory Commission report July 22, 2011 files.dep.state.pa.us

189. Governor Corbett said "no amount of economic benefit would justify the degradation of our land, air, or water.": Governor's Marcellus Shale Advisory Commission report July 22, 2011 Ibid

189. "We must not lose this moment; it's the economic cornerstone of the commonwealth's recovery from the rescission." Ibid

Chapter 9: OUR DYSFUNCTIONAL GOVERNMENT

194. "It's so bad around here, that they filibuster their own bills": E.J. Dionne "Where does the buck stop?" Washington Post

194. "Working with my Senate colleagues reminds me of chasing one of these little pigs in a greased pig contest" MSNBC May 7, 2014 www.msnbc.com

195. Mark Russell calls George Bush a "Moron" and, "It's cheaper than taking Prozac." The Mark Russell Show PBS.org

196. Story of Prescott Bush: In general, see "How Bush's grandfather helped Hitler's rise to power" Ben Aris and Duncan Campbell Sept 25, 2004 www.theguardian.com

197. Bohemian club: "Dobelle used state funds to mingle at club" Patrick Johnson pjohnson@repub.com

197. "The public be damned!" Who rules America? Allan Lichtman, contributor Aug 12, 2014 thehill.com

198. John Rockefeller: In general, see "John D. Rockefeller" PBS.org

198. The Michigan Copper Country miner's strike: Dec. 17, 2013 PBS.org

199. The federal gas tax: "Nation needs highway, bridge funds" May 18, 2014 The Republican

199. Energy credits: Jeff Plungis, Bloomberg News "Energy credits to carmakers for emissions goals" May 15, 2014 www.blomberg.com

199. Jerrold Nadler D-NY "can't afford to spend money on a program the military says it does not yet need or work": Frontline documentary

200. Government deficit: www.treasurydirect.gov

200. Corporate capture: Suzy Khimm, "How much did the financial crisis cost us? $12.8 trillion one group says" Sept. 16, 2012 www.washingtonpost.com

200. The Big Dig: "True cost of Big Dig exceeds $24 billion with interest" Eric Moskowitz July 10, 2012 www.boston.com

200. Denver airport: In general, see Denver International Airport, wikipidia.org

201. The Bridge to Nowhere: A National Embarrassment" www.heritage.org

201. It's estimated it will cost us $3.6 trillion by 2012: www.infrastructure.org

202. According to Parade writer Paul Taylor… "half of our entire federal budget": Paul Taylor, Boomers and Millennials Bridging the Generation Gap" Apr 5 2014 parade .condenast.com

202. "Both the social security trust fund and one of Medicare's two trust funds will be broke"…: Ibid

202 Government expenditures: Douglas Elmendorf, "The economic and Budget Outlook, "Congressional Budget Office, May 13 2010, www.cbo.gov.

202. Overgenerous government: Jonnelle Marte "10 things social security won't tell you" WSJ Sunday June 30, 2014

203. Jimmy Carter, Ronald Reagan and Paul Volker: In general, see Jeff Madrick "The Age of Greed" chapter 11

205. The flood insurance program www.fema.gov

206. Elizabeth warren says the "fortune 500 companies' pay nothing in taxes": PBS News hour May 19, 2014

206. According to a Jan.2012 report by Foreign Policy: Jan 2012 www.foreignpolicy.com

206. 100 million in his IRA's: Laura Saunders "How IRA's Can Favor an Already-Affluent Society The Republican

206 "His personal finances are a poster child of what's wrong with the American tax system": "Romney Parks Millions in Cayman Islands" Jack Blum Jan 18, 2012 abcnews.go.com

207. And his private equity company Bain Capital has "138 secretive offshore funds:" "social Welfare": www.irs.gov

207. The corporate share of taxes has gone "from 30% of federal revenue to just over 6% since the 1950's": Mark Shields "Renouncing citizenship for profit" The Washington Post May 28, 2013

207. As Mark Shields of the Washington Post points out: ibid

209. The IRS statutory provisions says "Organizations exempt under IRC 501©(4)may not allow to have any part of their net earnings to inure to the benefit of any private shareholder or individual.": www.irs.gov

210. "Exclusively for the promotion of welfare": Ruth Marcus "Toxic politics secret source" May 22, 2013 Washington Post

210. In 2012 the Center for Responsive Politics estimated: Center for Responsive Politics

211. "50 engineers lawyers and other experts": www.washingtonpost.com

214. California's $4.2 billion surplus: Jennifer Medina "With Surplus in Hand, California Eyes Debt" Jan 20, 2014 The Times Editorial board www.nytimes.com "Stash away California's budget surplus" Nov 20, 2013 www.latimes.com

Chapter10: TWO BANK MELTDOWNS IN TWENTY YEARS AND OTHER SCAMS

217. The near meltdown of 1907: "panic of 1907" wickipedia.com

217. By the second quarter of 2014: Ryan Tracy "Banks Lending Expands" Aug 31, 2014 WSJ Sunday

217. Mega-banks renting out New York City offices: CBS News April 29, 2014

218. Then finally the "BIG BANG" came in 2008: Bob Ivry, Bradley Keoun and Phil Kuntz "Secret Fed Loans Gave Banks $13 billion Undisclosed to congress" Nov 27, 2011 www.bloomberg.com

218. Fed Chairman Ben Bernanke: "the worst financial collapse in global history and 12 of the 13 most important financial institutions in the U.S. were at risk of failure within a period of a week or two.": Pedro Nicolaci da Costa "Like old Times" Aug 31, 2014 Real Time Economics blog WSJ.com

219. The Bloomberg News reported Morgan Stanly took out 107 billion....: Bob Ivry, Bradley Keoun and Phil Kuntz "Secret Fed Loans Gave Banks $13 billion Undisclosed to congress" Nov 27, 2011 www.bloomberg.com

219. The Fed wound up committing 7.77 Trillion dollars to the banks from 1985 to 2009, culminating with the $1.2 trillion bailout on Dec. 5, 2008: Ibid

220. "one of the strongest and most stable major banks in the world.": Nov. 26, 2008: Ibid

220. Then they bundled most of the "$10 trillion": Al Lewis "Mortgages for the Masses" WSJ SUNDAY May 18, 2014

220. Fabrice Tourre story: multiple sources

221-222. Countrywide and fraudulent mortgages: In general, see "Inside the Meltdown" Feb 17, 2009 Frontline pbs.org

221. One third of them underwater by 2012: Conner Dougherty "underwater homes Impede Housing Recovery" WSJ May 25, 2014

221. "Were professionals who knew about their deals and what marketing strategy was all about." "Basically you sell your crap to get rid of your risk": In general, see "Inside the Meltdown" Feb 17, 2009 Frontline pbs.org

228. $772 million in consumer refunds and civil penalties: www.usatoday.com April 9, 2014

231. "You should put the interest of the country ahead of the bankers!": "Inside the meltdown" Frontline 2013 PBS

231. "There shouldn't be any consumer protection system at all.": Ibid

CHAPTER 11: NEW YORK CITY AND THE MEDIA

236. It was summed up best: "Ghost busters two" 1989 www.ask.com

237. On April 7, 2014: NBC News www.nbcnews.com

238. Telecommuting: In general, see "Telecommuting has pros, cons" Joyce Russell Washington Post June 30, 2013 The Republican

239. ABC morning news reported New Yorkers give their kids over $13: Feb. 25, 2015

240. and Yuppie parents: Roxanne Roberts "Designing parents raiding the dorm" The Washington Post Aug 31, 2014

240. I saw one family on TV: In general, see Good Morning America (GMA)

243. Marilyn Preston points out: Marilyn Preston "Scorching truth: Sunscreen may give you cancer" Energy Express June 1, 2014 The Republican

245. Statistics used in imaginative ways are from various Sunday editions of the Republican newspaper. Ibid

245. State of the Union address: wwlp Jan 19, 2014

246. The Anglo-French Sykes-Picot Agreement: "Sykes-Picot Agreement" The editors of the encyclopedia Britannica www.britannica.com

248. 75% of singles looking for love from perfect strangers: ABC 40 news Feb 14, 2015

258. Advertisers have gotten TV stations to speed up their shows: CBS Evening News Feb 20, 2015

CHAPTER 12: ELECTRONICS - ENVIRONMENTAL AND SOCIAL GENOCIDE OR SAVIOR?

260. Newsflash: ABC Morning News Mar 24, 2015

261. The WSJ's Priya Anand: Priya Anand "10 THINGS ... Con Artist Won't tell you" 27 Apr. 2014 WSJ, The Republican

263. "Social media is everywhere and you can't get away from it.": GMA

264. According to a report in May 2014; 1 out of 5 kids claims to have been bullied: wwlp.com May 4, 2014

264. Dartmouth College got hammered: "Dartmouth battles online 'rape problem'" April 13, 2014 Ibid

CHAPTER 13: MEDICAL/INSURANCE FRAUD - ARE WE JUST GUINEA PIGS

280. We consume 99% of all hydrocodone and 80% of all opioid pills: "Northwestern DA tackles opioid abuse" editorial Sept 14, 2014 The Sunday Republican

280. A Medicare government report: "Medicare pay list may open door to more data" April 13, 2014 Bloomberg News

281. "hundreds of millions of dollars": "Executive accused in China drug bribery" May 15, 2014 The Republican

281. "Pfizer has more than $51 billion in annual revenue": Al Lewis "Pfizer's New Tax Remedy" May 5, 2014 Ibid

281. AstraZeneca was fined $7.9 million for kickbacks: "AstraZeneca to pay $7.9 million over kickback allegations" Feb 12, 2015 Ibid

281. drug overdose "is now the leading cause of death": Ronald Dunlop, "A physicians perspective on opiate abuse" April 13, 2014 Ibid

281. "38,000 annual drug overdose deaths of which 60%": Ibid

283. In a report by Marilyn Preston: Good to skip your annual checkups? 13 Apr. 2014 Ibid

288. Forbes reports in 2013: Evan Albright "Medicare Reports Fraud and Waste Grew In 2013 After Years of Decline" Dec 20, 2013 www.forbes.com

288. Some get over 10 million a year: Bloomberg news "Medicare pay list may open door to more data" April 13, 2014 www.bloomberg.com

289. Doctors are even giving it to an estimated 10,000 toddlers: Editorial "Toddlers don't need ADHD medications" May 22, 2014 The Republican

289. Dr. Leonard Sax: "Boys are not doing just fine" Esther Cepeda Apr 9, 2015 Washington Post

297-299. For-Profit Assisted Living Facilities is in part a synopsis of a documentary by Frontline. pbs.org and personal contact.

CHAPTER 14: THE LEGAL SYSTEM

300. With a country of over a million attorneys: Paul Grobman "Vital Statistics"

301. The long arm: "Players to receive payments" AP June 1, 2014

309. charged with mail fraud, conspiracy to commit mail fraud and racketeering: "Top official says he was mum on hiring misfires": Shira Schoenberg May 13, 2014 The Republican

312. "Marijuana use, gun control, health insurance requirements and identification standards for driver's licenses." AP David A. Lieb "Federal nullification efforts mounting" Ibid June 23, 2013

318. Prisons: In general, see Center for Media and Democracy www.prwatch.org

CHAPTER 15: SPORTS

321. $37,500 by 1934: "1934 New York Yankees Roster" www.baseball almanac.com

321. Babe Ruth: "Babe Ruth Biography" espn.go.com

328. High school football: In general, see Football High: Frontline Apr 12, 2011 pbs.org

CHAPTER 16: RELIGION

334. Paragraph 2; In general, see "Despite rise of the 'nones,' US remains religious nation" Michael Gerson The Washington Post, The Republican March 31, 2013

336. George Washington University: "Georgetown University – about" www.georgetown.edu

CHAPTER 17: MILITARY

341. U.S. Army Colonel Lawrence Wilkerson drops a bomb: Dec 22, 2015 Former Bush official Lawrence Wilkerson exposes the corruption inside the establishment and says "America's ship is sinking." Tyler Durden Zero hedge Dec 20, 2015

341. US General Wesley Clark, Ex Supreme Allied Commander NATO: Pakistan Defense's video Dec 23, 2015

343. "Mr. Gorbachev tear down this wall!": "Remembering Reagan's "Tear Down This Wall" speech 25 years later" June 12, 2012 CBS news www.cbsnews.com3.

344. Our military budget peaked at $851.3 billion and now sits at $756.4 billion for 2015: Kimberly Amado U.S. Military Budget How Much the U.S. Spends on Defense Will Surprise You about.com

348. In 2009 Katherine McIntire Peters reported: Katherine McIntire Peters, "Defense Budget Portends Difficult tradeoffs," Aug. 12, 2009 www.govexec.com

350. "at risk of being lost or forgotten": Kevin Freking, AP "Warnings on patient waits go back years" June 1, 2014 The Republican

351-352. Woman in the armed service: In general, see "Parris Island leader says woman can handle combat" Susanne Schafer AP March 17, 2013351. When the moon hits your eye: Dean Martin

CHAPTER 18: THE PRESIDENTIAL ADDRESS

357. Insider Jeb Bush: "Jeb Bush hinting at presidential run" Phillip Rucker and Matea Gold The Washington Post Feb 14 2014

EPILOGUE: CAN AMERICA BE SAVED?

364-366. Teddy Roosevelt is a compilation of many resources and mediums:

368. And Smith and Wesson is still: "Food Truck Fare Part of Smith and Wesson's 'Celebration of Heroes" Anne Gerard Flynn, The Republican May 15, 2014

Acknowledgments

To the people of the United States of America: This book would not have been possible without you. Thank You!

www.ingramcontent.com/pod-product-compliance
Lightning Source LLC
Chambersburg PA
CBHW060834280326
41934CB00007B/773